FORTRAN with Problem Solving: A Structured Approach

Robert J. Bent
George C. Sethares

FORTRAN with Problem Solving: A Structured Approach

Brooks/Cole Series in Computer Science

Business BASIC
Robert J. Bent and George C. Sethares

BASIC: An Introduction to Computer Programming
Robert J. Bent and George C. Sethares

Beginning BASIC
D. K. Carver

FORTRAN with Problem Solving: A Structured Approach
Robert J. Bent and George C. Sethares

FORTRAN with Problem Solving:
A Structured Approach

Robert J. Bent
George C. Sethares
Bridgewater State College

Brooks/Cole Publishing Company
Monterey, California

Dedicated to Costas H. Sethares
and to the memory of
Mary C. Sethares
Catherine A. Bent
John J. Bent

Brooks/Cole Publishing Company
A Division of Wadsworth, Inc.

© 1981 by Wadsworth, Inc., Belmont, California 94002.
All rights reserved.
No part of this book may be reproduced, stored in a retrieval system,
or transcribed, in any form or by any means—electronic,
mechanical, photocopying, recording, or otherwise—
without the prior written permission of the publisher,
Brooks/Cole Publishing Company, Monterey, California 93940,
a division of Wadsworth, Inc.

Printed in the United States of America

10 9 8 7 6 5 4 3 2 1

Library of Congress Cataloging in Publication Data

Bent, Robert J   1934–
    FORTRAN with problem solving.

    Includes index.
    1. FORTRAN (Computer program language)   2. Problem
solving.   I. Sethares, George C., 1930–   joint
author.   II. Title.
QA76.73.F25B46   001.64′24   80–28581
ISBN 0–8185–0436–6

Acquisition Editor: *James F. Leisy, Jr.*
Manuscript Editor: *Kirk M. Sargeant*
Production Editor: *Cece Munson*
Interior Design: *Katherine Minerva*
Cover Design and Photo: *Stan Rice*
Illustrations: *VMH Visual Communications*
Typesetting: *Graphic Typesetting Service, Los Angeles, California*

Preface

This book is intended for an audience with no prior programming experience. A mathematics background of elementary algebra is sufficient for most of the material. The many worked-out examples illustrate how the FORTRAN programming language can be used both in a data-processing and in a scientific environment. The examples and the numerous problem sets are drawn from a wide range of application areas, including business, economics, personal finance, the social and natural sciences, mathematics, and statistics.

We wrote this book with two principal goals in mind. First, we felt it important to present the elements of FORTRAN so that meaningful computer programs could be written at the earliest possible time. We adhere to the notion that one learns by doing. As a result, problem solving is emphasized from the very beginning, and the various aspects of the FORTRAN language are introduced only as needed. Our second goal was to write a book that would serve as a general introduction to computer programming, not just to a programming language. Simply describing a variety of computer applications and ways to go about writing FORTRAN programs for these applications does not constitute an introduction to programming. What is required is a consideration of the entire programming process. The approach we have taken toward this objective is to introduce programming principles only as they can be understood and appreciated in the context of the applications being considered. For example, a beginner can easily appreciate the need to identify what values must be input and what form the output should take. Hence, these steps are introduced early. On the other hand, the value of modularization—that is, breaking down a long and possibly complex task into more manageable subtasks—is not so easily grasped in the context of the straightforward programming problems first encountered. As natural as modularization may appear to an experienced programmer, a beginner must "see" its usefulness before being convinced of its value. Thus, although several of the early examples illustrate the method of problem segmentation in very simple programming situations, it is not discussed as a general programming principle until later in the book.

All FORTRAN programs appearing in this text conform to the American National Standards Institute (ANSI) document, ANSI X3.9-1978, commonly referred to as FORTRAN 77. We have taken considerable care to avoid those parts of FORTRAN 77 that are not widely implemented or that are not essential to writing "good" programs. We *have* used the IF–THEN and IF–THEN–ELSE statements. Although they are not implemented on older FORTRAN systems, they represent a major improvement in the FORTRAN language. Their use not only simplifies the coding process but can significantly improve the readability of FORTRAN programs. As shown in Chapter 6, any program containing IF–THEN and IF–THEN–ELSE statements is easily modified to run on FORTRAN systems that do not allow these statements.

A few remarks are appropriate concerning the organization of this text. The first two chapters are introductory. Chapter 1 contains a brief introduction to computer science and to some of the terminology associated with computers. The term *compiler* described in this chapter is used throughout the text; hence, an understanding of what a compiler does is essential. Other than this, Chapter 1 may be read at any time. Chapter 2 contains an introduction to problem solving. The term *algorithm* is defined, and the sense in which computer programs and algorithms are equivalent is explained. This chapter must not be skipped.

Chapters 3–7 contain a description of what may be called elementary FORTRAN programming. Included are descriptions of the assignment statement, as used to perform numerical calculations; the READ, WRITE, and PRINT statements, as used for elementary input and output operations; and the control statements IF, GO TO, and DO. FORMAT statements, which often cause considerable difficulty for beginners, are described in parts. The simplest forms of the FORMAT statement needed to produce meaningful output are taken up in Chapter 3. The simplest forms needed to transfer numerical input data to the computer are described in Chapter 5. In Chapter 8, we give a more detailed description of FORMAT statements used for input/output operations involving numerical data; in Chapter 12, we describe the form needed for processing nonnumerical character data; and in Chapter 16, the forms needed for logical, complex, and double precision data are described. In each case, the material is written so that it can easily be taken up earlier, should that be desired. Also included in these chapters on elementary FORTRAN are descriptions of the two modes of operation used in FORTRAN programming: the batch processing mode and the conversational, or time-sharing, mode. These two computing environments are described in Chapter 4 and essentially all of the material following this chapter is appropriate in both environments. Situations where different methods apply are clearly identified.

The intermediate and advanced topics covered in Chapters 8–16 need not be taken up in the order of their appearance. Indeed, much of this material is presented in such a way that it can be taken up much earlier. For instance: the intrinsic functions (Sections 10.1–10.2) can be taken up any time after the logical IF statement is introduced in Chapter 6; statement functions (Sections 10.3–10.4) can be taken up just after Chapter 8; the material in Sections 12.1–12.4 on processing character data can be understood any time after the DATA statement is introduced in Chapter 8; and data files (Sections 14.1–14.4) can be taken up any time after Chapter 8. Included in these chapters on intermediate and advanced programming is a separate chapter (Chapter 15) on sorting and searching. Although some of this material is difficult, the chapter should not be omitted; at the very least, a method should be learned for sorting large files that will not fit in the computer's memory at one time.

Section 6.9, which describes the method of top-down programming, must not be skipped, for in many respects it is the most important section in the book. It not only brings together many of the programming principles learned in Chapters 2–6, but also describes the single most useful approach to programming that is known. No introduction to programming can be considered complete without an understanding of and a facility with the method of top-down programming.

We wish to take this opportunity to acknowledge the helpful comments of our reviewers: Charles Downey of the University of Nebraska at Omaha, Kendall E. Nygard of North Dakota State University, and Charles Pfleeger of the University of Tennessee. We feel that their many thoughtful suggestions have led to a greatly improved text.

A very special thanks goes to Patricia Shea, our typist, proofreader, debugger, and consultant on matters of form. Many of her suggestions concerning the text format have been adopted, and her meticulous concern for detail was indispensable. Finally, we are happy to acknowledge the fine cooperation of the staff at Brooks/Cole Publishing Company.

Robert J. Bent
George C. Sethares

Contents

4 Loading and Running a Program   35

5 Processing Input Data   53

6 The Computer as a Decision Maker   81

7 Loops Made Easier—The DO Statement   117

8 More on Input-Output Programming   145

9 Arrays and Subscripted Variables   165

10 Functions   211

11 Subprograms   227

12 Processing Character Data   255

1

Computer Systems

An electronic computer system has the ability to store large quantities of data, to process these data at very fast rates, and to present the results of this processing in ways that are meaningful to the task at hand. Thus, if the task is to prepare a payroll, employee data will be stored in the computer, the computer will process these data to calculate relevant wage statistics, and the results will be presented in printed form, possibly including paychecks. This payroll example illustrates the three principal tasks involved in any computer application: data must be presented to the computer (**INPUT**), data must be processed (**PROCESS**), and results must be presented in a meaningful way (**OUTPUT**). (See Figure 1.1.)

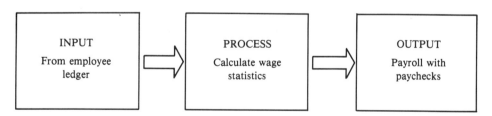

FIGURE 1.1. An INPUT–PROCESS–OUTPUT diagram.

The purpose of this chapter is not to convince you that a computer can "do" many things, nor even to indicate the computer applications you will be able to carry out after completing this text. Rather, the objectives of this chapter are to introduce you to the types of computer equipment you may encounter, to describe what a computer program is, and to introduce certain terminology that is helpful when talking about computers.

1.1 Computer Hardware

Central to every computer system is an electronic computer whose principal function is to process data. The computer component that does this is called the **central processing unit (CPU).** The CPU contains an **arithmetic unit,** consisting of circuitry that performs a variety of arithmetic and logical operations, and a **control unit,** which controls all electrical signals passing through the computer. In addition to the CPU, every computer has a **memory unit** which can store data, and from which data can be retrieved for processing. Fortunately, you need not understand how a computer processes data to make a computer work for you. The circuitry in a computer is not unlike that in an ordinary pocket calculator, and all who have used calculators know that no knowledge of their circuitry is needed to use them.

Data must be transmitted to the computer (*Input*), and results of the processing must be returned (*Output*). Devices meeting these two requirements are called **input** and **output (I/O) devices.** The I/O devices you are most likely to encounter in your introduction to computer programming are as follows.

Teletypewriter and Video Terminals: These serve as both input and output devices. On a teletypewriter (Figure 1.2) you transmit information to the computer simply by typing it at the teletypewriter keyboard and the computer transmits the results back to the teletypewriter, which produces a printed copy for you. A video terminal (Figure 1.3) works the same way except that the results are displayed on a video screen.

Card Readers: Information can be transferred to punched cards for submission to a computer. (This process is discussed in Chapter 4.) A card reader (Figure 1.4) is used to "read" the information punched on these cards and transmit it to the computer. Card readers serve only as input devices.

Line Printers: A line printer (Figure 1.5) serves only as an output device. As indicated by its name, an entire line of output is printed simultaneously. Computer systems that use card readers for input usually use line printers for output.

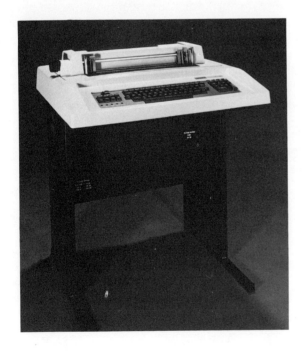

Figure 1.2 (above) ASR Model 43 Data Terminal with paper tape unit. (Courtesy of Teletype Corporation.) (left) DECwriter LA-36 Terminal. (Courtesy of Digital Equipment Corporation.)

FIGURE 1.3. Digital VT100 Video display with keyboard. (Courtesy of Digital Equipment Corporation.)

FIGURE 1.4. Card reader. (Courtesy of Control Data Corporation.)

FIGURE 1.5. Dataproducts' B-Series band printer. (Courtesy of Dataproducts Corporation.)

Most modern computer systems are equipped with storage devices other than the memory unit. They are called *external* (or *secondary*) storage devices because they are not a part of the computer as is the memory unit. The most common external storage devices are as follows.

Magnetic-tape units: Information is stored on magnetic tapes as sequences of magnetized "spots." Although tape units can be rather "large" (Figure 1.6), some computer systems (especially microcomputer systems) use ordinary cassette tape recorders. Data are "read" from a tape by reading through the tape sequentially until the desired data are found. For this reason, tape units are called sequential access devices.

Disk-storage units: (Figure 1.7) Information is stored on rotating disks that resemble phonograph records. However, the disks have no grooves; the data are stored as sequences of magnetized spots appearing on concentric circles. A disk unit will contain one or more disks, each with one or more read/write heads. Disk units are called random access devices. This term indicates that data stored on any part of a disk can be accessed directly without having to read through the entire disk to find the desired data.

FIGURE 1.7. IBM 5444 Disk unit. (Courtesy of IBM Corporation.)

FIGURE 1.6. Magnetic tape unit. (Courtesy of Honeywell Information Systems.)

Data terminals, card readers, tape units, disk units, and all other mechanical and electrical devices other than the computer itself are referred to as **computer peripherals.** The computer and all peripherals constitute what is called the **hardware** of the computer system. Figure 1.8 illustrates the flow of information between a computer and its peripherals.

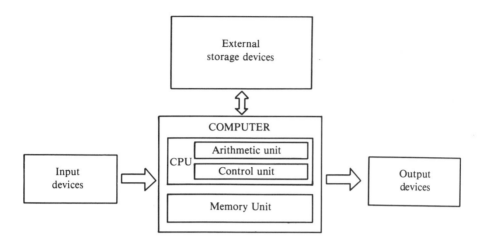

FIGURE 1.8. Flow of information through a computer system.

1.2 Computer Software

The physical components, or hardware, of a computer system are inanimate objects. They cannot prepare a payroll or perform any other task, however simple, without human assistance. This assistance is given in the form of instructions to the computer. A sequence of such instructions is called a **computer program,** and a person who determines what these instructions should be is called a programmer.

The precise form that instructions to a computer must take depends on the particular computer system being used. **FORTRAN** (FORmula TRANslation) is a carefully constructed English-like language used for writing computer programs. Instructions in the FORTRAN language are designed to be understood by people as well as by the computer. Even the uninitiated will understand the meaning of this simple FORTRAN program:

```
TERM1=3
TERM2=9
SUM=TERM1+TERM2
PRINT SUM
STOP
END
```

A computer is an electronic device and understands an instruction such as TERM1 = 3 in a very special way. An electronic device can distinguish between two distinct electrical states. Consider, for instance, an ordinary on/off switch for a light fixture. When the switch is in the "on" position, current is allowed to flow and the light bulb glows. If we denote the "on" position by the number 1 and the "off" position by the number 0, we can say that the instruction 1 causes the bulb to glow and the instruction 0 causes it not to glow. In like manner, we could envision a machine with two switches whose positions are denoted by the four codes 00, 01, 10, and 11, such that each of these four codes causes a different event to occur. It is this ability to distinguish between two distinct electrical states that has led to the development of modern computers. Indeed, modern computers are still based on this principle. Each computer is designed to "understand" a certain set of primitive instructions. On some computers these instructions take the form of sequences of 0's and 1's, but their precise form is not important to the beginner. All such primitive instructions that are meaningful to a particular computer are together called the **machine language** for that computer.

You will not be required to write programs in machine language. The computer you use will contain a **compiler,** which automatically translates your FORTRAN instructions into equivalent machine-language instructions that are then executed by the computer (Figure 1.9). Thus, when the six-line FORTRAN program shown above is presented to the computer, the compiler produces an equivalent machine-language program that instructs the computer to perform the specified task. The FORTRAN program is called the **source program** and the machine-language program is called the **object program.**

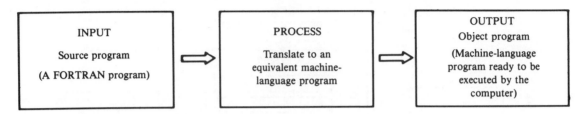

FIGURE 1.9. INPUT–PROCESS–OUTPUT diagram for a FORTRAN compiler.

FORTRAN compilers are themselves computer programs. They are called **system programs** because they are an integral part of the computer system being used. The FORTRAN programs appearing in this text, as well as the programs you will write, are called **application programs.** They are not an integral part of the computer system, so they are not called system programs. All computer programs, both system programs and application programs, are called **computer software.** The term *software* refers not only to computer programs, but also to any documentation, such as manuals and circuit diagrams, concerned with the operation of computers.

In addition to a FORTRAN compiler, your system will most likely include other system programs. These include programs to produce printed listings of your programs, to "save" your programs on secondary storage devices for later use, to assist you in finding errors in the programs you write, and, most important of all, a program called the **operating system** that exercises general control over the entire system. The operating system allows you to issue commands to the computer to "call up" and execute any of the other system programs provided.

The emergence of computer science as a new discipline has been accompanied by a proliferation of new words and expressions. They are useful for talking about computers but are, for the most part, absolutely unnecessary if your objective is to learn a computer language such as FORTRAN to assist you in solving problems. In our discussion of computer hardware and software, we have attempted to introduce only fundamental concepts and frequently used terminology. If this is your first exposure to computers, you may feel lost in this terminology. Don't be disheartened: much of the new vocabulary has already been introduced. You will become more familiar with it and recognize its usefulness as you study the subsequent chapters. You will also find it helpful to reread this chapter after you have written a few computer programs.

1.3 Review True-or-False Quiz

1. The principal function of a computer is to process data.   T   F
2. The term *arithmetic unit* is another name for the CPU.   T   F
3. I/O devices, external storage devices, and the central processing unit are called computer peripherals.   T   F
4. Card readers and video terminals can be used as input devices but cannot be used as output devices.   T   F
5. Disk storage units are called *random access devices* because information stored on a disk is accessed by randomly searching portions of the disk until the desired data are found.   T   F
6. Tape units are called *sequential access devices* because information is read from a tape by reading through the tape until the desired data are found.   T   F

7. The function of a FORTRAN compiler is to translate FORTRAN programs into machine language.   T   F
8. A FORTRAN compiler is part of the hardware of a computer system.   T   F
9. A FORTRAN program written to solve a particular problem may accurately be called a system program.   T   F
10. The machine-language program obtained when a FORTRAN program is compiled is called the object program.   T   F
11. An operating system is a computer system.   T   F
12. The expressions *computer software* and *computer program* are synonymous.   T   F

Problem Solving

A computer program consists of a sequence of instructions to the computer. These instructions describe a step-by-step process for carrying out a specified task. Such a process is called a *procedure,* or an *algorithm.* Algorithms have been with us since antiquity: the familiar division algorithm was known and used in ancient Greece; the activities of bookkeepers have always been guided by algorithms (an algorithm to determine a tax assessment, an algorithm to calculate a depletion allowance, and so on); even the instructions for assembling a child's new toy are often given as an algorithm.

Since a computer program describes an algorithm, the process of writing computer programs can be equated to the process of discovering algorithms. For this reason, an understanding of what is, and what is not, an algorithm is indispensable to a programmer.

2.1 Algorithms

An algorithm is a prescribed set of well-defined rules and processes for solving a problem in a finite number of steps. Here is an algorithm giving instructions for completing a financial transaction at a drive-in teller port.

    a. Press the call button.
    b. Remove the carrier from the tray.
    c. Place your transaction inside the carrier.
    d. Replace the carrier.
    e. When the carrier returns, remove the transaction.
    f. Replace the carrier.

To see that these six steps describe an algorithm, we must verify that each step is well defined and that the process stops in a finite number of steps. For example, step (a) requires that there be only one call button, and step (b) requires that there be but one tray containing a single carrier. Having verified that each step is well defined, and noting that the process is obviously finite, we are assured that the process does indeed describe an algorithm. In addition, it should be clear that the algorithm "does" what is claimed.

The previous example illustrates the following three properties of any algorithm.

1. Each step must be well defined—that is, unambiguous.
2. The process must halt in a finite number of steps.
3. The process must "do" what is claimed.

Following are two additional examples to help you gain an understanding of what an algorithm is and some practice with the process of discovering algorithms.

EXAMPLE 1. Let's find an algorithm to calculate the year-end bonus for all salaried employees in a firm. Employees are to be paid 3% of their annual salary or $400, whichever is larger.

To carry out this task, a payroll clerk might proceed as follows.

a. Open the employee ledger.
b. Turn to the next employee's account.
c. Determine the employee's bonus.
d. Write the employee's name and bonus amount on the bonus sheet.
e. If all bonuses have not been determined, return to step (b).
f. Close the ledger.

It is not difficult to see that these six instructions constitute an algorithm. Each step is well defined, and, since a business can employ only a finite number of people, the algorithm will terminate in a finite number of steps. Moreover, if this algorithm is followed, all employee bonuses will be determined as specified.

Although the algorithm "does" what was asked, the process could be made more specific by including more detail in step (c). Recalling the method specified for calculating bonus amounts, we can substitute the following for step (c).

c1. Multiply the employee's salary by .03 to obtain a tentative bonus.
c2. If the tentative bonus is at least $400, go to step (d).
c3. Set the bonus to $400.

Making this change, or *refinement,* we obtain the following more detailed algorithm.

a.   Open the employee ledger.
b.   Turn to the next employee's account.
c1. Multiply the employee's salary by .03 to obtain a tentative bonus.
c2. If the tentative bonus is at least $400, go to step (d).
c3. Set the bonus to $400.
d.   Write the employee's name and bonus amount on the bonus sheet.
e.   If all bonuses have not been determined, return to step (b).
f.   Close the ledger.

Remark 1: The first algorithm is more general than the second. It describes a process one might follow to determine employee bonuses, however they are to be calculated. The second algorithm can be used only if bonuses are calculated as specified in the problem statement.

Remark 2: It is somewhat easier to verify that the first algorithm "does" what was asked. This is because of, and not in spite of, the detail not present in the algorithm. Having verified that the first algorithm is correct, all that is required to verify that the second algorithm is also correct is to check that steps (c1), (c2), and (c3) describe the same task as step (c) of the first algorithm.

EXAMPLE 2. Let's find an algorithm to determine the largest number in a list of ten numbers.

One way to determine the largest number in a list of ten numbers is to read them one at a time, remembering only the largest of those already read. To help us give a precise description of this process, let's use two symbols as follows:

LARGE to denote the largest of those numbers already read.
NUM to denote the number currently being read.

The following algorithm can now be written.

a. Read the first number and denote it by LARGE.
b. Read the next number and denote it by NUM.
c. If LARGE is at least as large as NUM, skip the next step.
d. Assign the number NUM to LARGE.
e. If all ten numbers have not been read, go to step (b).
f. Print the value of LARGE and stop.

Remark: If the ten numbers are written on a sheet of paper, a person could simply look them over and select the largest. However, this process is heuristic and does not constitute an algorithm.* To see that this is so, imagine many hundreds of numbers written on a large sheet of paper. In this case, selecting the largest simply by looking over the numbers can easily result in an error. What is needed is an orderly process that will ensure that the largest number is selected. Examining numbers one at a time, as was done in the algorithm, is such an orderly process.

2.2 Variables

Algorithms can often be easily and clearly stated if symbols are used to denote certain quantities. Symbols are especially helpful when used to denote quantities that may change during the process of performing the steps in an algorithm. The symbols LARGE and NUM used in Example 2 of the preceding section are illustrations of this practice. (It would be instructive to write down the algorithm of Example 2 without using symbols.)

A quantity that can change during a process is called a *variable quantity,* or simply a *variable.* A symbol used to denote such a variable quantity is the name of the variable. Thus, LARGE and NUM, in Example 2, are names of variables. However, it is a common practice to refer to the symbol as being the variable itself, rather than just its name. For instance, step (f) of the algorithm for Example 2 says to print the value of LARGE. Certainly, this is less confusing than saying "Print the value of the variable whose name is LARGE."

Each of the examples in Section 2.1 concerns an algorithm describing a process to be carried out by people. A computer programmer must be concerned with algorithms describing processes to be carried out by a computer. This means that each step must describe an action that a computer can perform. This constraint is not so restrictive as it may appear. Computer languages, such as FORTRAN, contain instructions to assign numerical values to variables, to perform arithmetic operations, to compare numerical quantities and transfer control to different instructions depending on the result of this comparison, and to print numerical values. Each step in the algorithm of Example 2 represents one of those four types of action, which means that the algorithm does indeed describe a process that can be carried out by a computer.

Even instructions that appear to have nothing at all to do with computers can sometimes describe meaningful computer operations. As you progress through your study of FORTRAN, you will find that

---

*A *heuristic process* is one involving exploratory methods. Solutions to problems are discovered by a continual evaluation of the progress made toward the final result. For instance, suppose you come upon an old map indicating that a treasure is buried in the Black Hills. You may be able to work out a plan that you know will lead to the location shown on the map. *That's an algorithm.* However, suppose you can find no such plan. Determined to find the location, or to verify that the map is a fake, you decide upon a first step in your search, with no idea of what the next step will be. *That's exploratory.* Carrying out this first step may suggest a second step, or it may lead you nowhere, in which case you would try something else. Continuing in this manner, you may eventually find the location, or you may determine that the map is a fake. But, it is also possible that the search will end only when you quit. Whatever the outcome, the process used is heuristic. Someone else using this process will undoubtedly carry out entirely different steps and perhaps reach a different conclusion.

statements such as "Open the employee ledger," as found in the algorithm of Example 1, can indeed correspond to actions a computer can carry out.

The problems at the end of this chapter are designed to give you practice with the process of discovering algorithms. At this point it is not important that the individual steps in an algorithm correspond to actions that a computer can perform. A knowledge of what constitutes an admissible instruction to a computer will come as you gain experience in working with the FORTRAN language. What is important is that the individual steps are easy to understand and that the process described is an algorithm that, when carried out, does what is asked.

We conclude this chapter with a third example illustrating the process of discovering algorithms.

EXAMPLE 3. Find an algorithm to prepare a depreciation schedule for a capital investment whose cost is $10,000, whose salvage value is $2,000, and whose useful life is five years. Use the straight-line method. (The straight-line method assumes that the value of the capital item will decrease by one-fifth of $8,000 (cost − salvage value) during each of the five years.)

For each year, let's agree to write one line showing the year, the depreciation allowance for that year, and the cumulative depreciation. A person carrying out this task might proceed as follows:

a. Look up the cost ($10,000), the salvage value ($2,000), and the useful life (five years).
b. Determine the depreciation allowance for one year.
c. Subtract the depreciation allowance from the book value (initially the cost).
d. Add the depreciation amount to the cumulative depreciation (initially zero).
e. Write one line showing the year, the depreciation allowance for that year, and the cumulative depreciation.
f. If the schedule is not complete, go to step (c).
g. Stop.

Let's modify this algorithm to apply to capital items whose cost, salvage value, and useful life are known but are not necessarily equal to those given in the problem statement.

To help describe this more general algorithm, let's first choose variable names to denote the various quantities of interest.

BVAL   = book value. (The initial value is the cost.)
SVAL   = salvage value.
LIFE   = useful life in years.
DEPR   = depreciation allowance for one year: (DEPR = (BVAL − SVAL)/LIFE).
CMDEPR = cumulative depreciation (initially zero).

The following algorithm describes one way to carry out the specified task.

a. Assign values to BVAL, SVAL, and LIFE.
b. Assign the value $0.00 to CMDEPR.
c. Calculate DEPR = (BVAL − SVAL)/LIFE.
d. Subtract DEPR from BVAL.
e. Add DEPR to CMDEPR.
f. Write one line showing the year and the values DEPR and CMDEPR.
g. If the schedule is not complete, go to step (d).
h. Stop.

Remark: It is not often that a problem statement exactly describes the problem to be solved. Problem statements are usually written in a natural language, such as English, and thus are subject to the ambiguities inherent in natural languages. Moreover, they are written by people, which means that they are subject to human oversight and error. An algorithm describes a precise, unambiguous process for carrying out a task. Thus the task to be performed must be clearly understood. If it appears ambiguous, the ambiguities must be resolved. If it appears that one thing is being asked where another is actually desired, the difference must be resolved. For instance, the problem statement in the present example asks for only a very limited algorithm (a book value of $10,000, a salvage value of $2,000, and a useful life of five years), when what is really desired is the more general algorithm that has a wider application.

Skill in algorithm discovery must be developed by practice. The problem-solving methods begun in this chapter will be emphasized throughout the text. If you study the examples carefully and work a good selection of the problems at the end of each section, you will have ample opportunity to improve your problem-solving ability.

2.3 Problems

Problems 1–4 refer to the following algorithm, which is intended for completing an invoice:

   a. Let AMOUNT = 0.
   b. Read QTY and PRICE of an item.
   c. Add the product QTY × PRICE to AMOUNT.
   d. If there is another item, go to step (b). Otherwise, continue with step (e).
   e. If AMOUNT is not greater than $500, go to step (h). Otherwise, continue with step (f).
   f. Evaluate the product .05 × AMOUNT.
   g. Subtract this product from AMOUNT.
   h. Record the value AMOUNT and stop.

1. What interpretation could be given to the product appearing in step (f)?
2. What purpose would you say is served by step (e)?
3. If the values (10, $3.00), (50, $8.00), and (25, $12.00) are read by step (b), what value will be recorded by step (h)?
4. If the values (100, $2.00) and (50, $1.00) are read by step (b), what value will be recorded by step (h)?

Problems 5–8 refer to the following algorithm, which is intended for use by a payroll clerk as a preliminary step in the preparation of a payroll:

   a. Read a time card.
   b. If the number of hours worked (NHOURS) does not exceed 32, let G = X = 0 and go to step (e). Otherwise, continue with step (c).
   c. Evaluate 6 × (NHOURS − 32) and assign this amount to both G and X.
   d. Let NHOURS = 32.
   e. Evaluate 4 × NHOURS and add this amount to G.
   f. Write the amounts G and X on the time card.
   g. If there is another time card, go to step (a). Otherwise, stop.

5. If the numbers of hours shown on the first four time cards are 20, 32, 40, and 45, respectively, what amounts will be written on these cards?
6. What meaning do G and X have?
7. What is the base hourly rate for each employee?
8. What is the overtime rate?

What will be printed when each algorithm shown in Problems 9–12 is carried out?

9. a. Let SUM = 0 and N = 1.
   b. Add N to SUM.
   c. If N < 6, increase N by 1 and return to step (b). Otherwise, continue with step (d).
   d. Print the value SUM and stop.
10. a. Let PROD = N = 1.
   b. Print the values N and PROD on one line.
   c. Increase N by 1.
   d. If N exceeds 6, stop. Otherwise, continue with the next step.
   e. Multiply PROD by N and go to step (b).

11. a. Let A = B = 1 and NUM = 3.
   b. Evaluate A + B and assign this value to F.
   c. If NUM does not exceed 9, increase NUM by 1 and proceed to step (d). Otherwise, print the value F and stop.
   d. Assign the values of B and F to A and B, respectively, and go to step (b).

12. a. Let NUM = 56, SUM = 1, and D = 2.
   b. If D is a factor of NUM, add D to SUM and print D.
   c. If D ≥ NUM/2, print SUM and stop.
   d. Increase D by 1, and go to step (b).

Write an algorithm to carry out each task specified in Problems 13–19.

13. A retail store's monthly sales report shows, for each item, the fixed cost, the sale price, and the number sold. Prepare a three-column report with the column headings ITEM, GROSS SALES, and INCOME.

14. Each of several three-by-five cards contains an employee's name, Social Security number, job classification, and date hired. Prepare a report showing the names, job classifications, and complete years of service for employees who have been with the company for more than ten years.

15. A summary sheet of an investor's stock portfolio shows, for each stock, the corporation name, the number of shares owned, the current price, and the earnings as reported for the most recent year. Prepare a six-column report with the column headings CORP. NAME, NO. OF SHARES, PRICE, EARNINGS, EQUITY, and PRICE/EARNINGS. Use this formula: Equity = No. of Shares × Price.

16. Each of several cards contains a single number. Determine the sum and the average of all of the numbers. (Use a variable N to count how many cards are read and a variable SUM to keep track of the sum of the numbers already read.)

17. Each of several cards contains a single number. On each card, write the letter G if the number is greater than the average of all of the numbers. Otherwise, write the letter L on the card. (You must read through the cards twice: once to find the average, and a second time to determine whether to write the letter G or the letter L on the cards.)

18. A local supermarket has installed a check-validation machine. To use this service, a customer must have previously obtained an identification card containing a magnetic strip and also a four-digit code. Instructions showing how to insert the identification card into a special magnetic-strip reader appear on the front panel. To validate a check, a customer must present the identification card to the machine, enter the four-digit code, enter the amount of the check, and place the check, blank side toward the customer, in a special clearly labeled punch unit. To begin this process, the CLEAR key must be depressed, and, after each of the two entries has been made, the ENTER key must be depressed. Prepare an algorithm giving instructions for validating a check.

19. Write an algorithm describing the steps to be taken to cast a ballot in a national election. Assume that a person using this algorithm is a registered voter and has just entered the building in which voting is to take place. While in the voting booth, the voter should simply be instructed to vote. No instructions concerning the actual filling out of a ballot are to be given.

2.4 Review True-or-False Quiz

1. The terms *algorithm* and *process* are synonymous.   T   F
2. The terms *algorithm* and *procedure* are synonymous.   T   F
3. A computer program should describe an algorithm.   T   F
4. Every algorithm can be translated into a computer program.   T   F
5. The expression *heuristic process* refers to a procedure.   T   F
6. It is always easier to verify the correctness of an algorithm that describes a very specific task than the correctness of a more general algorithm.   T   F
7. The expressions *variable quantity* and *variable* are used synonymously. Both refer to a quantity that can change during a process.   T   F

3

A First Look at FORTRAN

Here is a FORTRAN program whose purpose is described in the first line:

```
C PROGRAM TO AVERAGE THREE NUMBERS.
C     A, B, AND C DENOTE THE NUMBERS.
C     AV DENOTES THE AVERAGE.
      A=12.25
      B=19.40
      C=17.10
      AV=(A+B+C)/3.0
      WRITE(6,10)AV
   10 FORMAT(1X,'AVERAGE IS',F7.2)
      STOP
      END
```

If a computer carries out the instructions in this program, it will produce the following output:

```
AVERAGE IS   16.25
```

The lines in this program are called **FORTRAN statements.** The first three are *comment lines* and serve only as program documentation. The next four lines associate certain numerical values with certain symbols. For example, the first of these associates the value 12.25 with the symbol A and the last associates the average 16.25 of the three numbers 12.25, 19.40, and 17.10 with the symbol AV. The WRITE statement causes the value associated with AV to be printed according to the output format specified in the FORMAT statement. Finally, the STOP statement terminates execution. The END statement simply informs the FORTRAN compiler that there are no more statements to compile.

Unlike a natural language such as English, a programming language such as FORTRAN must not allow ambiguous statements. Although we as humans can deal with ambiguities, a computer cannot; computers must be told precisely what to do. For this reason, the FORTRAN syntax (rules of grammar) is very precise and must be followed exactly. The purpose of this chapter is to describe how the statements introduced in the foregoing example can be used to form admissible FORTRAN programs. A complete description of these statements is not intended at this time; our immediate goal is to provide you with the minimal information needed to understand and write some FORTRAN programs.

3.1 Numerical Constants and Variables

FORTRAN allows you to represent numbers much as in ordinary arithmetic. For example, if you wish to include the number 23 in a program, you may write it as 23.00, 23., 23, or even 023. However, the way the computer stores and manipulates numbers depends very much on how they are written. In particular, the presence or absence of a decimal point in a number such as 23 may affect the results of a computation. In what follows you will see that the expressions

23./5.   and   23/5

are evaluated differently. The first will be 4.6 as expected, but the second will be 4, which is not expected. The reason for this discrepancy is explained in Section 3.3.

In FORTRAN, each datum to be processed has a *type*. The two most common numerical data types are *integer* and *real*. A number has the type *integer* if it contains no decimal point. Numbers that include a decimal point are of the type *real*.

Integer-type constants			Real-type constants		
23	023	+23	23.	23.00	+19:12
0	−247	207004	0.	0.00315	−5278.

The use of commas and dollar signs in numbers is not allowed; using 93,000 or \$93000 to represent 93000 will result in an error.

Very small numbers, such as 0.000000000000193, and very large numbers, such as 2470000000000, generally cannot be written as shown. There is a limitation on the number of significant digits allowed by a FORTRAN compiler. This limit depends on the system being used but is usually at least seven. An alternate form for real constants, called the *exponential form,* allows you to present such numbers to the computer for processing. The exponential form, together with its meaning, is

$$nEm = n \times 10^m.$$

Here n denotes either an integer or decimal and m denotes an integer. E stands for "exponent" and nEm is read "n times ten to the power m." Normally, exponents are limited to two-digit numbers, but some systems allow three-digit exponents.

Real constant	Meaning	Value
1.93E2	1.93×10^2	193.
1.93E−13	1.93×10^{-13}	.000000000000193
2.47E12	2.47×10^{12}	2470000000000.
200E−08	200×10^{-8}	.000002
.12345E04	$.12345 \times 10^4$	1234.5
1E5	1×10^5	100000.

A FORTRAN **variable** is an entity that has a *name* and a *type*. The name can be any sequence of one to six* alphanumeric characters (letters A–Z and digits 0–9) the first of which is a letter.

Admissible variable names	Inadmissible variable names	
X	3RD	(Begins with a digit.)
ANSWER	TOTAL DUE	(Too many characters.)
T3275	S − 200	(− is not allowed.)
GROUP9	SSN.	(The period is not allowed.)

The type of a variable can be declared with a **type statement** as illustrated by the following INTEGER and REAL statements:

INTEGER COUNT, ITEM, TOTAL
REAL MEAN, RATE, SUM, TIME

The first declares COUNT, ITEM, and TOTAL as integer variables and the second declares MEAN, RATE, SUM, and TIME as real variables.

If a variable is not declared in a type statement, FORTRAN assumes it to be of type integer if its name begins with one of the letters I, J, K, L, M, or N; otherwise, it is taken as a real variable.

Variables that are not declared in type statements	
Integer variables	Real variables
ISUM	SUM
NTOTAL	TOTAL
MEAN	AMEAN
KOUNT1	COUNT1
L1432X	A1432X

In this text, the assumption is that the type of each variable (whether it appears in a program, in the text, or in an exercise) is determined by the first letter of its name, unless explicitly declared in a type statement.

A FORTRAN compiler associates a storage unit in the computer's memory with each integer and real variable name. Storage units corresponding to integer variables will contain integer constants, and storage units corresponding to real variables will contain real constants. (The computer actually uses different methods to store data of different types.)

As noted in Chapter 2, we will not distinguish between a variable and its name. Thus, we will say "the variable SUM" when we mean "the variable whose name is SUM." Moreover, we will make frequent use of expressions such as "the value of SUM." Certainly, this is simpler than the more precise statement "the contents of the storage unit associated with the variable named SUM."

3.2 Problems

1. Write each of the following as a FORTRAN integer constant.
   a. 275.00   b. −124.0   c. 6.2×100 d. $-190 \div 2$
   e. 1.35×10^4 f. 21,743   g. $200   h. 910000E − 03

2. Write each of the following as a FORTRAN real constant, in both the decimal and exponential forms.
   a. 2,346   b. 265×10^2 c. $146 \div 10$ d. 1.2×10
   e. 0.000123   f. 1,235,000   g. 0.00056×10^4 h. $10^3 \times 10^2$

*Some systems allow more than six characters in a variable name, but such names should be avoided. Your programs will not be transportable to other computer systems. There are a few systems that require that fewer than six characters be used.

3. Express each of the following FORTRAN real constants as an ordinary decimal number.

    a.   2.934000E04   b. 0.1230E + 02   c. 0.101E − 01
    d.   0.001E3   e. 1.00002E + 5   f. 1E − 13

4. Which of the following are inadmissible symbols for FORTRAN constants? Explain.

    a.   12,305   b. 12 + 13   c. 1.200E − 04
    d.   00.123   e. 34E0.5   f. 1.32E00
    g.   0.0   h. 0.   i. 0

5. Which of the following are inadmissible FORTRAN variable names? Explain. What are the types of those that are admissible?

    a.   SCORE   b. JSCORE   c. N-SCORE
    d.   ANS.   e. NUMBER   f. 3TAG
    g.   NUM1   h. HI-LOW   i. EMPLOYEE
    j.   I3TAG   k. SIX666   l. EMP#12

3.3 Arithmetic Operations and Expressions

FORTRAN uses the following symbols to denote the arithmetic operations:

FORTRAN symbol	Meaning	Priority
**	Exponentiation	Highest
*	Multiplication	Intermediate
/	Division	
+	Addition	Lowest
−	Subtraction	

      These operation symbols can be combined with constants and variables to form arithmetic expressions such as 9 − 5 + 2, 4.74/1.7 + 5.33/4.1, and COST + 0.09*COST. When such expressions are evaluated by the computer, the order in which the operations are performed is determined first by the indicated priority and then, in any priority class, from left to right. The single exception to this rule concerns the occurrence of two or more exponentiation operations ** in an arithmetic expression, and this will be discussed in Section 3.4.

EXAMPLE 1. In the following expressions the circled numbers indicate the order in which the operations will be performed by the computer.

                  ① ②
  a. 9 − 5 + 2 =
        4   + 2 =
           6

      Since + and − have the same priority, they are performed from left to right. Note that performing the + first gives the incorrect value: 9 − (5 + 2) = 9 − 7 = 2.

           ①   ③   ②
  b. 4.74 / 1.7 + 5.33 / 4.1 =
        2.2   + 5.33 / 4.1 =
        2.2   +   1.3   =
           3.5

③ ① ②

c. 2 +   6 / 2 * 3 =
    2 +   3   * 3 =
    2 +   9   =
                 11

Since / and * have the same priority they are performed from left to right. Note that performing the * first gives the incorrect value 3.

Expressions such as $+5$, -1.2, $+A$, and $-B$ are also allowed in FORTRAN. Both A and $+A$ have the same meaning, and $-A$ denotes the negative of A. When $+$ and $-$ are used in this manner, they are called *unary operations* and are also of the lowest priority.

EXAMPLE 2. In the following, NUM1 $= 3$, NUM2 $= -2$, and NUM3 $= 4$.

FORTRAN expression	Value of the expression
$-2**4$	-16 (not 16)
$-$NUM1	-3
$-$NUM2	2
$+$NUM2	-2
$-$NUM1$+$NUM2	-5
$-5*$NUM1$+4$	-11
$1-3**$NUM3	-80
$12/$NUM2$*$NUM1	-18 (not -2)

Parentheses may be used in FORTRAN expressions just as in ordinary algebra. They are used to override the normal order in which operations are performed and also to help clarify the meaning of numerical expressions. For example, 5.1/4.3*2.7 and (5.1/4.3)*2.7 have the same meaning in FORTRAN but the second form shown is less likely to be misinterpreted. A third use of parentheses in FORTRAN is explained in Example 3.

EXAMPLE 3. In the following, X $= 6.5$, Y $= 2.5$, and Z $= -1.5$.

FORTRAN expression	Value of the expression
0.5*(X+Y)	4.5
(X+Y)/(X+Z)	1.8
X*(Y+Z)+(Y+Z)	7.5
(−Y)**2	6.25
−Y**2	−6.25
Y*(−Z)	3.75

Remark: The parentheses surrounding $-Z$ in X*($-Z$) are necessary in order that two operation symbols do not appear adjacent to each other. Failure to observe this rule will result in an error.

An arithmetic expression containing only integer constants and variables is evaluated by the computer as an integer constant. The expression 23/5 will not be evaluated as 4.6 since this is not an integer. Rather, the fractional part (.6) will be dropped to yield

23/5 $= 4$

This is called **integer arithmetic**—all operands and all results are integers. The computer does this by truncating noninteger values—that is, by dropping the fractional part. Thus, $(-23)/5 = -4$ since the fractional part (.6) of the quotient -4.6 is dropped.

EXAMPLE 4. Some integer expressions and their evaluation.

a.   2 + 7/2 − 1 =   (7/2 = 3.5 is truncated to 3.)
     2 + 3 − 1 =
         5   − 1 =
                4

b.   1/2**2 =
        1/4 =   (1/4 = 0.25 is truncated to 0.)
         0

c.   (−2)/5 + 7 =   ((−2)/5 = −0.4 is truncated to 0.)
        0 + 7 =
           7

d.   1000*2**(−3) =   (2**(−3) = 2^{-3} = 0.125 is truncated to 0.)
       1000*0   =
              0

An arithmetic expression containing only real constants and variables is evaluated by the computer as a real constant. Unlike integer arithmetic, such real expressions will be evaluated as in ordinary arithmetic.

When using the operators **, *, /, +, and −, to form arithmetic expressions, the two operands should be of the same type—that is, both integers or both reals. The single exception to this rule is the form *real**integer*. This form will always be evaluated as a real. The reason that all FORTRAN compilers allow this mixed form is explained in Section 3.4.

EXAMPLE 5. Admissible and inadmissible FORTRAN expressions.

Expression	*Discussion*
N+I/(M+3)	Admissible. Contains only integer data.
A+(2.15)*B	Admissible. Contains only real data.
N+I/(A+B)	Inadmissible. The division operator has integer and real operands (I and A + B).
X**(N+1)	Admissible. X is a real and N + 1 is an integer, so, this is of the form *real**integer,* which is allowed.
A+B**(4+I/(J+K))	Admissible. 4 + I/(J + K) is an integer so the expression is of the form A + B***integer*. B***integer* is allowed and has a real value, so both operands A and B***integer* for the + operator are of type real.
(ISUM/N)*Y	Inadmissible. The operands for the operator * are ISUM/N, an integer, and Y, a real.

Expressions involving operators whose operands are of different types (other than the form *real**integer*) are called **mixed-mode** expressions. They are allowed on some, but not all, FORTRAN systems. Programs including mixed-mode expressions will not always be transportable to other computers. They can also be very difficult to understand and, hence, to correct or modify. Indeed, the source of many frustrations, especially for beginners, is found in the misuse of mixed-mode expressions. The policy in this text is to avoid them entirely.

There are times when you may find that a real number must be divided by an integer. For example, suppose SUM denotes the sum of a collection of real numbers and ICOUNT denotes how many numbers were added to obtain this sum. To find the average of these numbers we might write

SUM/ICOUNT

But this is a mixed-mode expression. FORTRAN allows you to get around this difficulty by writing

SUM/FLOAT(ICOUNT)

FLOAT is one of many FORTRAN *functions*. Its effect is to convert an integer to a real. Thus, if ICOUNT = 184, then FLOAT(ICOUNT) = 184., a real constant. This means that both operands SUM and FLOAT(ICOUNT) are of the same type so that SUM/FLOAT(ICOUNT) is not a mixed-mode expression.

3.4 The Exponentiation Operator **

In this section we discuss three topics:

1. the form *real**integer,*
2. roots of numbers, and
3. the form a**b**c

When a FORTRAN compiler encounters an expression such as X**2, it compiles it as if it were X*X—that is, as a multiplication both of whose operands are real. Similarly, X**(−2) is compiled as 1./(X*X), which also involves only real type data. A similar situation holds whenever integer exponents are encountered.

Expression	Method of Evaluation
X**3	(X*X)*X
X**(−3)	1./((X*X)*X)
2.**(−2)	1./(2.*2.) (=.25)

In each case, the form *real**integer* is compiled as an expression involving only real data; hence it is not regarded as a mixed mode expression.

Note: Expressions such as X**0.5 and X**2.0, which involve real exponents, are executed by a more complicated and lengthy process involving logarithms. Since X**2. and X**2 both represent the same algebraic expression x^2, the second form, with the integer exponent, should be used. In general, using integer exponents, where possible, results in the most efficient use of your computer resources.

Roots of numbers are indicated in FORTRAN by using the exponentiation operator **. Recall from algebra that

$$\sqrt{9} = 9^{1/2} = 3.$$

In FORTRAN, we write this as

9.**0.5   or   9.**(1./2.)

When taking roots, the exponent must be real. For example, 9.**(1/2) = 9.**0, since the value of the integer expression 1/2 is 0. Certainly, this is not the square root of 9: indeed, 9.**0 = 9^0 = 1.

EXAMPLE 6. In the following, M = 4, X = 4.0, and Y = 5.0.

Algebraic expression	An equivalent FORTRAN expression	Value
$\sqrt{x}$	X**0.5	2.
$\sqrt{x+y}$	(X+Y)**(1./2.)	3.
$\sqrt[3]{2x}$	(2.*X)**(1./3.)	2.
$\sqrt[m]{x^2}$	(X**2)**(1./FLOAT(M))	2.
$\sqrt[m]{81}$	81.**(FLOAT(M)**(−1))	3.

Caution: FORTRAN is not designed to take roots of negative numbers. For example, the cube root of −8 is −2, but the FORTRAN expression (−8.)**(1./3.) does not give this value. An expression with a real exponent, such as A**B, will result in an error if A is negative. As you progress in the study of FORTRAN you will find ways around such difficulties.

The expression X**Y**Z represents an exception to the rule that states that operations of the same priority are evaluated from left to right. On some systems it is evaluated as X**(Y**Z), on others as (X**Y)**Z, and on still others it is not allowed. The safest, and best, policy is always to use parentheses. The FORTRAN standard ANSI X.3 − 1978* specifies that exponentiations are to be evaluated from right to left, and operations of lower priorities from left to right. Although this may seem confusing, it is in total agreement with the conventions of ordinary algebra.

3.5 Problems

1. Evaluate the following FORTRAN expressions.
   a. 12./(1.+2.)
   b. 12/(1+2)
   c. −4+2
   d. −(4+2)
   e. (−4)+2
   f. 2−4
   g. 1./2./2.
   h. 1/2/2
   i. 1/2*2
   j. 2*1/2
   k. 2**3
   l. 2.**3
   m. −2.*3./8.*12.
   n. −2*3/8*12
   o. FLOAT(16)**0.5

2. For A = 3.0, B = 9.0, M = 5, and N = 2, evaluate the following.
   a. A+3.0/B
   b. (A+B)/A*B
   c. B/A*B
   d. A+B**2
   e. B**0.5−A
   f. M**N
   g. FLOAT(M)**N
   h. B**(M/N)
   i. B**(FLOAT(M)/FLOAT(N))
   j. M/N+N
   k. M/(N+M)
   l. M−(M/N)*N

3. Some of the following are not admissible FORTRAN expressions. Explain why. You are to assume that mixed mode expressions are not allowed.
   a. (X+SUM)Y
   b. X2**3
   c. M7**3.0
   d. (A+B)/74
   e. 2X**2
   f. N+(+N)
   g. A3−(−A3)
   h. A**−N
   i. (A−B)/−A
   j. −(A+2B)
   k. −(M+2N)
   l. X+Y/FLOAT(I+J)

4. Some of the following are admissible FORTRAN expressions and some are not. Rewrite those that are not and then evaluate all of them. (Mixed mode expressions are not admissible.)
   a. (−3+ −7)*2
   b. 2+(2)
   c. −2**2*3
   d. (7+2)/−4
   e. (−3)**2
   f. −3**2
   g. 2(3.1+2.2)
   h. −3+(−3+1)
   i. 7.0*1.2E−03
   j. 7*1.2E−03
   k. 7.*12E2
   l. 9**1/2
   m. 9**(1./2.)
   n. 9.**1./2.
   o. (2+7+6)/FLOAT(3)

5. Following are some mathematical expressions and corresponding FORTRAN expressions. The FORTRAN expressions are incorrect; that is, they do not do what is intended. Correct them.
   a. $5x + 2y$,   5X+2Y
   b. $\frac{1}{ab}$,   1/A*B
   c. $\frac{a + b}{c + d}$,   A+B/C+D
   d. $2x^2 − 9$,   2*X**2−9
   e. $\frac{m + n}{2}$,   (M+N)/2
   f. $\sqrt{x^2 + y^2}$,   (X**2+Y**2)**(1/2)

3.6 Assigning Values to Variables

In Section 3.3 you saw how to write arithmetic expressions in a form acceptable to the computer. You will now learn how to instruct the computer to evaluate such expressions.

*Hereafter referred to as "the FORTRAN standard."

The following program was listed at the outset of this chapter:

```
C PROGRAM TO AVERAGE THREE NUMBERS
C     A, B, AND C DENOTE THE NUMBERS
C     AV DENOTES THE AVERAGE
      A=12.25
      B=19.40
      C=17.10
      AV=(A+B+C)/3.0
      WRITE(6,10)AV
   10 FORMAT(1X,'AVERAGE IS',F7.2)
      STOP
      END
```

Each line shown is called a FORTRAN **statement** and a collection of FORTRAN statements is called a FORTRAN **program.** Certain of the FORTRAN statements are called *executable* because they represent instructions to the computer to carry out specific tasks during program execution. All others are called *nonexecutable*. The executable statements in the program shown are

A = 12.25
B = 19.40
C = 17.10
AV = (A + B + C)/3.0
WRITE(6,10)AV
STOP

The first three assign values to variables, the fourth evaluates the expression (A + B + C)/3.0 and assigns this value to the variable AV, and the fifth instructs the computer to print the value of AV. The statements (executable statements) in a FORTRAN program are performed in the order in which they are written unless some instruction overrides this order.

The four statements

A = 12.25
B = 19.40
C = 17.10
AV = (A + B + C)/3.0

are called **assignment statements**—each *assigns* a value to a variable. The general form of the FORTRAN assignment statement is

v = e

where **v** denotes a variable name, and **e** denotes a FORTRAN expression that may simply be a constant. This statement directs the computer to evaluate the expression **e** and then assign this value to the variable **v** (more precisely, the value of **e** is stored in the storage unit associated with the variable name **v**). The variable **v** and the expression **e** need not be of the same type. However, since only integer constants can be assigned to integer variables, and real constants to real variables, the value of **e** will be converted to the type of **v** before it is stored. We illustrate by example.

EXAMPLE 7. In the following I = 5, A = 2.0, B = −2.0, and C = 3.0.

Assignment statement	After execution	
S = A + B + C	S has the *real* value 3.	
T = C/A + B	T has the *real* value − .5.	
X = 37	X has the *real* value 37.	(The integer 37 is converted to a real.)

Assignment statement	After execution	
N = 22.91	N has the *integer* value 22.	(The real 22.91 is truncated to the integer 22.)
M = C/B	M has the *integer* value 1.	(The real 3./2. = 1.5 is truncated to the integer 1.)
Y = I/J	Y has the *real* value 2.	(5/2 = 2 since I/J must be an integer. This integer 2 is then converted to a real.)
K = J/I	K has the *integer* value 0.	(2/5 = 0 since J/I must be an integer.)
IX = J**I	IX has the *integer* value 32.	($2**5 = 2^5 = 32$, an integer.)
Z = A**I	Z has the *real* value 32.	($2.**5 = 2.^5 = 32.$, a real.)

Blank spaces may be used to improve the appearance and legibility of any FORTRAN statement. With but few exceptions, which will be explained as needed, the computer ignores all blanks in FORTRAN statements. Thus, the following three statements are equivalent.

        AV = (A + B + C)/3.0
        AV = (A + B + C)/3.0
        AV = (A + B + C) / 3. 0

Good programming practice dictates that this freedom in spacing be used to advantage; a program should be easy to read.

EXAMPLE 8. Here is a FORTRAN program ready to be submitted to the computer and run. (The procedure for doing this is described in the next chapter.) The columns to the right of the program show how the values of the variables change during program execution.

The program	After execution of each instruction		
	Value of P	Value of Q	Value of ONE
ONE = 1	–	–	1.
P = 12	12.	–	1.
Q = P/2. + ONE	12.	7.	1.
P = Q/2. + ONE	4.5	7.	1.
Q = P/2. + ONE	4.5	3.25	1.
STOP			
END			

Remark 1: Note that no values are shown for P and Q prior to their being assigned values by assignment statements. Some, but not all, FORTRAN compilers assign initial values of zero to all numerical variables.

Remark 2: Newly written programs may not do what they were meant to do. The programmer must find and correct all errors. The errors are called *bugs,* and making corrections is referred to as *debugging* the program. A very useful debugging technique is to pretend that you are the computer and prepare a table of successive values of program variables, as was done in this example. The process of preparing such a table of values is called *tracing;* the table is called a *trace.*

The FORTRAN statement

        N = N + 1

does not mean that N is equal to N + 1 (since that is impossible). It means that the expression on the right, N + 1, is evaluated, and the value obtained is assigned to the variable on the left, N. For example, the effect of the two lines

        N = 5
        N = N + 1

is that the value 6 is assigned to N. Similarly, the statement

S = S + Y

evaluates S + Y and then assigns this new value to S.

EXAMPLE 9. In the following, M = 10, N = 8, S = 3.0, Y = -2.0, and Z = 6.0.

Assignment statement	After execution
S = S + Y	S has the value 1.
M = M - 1	M has the value 9.
N = 35 - 3*N	N has the value 11.
Z = 13. + 2.*Z	Z has the value 25.

3.7 Problems

1. Which of these are incorrect FORTRAN assignment statements? Explain.
a. X = (A + B)C
b. M = M1 - M2
c. 2FJ = Y - ZZZ
d. B = A*A*A
e. VALUE135 = 41 + 4*Y
f. I + J = K
g. X = 2.3E - 05
h. Y = 4E0.5

2. Write assignment statements to perform the indicated tasks. Do not use mixed-mode expressions.
a. Assign the value 7 to M.
b. Assign the value of the expression S + X to X.
c. Increase the value of N by 7.
d. Increase the value of S by 7.
e. Assign the tenth power of 1.0 + R to A.
f. Replace the value of H by double its value.
g. Decrease the value of X by twice the value of Y.
h. Increase the value of Y by the value of M.

3. Let I = 5, J = 3, X = 3.0, Y = 5.0, and Z = 2.0. Explain the effect of each of the following assignment statements.
a. A = X + Y/Z
b. Z = 2.*Z
c. K = Z*(X/Y)
d. A = Z*(X/Y)
e. T = (I + J)/3
f. N = (I + J)/3
g. S = Y/X + FLOAT(I)/FLOAT(J)
h. S = Y/X + FLOAT(I/J)
i. P = Z**(I - J + 1)
j. M = J**J

4. Complete the following traces as was done in Example 8.

a. The program	Value after execution		
	I	J	K
I = 1	1	–	–
J = 2	1	2	–
K = 1			
K = K + J			
I = J**2			
J = K - J + I			
K = K - 1			
J = I*J			
I = J/I			
STOP			
END			

b. *The program* — *Value after execution*

b. The program	N	M
N = 1	1	–
M = N*(N + 1)		
N = N + 1		
M = N*(N + 1)		
N = N + 1		
M = N*(N + 1)		
STOP		
END		

c. *The program* — *Value after execution*

c. The program	X	Y	I
X = 1.5	1.5	–	–
Y = 3.0/(2.*X + 2.)			
X = − X			
Y = 3.0/(2.*X + 2.)			
I = 3.*X			
I = − I			
I = 2**I			
STOP			
END			

3.8 Printing Results—The WRITE, PRINT, and FORMAT Statements

Every computer language is designed so that results can be made available in a usable form. This may mean producing a printed report, displaying the results on a video screen, or recording the results on magnetic tape or disk or even on cards by means of a card punch machine.

There are two FORTRAN statements for producing output, the WRITE and PRINT statements. These two statements are most often used in conjunction with FORMAT statements that specify the precise form of the output. When used with FORMAT statements, they are called **formatted WRITE** and **formatted PRINT statements.** The example listed at the outset of this chapter contains the following formatted WRITE statement:

```
     WRITE(6,10)AV
10 FORMAT(1X,'AVERAGE IS',F7.2)
```

The WRITE statement instructs the computer to print the value of AV in the form specified in the FORMAT statement labeled 10.* The 6 appearing in the WRITE statement tells the computer which output device to use. We'll use the device number 6 to specify a printer or video screen as the output unit. The first item, 1X, in the FORMAT statement is used for carriage control. It causes nothing to be printed but causes the output to appear on a new print line. We'll use the characters 1X to begin every output FORMAT statement until carriage control characters are explained more fully in Chapter 8. The expression 'AVERAGE IS' appearing next in the FORMAT statement causes all characters, including blanks, enclosed in quotes to be printed. Finally, the expression F7.2 tells the computer to print the value of AV by using seven print positions, including two digits to the right of the decimal point.

---

*Any FORTRAN statement can be labeled with a one- to five-digit statement number. Uses of such labels, other than referencing FORMAT statements, will be explained as needed.

The following somewhat simpler PRINT statement can be used to accomplish the same thing:

```
    PRINT 10,AV
10 FORMAT(1X,'AVERAGE IS',F7.2)
```

This formatted PRINT statement is equivalent to the formatted WRITE statement except that the device number 6 is not needed—the output is automatically produced at your printer or video display.

The WRITE statement is allowed on all FORTRAN systems; the PRINT statement is allowed on most. In what follows, we'll describe how to use the WRITE statement and in each situation will show how the same thing can be accomplished with the PRINT statement.

The general forms of the WRITE and FORMAT statements are

WRITE(u,f)list
f   FORMAT(fs)

> When using PRINT, use
>
> **PRINT f,list**
> **f   FORMAT(fs)**

The items **list, fs, u,** and **f** are as follows:

list   denotes a list of variable names separated by commas. Whatever values are currently assigned to these variables will be output.

fs   denotes a format specification consisting of a list of *edit descriptors,* such as F7.2 and 'AVERAGE IS' in the example. In this section, four of the many edit descriptors allowed in FORTRAN will be described.

u   denotes an unsigned integer that specifies which output unit should be used. In this text we use **u** = 6 to specify a printer or a video screen as the output unit. (The integer **u** is not used when using PRINT.)

f   denotes an unsigned integer used to label a FORMAT statement. All FORMAT statements must be labeled. The occurrence of **f** in a WRITE or PRINT statement instructs the computer to output the values of the variables included in **list** according to the format specification in the statement labeled **f.**

The next four examples illustrate four of the edit descriptors that can appear in a format specification.

EXAMPLE 10. Here is a program to produce integer output (the edit descriptor Iw):

```
    INTEGER COUNT,SUM
    SUM=5+11+7+2
    COUNT=4
    WRITE(6,10)COUNT,SUM                or, PRINT 10,COUNT,SUM
10 FORMAT(1X,I2,I5)
    STOP
    END
```

Output: (Δ denotes a blank space.)

Δ4ΔΔΔ25

The edit descriptor I2 tells the computer to print the first value (value of COUNT) using two print positions. Since COUNT = 4 has only one digit, it is printed as Δ4; that is, it is right justified in the two allotted positions with a blank appearing in the unused position. The second descriptor I5 causes the second value SUM to be printed right justified in the next five print positions. Since SUM = 25, this value is printed as ΔΔΔ25.

Remark 1: If the descriptor I5 is replaced with I2, the value 25 will be printed in the two allotted positions with no leading blanks. This means that the output will appear as Δ425. Specifying more print positions than are actually needed for a number, as was done in the example, is one way to ensure that numbers will be separated in the output. Another way to accomplish this is shown in Example 12.

Remark 2: When using a descriptor such as I2, you must specify enough print positions to accommodate whatever values are to be printed. If the number being printed is negative, the digits and the minus sign must fit. Thus, I2 is adequate for printing the integers 4, −7, or 28, but not for printing −29 or 219. What happens when you do not specify enough room for values being printed is system dependent and will not be discussed here.

EXAMPLE 11. Here is a program to produce real output (the edit descriptor Fw.d):

```
    VAR1=12.328
    VAR2=-194.22
    WRITE(6,11)VAR1,VAR2
 11 FORMAT(1X,F8.2,F8.2)
    STOP
    END
```

or, PRINT 11,VAR1,VAR2

Output:

ΔΔΔ12.33Δ-194.22

The first edit descriptor F8.2 tells the computer to print the first value (value of VAR1) using eight print positions. The 2 in F8.2 says that two digits are to be printed to the right of the decimal point. (The decimal point will use one of the eight print positions.) Since the value 12.328 of VAR1 must be printed with only two fractional digits, it is first rounded to 12.33. This number requires only five of the eight positions allotted, so it is printed as ΔΔΔ12.33; that is, it is right justified in the space provided, with blanks appearing in the unused positions.

The value −194.22 of VAR2 is then printed according to the next descriptor, which again is F8.2, as Δ−194.22.

Remark 1: If the second descriptor is replaced with F7.2, the output will be ΔΔΔ12.33−194.22 (see Remark 1 in Example 10).

Remark 2: When using the F descriptor, space must be provided for the decimal point and also for a possible minus sign. In addition, numbers smaller in magnitude than 1 are printed with a zero preceding the decimal point. For example, .132 is printed as 0.132 and −.74 is printed as −0.74. Thus, for such small numbers, space must also be provided for the leading zero.

EXAMPLE 12. Here is a program to illustrate the spacing descriptor X:

```
    NUM1=-145
    VAR1=-NUM1
    WRITE(6,12)NUM1,VAR1
 12 FORMAT(1X,I4,3X,F7.0)
    STOP
    END
```

or, PRINT 12,NUM1,VAR1

Output:

-145ΔΔΔΔΔΔ145.

The integer value −145 of NUM1 is printed using the descriptor I4. Since −145 requires four print positions, it uses all four specified in I4. Then, the descriptor 3X produces three blanks in the output. The next value to be printed is the real value 145. of the real variable VAR1, hence a real descriptor appears next in the format specification. F7.0 specifies that the value of VAR1 is to be printed using seven positions with no digits to the right of the decimal point. Thus, ΔΔΔ145. is output.

FORTRAN allows you to have messages printed during program execution. These messages are called **character strings;** they can contain any of the individual characters allowable on your system and they must be enclosed within single quotation marks.* The character string together with its quotation marks is called a **string constant.** These character strings can serve as headings or as identifying labels for printed results. The following example illustrates how this can be done.

EXAMPLE 13. Here is a program to calculate the sales tax (5%) on an automobile listing at $5,320.00:

```
    WRITE(6,10)
 10 FORMAT(1X,'TAX COMPUTATION PROGRAM')
    PRICE=5320.00
    RATE=0.05
    TAX=RATE*PRICE
    WRITE(6,11)TAX
 11 FORMAT(1X,'SALES TAX=',F8.2)
    STOP
    END
```

or, PRINT 10

or, PRINT 11,TAX

Output:

```
TAX COMPUTATION PROGRAM
SALES TAX=ΔΔ266.00
```

The first WRITE statement includes no variables; hence the format specification in the FORMAT statement labeled 10 does not require an I or an F descriptor. However, the string constant 'TAX COMPUTATION PROGRAM' causes the character string TAX COMPUTATION PROGRAM to be printed as shown in the output.

The second WRITE statement includes the real variable TAX, hence the format specification in the statement labeled 11 contains the real descriptor F8.2. The string constant 'SALES TAX =' appears before F8.2 so the character string SALES TAX = is printed prior to the value 266. of the variable TAX.

Remark: The value 266. of the variable TAX is printed as ΔΔ266.00, as shown in the output. The two fractional digits specified in the descriptor F8.2 are always printed, even if they are both zero.

The preceding examples illustrate four ways to control the output of a FORTRAN program. In Chapter 8 you will see that there are other ways to construct format specifications. However, the four descriptors we have considered are four of the most widely used and will suffice for many applications. Following is a summary of these edit descriptors.

Edit Descriptor	*Description*
I*w*	*w* denotes an unsigned integer indicating that an integer datum is to be output using *w* positions. If the datum requires fewer than *w* positions, it will be printed right-justified with leading blanks.
F*w.d*	*w* denotes an unsigned integer and indicates that a real datum is to be output using *w* positions. *d* also denotes an unsigned integer and indicates that *d* digits are to be printed to the right of the decimal point. If the datum to be output has more

*A single quote in a string is represented by two single quotes. For instance 'THAT''S ALL FOLKS!' represents THAT'S ALL FOLKS!

than *d* fractional digits it is rounded to *d* decimal places. If the datum requires fewer than *w* positions, it will be printed right-justified with leading blanks.

*n*X   *n* denotes an unsigned integer and indicates that *n* blanks are to be output. 1X may be written as X. (When 1X appears first in an output specification, it is a carriage control character as explained in Chapter 8.)

'----'   denotes the character string consisting of all characters, including blanks, enclosed within the single quotes. On some systems, a quoted string such as 'AVERAGE IS' must be written as *AVERAGE IS*, while others require the Hollerith notation 10HAVERAGE IS. The Hollerith descriptor *n*H specifies that the *n* characters, including blanks, immediately following the letter H constitute a string equivalent to one specified by enclosing the *n* characters in single quotes.

Many systems, especially time-sharing systems, allow **unformatted WRITE** and **PRINT statements.** For example, the statement

PRINT,I,A,B

will cause the values of I, A, and B to be printed on one line. Similarly, the statement

PRINT,'AVERAGE IS',AV

will produce the following output:

AVERAGE IS (value of AV)

In general, unformatted WRITE and PRINT statements are written in exactly the same way as formatted WRITE and PRINT statements, except that the statement label referring to a FORMAT statement is omitted. Thus, the general forms of the unformatted WRITE and PRINT statements are

WRITE(u)a,b,c,. . .

and

PRINT,a,b,c,. . .

where **a, b, c,** . . . denote variable names or quoted strings and **u** denotes an unsigned integer specifying an output device. Either statement will print the indicated items on one line in a form determined by the computer rather than by the programmer. If there is insufficient space on one line for all of these items, more than one line will be used.

3.9 Comments as Part of a Program

The program listed at the outset of this chapter begins with the following three lines:

```
C PROGRAM TO AVERAGE THREE NUMBERS.
C    A, B, AND C DENOTE THE NUMBERS.
C    AV DENOTES THE AVERAGE.
```

These three FORTRAN statements are included to indicate the purpose of the program and to identify what quantities the variables A, B, C, and AV represent. They are called comment lines. They cause nothing to happen during program execution. Their sole purpose is to allow you to include documentation as part of a program.

EXAMPLE 14.

```
C PROGRAM TO DETERMINE THE RATE OF RETURN
C GIVEN THE CURRENT PRICE AND EARNINGS.
C    P DENOTES THE CURRENT PRICE OF A SECURITY
```

```
C      E DENOTES THE RECENT ANNUAL EARNINGS
C      R DENOTES THE RATE OF RETURN
       P=80.00
       E=6.00
C CALCULATE AND PRINT THE RATE OF RETURN
       R=100.*E/P
       WRITE(6,100)R
   100 FORMAT(1X,'RATE OF RETURN',X,F6.2)
       STOP
       END
```

> or, PRINT 100,R

Output:

```
RATE OF RETURNΔΔ7.50
```

In this program, comments are used for three different purposes: to give a brief description of the program (first two lines), to describe the quantities represented by the variables used (next three lines), and to describe the action of a group of programming lines (the last comment describes the purpose of the next three lines). Using comments in this manner is an excellent programming practice. Your programs will be easier to read and understand, easier to debug, and easier to modify at some later date (should that be required).

3.10 Problems

1. Which of these are incorrect FORTRAN statements? Explain.

a. `WRITE(6 10)A+B+C`

b. `WRITE M,N,J`

c. `WRITE(6,12)'SUM IS',S`

d. `25 FORMAT(1X I4 I7 F5.1)`

e. `35 FORMAT(1X,DEPT IS,I5)`

f. `10. FORMAT(1X,I6,'XX',I3)`

2. Let N1 = 12, N2 = 36, and X = 1.239E03. Exactly what output will be produced by the following formatted WRITE statements?

a.
```
    WRITE(6,10)N1,N2
 10 FORMAT(1X,I7,I5)
```

b.
```
    WRITE(6,11)N1,N2,N1
 11 FORMAT(1X,I5,I5,I5)
```

c.
```
    WRITE(6,12)N2
 12 FORMAT(1X,5X,'LARGEST ',12)
```

d.
```
    Y=N1+N2
    WRITE(6,13)N1
 13 FORMAT(1X,5X,'FIRST',I4)
    WRITE(6,14)Y
 14 FORMAT(1X,'SUM=',F8.3)
```

e.
```
    Y=FLOAT(N1+N2)/70.
    WRITE(6,15)Y
 15 FORMAT(1X,'ANSWER',F12.3)
```

f.
```
    Z=(N1+N2)/70
    WRITE(6,16)Z
 16 FORMAT(1X,4X,'RESULT',F8.2)
```

g.
```
    WRITE(6,17)
    WRITE(6,18)N1,N2
 17 FORMAT(1X,'TWO NUMBERS')
 18 FORMAT(1X,I5,I5)
```

h.
```
    I=X
    WRITE(6,19)X,I
 19 FORMAT(1X,F10.2,I6)
```

3. Let N1 = 70, N2 = 48, and X = 138.827. Exactly what will be printed by the following formatted PRINT statements?

a.   b.

```
a.        PRINT 20,N1,N2
       20 FORMAT(1X,I7,I5)
```

```
b.        PRINT 21,X,N2
       21 FORMAT(1X,F8.2,I3)
```

```
c.        S=N1+N2
          PRINT 22,N1,N2
       22 FORMAT(1X,'NUMBERS',I3,I3)
          PRINT 23,S
       23 FORMAT(1X,'SUM',1X,F6.2)
```

```
d.        T=FLOAT(N2)/FLOAT(N1)
          PRINT 26,T
       26 FORMAT(1X,'QUOTIENT',F12.3)
```

```
e.        Q=N1/N2
          PRINT 27,Q
       27 FORMAT(1X,'QUOTIENT',F6.2)
```

```
f.        PRINT 28
          PRINT 29,N1,X
       28 FORMAT(1X,'TWO NUMBERS')
       29 FORMAT(1X,I5,F8.0)
```

4. The following program segments do not do what is claimed. Explain. Correct each so that it behaves as described.

```
a.  C DIVIDE X BY Y
          X=26.
          Y=13.
          QUOTIENT=X/Y
          WRITE(6,10)Q
       10 FORMAT(1X,'QUOTIENT',I4)
```

```
b.  C ADD X AND Y
          X=13.12
          Y=20.5
          SUM=X+Y
          WRITE(6,11)SUM
       11 FORMAT(1X,'SUM',SUM)
```

```
c.  C PRINT THE FOLLOWING
    C     TEA FOR TWO
          WRITE(6,13)
       13 FORMAT(1X,'TEA','FOR','TWO')
```

```
d.  C PRINT THE FOLLOWING
    C     WET
    C     PAINT
          WRITE(6,14)
          WRITE(6,15)
       14 FORMAT(1X,5X,'WET')
       15 FORMAT(1X,5X,'PAINT')
```

5. Replace each WRITE statement in Problem 4 with an equivalent PRINT statement and then explain why the resulting program segments do not do what is claimed. Correct them so that they behave as described.

6. Complete the following traces; show the values of variables and what is output, following execution of each program statement.

a.

	X	Y	S	Output
X=12.69	12.69	-	-	
WRITE(6,10)X	12.69	-	-	X=△△△13.
Y=5				
S=X+Y				
WRITE(6,11)Y				
WRITE(6,12)S				
10 FORMAT(1X,'X=',F6.0)				

```
11 FORMAT(1X,F6.2)

12 FORMAT(1X,'SUM IS',F7.1)

   STOP

   END
```

b.

```
   X=14.915

   PRINT 20,X

   Y=X+6.003

   PRINT 21,Y

   P=Y*1E1

   PRINT 22,P

20 FORMAT(1X,F6.0)

21 FORMAT(1X,'Y=',F8.2)

22 FORMAT(1X,F10.1)

   STOP

   END
```

X	Y	P	Output
14.915	-	-	
14.915	-	-	ΔΔΔ15.

3.11 Review True-or-False Quiz

1. $2+3$ is a numerical constant in FORTRAN.   T   F
2. $A3 = A3*A3$ is an admissible FORTRAN statement.   T   F
3. If $N = 3$, the statement $1 + N**2 = M$ assigns the value 10 to the variable M.   T   F
4. $1.0E01 = 10$.   T   F
5. $123E - 8 = .00000000123$ T   F
6. $(A + B)**.5$ and $(A + B)**(1/2)$ have the same meaning in FORTRAN.   T   F
7. If A has the value -27.00, the statement $B = A**(1./3.)$ assigns the value $-3.$ to B.   T   F
8. Parentheses may be used only to override the normal order in which operations are
   performed by the computer.   T   F
9. Comment lines are often used to explain the purpose of groups of program statements.   T   F
10. The sole purpose of comment lines is to document a program.   T   F
11. The statement $K = K + 1$ is an admissible assignment statement but will result in an
    error because there is no value K for which $K = K + 1$.   T   F
12. There is nothing wrong with the assignment statement $Y = SUM/FLOAT(NUMBER)$.   T   F
13. The statement $SUM = NUM1 + NUM2$ is inadmissible because SUM and NUM1
    + NUM2 are of different types.   T   F
14. Every FORMAT statement must have a statement label.   T   F
15. The value of the integer variable NUM can be output by using the edit descriptor
    F6.2; however, if this is done, two zeros will appear to the right of the decimal point.   T   F

4
Loading and Running a Program

Chapter 3 presented examples of FORTRAN programs ready to be transmitted to the computer for execution. Computer systems differ in how this can be done but they all fall into two major categories: **conversational systems** and **batch processing systems.** Conversational systems allow you to interact with the computer during the preparation and execution of a program. Everything takes place while you are seated at a computer terminal, and you are in complete control of the computer's operations. Batch processing systems allow little or no interaction. They require that a complete job, including the program, the data to be processed, and certain instructions to the computer concerning the task to be performed, be submitted at one time. Usually, this involves a punched card operation in which all information is transferred to punched cards before being submitted to the computer. Conversational and batch processing systems are described in Sections 4.1 and 4.3, respectively. These two sections are completely independent and may be taken up in either order. We then conclude this chapter with a section on writing your first FORTRAN program.

4.1 Conversational Computer Systems

The first step in using a conversational computer system is to establish communication with the computer. When this has been accomplished you are *on line*. If you are using a small computer system dedicated to a single user, going on line can be as simple as pressing a button or turning a knob. However, conversational systems most often are time-sharing systems allowing simultaneous access to the computer's resources by many users. In such cases, going on line involves a slightly more complicated log-in procedure. The usual situation is as follows.

1. You initiate the log-in procedure by activating a switch and possibly dialing the computer site.

2. The time-sharing system identifies itself by printing an appropriate message.
3. You enter a *user number* and a *password* as directed by the computer. If they are recognized by the computer as identifying an authorized user, you are on line.
4. At this point you must respond to a number of prompts by the computer. For your first session at a terminal, this will involve identifying FORTRAN as the language to be used, specifying that you will type in a new program, and assigning a name to this program.

Following is the printout generated during a log-in to a typical time-sharing system. The underlined characters are printed by the computer.

(The time-sharing system identifies itself.)
USER NUMBER: ABC652   (The user number ABC652 is typed.)
PASSWORD: (The password is typed but not displayed at the terminal.)
SYSTEM: FORTRAN   (The FORTRAN language is selected.)
NEW OR OLD: NEW   (A new program will be typed.)
NEW FILE NAME: PROG2   (The name PROG2 is chosen.)
READY   (The computer is now ready for you to type in a program or to type any command allowed by the time-sharing system.)

Here is a short FORTRAN program ready to be transmitted to the computer:

```
C SALES TAX COMPUTATION
  RATE=0.05
  PRICE=5329.00
C CALCULATE THE TAX
  TAX=RATE*PRICE
  STOP
  END
```

We'll now show how this program can be entered when operating in a time-sharing or conversational environment. The procedure for submitting the same program when operating a batch processing environment is described in Section 4.3.

Each FORTRAN statement must be preceded by an unsigned integer called a *line number*. Different statements must have different line numbers. Line numbers are not to be confused with the statement numbers used to label FORTRAN statements such as FORMAT statements. Line numbers are used for editing purposes and are not part of the FORTRAN program; for instance, the FORTRAN compiler processes the program statements in the order of increasing line numbers. While typing a program, the following rules apply:

1. The letter C immediately following a line number indicates a comment line.
2. Any nonblank character other than C or a digit 0 to 9 immediately following the line number indicates that the line is a continuation of the preceding line. If you use continuation lines, you should consult your FORTRAN manual for possible restrictions on their use.
3. In all other cases, a blank space must appear in the position immediately following the line number and the FORTRAN statement can begin in the next position.

Following these rules, the given program can be entered by typing the following:

```
100C SALES TAX COMPUTATION
110 RATE=0.05
120 PRICE=5329.00
130C CALCULATE THE TAX
140 TAX=RATE*PRICE
150 STOP
160 END
```

After each line is typed, it is entered by depressing the RETURN key (sometimes labeled ENTER).

Spaces may be used to improve the appearance and readability of programs. Spaces appearing in FORTRAN statements are ignored during compilation. The one exception is that spaces appearing in string constants, such as 'TEA FOR TWO', are not ignored.

Our SALES TAX program contains no output statement, so, if it is executed, nothing will be printed. To rectify this situation you can add the following lines simply by typing them:

```
145 WRITE(6,10)TAX
148 10 FORMAT(1X,'SALES TAX=',F8.2)
```

Conversational systems allow you to enter these lines out of their natural numerical order; the program will still be executed according to the sequence of line numbers from smallest to largest. Thus, if a line is omitted in the initial typing of a program, it can be inserted at any time simply by typing it. Choosing line numbers that increase by some other increment than 1 (10 is very popular) allows you to use the line numbers omitted for this purpose.

A printed list of all program statements already transmitted to the computer can be obtained by typing LIST. This is the first of several commands called **system commands.** A system command has no line number and is not part of a FORTRAN program. It is an instruction to the computer to perform a specific task at the time the command is issued. We illustrate for the SALES TAX COMPUTATION PROGRAM:

```
LIST                                          (You type this.)

100C SALES TAX COMPUTATION                    (This is printed by the computer.)
110 RATE=0.05
120 PRICE=5329.00
130C CALCULATE THE TAX
140 TAX=RATE*PRICE
145 WRITE(6,10)TAX
148 10 FORMAT(1X,'SALES TAX=',F8.2)
150 STOP
160 END

READY
```

Note that the statements with line numbers 145 and 148 have been inserted in their proper places even though they were actually typed after line 160 was typed. READY is the computer's signal that it is ready for you to make another entry.

When you are reasonably certain that the program has been typed correctly, you can cause it to be executed with the system command RUN. This command instructs the computer to compile your program and then execute it. We illustrate with the program just listed:

```
RUN                                           (You type this.)

SALES TAX=  266.45                            (This is printed by the computer.)

READY
```

During a session at the terminal it is almost inevitable that typing errors will occur. The simplest way to correct a typing error is to retype the entire line, including the line number. This action will replace the incorrect line with the latest version entered. An entire line can be deleted from a program simply by typing its line number and then depressing the RETURN key. Conversational systems provide other editing features that can be helpful during preparation of a program. These differ from system to system so they will not be described here.

EXAMPLE 1.

```
10 X=5.12                    (You type this.)
20 Y=3.12
30 Z=1.95
40 X-Y=DIFF
50 WRITE(6,10)DIFF
60 10 FORMAT(I5)
70 STOP
80 END
60 10 FORMAT(1X,F7.2)
40 DIFF=X-Y
30
LIST
```

```
10 X=5.12                    (This is printed by the computer.)
20 Y=3.12
40 DIFF=X-Y
50 WRITE(6,10)DIFF
60 10 FORMAT(1X,F7.2)
70 STOP
80 END
```

READY

Lines 60 and 40 were retyped. The edit descriptor I5 in the original line 60 was inappropriate for printing the value of the real variable DIFF, and line 40 contained a syntax error. Line 30 was not needed, so it was deleted by typing the line number 30 and then depressing the RETURN key.

You may not always be fortunate enough to detect syntax errors before attempting to "run" your program. Should you issue the RUN command for such an incorrect program, appropriate *error messages* will be printed. These messages will indicate the type of error and, on many systems, the line number on which the error occurs. The exact form of such messages depends on the system you are using. The following example illustrates how such error messages can be of help in correcting a program.

EXAMPLE 2.

```
10 X=7                       (You type this.)
20 X+9=Z
30 WRITE(6,10)Z
40 STOP
RUN
```

```
ILLEGAL STATEMENT AT 20                  (This is printed by the computer.)
NON-EXISTENT STATEMENT REFERENCED AT 30
END NOT LAST AT 40
     3 FORTRAN COMPILATION ERRORS
```

READY

```
20 Z=X+9                     (You type this.)
35 10 FORMAT(1X,'ANSWER IS',F7.2)
50 END
RUN
```

```
ANSWER IS  16.00
```
                                         (This is printed by the computer.)

```
READY
```

Remark: Some, but not all, FORTRAN systems recognize certain syntax errors as soon as you make them, rather than during compilation.

As illustrated in the following example, error messages are sometimes printed even though a program contains no syntax errors.

EXAMPLE 3. A program to compute the ratio

$$\frac{COST + MARKUP}{COST - MARKUP}$$

```
10C C DENOTES THE COST
20 C=100.
30C AM DENOTES THE MARKUP
40 AM=100.
50 R=(C+AM)/(C-AM)
60 WRITE(6,10)R
70 10 FORMAT(1X,'RATIO=',F7.2)
80 STOP
90 END
RUN

     DIVISION BY ZERO AT 50

READY
```

This program is syntactically correct. When run, the computer assigns 100 to C (line 20), 100 to AM (line 40), and then attempts to evaluate the expression in line 50. The error message tells you that the computer does not "know" how to divide by zero.

Errors of this type are called *run-time errors*, whereas syntax errors are referred to as *compile-time errors*.

Unfortunately, errors are not always detected by the computer. The following example illustrates such a situation.

EXAMPLE 4.

```
10C COMPUTE THE AVERAGE OF M AND N.
20C THIS PROGRAM IS SYNTACTICALLY CORRECT
30C BUT PRODUCES INCORRECT RESULTS.
40 M=10
50 N=5
60 AV=(M+N)/2
70 WRITE(6,10)AV
80 10 FORMAT(1X,'AVERAGE IS',F6.2)
90 STOP
99 END
RUN

AVERAGE IS  7.00

READY
```

The computer does precisely what you instruct it to do; it does not do what you meant it to do. The programming error in line 60 is an error in the logic of the program and is not a syntax error. It can be written correctly as 60 AV = FLOAT(M + N)/2.0. Such errors are often very difficult to find.

If a system command (rather than a programming line) is typed incorrectly, the system will respond with a message indicating that the command is unrecognizable. Thus, you needn't worry about harming the system with novice mistakes.

4.2 Problems

In Problems 1–4, assume that the lines shown are typed immediately after you have logged in. What will be printed if the LIST *command is entered? The* RUN *command?*

1.
```
10 M=14
20 N=M-5
30 WRITE(6,20),N
40 20 FORMAT(1X,'DIFF',I4)
50 STOP
10 M=24
60 END
30 WRITE(6,20)N
```

2.
```
10 WRITE(6,21)
10C DISCOUNT PROGRAM
20 PRINT=125.50
30 DISC=0.1*PRICE
40 WRITE(6,22)DISC
50 STOP
60 21 FORMAT(1X,'DISCOUNT PROGRAM')
70 22 FORMAT(1X,'DISCOUNT',F8.2)
80 END
```

3.
```
100C---DIVISION ALGORITHM
110    INTEGER N,D,Q,R
120 N=17
130 D= 7
140 Q=N/D
150 R=N-Q*D
160 WRITE(6,10)Q,R
120 N=27
170 WRITE(6,10)Q,R
180 STOP
190 10 FORMAT(1X,'QUOTIENT:',I4,5X,'REMAINDER:',I4)
200 END
```

4.
```
10 X=5.
20 Y=X/4.+X**2
30+ +3.*X+20.
40+ -11.25
50 WRITE(6,10)X,Y
60 10 FORMAT(1X,F10.4,3X,F10.4)
50 WRITE(6,10)Y,X
40
65 STOP
70 END
```

The programs in Problems 5–8 contain one or more bugs—either syntax errors (violations in the FORTRAN *rules of grammar) or programming errors (errors in the logic of a program). Find each bug, tell which type of error it is, correct the programs, and show what will be printed if the corrected programs are run.*

5.
```
10C PROGRAM TO COMPUTE SIX
20C PERCENT OF $23,000.
30 D=23,000.
40 R=6.
50 A=R*D
60 WRITE(6,10)A
70 10 FORMAT(1X,'ANSWER',F8.2)
80 STOP
90 END
```

6.
```
10C PROGRAM TO AVERAGE 2 NUMBERS
20 NUM1=24
30 NUM2=15
40 MEAN=(NUM1+NUM2)/2
50 WRITE(6,10),MEAN
60 10 FORMAT(1X,'MEAN IS',F6.1)
70 STOP
```

```
7.  10C PROGRAM TO FIND A SOLUTION    8.  10 COMMENT--ASSIGN VALUES
    20C X TO THE FOLLOWING EQUATION       20       M=5
    30C        35X+220=0                  30       N=8
    40 A=35.                              40 COMMENT--INTERCHANGE M AND N
    50 B=220.                             50       M=N
    60 A*X+B=0                            60       N=M
    70 WRITE(6,10)X                       70 WRITE(6,10)M,N
    80 10 FORMAT(1X,'X=',F9.4)            80 10 FORMAT(1X,F5.0,2X,F5.0)
    90 STOP                               90 STOP
    99 END                                99 END
```

4.3 Batch Processing Systems

In this section we describe how a FORTRAN program can be transferred to *punched cards* for submission to the computer. Figure 4.1 shows a card that has been punched to record a FORTRAN statement.

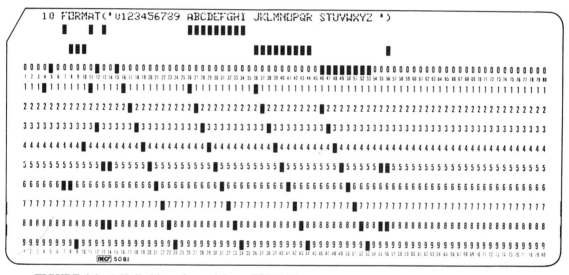

FIGURE 4.1. A Hollerith card containing a FORMAT statement.

Each card has 80 numbered columns and each column can be used to record (punch) a single character. Such cards are also called *Hollerith cards* after Herman Hollerith, a statistician and inventor who developed the first punched card operation for use in tabulating the United States Census in 1890.

The following rules must be followed in punching FORTRAN statements onto cards:

Column 1	A letter C in column 1 indicates that the card contains a comment line. The comment itself may be punched anywhere in columns 2 through 72.
Columns 1–5	Statement numbers (labels) are punched here. The common practice is to punch them right-justified in these five positions and leave the leading unused positions blank (unpunched). Statement numbers are not to be confused with the line numbers required on time-sharing systems.
Columns 7–72	The FORTRAN statement is punched here. It need not begin in column 7. Blanks in these 66 columns are ignored during compilation. The one exception is that blanks appearing in string constants such as 'TEA FOR TWO' are not ignored.
Column 6	Any character other than blank or zero that is punched in column 6 indicates that columns 7–72 contain a continuation of the preceding card. A common practice is to use the digits 1 to 9. Thus, if a long

FORTRAN statement requires four cards, column 6 is left blank on the first card, and contains 1, 2, and 3, respectively, on the next three cards. Should you use continuation cards, you should consult your system's FORTRAN manual to determine what restrictions are imposed on their use.

Columns 73–80   Whatever is punched in these columns is ignored by the computer; usually they are left blank. Some people punch numbers (called sequence numbers) in these columns to indicate the order in which the cards should appear. If this is done, a dropped deck of cards is easily reassembled.

EXAMPLE 5. Here is a short FORTRAN program shown with the corresponding punched cards:

```
C SALES TAX COMPUTATION
      RATE=0.05
      PRICE=5329.00
C     CALCULATE THE TAX
      TAX=RATE*PRICE
      WRITE(6,10)TAX
   10 FORMAT(1X,'SALES TAX=',F8.2)
      STOP
      END
```

Cards are punched by using a *card punch machine* called a **keypunch** (Figure 4.2). A keypunch has a keyboard not unlike an ordinary typewriter keyboard. Any character typed is recorded as a column of from 1 to 3 punched holes on the card. On many modern keypunches the cards are *interpreted* for you; that is, each character is printed at the top edge of the card directly above the corresponding punched holes. Instructions concerning the operation of your keypunch can be obtained from your computer center or from your instructor. Operating a keypunch is not difficult and can be learned in one short session.

A program to be keypunched should be written on a FORTRAN **coding sheet** as shown in Figure 4.3. The coding sheet has 80 columns corresponding to the 80 columns on a card. The program is written on this coding sheet so that each line corresponds *exactly* to what will be punched on a single card. Some coding sheets have only 72 columns, which simply means that sequence numbers will not be shown on the sheet.

A program carefully written on a coding sheet can be transferred to punched cards by a person who

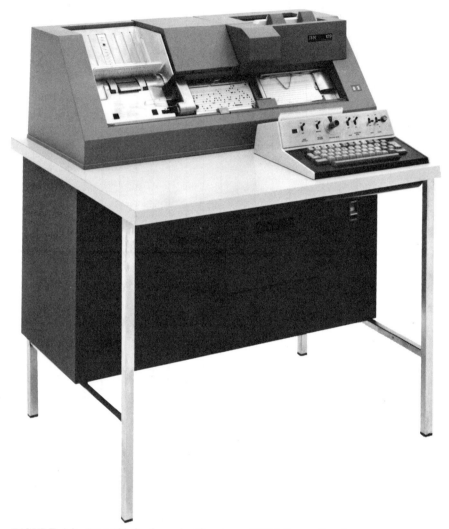

FIGURE 4.2. IBM 129 Card punch. (Courtesy of IBM Corporation.)

knows nothing at all about FORTRAN. Many computer centers employ keypunch operators who perform this service. In such cases you *must* submit your programs on coding sheets.

Punched cards are transmitted to the computer by means of a **card reader** (see Figure 1.4). It is not unusual for a card reader to process (read) 1000 or more cards per minute. The information read into the computer is placed in a file that may contain many other jobs. These jobs are scheduled and processed under the control of a *supervisory program* called the **operating system.** The operating system can process many different types of jobs. One job may involve compiling and executing a FORTRAN program, another may involve processing a COBOL program (COBOL is another computer language designed principally for business applications), and still another may involve executing a FORTRAN program that was compiled at an earlier time.

Because the operating system performs a variety of different tasks, it needs to "know" certain things about each job that is submitted. This information is transmitted to the computer on punched cards, called **control cards.** Control cards contain such items as a program name, an account number, the type of program being submitted (FORTRAN, COBOL, and so on), the estimated running time, the estimated memory requirements, and so forth. Normally, very few control cards are needed and the same cards may be used for jobs that are similar. The precise form that such cards must take is system dependent and can be found in the operating manual for your system.

In addition to including control cards and FORTRAN cards, you may also include cards containing data to be processed by the FORTRAN program. These data cards and their use are described in Chapter 5. The entire collection of cards that you submit for processing is called a **job deck.** If the language being used is FORTRAN, the job deck is also called a FORTRAN *deck* or FORTRAN *package*.

PROBLEM Sales Tax

PROGRAMMER P. Shea

FORTRAN STATEMENT

```
C SALES TAX COMPUTATION
  RATE=0.05
  PRICE=5329.00
C CALCULATE THE TAX
  TAX=RATE*PRICE
  WRITE(6,10)TAX
10 FORMAT(1X,'SALES TAX=',F8.2)
  STOP
  END
```

FIGURE 4.3. Sales tax program written on a coding sheet.

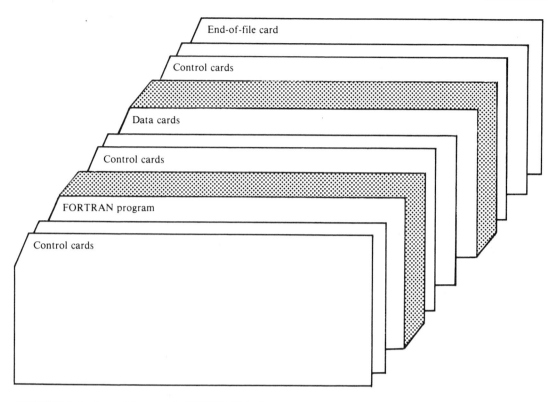

FIGURE 4.4. General layout of a FORTRAN deck.

The order of the cards in a job deck is important. Control cards are placed on top of the deck followed by the FORTRAN cards and finally the data cards (should there be any). Additional control cards are placed between the FORTRAN cards and the data cards, and also at the bottom of the deck. Figure 4.4 shows the general layout of a FORTRAN deck. Figure 4.5 shows a complete FORTRAN deck, which does not require data cards. In all likelihood your control cards will differ from those shown. The illustration is included here to show that control cards generally are not complicated or numerous.

When operating in a batch processing environment, a complete job must be submitted to the computer at one time. The job deck represents the most common, but not the only, way to do this. Some large computer systems allow you to create a file containing a complete job while operating in a time-sharing mode. The file must contain essentially the same items as an equivalent job deck. This file can then be submitted to the operating system for processing by typing appropriate commands at the terminal keyboard, thus entirely avoiding the use of punched cards. Once the job is submitted, it is handled in the same way that punched card decks are handled.

The usual output device for batch processing systems is a line printer (see Figure 1.5). A line printer prints an entire line at once, and speeds of over 1,000 lines per minute are not uncommon. Normally, the printout for a particular job will include items other than the output generated by the program. These items may include a section identifying the job, a program listing, and, possibly, diagnostic messages identifying compilation and run-time errors.* If the program is not correct, the job deck must be changed and resubmitted. The diagnostic messages should help you in this task. The messages may or may not be clear; your FORTRAN manual should help you interpret those that are not clear.

A job deck should be prepared carefully. A single incorrect character can cause an entire job to be aborted. Each unnecessary time you submit a job wastes not only your time but also that of the computer

---

*Compilation (compile-time) errors occur when the FORTRAN syntax is violated. Most often these are typing errors. Run-time errors are errors that are recognized during program execution. For example, the FORTRAN assignment statement $X = A/B$ will always compile correctly since it is syntactically correct, but, if B has a zero value, an error will occur during program execution.

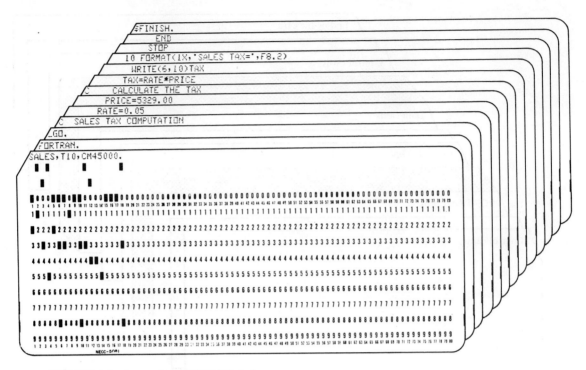

FIGURE 4.5. A complete FORTRAN deck.

center's personnel. Moreover, the number of times a job can be submitted (*turnarounds*)* in a day is limited. Some computer centers allow only three or four turnarounds a day; many even have fixed times when the card reader is in operation. Consideration of such factors is particularly important when programming tasks must be completed within a fixed time period.

4.4 Problems

Write each of the programs shown in Problems 1–4 on a coding sheet in a form acceptable to a keypunch operator.

1.
```
C CALCULATE SIX PERCENT OF D
  D=23000.
  ANSWER=0.06*D
  WRITE(6,100)ANSWER
  100 FORMAT(1X,,'SIX PERCENT
  IS',F9.2)
  STOP
  END
```

2.
```
C AVERAGE 2 NUMBERS
C VAR1 AND VAR2
  VAR1=24.
  VAR2=15.
C CALCULATE THE AVERAGE
  AV=(VAR1+VAR2)/2.
  WRITE(6,200)AV
  200 FORMAT(1X,'MEAN IS',F8.2)
  STOP
  END
```

3.
```
C DISCOUNT PROGRAM
C P DENOTES THE PRICE
C R DENOTES THE DISCOUNT RATE
  P=125.
  R=0.15
```

4.
```
C---DIVISION ALGORITHM---
  INTEGER N,D,Q,R
C N=DIVIDEND
C D=DIVISOR
C Q=QUOTIENT
```

---

*Whereas the term *turnarounds* refers to the number of times a job can be submitted, *turnaround time* refers to the time to complete a job—that is, to load, process, and make the printout available to the user.

```
C CALCULATE THE DISCOUNT D AND        C R=REMAINDER
   SALES PRICE S.                       N=17
   D=R*P                                D=7
   S=P-D                                Q=N/D
   WRITE(6,10)D                         R=N-Q*D
   WRITE(6,11)S                         WRITE(6,10)Q,R
10 FORMAT(1X,'DISCOUNT:',F7.2)       10 FORMAT(1X,'QUOTIENT=',I4,
11 FORMAT(1X,'SALES PRICE:',            5X,'REMAINDER=',I4)
   F8.2)                                STOP
   STOP                                 END
   END
```

Problems 5 and 6 are on pages 48 and 49. If the programs in Problems 5 and 6 are transferred to punched cards, exactly as indicated on the coding sheets, they will not do what is claimed. Find and correct all errors.

4.5 On Writing Your First Program

You are now ready to write your first program. Even for very simple problems, certain steps should be followed. Experience has shown that the following approach to problem solving is applicable both to simple and complex problems.

1. Be sure you thoroughly understand what is being asked in the problem statement. A good way to do this is to identify the following items:
   Input: Data to be presented to the computer for processing. (For now, such data will be numerical data. Later we will consider how character data, such as lists of names, can be processed by the computer.)
   Output: The results called for in the problem statement. This may involve identifying both output values and the form in which they are to be printed.
2. Identify what, if any, mathematical equations will be needed. For example, to convert degrees Celsius to degrees Fahrenheit, you could use the equation $F = (9/5)C + 32$.
3. Find and describe a step-by-step process (algorithm) that, if carried out, will result in a correct solution. For simple programming tasks, this step usually is not difficult. For example, to convert degrees Celsius to degrees Fahrenheit you could use the following algorithm:
   a. Assign a value to C (degrees Celsius).
   b. Calculate $F = (9/5)C + 32$.
   c. Print the result F and stop.
4. Write the program statements to carry out the algorithm you have described. This is called *coding the program.* Be sure to include adequate and meaningful comment statements.
5. Debug the program. This means running it to test for syntax errors and also to convince yourself that the program will produce correct results.

EXAMPLE 6. Write a program to calculate the simple interest and the amount due for a loan of P dollars, at an annual interest rate R, for a time of T years. Use the program to find the interest and amount due when $P = 3250.00$, $R = 0.0925$, and $T = 2.5$.

A quick reading of this problem statement shows that the input and output values are as follows:

Input: P, R, and T.
Output: Simple interest and the amount due.

We should all recognize the familiar formulas that govern this situation.

Simple interest: $INTRST = P \times R \times T$
Amount due: $AMTDUE = P + INTRST$

PROBLEM _____ 5 _____

PROGRAMMER _____ P. Shea _____

PAGE __ 1 __ OF __ 1 __

DATE __ March 15, 1981 __

FORTRAN STATEMENT

```
C  ADDITION PROGRAM
C  ASSIGN VALUES
X=5.0
Y=6.7
Z=X+Y
C  PRINT THE SUM
WRITE (6,10) SUM
10 FORMAT (1X,F7.2)
STOP
END
```

5.

PROBLEM ___6___

PROGRAMMER ___P. Shea___

PAGE ___1___ OF ___1___

DATE ___March 15, 1981___

FORTRAN STATEMENT

```
C COMMENT 8.75 PERCENT OF X
  X=12,500
  R=0.0875
C COMMENT FIND AND PRINT THE ANSWER
  ANSWER=X*R
C WRITE 6 10 ANSWER
10 FORMAT(1X F10.2)
  STOP
  END
```

Knowing these formulas, we can write the following algorithm:
a. Assign values to P, R, and T.
b. Calculate the interest, INTRST, and the amount due, AMTDUE.
c. Print the results (INTRST and AMTDUE) and stop.

To code this algorithm correctly, we should note that all quantities involved are best represented by real variables: P, INTRST, and AMTDUE are dollar amounts; R denotes an interest rate (0.0925 in the problem statement); and T denotes time in years that may be fractional (2.5 in the problem statement).

The Program:

```
C SIMPLE INTEREST PROGRAM
      REAL AMTDUE,INTRST,P,R,T
C      P DENOTES AMOUNT OF LOAN
C      R DENOTES ANNUAL INTEREST RATE
C      T DENOTES TERM OF LOAN IN YEARS
C      ASSIGN VALUES TO P, R, AND T
      P=3250.00
      R=0.0925
      T=2.5
C      CALCULATE THE INTEREST AND THE AMOUNT DUE.
      INTRST=P*R*T
      AMTDUE=P+INTRST
C      PRINT THE RESULTS
      WRITE(6,10)INTRST,AMTDUE
   10 FORMAT(1X,'INTEREST:',F8.2,10X,'AMOUNT DUE:',F8.2)
      STOP
      END
```

Output:

```
INTEREST:  751.56          AMOUNT DUE: 4001.56
```

Remark 1: To find the interest and amount due for other simple interest loans, it is necessary to change the three lines that assign values to P, R, and T. In Chapter 5 you will see how different values can be assigned to P, R, and T without having to change program statements.

Remark 2: Notice that the three steps in the algorithm written for this program are used as comment lines. Not only does this emphasize how the coding process follows from the algorithm, but it also suggests that each step in an algorithm should contain enough detail so that it is easily coded. Writing algorithms according to this principle and using the individual steps of the algorithm as comment lines are excellent programming practices.

The development of programming habits, both good and bad, begins with your first program. At the end of this chapter you will be asked to write some programs. To learn good habits from the start, you should follow the five steps suggested in this section. Coding should almost never be your first step.

4.6 Problems

Following are a number of tasks to be performed. Write a FORTRAN program for each. Use WRITE or PRINT statements to label all output values, and also include comment lines as suggested in Section 3.9.

1. Compute the selling price S for an article whose list price is PRICE, if the rate of discount is D%.
2. Compute the original price if an article is now selling at S dollars after a discount of D%.
3. Compute the state gasoline tax S in dollars paid by a driver who travels M miles per year if the car averages MPG miles per gallon and the tax is T cents per gallon.

4. Find the commission C on sales of S dollars if the rate of commission is R%.
5. Find the principal P that, if invested at a rate of interest R for time T years, yields the simple interest SI. (Recall that SI = PRT.)
6. Compute the weekly salary, both gross (GSAL) and net (SALNET), for a person who works H hours a week for D dollars an hour (no overtime). Deductions are S% for state taxes and F% for federal taxes.
7. Compute the area of a triangle of base B and height H.
8. Compute the volume and surface area of a rectangular solid.
9. Compute the area of a triangle whose sides are a, b, and c. (Heron's formula for such a triangle is $A = \sqrt{s(s-a)(s-b)(s-c)}$ where $s = (a+b+c)/2$.
10. Compute the area and circumference of a circle given the radius. (Use $\pi = 3.14159$.)
11. A tin can is H inches high and the radius of its circular base is R inches. Calculate the volume and surface area. (Volume = area of base × height. Curved surface area = circumference of base × height.)
12. Compute the batting average AV of a baseball player who has SNGL singles, DBLE doubles, TPLE triples, and HR home runs in AB times at bat. (AV = number of hits/number of times at bat.)
13. Compute the slugging percentage P of the baseball player described in Problem 12. (P = total bases/number of times at bat.)
14. Find the total cost COST of four tires if the list price of each is PRICE dollars, the federal excise tax is FET dollars per tire, and the sales tax is S%.
15. Compute the total cost COST of a sofa listed at PRICE dollars selling at a discount of D% if the sales tax is S%.
16. Find the total taxes TAX on the McCormick property assessed at D dollars if the rate is R dollars per $1,000. In addition, if the community uses S% of all taxes for schools, find how much of the McCormick tax is spent for schools.
17. The market value of a home is VAL dollars, the assessment rate is A% of the market value, and the tax rate is R dollars per $1,000. Calculate the property tax.

4.7 Review True-or-False Quiz

1. Each step in an algorithm for a computer program should correspond to a single program statement. T F
2. Coding a FORTRAN program involves the process of determining the programming lines to carry out a known algorithm. T F
3. A good programming practice is to choose comment lines to correspond to the individual steps in an algorithm. T F
4. The identification of what input values are required in a program should be made before an algorithm has been written, whereas the identification of what output values are required is best made after the algorithm has been described. T F
5. The only difference between a conversational time-sharing system and a batch processing system is that the former uses a time-sharing terminal as the principal link between a user and the computer, whereas the latter normally uses punched cards and a line printer. T F

Numbers 6–13 concern conversational systems.

6. Line numbers, but not necessarily statement numbers, must be used for every FORTRAN statement. T F
7. If the line number of a FORMAT statement is 240, the statement WRITE(6,240)X,Y will cause the current values of X and Y to be printed according to the format specification contained in this FORMAT statement. T F
8. It is not necessary to include a blank space between a line number and a statement number. T F
9. FORTRAN statements are compiled in the order in which they are typed. T F
10. System commands are carried out as soon as they are issued. T F

11. A program statement may be deleted from a program by typing its statement number and immediately depressing the RETURN key.   T   F
12. A program containing no syntax errors can cause error messages to be printed when it is run.   T   F
13. A program statement can be changed by retyping it with a new line number.   T   F

Numbers 14–20 concern batch processing systems.

14. The programming line 10 FORMAT(1X,'SUM IS',F7.3) must be punched somewhere in columns 7–72.   T   F
15. When the assignment statement QTY = X + Y is punched on a card, the letter Q must appear in column 7.   T   F
16. When using cards, a C punched in column 1 or in column 6 indicates that the card contains a comment line.   T   F
17. Hollerith cards, which are named after Herman Hollerith, are similar to the cards used in a batch processing environment except that their principal use is in census tabulations.   T   F
18. On batch processing systems, the usual input device is a card reader and the usual output device is a line printer; however, some batch systems allow other input and output devices.   T   F
19. The expressions *turnaround time* and *turnarounds* are synonymous.   T   F
20. Principally, coding sheets are used for documentation. They serve no other purpose.   T   F

5

Processing Input Data

In Chapter 3 you saw how to assign numerical values to variables by using assignment statements. For example, a program to perform calculations involving the numbers 12.57 and 27.48 can be written by using the following two assignment statements:

A = 12.57
B = 27.48

Doing this means that the data to be processed (12.57 and 27.48) are included as part of the program. The typical programming task involves writing a program to process data that are either unknown or that will be different each time the program is run. For instance, a program to produce an inventory report will most certainly involve different data each time it is run. Such data cannot be included as part of a program. FORTRAN alleviates this difficulty by allowing data to be transferred to the computer from sources external to the program, including punched cards, time-sharing terminal keyboards, and magnetic tapes and disks. The READ statement is used to assign these input data to program variables for processing. The process is called *reading*. In this chapter, we describe the simplest and most common methods of transmitting input data to the computer.

5.1 The READ Statement

Most often, READ statements are used with FORMAT statements. The READ statement contains a list of variables that are to be assigned values during program execution, and the FORMAT statement contains a description of how the computer is to interpret the input data. When used with a FORMAT statement, a READ statement is called a **formatted** READ statement.

The two programming lines

```
   READ(5,10)J,K
10 FORMAT(I4,I5)
```

describe a formatted READ statement. The 5 appearing in the READ statement tells the computer which input device to use. We'll use the device number 5 to specify the terminal keyboard or the standard card reader.

The first edit descriptor I4 tells the computer to interpret the first four characters of the input data as a value for the first variable J. The second edit descriptor I5 says to interpret the next five characters of the input data as a value for the second variable K. In all, nine characters must be input. If you wish to assign 93 to J and 85 to K, the input data must be

$\Delta\Delta93\Delta\Delta\Delta85$

or, equivalently,

009300085

On input, the nonprinting blank character (denoted by Δ) is interpreted as a zero.

In a time-sharing environment, these nine characters are typed on one line at the terminal keyboard. In a punched-card environment, they are punched in the first nine columns of a card. Aspects of the READ statement peculiar to conversational and batch systems are described in Sections 5.3 and 5.4, respectively.

The nine-character string $\Delta\Delta93\Delta\Delta\Delta85$ is called an **input record.** An input record can be any string of characters; it does not have to consist only of numerical digits and blanks. As we just saw, the edit descriptors in a FORMAT statement tell exactly how an input record is to be interpreted in assigning values to variables. Every character (including blanks) in the input record counts, and the exact position of each character is significant. In what follows, an input record such as $\Delta\Delta93\Delta\Delta\Delta85$ will be displayed in the following form so that the exact position of each character can readily be seen:

```
          1         2         3
123456789012345678901234567890
   93    85
```

EXAMPLE 1. This example illustrates how a single input record can be interpreted differently by different formatted READ statements. Parts (a), (b), and (c) all refer to the following input record:

```
          1         2         3
123456789012345678901234567890
   56    842
```

a. The formatted READ statement

```
   READ(5,10)N1,N2
10 FORMAT(I4,I6)
```

"reads" the given input record to obtain the values

N1 = 56
N2 = 842

The first edit descriptor I4 tells the computer to use the first four characters $\Delta\Delta56$ to obtain the value 56 for N1. The second edit descriptor I6 says to use the next six characters $\Delta\Delta\Delta842$ to obtain the value 842 for N2.

b. The formatted READ statement

```
   READ(5,11)N1,N2
11 FORMAT(I4,I4)
```

reads the input record to obtain the values

N1 = 56
N2 = 8

Here both descriptors are I4, so the first four characters ΔΔ56 are used to assign 56 to N1 and the next four characters ΔΔΔ8 are used to assign 8 to N2. In this case, the final two characters 42 in the input record simply are not used.

c. The formatted READ statement

```
   READ(5,12)N1,N2,N3
12 FORMAT(I3,I3,I3)
```

reads the input record to obtain the values

N1 = 5
N2 = 600
N3 = 84

All three edit descriptors are I3, so the first three characters ΔΔ5 are used to assign 5 to N1, the next three characters 6ΔΔ are used to assign 600 to N2, and the next three characters Δ84 are used to assign 84 to N3. In this case, the final character 2 is not used.

As shown in parts (b) and (c) of Example 1, a READ statement may use only part of an input record: the remainder is simply ignored. That part of a record that is used is partitioned into *fields*. A field consists of all characters referenced by a single edit descriptor. For example, in part (a) of Example 1, the record ΔΔ56ΔΔΔ842 is partitioned into the two fields ΔΔ56 and ΔΔΔ842. In part (b), we have the fields ΔΔ56 and ΔΔΔ8, since values for N1 and N2 are both obtained by using the descriptor I4. The remaining characters (42) are ignored. Similarly, in part (c) we have the three fields ΔΔ5, 6ΔΔ, and Δ84.

The term *field* provides us with a convenient way to refer to parts of a record. For instance, since blanks are interpreted as zeros, we can now state the following rule. An integer appearing in an input record must be right-justified (in the rightmost positions) in its field.

The general form of the READ statement with its corresponding FORMAT statement is

READ(u,f)list
f FORMAT(fs)

> Many systems allow the form
>
> **READ f, list**
> **f FORMAT(fs)**

The items **list, fs, u,** and **f** are as follows:

list   denotes a list of variables separated by commas. Values will be assigned to these variables from one or more input records. If **list** is omitted, an input record is skipped.

fs   denotes a format specification that specifies how input records are to be interpreted by the computer. In this chapter, we'll use only the edit descriptors Iw, Fw.d, and nX. Other edit descriptors that can be used with formatted READ statements will be described as needed.

u   denotes an unsigned integer that specifies which input unit should be used. In this text we'll use **u** = 5 to specify the terminal keyboard or the standard card reader as the input unit. Note that the second form of the READ statement does not include **u.** When used it assumes the terminal keyboard or standard card reader as the input device.

f   denotes an unsigned integer used to label a FORMAT statement. The occurrence of **f** in the READ statement instructs the computer to assign values to the variables appearing in **list** according to the edit descriptors in **fs.**

The next two examples show two ways to input values for *real* variables.

EXAMPLE 2. We describe how the formatted READ statement

```
    READ(5,20)A,B
 20 FORMAT(F5.2,F6.3)
```

interprets the input record

```
          1         2         3
12345678901234567890123456789 0
56347 -4273
```

to obtain the values

A = 563.47
B = − 4.273

The 5 in the edit descriptor F5.2 tells the computer to use the first five characters 56347 of the input record to obtain a value for A. The 2 in F5.2 indicates that the rightmost two characters 47 are fractional digits. Hence, 563.47 is assigned to A. Similarly, the descriptor F6.3 tells the computer to use the next six characters Δ − 4273, with the rightmost three characters 273 as fractional digits, to obtain the value − 4.273 for B.

EXAMPLE 3. Decimal points may be included in an input record. We illustrate by describing how the formatted READ statements

```
    READ(5,21)X,Y,N
    READ(5,21)A,B
 21 FORMAT(F6.3,F9.0,I3)
```

interpret the input records

```
          1         2         3         4
1234567890123456789012345678901234567890
  2.1 -31.6      27
 62.58    657.26
```

to obtain the values

X = 2.1
Y = − 31.6
N = 27
A = 62.58
B = 657.26

Whenever a decimal point appears in an input field corresponding to an F descriptor, the decimal point overrides that portion of the F descriptor that would otherwise specify the location of the decimal point. When the first READ statement is executed, the descriptor F6.3 determines the six-character field ΔΔ2.1Δ (note that the decimal point counts as one of the six characters). Since this field contains a decimal point, the value 002.10 or, equivalently, 2.1 is assigned to X; the 3 in F6.3 has no effect whatever, in this case. Similarly, the nine-character field $-31.6\Delta\Delta\Delta\Delta$, determined by the 9 in F9.0, is interpreted to obtain the value -31.6 for Y. The next three characters $\Delta27$ are interpreted by I3 to obtain the value 27 for N.

The second READ statement then reads the second input record to obtain the values 62.58 and 657.26 for A and B, respectively.

Remark 1: If the decimal point for a real datum is included in an input field, the number can appear anywhere in the field. In this example, the value 2.1 appears in positions 3, 4, and 5 of a six-character field, whereas -31.6 appears in the leftmost five positions of a nine-character field.

Remark 2: Both real and integer variables may appear in the same READ statement. The corresponding FORMAT statement and input record must be written so that real values are assigned to real variables and integer values to integer variables.

Remark 3: Only two variables (A and B) appear in the second READ statement, but there are three edit descriptors in the referenced FORMAT statement. The last descriptor, I3, is simply ignored in this case.

It should be clear that great care should be exercised in writing formatted READ statements and their corresponding input records. One careless mistake, such as leaving a blank position in an input field where none was intended, can cause a serious error. If you are fortunate, the error will be detected by the computer and helpful diagnostics will be printed. If you are not so fortunate, the computer may simply produce incorrect results. Such errors can be very difficult to find and may even go undetected.

5.2 Problems

1. Complete the table by using the following formatted READ statement:

```
   READ(5,10)NUM
10 FORMAT(I6)
```

Characters in positions 1–6 of input record	Resulting value of the variable NUM
a. $\Delta\Delta\Delta653$	
b. $+\Delta\Delta5\Delta0$	
c. $\Delta-43\Delta\Delta$	
d. $74300\Delta6$	
e. $8\Delta5\Delta43$	
f. $-\Delta043\Delta$	
g. $\Delta\Delta\Delta\Delta\Delta\Delta$	

2. Complete the table by using the following formatted READ statement:

```
   READ(5,20)ALPHA
20 FORMAT(F7.2)
```

Characters in positions 1–7 of input record	Resulting value of the variable ALPHA
a. ΔΔΔ5376	
b. Δ84Δ8Δ5	
c. 834ΔΔΔ4	
d. 541Δ3.7	
e. 0ΔΔ4.43	
f. -351Δ53	
g. Δ+4.693	
h. -1.864Δ	

In Problems 3–7 determine the values assigned to the variables in the READ statements by using the given input records.

3.
```
      READ(5,35)N1,N2,N3
   35 FORMAT(I4,I3,I5)
```

```
          1         2         3
12345678901234567890123456 7890
   64+31851624
```

4.
```
      READ(5,36)ITEM1,ITEM2
      READ(5,36)LENGTH
   36 FORMAT(I10,I10)
```

```
          1         2         3
12345678901234567890123456 7890
    11246     22458      1732
       25        26        27
```

5.
```
      READ(5,37)ID,RATE,HOURS
   37 FORMAT(I5,F10.2,F5.1)
```

```
          1         2
12345678901234567890
 8715      1085  445
```

6.
```
      READ(5,38)X,Y,Z
   38 FORMAT(F5.0,F5.0,F5.0)
```

```
          1         2
12345678901234567890
 2.4 -7.9      +28.6
```

7.
```
      READ(5,39)COUNT,NAME,VALUE
      READ(5,39)SALE,NEXT
   39 FORMAT(F7.2,I5,F8.3)
```

```
           1         2
 12345678901234567890
      355 442    278625
    2.45    356  7.125
```

8. Give a READ statement and an input record so that A = 443.5, B = 21.62, I = 21, and J = 3 if the FORMAT statement is

```
   20 FORMAT(F5.1,F9.3,I6,I2)
```

9. Give a READ statement and an input record so that C = 42.3, D = 84., M = 6, BETA = 8.35, and NUM = 7 if the FORMAT statement is

```
   80 FORMAT(F6.1,F8.0,I3,F4.2,I2)
```

10. Give READ statements and input records so that N1 = 12, N2 = 75, and N3 = 164 if the FORMAT statement is

```
   13 FORMAT(I5)
```

11. Give READ and FORMAT statements so that X = 42.78, Y = 904.2, N1 = 43, and MEM7 = 506 if the input records are

```
           1         2         3
 123456789012345678901234567890
      4278        43
    9042     506
```

12. Give READ statements and a single FORMAT statement so that I = 27, J = 90, A = 15.139, and B = 2.8, if the input records are

```
           1         2         3         4         5         6
 1234567890123456789012345678901234567890123456789012345678901234567890
    27     15.139
    9          28
```

5.3 Transmitting Input Data on Conversational Systems

To enter input data on conversational systems you simply type the input record at the terminal.

EXAMPLE 4.

```
100C A PROGRAM TO INPUT TWO INTEGERS
110C AND PRINT THEIR SUM
120 INTEGER J,K,SUM
130 READ(5,20)J,K              or READ 20,J,K
140 20 FORMAT(I4,I5)
150 SUM=J+K
160 WRITE(6,10)SUM             or PRINT 10,SUM
170 10 FORMAT(1X,'SUM IS',I6)
180 STOP
190 END
```

When line 130 is executed the system will print a "?" followed by one blank space. It will then wait for you to type values for J and K as specified in the FORMAT statement at line 140. To assign 253 to J and 746 to K, you enter the record

```
         1         2         3
123456789012345678901234567890
 253   746
```

by typing Δ253ΔΔ746. Let's run this program.

RUN Ⓡ

?ΔΔ253ΔΔ746 Ⓡ   (Underlined characters are printed by the computer. The
SUM IS   999   symbol Ⓡ denotes the RETURN or ENTER key on
                                    your terminal keyboard.)

READY

Remark: The input record must be consistent with the format specification used to interpret the input data, and all characters comprising the record must be typed. In this program, a nine-character input record is required, regardless of the values to be assigned to J and K. To assign 1 to J and 2 to K, you must type ΔΔΔ1ΔΔΔΔ2; anything else, other than using zeros for blanks, is incorrect. This awkward situation can be avoided only if the system being used allows unformatted READ statements as described in Section 5.6.

READ statements, calling for values to be typed at a terminal, should always be preceded by WRITE or PRINT statements that print a message describing what values are to be typed. This practice is illustrated in the following example.

EXAMPLE 5. Here is a program to calculate the commission on the sale of an item sold for AMT dollars if the rate of commission is 5.5%:

```
100C PROGRAM TO CALCULATE 5.5 PERCENT COMMISSIONS
110C      AMT=AMOUNT OF SALE
120C      COMM=COMMISSION
130 R=0.055
140 WRITE(6,10)                           or PRINT 10
150 10 FORMAT(1X,'AMOUNT OF SALE-USE THE FORM XXXXX.XX')
160 READ(5,20)AMT
170 20 FORMAT(F8.2)
180 COMM=R*AMT
190 WRITE(6,11)COMM                       or PRINT 11,COMM
200 11 FORMAT(1X,'COMMISSION IS ',F8.2)
210 STOP
220 END
RUN Ⓡ
```

AMOUNT OF SALE-USE THE FORM XXXXX.XX   (Underlined characters are printed by the com-
?Δ   puter.)

At this point you follow the instructions and type the amount of the sale in the form shown. Let's complete this run as follows:

?ΔΔΔ625.00
COMMISSION IS   34.38

READY

To run this program again, for a different sales amount, nothing in the program needs to be changed. You simply respond to the question mark by typing the new sales amount.

Remark 1: For the run shown, the computer calculates 5.5% of 625.00 to obtain a commission of 34.375. This figure is then rounded to two decimal places to fit the output specification F8.2 in line number 200.

Remark 2: Note that none of the variable names used in this program is printed by the computer. The user is not asked to TYPE A VALUE FOR AMT nor does the computer print VALUE OF COMM IS 34.38. A user has no need to know what variable names are used in a program and should not be burdened with this information.

5.4 Transmitting Input Data on Batch Systems

On batch systems, the usual input device is the card reader and the input data are presented to the system in the form of punched cards. The cards are identical to the cards on which FORTRAN statements appear; however, all 80 columns can be used on data cards. No particular significance is given to the individual columns as it is when FORTRAN statements are keypunched. Figure 5.1 shows a data card punched to record a single input record containing the four amounts 1234.50, 2579.75, 61.59, and 123.75.

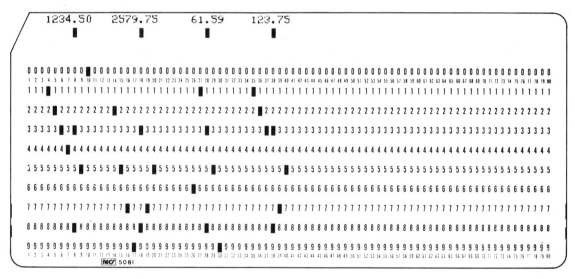

FIGURE 5.1. A data card.

A separate card must be used for each input record. For this reason, keypunches and card readers are called **unit record devices.** They punch and read one record (card) at a time.

Data cards containing all input records for a particular program run are included in the job deck as indicated in Section 4.3. During program execution the input records are read by READ statements in the order of their appearance in the job deck. Figure 5.2 shows a complete job deck including a short FORTRAN program and two data cards. (Your control cards will undoubtedly differ from those shown.) The program reads the two input records to obtain the sum of the first entries and the sum of the second entries on each card. To run this program again, with different input values, all that is necessary is to replace one or both of the cards. No change is made in the program or the control cards.

If the computer compiles and executes the program shown in Figure 5.2, the following output will be produced:

```
FIRST PAIR :  15.43  61.59
SECOND PAIR:  20.18  75.04
SUM OF FIRST ENTRIES:   35.61     SUM OF SECOND ENTRIES  136.63
```

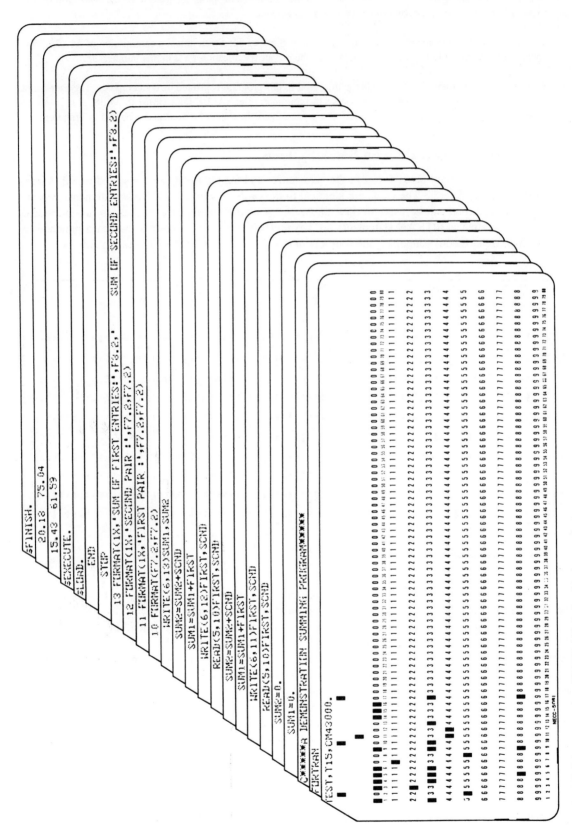

FIGURE 5.2. A complete FORTRAN deck with data cards.

The first two lines of output show what values were read from data cards. This is called *echoing*—values read from cards are printed back (echoed) under program control. In this example, the result is an improved output document.

5.5 Reading Portions of Input Records

The X descriptor can be used to skip over portions of input records. We illustrate with an example.

EXAMPLE 6. The formatted READ statement

```
     READ(5,10)ID,SLRY
10 FORMAT(I5,15X,F10.2)
```

interprets the input record

```
          1         2         3
123456789012345678901234567890
88207 1963    18 7.50   19750.00
```

to obtain the values

ID = 88207
SLRY = 19750.00

The edit descriptor I5 is used to obtain the value 88207 for ID as usual. The edit descriptor 15X then tells the computer to skip over the next 15 positions of the input record and begin reading data from position 21. Finally, the descriptor F10.2 interprets the ten-character field $\Delta\Delta$19750.00 to obtain 19750.00 for SLRY.

A common programming task is to write a program to process an existing collection of input records but to use only certain portions of each record. It is precisely in such situations that formatted READ statements using the X descriptor are most useful. Rather than preparing a new set of input records including only the needed information, the X descriptor can be used to skip over those parts of the existing input records that are not needed. On conversational systems, the input records will be read from a previously created file—the use of files is described in Chapter 14. On batch systems, the input records may appear on punched cards or on files.

EXAMPLE 7. This example illustrates how the X descriptor can be used to write formatted READ statements that read only selected portions of the following input record:

```
          1         2         3         4         5         6
123456789012345678901234567890123456789012345678901234567890
7245SANDERS,J.C.        M 19475  16   3
```

The information contained in this record is as follows:

Columns	Item	Number of positions
1–4	Identification number	4
5–24	Name	20
25	Sex	1
26–31	Salary in dollars	6
32–33	Not used	2
34–35	Years of service	2
36–37	Not used	2
38–39	Number of dependents	2

a. Consider the following READ/FORMAT pair:

```
   READ(5,22)SLRY
22 FORMAT(25X,F6.0)
```

The edit descriptor 25X tells the computer to skip over the first 25 positions of the input record and begin reading data from position 26. The next descriptor F6.0 interprets the six-character field Δ19475 to obtain the real value 19475. for SLRY.

b. Consider

```
   READ(5,23)ID,NDEP
23 FORMAT(I4,33X,I2)
```

First, the variable ID is assigned the integer value 7245. The descriptor 33X then says to skip over the next 33 positions and begin reading in position 38. The descriptor I2 then interprets the two-character field Δ3 to obtain the value 3 for NDEP.

Remark 1: In our description of the items and their locations in the input record, we included a third column showing the number of positions used for each item, including the number of positions in unused portions of the record. Having done this, determining how many positions appear between any two input fields is simply a matter of adding the numbers in this third column corresponding to the intervening items. Thus, the edit descriptor 33X was used in part (b) because the numbers 20, 1, 6, 2, 2, and 2 corresponding to the items between the *identification number* and the *number of dependents* add up to 33.

Remark 2: In Chapter 12 we'll describe how values other than numbers appearing in an input record can be processed. Until then, we'll continue to use the X descriptor to skip over such input data.

5.6 Unformatted READ Statements

The task of transmitting input data to the computer is greatly simplified by the use of unformatted READ statements—that is, READ statements that require no corresponding FORMAT statements. In this section we describe the two most common forms in use:

READ(u)list
READ,list

These are obtained from the two forms of the formatted READ statement (Section 5.1) by omitting the statement label **f.** The first conforms to the FORTRAN standard; the second does not, but is widely used and very convenient, if allowed.

To illustrate the first form, let's consider the statement

READ(5) A,B,M

This statement instructs the computer to read a record from input unit 5 to obtain values for A, B, and M. If the input record is

```
          1         2         3         4
12345678901234567890123456789012345678901234567890
42.4,73.84,2113
```

the assignments A = 42.4, B = 73.84, and M = 2113 are made. When using unformatted READ statements, the following rules apply:

1. Values in the input record must be delimited (separated) by commas. (A blank space is used optionally on some systems.)
2. The type of each value in the input record must agree with the type of the corresponding variable name in the READ statement.

3. The input record must contain at least as many values as the READ statement contains variables.
4. Values should appear in the input record in the exact form desired. The integer one thousand one is represented by 1001, not by 1ΔΔ1 as is possible with formatted READ statements. When inputting numerical values, it is safe to assume that all blanks will be ignored.

The action of the second form

READ,**list**

is identical to that of the first form except that the input unit is not specified. If allowed, it assumes the terminal keyboard or the standard card reader as the input unit. Thus, the statement

READ,A,B,M

will read the input record shown above to obtain A = 42.4, B = 73.84, and M = 2113, just as did the statement READ(5)A,B,M.

5.7 Programming with the READ Statement

We are now ready to write some FORTRAN programs using the READ statement to enter the input data. This section contains two short examples illustrating the programming process, from problem statement to the final program, as described in Section 4.5. In each case, READ statements are used to transmit input data to the computer for processing.

EXAMPLE 8. The cost to rent a car is $25 per day and 22 cents per mile. Determine the cost if the number of days and the number of miles is given.

Two values must be given (the number of days and the number of miles) and one value (the cost) must be determined. Let's use the following variable names:

Input: DAYS = number of days.
         MILES = number of miles.
Output: COST = rental cost.

Since the charge is $25 per day and 22 cents per mile, these three variables are related by the equation

COST = 25 × DAYS + 0.22 × MILES

Knowing this formula, we can write the following algorithm:

a. Assign values to DAYS and MILES.
b. Determine the rental cost.
c. Print the result.

Before this algorithm can be coded, we must decide how to assign values to DAYS and MILES. Available are the assignment and READ statements. Since we may use this program for different numbers of days and numbers of miles, the decision is easy: use a READ statement.

```
C******* CAR RENTAL PROGRAM *******
C    DAYS  = NUMBER OF DAYS
C    MILES = NUMBER OF MILES
C    COST = THE RENTAL COST
      INTEGER DAYS,MILES
      REAL COST
C ASSIGN VALUES TO DAYS AND MILES
      READ(5,10)DAYS,MILES
   10 FORMAT(I3,I5)
C DETERMINE THE COST
      COST=25.*FLOAT(DAYS)+0.22*FLOAT(MILES)
```

```
C PRINT THE RESULTS
      WRITE(6,11)
      WRITE(6,12)DAYS
      WRITE(6,13)MILES
      WRITE(6,14)COST
   11 FORMAT(1X)
   12 FORMAT(1X,'DAYS RENTED:',I3)
   13 FORMAT(1X,'MILES DRIVEN:',I5)
   14 FORMAT(1X,'RENTAL COST:',F8.2)
      STOP
      END
```

Input Data:

```
         1         2         3
12345678901234567890123456789 0
  3   515
```

Output:

```
DAYS RENTED:  3
MILES DRIVEN:  515
RENTAL COST:  188.30
```

Remark 1: The short discussion appearing just before the algorithm is called a **problem analysis.** It may simply contain a description of variables and how they are interrelated, as is the case here, or it may include a thorough analysis of alternative approaches to a solution. In any case, a problem analysis is the process of discovering a suitable algorithm.

Remark 2: The formatted WRITE statement

```
   WRITE(6,11)
11 FORMAT(1X)
```

is used for vertical spacing; it simply causes a blank line to appear in the printout. Another way to control vertical spacing in a printed document is shown in Chapter 8.

Remark 3: If this program is meant to be run on a conversational system, a WRITE or PRINT statement must be included to instruct the user concerning the values to be typed in response to the READ statement. Since a user must type exactly eight characters, three for DAYS and five for MILES, such a printed message may appear clumsy. A better solution is to use an unformatted READ statement and precede it with a statement such as

```
  WRITE(6,9)
9 FORMAT(1X,'ENTER: NUMBER OF DAYS,NUMBER OF MILES')
```

A typical run will then produce the following printout:

```
RUN
ENTER: NUMBER OF DAYS,NUMBER OF MILES
? 3,515

DAYS RENTED:  3
MILES DRIVEN:  515
RENTAL COST:  188.30

READY
```

EXAMPLE 9. Determine the yearly income and savings of a person whose weekly income and average monthly expenses are given.

Problem Analysis:

Two values must be specified (weekly income and monthly expenses) and two values must be determined (yearly income and savings). Let's agree to use the following variable names:

Input: WI = weekly income.
           EX = monthly expenses.
Output: YI = yearly income (note that YI = 52 × WI).
           YS = yearly savings (note that YS = YI − 12 × EX).

An algorithm for solving this problem can now be written.

a. Assign values to WI and EX.
b. Determine yearly income and savings.
c. Print results.

Let's agree to assign values to WI and EX with a READ statement and to print a four-line report showing the income, expenses, and savings amounts.

The Program:

```
C PROGRAM TO FIND YEARLY INCOME AND SAVINGS
C GIVEN THE WEEKLY INCOME AND MONTHLY EXPENSES
C   EX DENOTES MONTHLY EXPENSES
C   WI DENOTES WEEKLY INCOME
C   YI DENOTES YEARLY INCOME
C   YS DENOTES YEARLY SAVINGS
C
C ASSIGN VALUES TO WEEKLY INCOME AND MONTHLY EXPENSES
      READ(5,10)WI,EX
   10 FORMAT(F10.2,F10.2)
C COMPUTE YEARLY INCOME AND SAVINGS
      YI=52.*WI
      YS=YI-12.*EX
C PRINT THE RESULTS
      WRITE(6,11)
      WRITE(6,12)WI
      WRITE(6,13)EX
      WRITE(6,14)YI
      WRITE(6,15)YS
   11 FORMAT(1X)
   12 FORMAT(1X,'WEEKLY INCOME.....$',F8.2)
   13 FORMAT(1X,'MONTHLY EXPENSES..$',F8.2)
   14 FORMAT(1X,'YEARLY INCOME.....$',F8.2)
   15 FORMAT(1X,'YEARLY SAVINGS....$',F8.2)
      STOP
      END
```

Input Data:

```
        1         2         3         4
1234567890123456789012345678901234567890
   250.00    940.00
```

Output:

```
WEEKLY INCOME.....$  250.00
MONTHLY EXPENSES..$  940.00
YEARLY INCOME.....$13000.00
YEARLY SAVINGS....$ 1720.00
```

Remark: If this program is to be run on a conversational system, changes similar to those suggested in Remark 3 of Example 8 must be made.

5.8 Problems

Complete the following partial program so that it will perform the tasks specified in Problems 1–13. Be sure that the WRITE statement identifies the output but makes no reference to the variable names X or A.

```
READ(5,  )X
FORMAT(                    )
A=
WRITE(6   )A
FORMAT(1X,               )
STOP
END
```

1. Determine the equivalent weekly salary for a worker whose annual salary is X dollars.
2. Determine the equivalent hourly salary, assuming a 40-hour week, for a worker whose annual salary is X dollars.
3. Determine the total cost of an article whose selling price is X dollars if the sales tax is 4.5%.
4. Determine the weekly salary of a part-time employee working X hours at $3.47 per hour (no overtime).
5. Determine the cost per driving mile for a car that averages 19.2 miles per gallon if gasoline costs X cents per gallon.
6. Determine the average for the four grades of a student who has already received grades of 73, 91, and 62, if a grade of X is obtained on the fourth exam.
7. Convert inches to centimeters. (1 in. = 2.54 cm)
8. Convert centimeters to inches.
9. Convert degrees to radians. (One degree equals $\pi/180$ radians; use $\pi = 3.14159$.)
10. Convert radians to degrees.
11. Determine the area of a circle given its diameter.
12. Determine the diameter of a circle given its area.
13. Determine the distance A to the horizon as viewed over a smooth ocean from a vantage point X feet above sea level. (Consider the right triangle in the following diagram.)

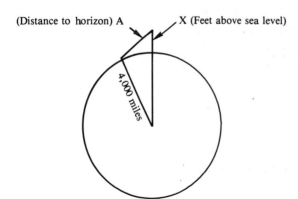

Write a program to perform each task specified in Problems 14–20. Use READ *statements to input data and* WRITE *or* PRINT *statements to label results.*

    For conversational systems: Use WRITE *or* PRINT *statements to describe values to be typed during program execution.*

    For batch systems: Be sure to "echo" all input values as described in Section 5.4.

14. For any three numbers A, B, and C, determine the three sums A + B, A + C, and B + C, and find the average of these sums.

15. For any three numbers P, Q, and R, determine the average AV, the differences P − AV, Q − AV, and R − AV, and the sum of these differences.

16. Semester grades are based on three one-hour tests and a two-hour final examination. The one-hour tests are weighted equally, but the final counts as two one-hour tests. (All exams are graded from 0 to 100.) Determine the semester average for a student whose grades are MARK1, MARK2, MARK3, and MARKF (F stands for final).

17. Janet and Jim are bricklayers. In one hour Janet can lay J1 bricks and Jim can lay J2. Determine how long it will take both of them to complete a job if the number of bricks required is known.

18. A baseball player is to be paid P dollars the first year of a three-year contract. Find the total dollar value of the contract over three years if the contract calls for an increase of I% the second year and J% the third year.

19. Determine the yearly gross pay, net pay, combined tax deductions, and retirement deductions for a person whose monthly salary is given. The combined tax rate is R%, and 6% of the gross salary is withheld for retirement.

20. A manufacturer produces three items that sell for $550, $620, and $1,750. A profit of 10% is realized on items selling below $1,000, and 15% is realized on all other items. Determine the profit before and after taxes for a particular year, given the quantity of each item sold. The current tax rate on profits is R%.

5.9 Processing Large Quantities of Data (A First Look at Loops)

FORTRAN contains several statements, called *control statements,* that allow you to override the normal sequential order in which programming lines are executed. This means that you can direct the computer to execute sections of a program repeatedly so that many hundreds of calculations are carried out with only a few programming lines. In this section we'll show how a single READ statement included in a program segment being repeated allows many input records to be read and processed during a single program run.

EXAMPLE 10. Here is a program segment to read and print one number from each of 50 input records:

```
    N=1
  1 READ(5,10)NUMBER
    WRITE(6,11)NUMBER
    N=N+1
    IF (N.LE.50) GO TO 1
```

The only new statement is the IF statement

```
IF (N.LE.50) GO TO 1
```

It is read "If N is less than or equal (.LE.) to 50, go to 1." Thus, if N is less than or equal to 50, program control is transferred back to the READ statement. If N is not less than or equal to 50, the normal sequential order in which statements are executed is not interrupted. This is what is meant by a loop. The four statements

```
  1 READ(5,10)NUMBER
    WRITE(6,11)NUMBER
    N=N+1
    IF (N.LE.50) GO TO 1
```

are executed over and over as long as N is less than or equal to 50. Finally, when N is greater than 50, control passes to whatever statement follows the IF statement.

The expression N.LE.50 appearing in the statement

IF (N.LE.50) GO TO 1

is called the condition of the IF statement; it specifies the condition that must be true for control to transfer to the statement labeled 1. The symbol .LE. is called a relational symbol since it specifies a relation (less than or equal to) between N and 50. FORTRAN allows you to form conditions for IF statements by using the six relational symbols shown in Table 5.1.

TABLE 5.1. FORTRAN relational symbols.

Relational symbol	Arithmetic symbol	Meaning
.EQ.	=	equal
.NE.	≠	not equal
.GT.	>	greater than
.GE.	≥	greater than or equal
.LT.	<	less than
.LE.	≤	less than or equal

Here are some correctly written IF statements. In each case, note that the two values being compared are both real or both integer as required.*

IF statement	Effect of the IF statement
IF (NUM.GT.100) GO TO 5	If NUM > 100, control passes to the statement labeled 5; otherwise, control passes to whatever statement follows the IF statement.
IF (AMT.EQ.0.0) GO TO 10	If AMT = 0.0, control passes to the statement labeled 10; otherwise, control passes to the next statement.
IF (N1.NE.N2) GO TO 15	If N1 ≠ N2, control passes to the statement labeled 15; otherwise, the normal sequential execution of the program statements is not interrupted.

EXAMPLE 11. Here is a program to read one value from each of five input records and print their sum:

```
    SUM=0.
    N=1
  1 IF (N.GT.5) GO TO 2
    READ(5,10)AMT
    SUM=SUM+AMT
    N=N+1
    GO TO 1
  2 WRITE(6,11)SUM
    STOP
 10 FORMAT(F7.2)
 11 FORMAT(1X,'SUM IS',F8.2)
    END
```

*FORTRAN compilers that allow mixed-mode expressions (see Section 3.3) also allow the two values being compared in an IF statement to be of different types. To keep your programs as transportable as possible, you should not take this liberty, even if allowed.

Input Data:

```
        1         2
1234567890123456789012345678 90
 125.40
 800.00
  17.55
 123.28
  50.00
```

Output:

```
SUM IS 1116.23
```

This program contains two control statements. The IF statement transfers control to the WRITE statement if the condition N > 5 is satisfied. The GO TO statement

```
GO TO 1
```

transfers control to the statement labeled 1. The GO TO statement is an unconditional transfer statement. It does not matter how often or under what circumstances the statement GO TO 1 is executed; control always passes to the statement labeled 1.

With this explanation of the two control statements, you should see that the action of this program is as follows:

a. Assign the initial value 0. to SUM and 1 to N.
b. If N is greater than 5, skip the next step.
c. Read a value for AMT, add this value to SUM, increase N by 1, and then repeat step (b).
d. Print the value of SUM and stop.

Remark 1: The IF and GO statements in this program are used to set up a loop in which the group of statements

```
READ(5,10)AMT
SUM=SUM+AMT
N=N+1
```

is executed five times. Indenting this group as shown in the program listing enhances the readability of the entire program. The practice of indenting program statements is not new to us. In several of the examples considered thus far, comment lines describing the meanings of variable names used in a program were indented. Other situations in which indentations should be used to improve the readability of your program will be mentioned as they arise.

Remark 2: If this program is meant to run in a conversational mode, a WRITE or PRINT statement must be included to instruct a user about the values to be typed in response to the READ statement. Placing the lines

```
   (WRITE 6,12)
12 FORMAT(1X,'FOLLOWING EACH ? ENTER AN AMOUNT IN THE FORM XXXX.XX')
```

just before the statement labeled 1—that is, before the loop is entered—and using the same input values, will cause the following printout:

```
FOLLOWING EACH ? ENTER AN AMOUNT IN THE FORM XXXX.XX
?   125.40
?   800.00
?    17.55
?   123.28
?    50.00
SUM IS 1116.23
```

Remark 3: If this program is meant to be run in the batch mode, you can "echo" each input value to ensure that numbers are being read correctly. Placing the lines

```
    WRITE(6,12)AMT
12 FORMAT(1X,F7.2)
```

immediately after the READ statement and using the same input records will cause the following printout:

```
    125.40
    800.00
     17.55
    123.28
     50.00
SUM IS 1116.23
```

A word of caution is in order. When using the GO TO and IF statements described in this section, great care must be taken to ensure that an orderly exit is made from every loop. For example, if you carelessly write

```
    READ(5,10)X
1 IF (X.EQ.0.) GO TO 2
    WRITE(6,11)X
    GO TO 1
2 STOP
```

and if the input value for X is 1.57, the computer will print

```
1.57
1.57
1.57
 .
 .
 .
```

and will not stop until someone notices what is happening and stops it manually. (The way to stop the computer in such a situation is system dependent and will not be considered in this text.)

The program shown in Example 11 finds the sum of exactly five input values. The program segment in Example 10 reads and prints exactly fifty input values. The typical programming application calls for a program to process a different number of values each time it is run. The next two examples illustrate two ways to do this.

EXAMPLE 12. Here is a program segment to read and print one number from each of COUNT input records. The first input record contains a value for COUNT.

```
    INTEGER COUNT,N,NUMBER
    READ(5,10)COUNT
    N=1
1 IF (N.GT.COUNT) GO TO 2
        READ(5,11)NUMBER
        WRITE(6,12)NUMBER
        N=N+1
    GO TO 1
2 (next statement)
```

The first READ statement reads an input record to obtain a value for COUNT. The rest of the program segment is identical to the program segment shown in Example 10 except that the number 50, which tells how many numbers to read and print, is replaced by COUNT. Thus, if COUNT = 50, fifty numbers will be read and printed; if COUNT = 5000, five thousand numbers will be read and printed.

Remark: Note that if the first input record contains 0, the condition N.GT.COUNT will be satisfied the first time the IF statement is executed. This means that control will pass immediately to the statement labeled 2 and no values will be read and printed.

As you progress in your study of programming, you will find that there are times when writing a loop such as the one in Example 12 is an appropriate way to process input data. However, you should be aware that you are forcing a user of your program to include a count of how many input records are to be processed as the first input value. A user should not be required to make this count, without good reason. For long lists, the task is boring and errors are likely. If the program is meant to be run in a conversational mode, the number of input values may not be known in advance. To avoid these difficulties, you can use a special value as the *last* input value rather than a count as the *first*. Such a value is called an **End-of-Data (EOD) tag.** Each time the READ statement is executed, the value or values read are checked for this EOD-tag. This technique is illustrated in the following example.

EXAMPLE 13. Here is a program segment to read a list of numbers and print their squares:

```
 C ****** EOD TAG IS 9999. ******
     1 READ(5,10)X
          IF (X.EQ.9999.) GO TO 2
          Y=X**2
          WRITE(6,11)X,Y
       GO TO 1
     2 (next statement)
```

The READ statement reads an input value for X and the condition X.EQ.9999. in the IF statement is tested. If it fails—that is, if X ≠ 9999.—control passes to the statement following the IF statement, X and its square are printed, and the statement GO TO 1 returns control to the READ statement. When the value 9999. is read for X (it must be included in the input values to effect an orderly exit from the loop), the condition X.EQ.9999. is satisfied and control passes out of the loop to the statement labeled 2.

The examples in this section illustrate only a limited form of the IF statement. Our objective has been to show how loops containing READ statements can be written for processing many input values. Other forms and uses of the IF statement are described in Chapter 6. The following rules apply in all cases.

1. The statement label appearing in a GO TO statement must be the label of an executable statement. Control cannot be transferred to a nonexecutable statement.
2. The two values being compared in the condition of an IF statement must be of the same type.
3. The condition of an IF statement must be enclosed in parentheses.

We conclude this chapter with an example illustrating the following programming practices stressed to this point:

1. To discover a correct algorithm, carefully analyze the problem statement and record this analysis in writing. Be sure to identify any input and output values.
2. Describe an algorithm that, if followed, will result in a correct solution to the problem. This should be done before any coding takes place.
3. Use comment statements to make your program more readable and to clarify what is being done at any particular point. The individual steps in your algorithm will suggest meaningful comment lines.

EXAMPLE 14. A man has a large house with many rooms. He wants to paint the walls and ceilings of each room, but, before buying the paint, he naturally needs to know how much paint is necessary. On the average, each window and door covers 20 sq. ft. According to the label, each quart of paint covers 110 sq. ft. Write a program that will allow the man to give the dimensions of each room and the number of doors and windows in each room and then determine how many quarts of wall paint and how many quarts of ceiling paint are needed for that room.

Problem Analysis:
Although this problem statement is somewhat lengthy it should not be difficult to identify the following input and output quantities.

Input: Length, width, and height of each room.
           Number of doors and windows in each room.
Output: Quarts of wall paint and quarts of ceiling paint needed for each room.

To determine how many quarts of wall paint are needed for a particular room we must determine the wall area (in sq. ft.) to be covered and divide this value by 110 since one quart of paint covers 110 sq. ft. Similarly, the amount of ceiling paint is obtained by dividing the ceiling area by 110.

Before attempting to write down a procedure for carrying out this task, let's choose variable names for the quantities of interest. Doing this will allow us to write a concise procedure by using variable names, rather than verbal descriptions for these quantities.

LEN,WIDTH,HGHT = the length, width, and height of a room (in ft).
           NUMDW = the number of doors and windows in a room.
           WAREA = the wall area, including doors and windows, in a room
                   (WAREA = 2(LEN + WIDTH) × HGHT).
          DWAREA = the area of the NUMDW doors and windows (DWAREA = 20 × NUMDW).
           CAREA = the area of a ceiling (CAREA = LEN × WIDTH).
          WPAINT = quarts of wall paint needed (WPAINT = (WAREA − DWAREA)/110).
          CPAINT = quarts of ceiling paint needed (CPAINT = CAREA/110).
            ROOM = the number of the room in question (this was not asked for, but a good programmer
                   will often provide the user with helpful results not specifically requested).

Using these variable names, we can write the following procedure. Note that the order in which the steps are taken is just how you might carry out this task with tape measure, pencil, and paper.

The Algorithm:
a. Read values for LEN, WIDTH, HGHT, and NUMDW.
b. If LEN = 0, stop. (Algorithms must halt.)
c. Determine the areas WAREA, DWAREA, and CAREA.
d. Determine how much paint is needed (WPAINT and CPAINT).
e. Print the room number ROOM and the values of WPAINT and CPAINT.
f. Go to step (a) and repeat the process for the next room.

This procedure is incomplete; it does not specify how the room number ROOM is to be increased as we pass from room to room. Of the many ways to accomplish this, perhaps the simplest is to precede step (a) with the statement Let ROOM = 0 and then modify step (e) to read

e1. Add 1 to ROOM.
e2. Print the values of ROOM, WPAINT, and CPAINT.

Before coding this algorithm, we must determine whether the variables should represent real data or integer data. Since LEN, WIDTH, HGHT, WAREA, DWAREA, and CAREA denote lengths and areas, they are best declared as real variables. Since NUMDW and ROOM denote counts, they are best declared as integer variables. This leaves WPAINT and CPAINT which denote numbers of quarts of paint. So that fractions of quarts are not lost (truncated), we'll declare them as real variables.

The program can now be coded. Note that the steps in the algorithm appear as comments in the program.

```
C ************* PAINT CALCULATOR PROGRAM *************
        INTEGER NUMDW,ROOM
        REAL LEN,WIDTH,HGHT,WAREA,DWAREA,CAREA,WPAINT,CPAINT
C INITIALIZE THE ROOM COUNTER
        ROOM=0
C READ VALUES FOR THE LENGTH,WIDTH,HEIGHT,AND
C NUMBER OF DOORS AND WINDOWS FOR ONE ROOM
      1 READ(5,10)LEN,WIDTH,HGHT,NUMDW
     10 FORMAT(F6.1,F6.1,F6.1,2X,I2)
           IF (LEN.EQ.0.) GO TO 2
C           CALCULATE AREAS
             WAREA=2.*(LEN+WIDTH)*HGHT
             DWAREA=20*NUMDW
             CAREA=LEN*WIDTH
C           FIND NUMBER OF QUARTS OF WALL AND CEILING PAINT
             WPAINT=(WAREA-DWAREA)/110.
             CPAINT=CAREA/110.
C           PRINT RESULTS FOR ONE ROOM
             ROOM=ROOM+1
             WRITE(6,20)ROOM,WPAINT,CPAINT
     20      FORMAT(1X,I4,7X,F5.2,8X,F5.2)
         GO TO 1
      2 STOP
        END
```

Input Data:

```
            1         2         3         4
1234567890123456789012345678901234567890
   13.0  13.0   9.0    5
   12.0   9.0   9.0    4
    8.0   5.0   9.0    2
   11.0   9.0   9.0    4
   10.0   8.5   9.0    4
    0.    0.    0.     0
```

Output:

```
   1        3.35         1.55
   2        2.71         0.98
   3        1.76         0.36
   4        2.55         0.90
   5        2.30         0.77
```

We are not quite finished. All values that the computer prints must be labeled. We conclude this example by showing how this can be done in a batch mode and in a conversational mode.

Batch Mode:

Headings can be printed for the three output columns by placing the following lines just before the READ statement—that is, before the loop is entered.

```
C PRINT COLUMN HEADINGS
      WRITE(6,21)
      WRITE(6,22)
```

```
 21 FORMAT(1X,'ROOM     QUARTS OF    QUARTS OF')
 22 FORMAT(1X,'NUMBER   WALL PAINT   CEILING PAINT')
```

With this addition, the printout will be as follows:

```
ROOM     QUARTS OF    QUARTS OF
NUMBER   WALL PAINT   CEILING PAINT
  1        3.35          1.55
  2        2.71          0.98
  3        1.76          0.36
  4        2.55          0.90
  5        2.30          0.77
```

As many data records as desired, each one containing the input values for a single room, can be used. But, regardless of the number of records, a final card containing the EOD-tag 0. for LEN must be included. For this program, a blank card will do—remember, on input, blanks are interpreted as zeros.

Conversational Mode:

Two changes must be made. The program segment that reads values for LEN, WIDTH, HGHT, and NUMDW must be modified so that a user is told what to do when confronted with a "?". In addition, the part of the program that prints the results must be changed so that all output values are labeled. Following is one way to make these two changes. Note that an unformatted READ statement is used to read values that are typed at a terminal keyboard.

```
C READ VALUES FOR LENGTH,WIDTH,HGHT,AND
C NUMBER OF DOORS AND WINDOWS FOR ONE ROOM
    1 WRITE(6,21)
      READ(5)LEN,WIDTH,HGHT
      WRITE(6,22)
      READ(5)NUMDW
   21 FORMAT(1X,'LENGTH,WIDTH,HEIGHT---TYPE 0.,0.,0. TO STOP')
   22 FORMAT(1X,'NUMBER OF DOORS AND WINDOWS')


C PRINT RESULTS FOR ONE ROOM
      ROOM=ROOM+1
      WRITE(6,23)ROOM
      WRITE(6,24)WPAINT
      WRITE(6,25)CPAINT
      WRITE(6,26)
   23 FORMAT(1X,'ROOM NUMBER:',I3)
   24 FORMAT(1X,'QUARTS OF WALL PAINT:',F5.2)
   25 FORMAT(1X,'QUARTS CEILING PAINT:',F5.2)
   26 FORMAT(1X)
```

With these changes, the printout for a typical run is as follows:

```
RUN

LENGTH,WIDTH,HEIGHT---TYPE 0.,0.,0. TO STOP
? 13.0,13.0,9.0
NUMBER OF DOORS AND WINDOWS
? 5
```

```
ROOM NUMBER:   1
QUARTS OF WALL PAINT: 3.35
QUARTS CEILING PAINT: 1.55

LENGTH,WIDTH,HEIGHT---TYPE 0.,0.,0. TO STOP
? 12.,9.,9.
NUMBER OF DOORS AND WINDOWS
? 4
ROOM NUMBER:   2
QUARTS OF WALL PAINT: 2.71
QUARTS CEILING PAINT: 0.98

LENGTH,WIDTH,HEIGHT---TYPE 0.,0.,0. TO STOP
? 0.,0.,0.

READY
```

5.10 Problems

1. The following programs do not do what is claimed. Find and correct all errors.

a.
```
C READ TWO NUMBERS AND PRINT
  THEIR DIFFERENCE (EOD-TAG IS 99.)
  1 READ(5,10)A,B
    DIFF=A-B
    IF (A.NE.99.) GO TO 1
 10 FORMAT(F5.2,F5.2)
 11 FORMAT(1X,'DIFFERENCE:',F7.2)
  2 STOP
```

b.
```
C READ AND PRINT TEN NUMBERS
      N=1
  1 IF (N.EQ.10) GO TO 2
      READ(5,20)NUM
      WRITE(6,21)NUM
      GO TO 1
 20 FORMAT(I7)
 21 FORMAT(1X,I7)
  2 STOP
```

c.
```
C FIND THE SUM OF 25
C INPUT VALUES
      N=1
  1 READ(5,30)X
    SUM=X
    N=N+1
    IF (N.LT.25) GO TO 1
    STOP
 30 FORMAT(F7.2)
```

d.
```
C READ 50 NUMBERS AND PRINT
C THOSE THAT ARE BETWEEN
C 77 AND 145, INCLUSIVE
```

```
      I=0
  1 IF (I.EQ.50) GO TO 2
      I=I+1
      READ(5,40)N
      IF (N.GE.77) GO TO 3
      IF (N.LE.145) GO TO 3
      GO TO 1
  3 WRITE(6,41)N
      GO TO 1
  2 STOP
 40 FORMAT(I3)
 41 FORMAT(1X,I5)
```

Problems 2–4 are appropriate for systems involving a punched card operation. In each case write a program to produce a printed report as specified. Make sure that each report has a title centered on the page, and that each column has an appropriate heading. Use an EOD-tag to terminate the input data cards.

2. Given the following bowling scores, print a four-column report showing the scores for the three strings and the average for each bowler.

String 1	String 2	String 3
171	178	179
180	171	183
165	175	185
190	195	197

3. Given the employee number and monthly sales, print a three-column report showing the employee number, monthly sales, and commission if the commission rate for each person is 6%.

Employee number	Monthly sales
34	$4,050
51	6,500
21	3,750
18	3,640
49	7,150

4. Given the employee number, monthly sales, and commission rate for each person, print a four-column report showing the employee number, the monthly sales, the commission rate, and the total commission.

Employee number	Monthly sales	Commission rate
401	$28,400	2%
513	34,550	2.5%
193	19,600	3%
184	14,500	2%
237	22,300	3.25%
207	31,350	1.5%

Problems 5–7 are appropriate for conversational systems. In each case, the user is to be instructed about what values are to be typed. In addition, all output is to be appropriately labeled. Use an EOD-tag to effect an orderly exit from each program.

5. You are given the input data shown in Problem 2. For each bowler, the three scores are to be typed to determine the average and the three-string total.
6. You are given the data shown in Problem 3. For each employee, the employee number and monthly sales figure are to be typed to obtain the commission amount, if the commission rate for each person is 6%.
7. You are given the data shown in Problem 4. The monthly sales and the commission rate for each employee are to be typed to obtain the commission earned.

5.11 Review True-or-False Quiz

1. Format specifications used to interpret input data may contain I, F, and X descriptors.   T F
2. If a real value is assigned by a READ statement, the input record must contain the decimal point.   T F
3. That part of an input record referenced by a single edit descriptor appearing in a format specification is called a field.   T F
4. Every value in an input record must appear right-justified in its field.   T F
5. Using one edit descriptor to read an input value and a different edit descriptor to print the same value is allowed.   T F
6. A value assigned to a variable by a READ statement using the edit descriptor F8.0 will have no fractional part.   T F
7. A single WRITE or PRINT statement can be used to print the headings for more than one column.   T F
8. Normally, formatted READ statements are used when operating in a time-sharing environment, whereas unformatted READ statements are used on batch systems.   T F
9. A problem analysis is the process of discovering a correct algorithm.   T F
10. It is possible for a program that contains just one READ statement to process five values from each of 1000 input records.   T F

6

The Computer as a Decision Maker

You have seen how to use the IF and GO TO statements to control the order in which program statements are executed. FORTRAN contains several control statements, including forms of the IF statement not yet considered. In this chapter we describe the forms of the IF statement allowed in FORTRAN and show how they can be used to advantage in several programming applications. In addition, flowcharts (diagrams showing the step-by-step flow of activity in the solution of a problem) and their usefulness in programming are considered.

6.1 The Logical IF Statement

An expression that is either true or false is called a logical expression. Thus, the condition N.GT.10 of the statement

IF(N.GT.10) GO TO 5

is a logical expression; it is true if N is greater than 10 and false if N is not greater than 10. For this reason, this IF statement is called a logical IF statement.

Including a GO TO statement in an IF statement, as illustrated in Chapter 5, represents a very limited use of the logical IF statement. The general form of the logical IF statement is as follows:

IF *(condition)* **s**

Here, **s** denotes any executable statement other than another logical IF statement or certain other control statements yet to be considered (DO, block IF, ELSE, and END IF). The *condition* is a logical expression—that is, an expression that is either true or false; it must be enclosed in parentheses. If it is true, the statement **s** is executed; otherwise, **s** is not executed. In either case control passes to the next program statement unless **s** causes a transfer of control to some other statement.

EXAMPLE 1. In each part of this example we are given values for certain variables and a logical IF statement. We are to tell what happens when the IF statement is executed.

a. With AMT = 58.50, consider

IF(AMT.LT.60.) WRITE(6,10)AMT

Since 58.50 is less than 60, the logical expression AMT.LT.60 is true. Hence, the WRITE statement is executed and control passes to the statement on the line following the IF statement.

b. With X = 0.5 and Y = 0.1, consider

IF(X**2.GT.Y) N=N+1

Since X**2 has the value 0.25 and Y has the value 0.1, the logical expression X**2.GT.Y is true. Hence, the assignment statement N = N + 1 is executed and control passes to the next line.

c. With M = 2 and N = 4, consider

IF(N.NE.2*M) STOP

Both N and 2*M have the value 4; hence, the condition N.NE.2*M is false. The STOP statement is not executed and control passes to the statement immediately following the IF statement.

d. With N = 33 and I = 11, consider

IF((N/I)*I.EQ.N) M=M+1

Since N/I has the value 3, (N/I)*I has the value 33. The condition is satisfied. M is increased by 1 and control passes to the statement on the next line.

e. With N = 16 and I = 5, consider

IF((N/I)*I.EQ.N) M=M+1

Since N/I has the value 3 (integer division, remember) (N/I)*I has the value 15. The condition is not satisfied. M is not increased and control passes to the statement on the next line.

Remark: Note that the two values being compared in each condition are both real or both integer. FORTRAN compilers that allow mixed-mode expressions also allow you to compare values of different types. To keep your programs as transportable as possible, you should not take this liberty.

You have seen how a logical IF statement can be used to construct a loop to process many input values (Section 5.9). In this section we illustrate other applications of logical IF statements.

EXAMPLE 2. Here is a program to count how many of three given numbers are less than 60:

```
C EXAMPLE 2: A COUNTING PROGRAM
C   N DENOTES THE COUNT
C   X, Y, AND Z DENOTE THE NUMBERS
      N=0
      READ(5,10)X,Y,Z
   10 FORMAT(F7.2,F7.2,F7.2)
C BEGIN COUNTING
      IF(X.LT.60.) N=N+1
      IF(Y.LT.60.) N=N+1
      IF(Z.LT.60.) N=N+1
      WRITE(6,20)N
   20 FORMAT(1X,I2,2X,'INPUT VALUES ARE LESS THAN 60.')
      STOP
      END
```

Input Data:

```
         1         2
12345678901234567890012345
  53.25  89.65  48.85
```

Output:

```
2  INPUT VALUES ARE LESS THAN 60.
```

The statement IF (X.LT.60.) N = N + 1 causes the assignment statement N = N + 1 to be executed if X is less than 60; otherwise, the statement N = N + 1 is skipped. In either case, control then passes to the next line. Thus the action of this program is as follows.

First, N is set equal to 0 and the values 53.25, 89.65, and 48.85 are assigned to X, Y, and Z, respectively, by the READ statement. The condition X.LT.60. in the first IF statement is *true* so the statement N = N + 1 is executed and N becomes 1. The condition Y.LT.60. is *false,* so the statement N = N + 1 in the second IF statement is skipped. The condition Z.LT.60. is *true,* so the statement N = N + 1 in the third IF statement is executed to give N = 2. Finally, the WRITE statement causes the output shown.

Example 2 illustrates the logical IF statement as a "decision maker." The IF statement is used to control which of two courses of action the computer should take—either add 1 to N or don't add 1 to N. Example 3 illustrates the use of the logical IF statement both as a decision maker and in the construction of a loop.

EXAMPLE 3. Here is a program to count how many of several input values are less than 60:

```
C EXAMPLE 3: A COUNTING PROGRAM
C  N DENOTES THE COUNT
C  X DENOTES AN INPUT VALUE
      N=0
C  EOD TAG IS 0.
    1 READ(5,10)X
      IF(X.EQ.0.) GO TO 2
      IF(X.LT.60) N=N+1
      GO TO 1
    2 WRITE(6,20)N
      STOP
   10 FORMAT(F7.2)
   20 FORMAT(1X,I3,2X,'INPUT VALUES ARE LESS THAN 60.')
      END
```

Input Data:

```
         1
123456789012345
  53.25
  89.65
  48.85
   0.0
```

Output:

```
2  INPUT VALUES ARE LESS THAN 60.
```

The two statements GO TO 1 and IF(X.EQ.0.) GO TO 2 set up a loop to read and process input values X until X = 0. is read. For each input value other than 0., the statement IF(X.LT.60.) N = N + 1 adds 1 to the counter N if X < 60, just as in Example 2.

EXAMPLE 4. Let's write a program to read two numbers A and B and print the message BOTH if both are negative and the message NOT BOTH otherwise.

Problem Analysis:
The logic of this problem is slightly complicated. First, the number A must be tested to determine if it is negative. If it is, then B must be tested. But as soon as a number being tested is not negative, the message NOT BOTH should be printed. A procedure for doing this is as follows.

a. Read values for A and B.
b. If A is not negative, print NOT BOTH and stop.
c. If B is not negative, print NOT BOTH and stop.
d. Print BOTH and stop.

The Program:

```
      READ(5,10)A,B
      IF(A.GE.0.) GO TO 1
      IF(B.GE.0.) GO TO 1
        WRITE(6,11)
        STOP
    1 WRITE(6,12)
      STOP
   10 FORMAT(F7.2,F7.2)
   11 FORMAT(1X,'BOTH')
   12 FORMAT(1X,'NOT BOTH')
      END
```

Remark: Beginning programmers are often tempted to begin coding a program without first describing the procedure to be followed. If this practice were followed for the problem at hand, we could easily be led into making the tests A.LT.0 and B.LT.0 rather than the tests A.GE.0 and B.GE.0. The result would be a program similar to the following:

```
      READ(5,10)A,B
      IF(A.LT.0.) GO TO 1
    2   WRITE(6,12)
        STOP
    1 IF(B.LT.0.) GO TO 3
        GO TO 2
    3 WRITE(6,11)
      STOP
   10 FORMAT(F7.2,F7.2)
   11 FORMAT(1X,'BOTH')
   12 FORMAT(1X,'NOT BOTH')
      END
```

This is a correct but rather poor program. It contains an additional GO TO statement (GO TO 2), which makes the logic more difficult to follow than that of the first program. There are no hard and fast rules for choosing between the two tests .LT. and .GE.; the "best" choice will be dictated by a carefully prepared algorithm.

Programming tasks calling for output documents in tabular form are not uncommon. Normally, these documents will consist of one or more columns of data, each with a descriptive column heading. Data to be printed need not be read from input records; they can all be generated by the computer during program execution, as is shown in the following example

EXAMPLE 5. Prepare a table of values, with column headings, for the expression $X^3 - 7X^2 + 13$ for all values of X between 0 and 1.

Problem Analysis:
The task, as stated, is impossible since there is an infinity of numbers between 0 and 1. Let's agree to evaluate the given expression for all X, begining with $X = 0$, in increments of 0.1. Using Y to denote the value of $X^3 - 7X^2 + 13$, we can write a procedure as follows:

a. Print column headings.
b. Let $X = 0$.
c. Let $Y = X^3 - 7X^2 + 13$.
d. Print X and Y on one line.
e. Add 0.1 to X, and go to step (c) if $X \leq 1$.
f. Stop.

```
C**TABLE OF VALUES FOR EXPRESSION IN STATEMENT 1**
C
C PRINT COLUMN HEADINGS
      WRITE(6,10)
C CALCULATE AND PRINT THE TABLE VALUES
      X=0.
    1 Y=X**3-7.*X**2+13.
        WRITE(6,20)X,Y
        X=X+0.1
      IF(X.LE.1.) GO TO 1
      STOP
   10 FORMAT(1X,'VALUE OF X',5X,'VALUE OF Y')
   20 FORMAT(1X,F7.1,10X,F6.3)
      END
```

Output:

```
VALUE OF X      VALUE OF Y
     0.0           13.
     0.1           12.931
     0.2           12.728
     0.3           12.397
     0.4           11.944
     0.5           11.375
     0.6           10.696
     0.7            9.913
     0.8            9.032
     0.9            8.059
     1.0            7.0
```

Remark 1: The executable statements

```
1 Y=X**3-7.*X**2+13.
     WRITE(6,20)X,Y
     X=X+0.1
  IF(X.LE.1.) GO TO 1
```

constitute the loop used to print the table values. Since the headings must be printed first, and only once, the statement that does this, WRITE(5,10), must appear before this loop is entered.

Remark 2: If you run this program, your computer may not print the last line of output. A computer stores numbers and does arithmetic in the binary number system. But some numbers, 0.1 is one of them, cannot be represented exactly as binary numbers (just as $\frac{1}{3} = .333\cdots$ cannot be represented exactly as a decimal number with finitely many digits). This means that calculations involving 0.1 will only be approximate. Thus, if 0.1 is represented in your computer by a slightly larger number, setting $X = 0$ and successively adding 0.1 to X ten times can result in a value of X that is slightly larger than 1. Should this happen, the condition (X.LE.1.) will be false and control will pass out of the loop without printing the value of Y for $X = 1$.

If your computer does not behave as it should, you can always fudge things so that it will. For instance, you can replace the condition (X.LE.1.) by the condition (X.LE.1.00001) to ensure that the final pass will be made through the loop.

In Example 1 (parts d and e) you saw that the integer expression (N/I)*I has the value N only if I is a factor of N. For instance, $(30/5)*5 = 30$, so 5 is a factor of 30, but $(30/4)*4 = 28$ (in integer arithmetic $30/4 = 7.5$ is truncated to give the value 7), so 4 is not a factor of 30. In the following example we determine if the integer FACT is a factor of the integer NUM with a logical IF statement that compares (NUM/FACT)*FACT with NUM.

EXAMPLE 6. Let's write a program for the following problem statement. A list of positive integers, terminated by the EOD-tag 9999, is to be input. For each integer, other than 9999, all factors and the sum of these factors are to be printed.

Problem Analysis:
Each time an integer, other than 9999, is read, all of its factors must be found, these factors must be printed, and the sum of these factors must be printed. Writing an algorithm to do this is not difficult if we omit the details.

Algorithm:
a. Read an integer.
b. If this integer is 9999, stop.
c. Find and print all factors of the integer, and also the sum of these factors.
d. Go to step (a).

We already know how to write program statements for steps (a), (b), and (d); only step (c) is troublesome. This leads us to ask how step (c) can be rewritten so that it can be coded more easily. But this is easy: the only possible factors of an integer are the integers from 1 up to the integer itself; hence, we should check all of these as possible factors. To help us describe this process further, let's use the following variable names:

NUM = any one of the input values.
FACT = a possible factor of NUM.
SUM = the sum of the factors of NUM.

Using these variable names, we can rewrite the algorithm as follows. Steps (c1) through (c4) describe step (c).

Algorithm (Refined):
a.   Read a value for NUM.
b.   If NUM = 9999, stop.
c1. Initialize: SUM = 0 and FACT = 1.
c2. If FACT is a factor of NUM, print FACT and add it to SUM.
c3. Add 1 to FACT and repeat step (c2) until FACT > NUM.
c4. Print SUM.
d.   Go to step (a).

In this refined algorithm, step (c2) is the only step that may be troublesome. But we know a simple test to determine if one number is a factor of another. In particular, FACT is a factor of NUM if (NUM/FACT)*NUM and NUM have the same value; otherwise, FACT is not a factor. In the following program we perform this test using a logical IF statement.

Remark: In this problem analysis, we took considerable care to proceed in an orderly way toward an algorithm that would be easy to understand and whose correctness would be fairly obvious. We started by subdividing the task described in the problem statement into four simpler tasks (the first algorithm). A more detailed procedure for carrying out step (c) was then written and inserted in the first algorithm to give us the refined algorithm. This approach to problem solving is not new to us (see Example 1 of Chapter 2). It is called the **method of step-wise refinement** and will be discussed and further illustrated in Section 6.9

The Program:

```
C PROGRAM TO DETERMINE THE FACTORS AND THE SUM OF THE
C FACTORS FOR ANY POSITIVE INTEGER.
        INTEGER FACT,NUM,SUM
C         NUM=THE CURRENT INPUT VALUE
C         FACT=A POSSIBLE FACTOR OF NUM
C         SUM=SUM OF THE FACTORS OF NUM
    1 READ(5,100)NUM
        IF(NUM.EQ.9999) STOP
        WRITE(6,101)NUM
        SUM=0
        FACT=1
    2   IF((NUM/FACT)*FACT.NE.NUM) GO TO 3
            WRITE(6,102)FACT
            SUM=SUM+FACT
    3   FACT=FACT+1
        IF(FACT.LE.NUM) GO TO 2
        WRITE(6,103)SUM
      GO TO 1
      STOP
  100 FORMAT(I6)
  101 FORMAT(1X,'FACTORS OF',IX,I6)
  102 FORMAT(1X,I6)
  103 FORMAT(1X,'SUM OF FACTORS IS',I8)
      END
```

Input Data:

```
          1         2         3         4
1234567890123456789012345678901234567890
     12
   1001
   9999
```

Output:

```
FACTORS OF      12
      1
      2
      3
      4
      6
     12
SUM OF FACTORS IS      28
FACTORS OF   1001
      1
      7
     11
     13
   1001
SUM OF FACTORS IS    1033
```

Remark 1: The only factor of NUM greater than NUM/2 is NUM itself. Hence, this program wastes a lot of time by testing numbers greater than NUM/2 as possible factors. To modify the program so that it will not test these numbers, only the statements SUM = 0 and IF(FACT.LE.NUM) GO TO 2 need to be changed. Explain how to do this.

Remark 2: If this program is to be run in a conversational mode, the READ statement must be preceded by a WRITE or PRINT statement telling a user how to respond to each question mark.

6.2 Compound Logical Expressions

Logical expressions can also be written using the logical operators .AND., .OR., and .NOT.. For example, the logical expression

(A.LT.B).OR.(A.LT.C)

is true if A is less than B or A is less than C, and otherwise is false. Expressions involving these logical operators are sometimes called compound logical expressions.

If le_1 and le_2 are logical expressions, the truth values (*true* or *false*) of the three logical expressions $(le_1).AND.(le_2)$, $(le_1).OR.(le_2)$, and $.NOT.(le_1)$ are as shown in Tables 6.1, 6.2, and 6.3.

TABLE 6.1. The .AND. operator.

le_1	le_2	$(le_1).AND.(le_2)$
true	true	true
true	false	false
false	true	false
false	false	false

TABLE 6.2. The .OR. operator.

le_1	le_2	$(le_1).OR.(le_2)$
true	true	true
true	false	true
false	true	true
false	false	false

TABLE 6.3. The .NOT. operator.

le_1	$.NOT.(le_1)$
true	false
false	true

EXAMPLE 7. The following illustrate typical uses of logical expressions containing the .AND. and .OR. operators.

a. The statement

   IF ((A.LT.0.).AND.(B.LT.0.)) GO TO 1

   will transfer control to the statement labeled 1 if both A and B are negative.

b. The statement

   IF ((M.GE.7).AND.(M.LE.28)) WRITE (6,10)

   will cause the statement WRITE(6,10) to be executed only if M is between 7 and 28, inclusive.

c. The statement

   IF ((M.LT.7).OR.(M.GT.28)) WRITE(6,11)

   will cause the statement WRITE(6,11) to be executed only if M is not between 7 and 28, inclusive.

Remark: The logical expression in part (b) is true only when M satisfies the double inequality $7 \leq M \leq 28$, whereas the logical expression in part (c) is true only when $M < 7$ or $M > 28$—that is, only when the double inequality $7 \leq M \leq 28$ is false. Thus, the two logical expressions ((M.GE.7).AND.(M.LE.28)) and .NOT.((M.LT.7).OR.(M.LE.28)) are *equivalent;* that is, for any value of M, they are both true or both false.

A logical expression may contain more than one of the operators .NOT., .AND., and .OR.. An expression such as

(M.EQ.0).OR.(A.LT.B).AND.(A.LT.C)

is an admissible logical expression. However, the order in which the .OR. and .AND. operators are executed matters. For example, suppose that M.EQ.0 is true while A.LT.B and A.LT.C are both false. Performing the .OR. first, we get

(true .OR. false).AND.(false)
= (true).AND.(false)   (using Table 6.2)
= false.   (using Table 6.1)

However, if the .AND. is performed first, we get

(true).OR.(false .AND. false)
= (true).OR.(false)   (using Table 6.1)
= true.   (using Table 6.2)

These two answers cannot both be correct. In FORTRAN, the following priorities are used:

Logical operator	Priority
.NOT.	highest
.AND.	intermediate
.OR.	lowest

In any logical expression the order in which the logical operators are performed is determined first by the indicated priority and then, in any priority class, from left to right. As with arithmetic expressions, parentheses may be used to override this order or simply to clarify what order is intended. Thus, the logical expression

(M.EQ.0).OR.(A.LT.B).AND.(A.LT.C)

is equivalent to the expression

(M.EQ.0).OR.((A.LT.B).AND.(A.LT.C))

If we want the .OR. to be performed first we must use parentheses and write

((M.EQ.0).OR.(A.LT.B)).AND.(A.LT.C)

EXAMPLE 8. This program reads five pairs of integers (I, J) and counts (KOUNT) how many of these pairs include only positive numbers:

```
      N=0
      KOUNT=0
    1 READ(5,10)I,J
        IF((I.GT.0).AND.(J.GT.0)) KOUNT=KOUNT+1
        N=N+1
      IF(N.LT.5) GO TO 1
      WRITE(6,11)KOUNT
   10 FORMAT(I5,I5)
   11 FORMAT(1X,I4,IX,'POSITIVE PAIRS WERE FOUND.')
      STOP
      END
```

Input Data:

```
         1
12345678901234
    19    27
   -23    48
   273     0
   147    65
   -24   -16
```

Output:

```
2  POSITIVE PAIRS WERE FOUND.
```

Remark: The readability of a program is often improved by the careful use of the operators .NOT., .AND., and .OR.. Using .AND. in this program allowed us to write a single IF statement to test two conditions. To write this program without using .AND., the two lines

```
IF((I.GT.0).AND.(J.GT.0)) KOUNT=KOUNT+1
N=N+1
```

could be replaced by the following lines:

```
  IF(I.LE.0) GO TO 2
  IF(J.LE.0) GO TO 2
  KOUNT=KOUNT+1
2 N=N+1
```

Certainly the first choice is easier to understand.

6.3 Problems

1. If A = 1, B = 2, and C = 3, which of the following logical expressions are true?
   a. A + B.LE.C
   b. A + B.GE.C
   c. 3.0.NE.C
   d. B**2.EQ.A + C
   e. A/C*B.LE.0.5
   f. 3. − (C/B).EQ.3. − C/B
   g. (A.LT.C).AND.(A + B.EQ.C)
   h. .NOT.((A.GT.B).OR.(C.GT.A))

2. Each of the following IF statements contains an error. Find it and explain whether it is a syntax error or a programming error.
   a. IF((X − Y)*(X + Y)) GO TO 1
   b. IF(M − N.LT.27),K = K + 1
   c. IF(M>N) STOP
   d. 5 IF(I.LT.J) GO TO 5
   e. IF(X.GT.FLOAT(N) WRITE(6,10)X
   f. IF SUM.EQ.TOTAL GO TO 3
   g. IF(.NOT.(I/3)) I = I + 1
   h. IF(A.LT.B.LT.C) WRITE(6,10)

3. Correct the following programs.
   a.
   ```
   C PROGRAM TO PRINT THE
   C ODD WHOLE NUMBERS THROUGH 15
       1 N=1
         WRITE(6,20)N
      20 FORMAT(1X,4I)
         N=N+2
         IF(N.LE.15) GO TO 1
         STOP
         END
   ```

b.
```
   C PROGRAM TO PRINT AN 8 PERCENT TAX
   C TABLE WITH COLUMN HEADINGS (PRICES FROM 100. TO 200.)
         PRICE=100.
       1 TAX=8.*PRICE
         WRITE(6,30)
         WRITE(6,40)X,TAX
         PRICE=PRICE+1.
         (IF PRICE.LE.200.) GO TO 1
      30 FORMAT(1X,'PRICE    TAX')
      40 FORMAT(1X,F6.2,4X,F5.2)
         STOP
         END
```

c.
```
   C PROGRAM TO PRINT A TABLE OF SQUARE
   C ROOTS WITH COLUMN HEADINGS
         N=2
         WRITE(6,20)
         R=N**1/2
       2 WRITE(6,30)N,R
         N=N+1
         IF(N.NE.100) GO TO 2
      20 FORMAT(1X,'NUMBER',4X,'SQUARE ROOT')
      30 FORMAT(1X,I4,7X,F8.4)
         STOP
         END
```

d.
```
   C TELL WHETHER ANY NON-ZERO
   C INTEGER IS POSITIVE OR NEGATIVE
       1 READ(5,10)N
         IF(N.EQ.0) GO TO 1
         IF(N.GT.0) WRITE(6,11)N
         STOP
         IF(N.LT.0) WRITE(6,12)N
         STOP
      10 FORMAT(I5)
      11 FORMAT(1X,I5,'IS POSITIVE')
      12 FORMAT(1X,I5,'IS NEGATIVE')
         END
```

4. Pretending that you are the computer, prepare a table showing the values of all variables and also what will be printed during execution of the following programs.

a.
```
         K=1
         M=1
       7 M=M*K
         WRITE(6,30)K,M
         K=K+1
         IF(K.LE.4) GO TO 7
      30 FORMAT(1X,I3,I10)
         STOP
         END
```

b.
```
         M=0
         N=5
      10 M=M+N
         WRITE(6,20)M
         N=-(N+1)
         IF(M.NE.-2) GO TO 10
      20 FORMAT(1X,I3)
         STOP
         END
```

```
c.    I=1
      WRITE(6,10)I
      J=1
      WRITE(6,10)J
   6  K=I+J
      WRITE(6,10)K
      I=J
      J=K
      IF(K.LT.5) GO TO 6
  10  FORMAT(1X,I4)
      STOP
      END
```

```
d.    I=0
      J=0
      K=11
   2  I=I+J+2
      IF (K.LT.I) GO TO 1
      J=J+1
      K=K-1
      IF (I.LT.K) GO TO 2
   1  WRITE(6,10)J
  10  FORMAT(1X,I5)
      STOP
      END
```

```
e.    A=1
      B=2
      C=3
   8  WRITE(6,10)A,B,C
      T=B
      B=C
      C=T
      WRITE(6,10)A,B,C
      T=C
      C=A
      A=T
      IF(A.NE.3.0) GO TO 8
  10  FORMAT(1X,F4.1,F4.1,F4.1)
      STOP
      END
```

```
f.    X=1.2
      N=2
   1  Y=X**N
      WRITE(6,10)N,Y
      N=N+1
      IF ((Y.LT.1.5).AND.(N.LT.5)) GO TO 1
      STOP
  10  FORMAT(1X,I2,2X,F8.2)
      END
```

Write a program to print each table described in Problems 5–17. Each table is to have a short title and each column is to have a heading.

5. The first column contains the number of miles (1, 2, 3, . . . , 10), and the second column gives the corresponding number of kilometers (1 mi = 1.6093 km).
6. The first column contains the number of inches (1, 2, 3, . . . , 36), and the second column gives the corresponding number of centimeters (1 in. = 2.54 cm).
7. The first column contains the temperature in degrees Celsius from −20 to 40 in steps of 2, and the second gives the corresponding temperature in degrees Fahrenheit (F = 9/5C + 32).
8. The first column gives the amount of sales (500, 1000, 1500, . . . , 5000), and the second gives the commission at a rate of 7.5%.
9. The first column contains the principal (50, 100, 150, . . . , 500), and the second column gives the corresponding simple interest for six months at an annual interest rate of 17.8%.
10. The first column gives the list price of an article ($25, $50, $75, . . . , $300), the second gives the amount of a 25% discount, and the third gives the corresponding selling price.
11. Ucall Taxi charges 85 cents for a ride plus 13 cents for each tenth of a mile. The first column gives the number of miles (0.1, 0.2, 0.3, . . . , 3.0), and the second gives the total charges.

12. The first column contains the number of years ($n = 1, 2, 3, \ldots, 10$), the second the amount in the account, and the third the interest earned at the end of n years on a principal of $1,000 at 6.5% compounded annually ($a = p(1 + r)^n$).

13. A three-column table showing the values of n, n^2, $\sqrt{n}$ for $n = 1, 2, 3, \ldots, 15$.

14. A three-column table showing the values of n, 2^n, and $\sqrt[n]{2}$ for $n = 1, 2, 3, \ldots, 16$.

15. A one-column table (list) containing the first ten terms of the arithmetic progression m, $m + n$, $m + 2n$, $m + 3n$, and so on. Integer values for m and n are to be assigned by a READ statement.

16. A one-column table (list) of the first 12 terms of the geometric progression a, ar, ar^2, ar^3, and so on. Real values for a and r are to be assigned by a READ statement.

17. An accurate sketch of the graph of $y = \sqrt{1.09}\, x^3 - \sqrt[3]{8.51}\, x^2 + (1.314x/1.426) - 0.8$ on the interval $1 \leqslant x \leqslant 3$ is required. To assist in this task, produce a table of the x and y values where the x's are in increments of 0.1.

Write a program to perform each task specified in Problems 18–30. Input values are to be read from cards or typed at a terminal keyboard, whichever is appropriate for the system you are using.

18. A salesperson's total weekly sales is to be input. Determine the commission earned if a commission of 5.3% is earned on the first $5,000 in sales and 2.1% is earned on any amount in excess of $5,000.

19. A person earns R dollars an hour with time-and-a-half for all hours over 32. Determine the gross pay for an N-hour week. (The input values are N and R.)

20. Two numbers M and N are to be input. If the sum of M and N is greater than 42, print 42. If not, increase M by 10 and N by 3, print the new M and N, and again check to see if the sum is greater than 42. Repeat this process until a sum greater than 42 is achieved.

21. Many numbers are to be input. For each, do the following. If it is between 17 and 35, inclusive, print BETWEEN. If it is less than 17, increase it by 5; if it is greater than 35, decrease it by 5. In either case print the value obtained and repeat the process until BETWEEN is printed. For example, if 54 is input, 49, 44, 39, and BETWEEN will be printed, and if 22 is input, the printout will be BETWEEN.

22. For any two integers M and N, print POSITIVE if both are positive, NEGATIVE if both are negative, and NEITHER in all other cases.

23. For any three numbers input, print ALL NEGATIVE if all are negative, ALL POSITIVE if all are positive, and NEITHER in all other cases.

24. For any real number X, determine the smallest positive integer I whose cube is greater than X.

25. For any input list, determine how many times a number is strictly larger than the one just before it. For example, if the list is 17, 3, 19, 27, 23, 25, the answer will be three, since $19 > 3$, $27 > 19$, and $25 > 23$.

26. A list of scores in the range 0 to 100 is to be examined to determine the following counts:
   C1 = number of scores less than 20.
   C2 = number of scores less than 40 but at least 20.
   C3 = number of scores less than 60 but at least 40.
   C4 = number of scores less than 80 but at least 60.
   C5 = number of scores not less than 80.
   Determine these counts for any list of input data.

27. A list of integers is to be input. Print only those integers that are even. (An integer is even if it is divisible by 2.)

28. A list of integers is to be input. Print those integers that are multiples of 5 or of 7.

29. One positive integer is to be input. Print the message PRIME, if it is prime and NOT PRIME otherwise. (An integer N is prime if $N > 1$ and its only factors are 1 and N.)

30. A list of integers is to be input. Print those that are prime.

6.4 Flowcharts and Flowcharting

The following diagram is a pictorial representation of a simple algorithm to recognize whether or not an input value is 5.

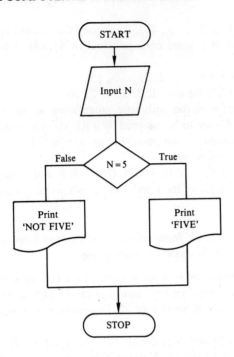

Such a pictorial representation of the sequence of steps in an algorithm or a program is called a **programming flowchart** or simply a **flowchart.** Flowcharts are useful for program documentation. In addition, it is often easier to prepare a pictorial description of a process to be followed than to attempt a detailed description in words. The flowchart is an excellent way to do this. Some of the components used to construct flowcharts can be seen in the following examples.

EXAMPLE 9. Here are two equivalent flowcharts for a program to print the numbers 100, 110, 120, . . . , 200:

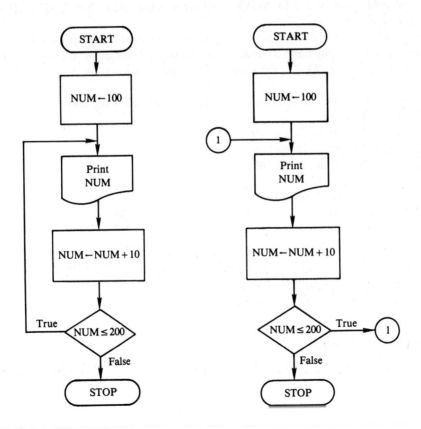

EXAMPLE 10. Here is a flowchart displaying the process of adding the integers from 1 to 10:

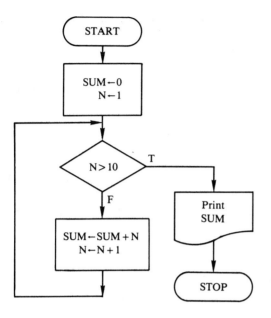

Remark 1: When two or more assignment statements are included in a single box they are evaluated from top to bottom.

Remark 2: Note that we have labeled the flow lines from the diamond-shaped decision symbol with the letters T and F for true and false, respectively.

In these examples, arrows connecting six different types of symbols are used to describe the sequence of steps in an algorithm. When possible, the flow should be directed from top to bottom or from left to right, as was done in these examples. Although there are many such flowchart symbols* in use, the six used here are adequate for displaying the flow of instructions for many FORTRAN programs. A brief description of how these symbols are used is given in Table 6.4.

The process of preparing a flowchart is called **flowcharting.** There are no fixed rules on how one should proceed toward the preparation of a flowchart; flowcharting must be practiced. However, it is helpful to determine *what* must be done before attempting to describe *how* to do it (a flowchart is concerned principally with *how* to carry out a task). If you don't do this, you will be confronted with the problem of determining not *what* must be done but what must be done *first*. This can be very difficult.

We conclude this section with two examples illustrating the process of flowcharting. Once a flowchart is prepared, the task of writing the program is reasonably routine; it consists only of coding the steps indicated in the flowchart.

*Flowchart symbols as proposed by the American National Standards Institute (ANSI) are described in "Flowcharting with the ANSI Standard: A Tutorial," by Ned Chapin, *Computing Surveys*, Vol. 2, No. 2, June 1970.

TABLE 6.4. Flowchart symbols.

The symbol	Its use
	To designate the start and end of a program.
	To describe any processing of data. If two or more assignment statements are included in one box, they are performed from top to bottom.
	To designate a decision that is to be made.
	To describe output that is to be printed by a line printer or at a time sharing terminal. If messages are to be printed, they will be enclosed in quotation marks.
	To indicate that data are to be read from cards. We also use it to indicate that data are to be input (typed) at a terminal keyboard.
	A connector—used to indicate the flow from one segment of a flowchart to another and also to avoid drawing long lines.

EXAMPLE 11. Construct a flowchart to find the largest and smallest numbers in a list of input values. The input list is terminated with the EOD-tag 9999.

Problem Analysis:

One way to determine the largest (smallest) number in a list is to read the numbers one at a time, remembering only the largest (smallest) of those already read. (This method was illustrated and discussed in Chapter 2, Example 2.) To help us give a precise description of this process, let's use the following variable names:

LARGE = largest of those numbers already read.
SMALL = smallest of those numbers already read.
NUM   = the number currently being read.

It is not difficult to construct a flowchart describing an algorithm for this task. First, we must read an input value and assign it to both LARGE and SMALL. Thus, we can begin with the following flowchart segment:

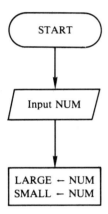

The next step is to read another input value and compare it with the EOD-tag 9999, to determine if the end of the input list has been reached. To display this step, we can add the following to our partial flowchart:

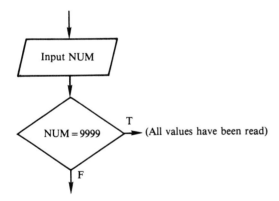

Note that while constructing the flowchart (that is, while discovering an algorithm), we always have a partial flowchart in front of us to help us decide what the next step should be. Continuing this process of flowchart construction, a flowchart such as the following will emerge:

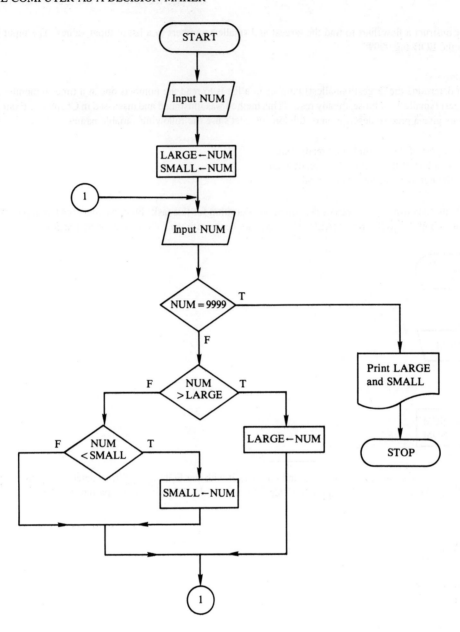

EXAMPLE 12. Construct a flowchart for a program to determine a salesperson's commission if the schedule is 4% on the first $2,000 in sales and 6% on everything in excess of $2,000.

Problem Analysis:
Let's denote the total sales by SALES and the commission by COMM. The following formulas govern this situation:

IF SALES ≤ 2000, COMM = .04 × SALES
IF SALES > 2000, COMM = .04 × 2000 + .06 × (SALES − 2000)

For any amount SALES, we must determine the commission COMM as indicated by these formulas. Having identified what must be done, we must show how to do it. First, we must read an input value for SALES. Let's assume that a sales amount of 0 means that all commissions have been determined and printed. This suggests the following flowchart segment to get us started:

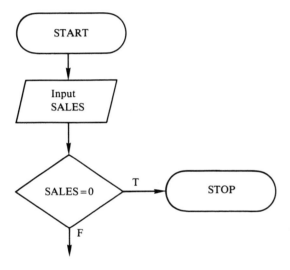

Next, we must compare SALES with 2000 to determine which of the commission formulas to use. This immediately gives rise to the following complete flowchart for the given problem statement. Note that including 0 as an EOD-tag allows many commissions to be calculated during a single program run. Although this was not specified in the problem statement, it is certainly a desirable feature to include in the program.

The Flowchart:

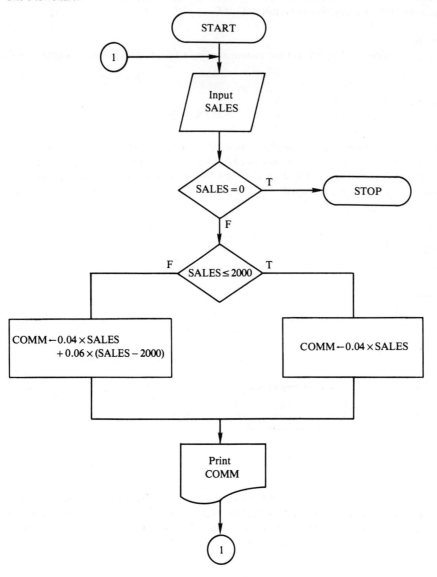

Remark: The flowchart segment,

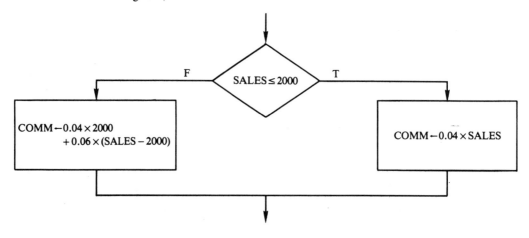

used to distinguish between the cases SALES ≤ 2000 and SALES > 2000, can be coded in many ways. Following are three ways to do this.

Program Segment 1:

```
IF(SALES.LE.2000.) COMM=.04*SALES
IF(SALES.GT.2000.) COMM=.04*2000.+.06*(SALES-2000.)
```

Program Segment 2:

```
  IF(SALES.LE.2000.) GO TO 1
     COMM=.04*2000.+.06*(SALES-2000.)
     GO TO 2
1 COMM=.04*SALES
2 (next statement)
```

Program Segment 3:

```
COMM=.04*SALES
IF(SALES.GT.2000.) COMM=.04*2000.+.06*(SALES-2000.)
```

Of these, the first is probably the easiest to read. The second is cluttered with GO TO statements and statement labels and is not particularly easy to follow. The third assigns the value of .04 × SALES to the variable COMM prior to determining which of the two formulas is appropriate. This constitutes a trick (called cleverness by some) and can lead to a program that is difficult to read. Although the two IF statements in Program Segment 1 have the same effect as the flowchart segment, they carry out the task in a different way. In particular, SALES is compared with 2000 to determine whether to execute the statement COMM = .04*SALES. Then SALES is again compared with 2000 to determine if the assignment statement in the second IF statement should be executed. The flowchart says to compare SALES with 2000, only once.

In Section 6.6 we'll describe a form of the IF statement that greatly simplifies coding such flowchart constructs.

6.5 Problems

Prepare a flowchart and then a program to accomplish each of the following tasks.

1. Input one number. If it is between 3 and 21, exclusive, print BETWEEN. Otherwise, print NOT BETWEEN.
2. Input two numbers. If either one is positive, print EITHER. Otherwise, print NEITHER.
3. Input three numbers. If the first is larger than the other two, print LARGEST. If it is smaller than the others, print SMALLEST. Otherwise, print NEITHER.
4. Calculate the sum $1 + 2 + 3 + \cdots + N$. N is to be input.
5. Calculate the sum $5 + 8 + 11 + 14 + \cdots + 98$.
6. Calculate the sum and average of any 20 input values. The input values are all to be integers.
7. Input a list of real numbers whose last value is 9999. Calculate the sum and average of all numbers input excluding the EOD-tag 9999.
8. Input a list of real numbers terminated with 9999. (9999. is an EOD-tag and is not considered to be in this list.) Print the largest number and also a count of how many numbers are included in the list.
9. (This is more difficult.) Input a list of real numbers as in Problem 8. Print the largest number in the list and also a count of how many numbers appear in the list before the first occurrence of this largest number. For example, if the list is {6, 9, 6, 12, 10, 5, 12, 7, 5}, the largest value is 12 and the count is three. (*Hint:* To determine the specified count you will need a variable to count the input values and another to "remember" the number of input values appearing before the "current" largest value.)

10. A salesperson's monthly commission is determined according to the following schedule:

Net sales	Commission rate
Up to $10,000	6%
Next $ 4,000	7%
Next $ 6,000	8%
Additional amounts	10%

Determine the monthly commission given the total monthly sales.

11. Andrew's parents deposit $500 in a savings account on the day of his birth. The bank pays 6.5% compounded annually. Construct a table showing how this deposit grows in value from the date of deposit to his 21st birthday.

12. Sally receives a graduation present of $1,000 and invests it in a long-term certificate that pays 8% compounded annually. Construct a table showing how this investment grows to a value of $1,500.

13. A young man agrees to begin working for a company at the very modest salary of a penny a week, with the stipulation that his salary will double each week. At the end of six months what is his weekly salary and how much has he earned in all?

6.6 Block IF Statements

Many FORTRAN compilers allow alternate forms of the IF statement called **block IF statements.** As you'll see, block IF statements can be used to simplify the coding process and at the same time improve the readability of your programs.

There are two types of block IF statements: the IF–THEN and the IF–THEN–ELSE statements. The form of an IF–THEN statement is shown in Figure 6.1 along with an equivalent flowchart segment. If the condition (logical expression) is true, the program segment (block) between the IF–THEN and END IF statements is executed. If the condition is false, the block is not executed. In either case, control then passes to the line following the END IF statement.

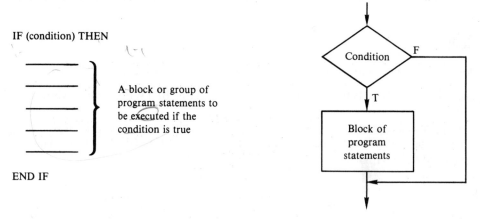

FIGURE 6.1. An IF–THEN statement.

EXAMPLE 13. A program segment to calculate the discount (DISC), tax (TAX), and amount due (CHARGE) for any amount (AMOUNT) over $200.00.

```
IF (AMOUNT.GT.200.) THEN
    DISC=0.20*AMOUNT
    PRICE=AMOUNT-DISC
    TAX=0.05*PRICE
    CHARGE=PRICE+TAX
    WRITE(6,10)AMOUNT,DISC,TAX,CHARGE
END IF
```

When the IF statement is executed, the condition AMOUNT.GT.200. is tested using the current value of AMOUNT. The five-line block that performs the necessary calculations and prints the results is executed only if this condition is true.

Remark: This program segment can be written without a block IF statement as follows:

```
IF (AMOUNT.LE.200.) GO TO 1
   DISC=0.20*AMOUNT
   PRICE=AMOUNT-DISC
   TAX=0.05*PRICE
   CHARGE=PRICE+TAX
   WRITE(6,10)AMOUNT,DISC,TAX,CHARGE
1 (next statement to be executed)
```

However, doing this introduces two sources of possible confusion. First, a GO TO statement and a statement label are introduced into the program. This can be confusing if the program already contains many GO TO statements and statement labels. Second, the condition AMOUNT.LE.200. does not display the condition under which the indicated calculations are to be carried out; rather, it displays the condition for *not* carrying out these calculations. The block IF statement is a positive statement; it says, "If the AMOUNT is greater than 200, then perform the following calculations."

The form of an IF–THEN–ELSE statement is shown in Figure 6.2 along with an equivalent flowchart segment. If the condition (logical expression) is true, the **THEN block** (program segment following the keyword THEN) is executed. If the condition is false, the **ELSE block** (program segment following the ELSE statement) is executed. In either case, control then passes to the line following the END IF statement.

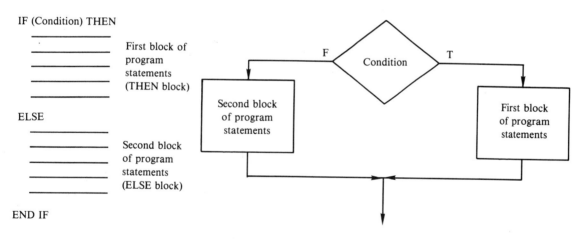

FIGURE 6.2. The IF–THEN–ELSE statement.

EXAMPLE 14. Here is a program segment to calculate a commission (COMM) of 4% on the first $2,000 in sales (SALES) and 6% on everything in excess of $2,000:

```
IF (SALES.LE.2000.) THEN
   COMM=.04*SALES
ELSE
   COMM=.04*2000.+.06*(SALES-2000.)
END IF
```

Three other ways to accomplish this same task were shown in Example 12 of Section 6.4. The IF–THEN–ELSE statement used here is especially easy to understand. Indeed, reading this program segment as if it were an English sentence explains precisely what it does.

The following slight modification of Example 13 illustrates that the programming lines comprising one block in a block IF statement may include another block IF statement. This is called *nesting*.

EXAMPLE 15.

```
IF (AMOUNT.GT.200.) THEN
    DISC=0.20*AMOUNT
    PRICE=AMOUNT-DISC
    IF (ISTAT.EQ.9) THEN
        TAX=0.0
    ELSE
        TAX=0.05*PRICE
    END IF
    CHARGE=PRICE+TAX
    WRITE(6,10)AMOUNT,DISC,TAX,CHARGE
END IF
```

Here, an IF–THEN–ELSE statement is included in the block of an IF–THEN statement. This program segment calculates the discount (DISC), tax (TAX), and amount due (CHARGE), just as in Example 13, except that no tax is charged if the tax status indicator ISTAT is 9.

Remark: Note that the IF and END IF statements used to form the IF–THEN statement appear at one level of indentation while the IF, ELSE, and END IF statements used to form the inner block IF statement appear at another level of indentation. Although you are not required to indent your program statements in this manner, the readability of your programs will be greatly improved if you do. Corresponding IF, ELSE, and END IF statements will appear at their own level of indentation with no intervening IF, ELSE, or END IF statements appearing at this same level of indentation. A person reading such a program can easily detect how the block IF statements were formed.

Rules for Block IF Statements

1. A block IF statement may be formed with an IF statement and an END IF statement or with an IF, ELSE, and END IF statement. The first form is called an IF–THEN statement and contains a single block; the second form is called an IF–THEN–ELSE statement and contains two blocks, a THEN block and an ELSE block.
2. Each block IF statement must have its own END IF statement. The number of block IF statements in a program must equal the number of END IF statements.
3. If any part of a first block IF statement is contained in a block of a second block IF statement, then the *entire* first block IF statement must be contained in this block. This is called nesting and was illustrated in Example 15.
4. The IF, ELSE, and END IF statements are executable statements. They may be labeled. For instance, the following is allowed:

```
  IF(A.EQ.B) THEN
      IF(M.LE.0) GO TO 1
      SUM=SUM+M
      M=M+1
1 END IF
```

However, it is a good programming practice to avoid labels when possible. Programs with many labels can be difficult to follow. This program segment can be written without the label as follows:

```
IF(A.EQ.B) THEN
   IF(M.GT.0) THEN
      SUM=SUM+M
      M=M+1
   END IF
END IF
```

Or, better still,

```
IF((A.EQ.B).AND.(M.GT.0)) THEN
   SUM=SUM+M
   M=M+1
END IF
```

6.7 The Arithmetic IF Statement

In this section we describe the **arithmetic** IF statement, a form of the IF statement that is rapidly going out of use, but that you may encounter should you be required to modify a previously written FORTRAN program. It is for this reason alone that we mention it at all.

The form of the arithmetic IF statement is

$$IF(e)s_1,s_2,s_3$$

where e denotes an arithmetic expression and s_1, s_2, and s_3 denote unsigned integers that are used as statement labels elsewhere in the program. The integers s_1, s_2, and s_3 need not be different. The expression e is evaluated and then control passes to the statement with label s_1, s_2, or s_3, depending on whether the value of e is less than 0, equal to 0, or greater than 0, respectively. The expression e must be enclosed in parentheses as shown.

EXAMPLE 16. In each part of this example we are given values for certain variables and an arithmetic IF statement. We are to tell what happens when the IF statement is executed.

a. With A = 1.5, B = 2.5, and C = 3.5, consider

   IF(A*B−C)17,18,19

   A * B − C has the value 0.25. Since this is greater than 0, transfer is made to the statement labeled 19.

b. With M = 7 and N = 2, consider

   IF(M/N−3)18,17,18

   M/N − 3 has the value 0 (recall that in integer arithmetic, 7/2 = 3). Control passes to the statement labeled 17. Note that in either of the cases M/N − 3 < 0 and M/N − 3 > 0, control will pass to the same statement, labeled 18.

c. With X = 1.5 and Y = 0.8, consider

   IF(X**2−(X+Y))101,100,100

   X**2 − (X + Y) = 2.25 − 2.3 = − .05. This value is less than 0 so control passes to the statement labeled 101.

Programs written with many statement labels and many GO TO statements have a cluttered appearance (they have been called spaghetti programs) and can be very difficult to understand. For this reason, you should avoid the arithmetic IF statement entirely. Not only does it force you to use statement labels, but it introduces three GO TO statements into a program (the three labels required in an arithmetic IF statement are, in fact, GO TO's).

6.8 Problems

1. What is printed by the following programs?

a.
```
    I=1
    J=50
  1 IF(I.GT.J) THEN
        WRITE(6,10)I
        STOP
    END IF
    I=I*(I+1)
    GO TO 1
 10 FORMAT(1X,I3)
    END
```

b.
```
    AMT=100.00
  1 TAX=.09*AMT
    IF(AMT.GT.120.) THEN
        WRITE(6,11)AMT
        STOP
    END IF
    AMT=AMT+TAX
    GO TO 1
 11 FORMAT(1X,F7.2)
    END
```

c.
```
  1 READ(5,12)X
    IF(X.LE.0.) STOP
    IF(X.GT.100.) THEN
        Y=X+.2*X
    ELSE
        Y=X+.1*X
    END IF
    WRITE(6,13)X,Y
    GO TO 1
 12 FORMAT(F7.0)
 13 FORMAT(1X,F7.2,2X,F7.2)
    END
```

Input Data:

```
         1
1234567890
   90.00
  120.00
  200.00
    0.
```

d.
```
    N=100
  1 IF(N.LT.50) THEN
        IF(N.GT.25) THEN
            N=N-10
            WRITE(6,14)N
        END IF
    ELSE
        N=N-30
    END IF
    N=N-1
    IF(N.GT.15) GO TO 1
    WRITE(6,14)N
    STOP
 14 FORMAT(1X,I3)
    END
```

2. Rewrite the following program segments by using block IF statements, but use no statement labels.

a.
```
    VAL=0.
    IF(SUM-100.)1,2,2
  1 VAL=.10*SUM
    N=N+1
  2 WRITE(6,10)N,VAL
```

b.
```
    IF(A+B)1,1,2
  1 N=N+1
    GO TO 3
  2 N=N-1
  3 WRITE(6,10)N
```

c.
```
    IF(X*Y)4,4,1
  1 IF(X) 2,3,3
  2 WRITE(6,10)
    GO TO 4
  3 WRITE(6,11)
  4 WRITE(6,12)X,Y
```

d.
```
    IF(M) 1,1,2
  1 WRITE(6,10)
    GO TO 5
  2 IF((M/2)*2-M)4,3,4
  3 WRITE(6,11)
    GO TO 5
  4 WRITE(6,12)
  5 WRITE(6,13)M
```

Construct a flowchart for each algorithm shown in Problems 3–8. In each case, write a corresponding program; use block IF statements as suggested by your flowcharts. Avoid GO TO statements and statement labels where possible.)

3. a. Input values for N, R, and T.
   b. If N ≤ 40, let S = N × R. Otherwise, let S = 40R + (N − 40)(1.5)R.
   c. Reduce S by the amount S × T.
   d. Print S and stop.

4. a. Input a value for N.
   b. If N > 0, print the integers from 1 up to N. Otherwise, print the integers from 0 down to N.
   c. Print the message GOODBYE and stop.

5. a. Input values for A and B.
   b. If A and B have the same sign (the condition for this is A × B>0), print POSITIVE or NEGATIVE according to whether A and B are positive or negative.
   c. Print "FINI" and stop.

6. a. Input an integer N.
   b. If N = 0, stop.
   c. Print EVEN if N is even; otherwise print ODD.
   d. Go to step (a).

7. a. Input values for X, Y, and Z.
   b. If X < Y, print Y − X and go to step (d).
   c. Print Z − X only if X < Z.
   d. Print X, Y, and Z.
   e. Stop.

8. a. Input a value for N.
   b. If N is less than or equal to 0, go to step (a).
   c. If N > 100, print VALUE IS TOO LARGE and go to step (g).
   d. If N > 50, calculate SUM = 50 + 51 + 52 + · · · + N and go to step (f).
   e. Calculate SUM = 1 + 2 + 3 + · · · + N.
   f. Print the value of SUM.
   g. Print the message GOODBYE and stop.

Write a program to perform each task specified in Problems 9–14.

9. If the wholesale cost of an item is under $100, the markup is 20%. Otherwise, the markup is 30%. Determine the retail price for all items whose wholesale costs are input. Use an EOD-tag to effect an orderly exit from the program.

10. Each salesperson earns a base weekly salary of $185.00. In addition, if a salesperson's total weekly sales exceed $1,000.00, a commission of 5.3% is earned on the first $5,000.00 in sales and 2.1% is earned on any amount in excess of $5,000.00. Determine the weekly pay, before deductions, for any salesperson whose total weekly sales amount is input. Use an EOD-tag to effect an orderly exit from the program.

11. Many real numbers are to be input. The number 0 is used as the EOD-tag. Determine the sum of all positive numbers and the sum of all negative numbers. Both sums are to be printed.

12. A list of numbers is to be input as in Problem 11. Determine and print the average of all positive numbers and the average of all negative numbers.

13. Several pairs (X,Y) of numbers are to be input. Any pair with X = Y serves as the EOD-tag. Determine and print counts of how many pairs satisfy X < Y and how many pairs satisfy X > Y.

14. A list of integers is to be input. Any integer less than 1 serves as the EOD-tag. Print the sum and a count of the even input values and also a sum and count of the odd ones.

6.9 Top-Down Programming

Programming is essentially a three-step process:

1. Carefully read the problem statement so that it is completely understood. If necessary, rewrite the problem statement to clarify what is being asked.

2. Discover and describe a procedure (algorithm) that, when followed, will lead to a solution to the problem.
3. Using the procedure described in step (2), write and debug the program.

For lengthy problem statements or for tasks that are intrinsically difficult, step (2) can be troublesome. When you are confronted with such a situation, there are several things you can do. The following have been suggested, both in the text and in the worked-out examples:

1. Identify all input and output values before attempting to find an algorithm.
2. Use descriptive variable names so that the values of interest can be referred to without having to use potentially confusing descriptions in words.
3. Identify what must be done before attempting to show how to do it. This means that the task should be broken down into simpler, more manageable subtasks.
4. Once you have identified what must be done, use diagrams (flowcharts) to help you determine how to carry out the task.

"We understand complex things by systematically breaking them down into successively simpler parts and understanding how these parts fit together. . . ."*

As natural as the idea of problem segmentation may appear, choosing subtasks that actually simplify matters may not be easy. Unfortunately, a formula for identifying appropriate subtasks is not known. What is known is a method that will help in your attempts to find such subtasks. This method was illustrated in Example 6 of Section 6.1. The task to be performed in that example was as follows:

Problem Statement:
A list of positive integers, terminated by the EOD-tag 9999, is to be input. For each integer, other than 9999, all factors and the sum of these factors are to be printed.

The approach taken was to begin with an algorithm containing as little detail as possible. The objective was to describe a procedure that would be easy to understand. The algorithm chosen was as follows:

a. Read an integer.
b. If this integer is 9999, stop.
c. Find and print all factors of the integer and also the sum of these factors.
d. Go to step (a).

That this algorithm describes a process for carrying out the stated task should be evident—in spite of the detail not present. For example, the algorithm contains no variable names (they were chosen later), and it does not tell "how" to find the factors or "how" to determine their sum. Details of any kind should be introduced only as needed; each time a detail is introduced, the complexity of the procedure increases. The algorithm was kept simple by considering "what" must be done, and not "how" it should be done.

The next step was to introduce variable names and show "how" the steps in the algorithm could be carried out. The variable names chosen were as follows:

NUM = any one of the input values.
FACT = a possible factor of NUM.
SUM = the sum of the factors of NUM.

The single step (c) (the only troublesome step) was then broken down into four simpler steps (c1) through (c4) to obtain the following more detailed algorithm:

a. Read NUM.
b. If NUM = 9999, stop.
c1. Initialize: SUM = 0 and FACT = 1.
c2. If FACT is a factor of NUM, print FACT and add it to SUM.
c3. Add 1 to FACT and repeat step (c2) until FACT > NUM.
c4. Print SUM.
d. Go to step (a).

*"Structured Programming with **go to** Statements," by Donald E. Knuth, *Computing Surveys*, Vol. 6, No. 4, December 1974.

This algorithm was then translated into a FORTRAN program. Knowing that the original four-step algorithm was correct, and also that the refinement of step (c) correctly carries out this task, we can be sure that this final seven-step algorithm is also correct.

The approach to problem solving illustrated in this example is called the **method of step-wise refinement** or **top-down programming.** You start at the top (the problem statement), break this task down into simpler tasks, then break these tasks into even simpler ones, and continue this process, all the while knowing how the tasks at each level combine, until the tasks at the lowest level contain whatever detail is desired.

The following two examples are designed to give you a better understanding of the method of top-down programming and how it is used. The first concerns the preparation of a sales report and illustrates the value of the top-down approach in producing printed documents. The second concerns a property of whole numbers and illustrates how the method can help in problems whose principal concern is *how* to do something and not *what* to do.

EXAMPLE 17. A clothing firm has retail stores in Miami, Tampa, and Orlando. Management desires a weekly sales report showing the week's sales for each store and the total sales for the week. In addition, a short report showing the amount and the day of the week of the greatest combined daily sales is to be prepared. Our task is to write a program to produce these two reports.

Problem Analysis:
To carry out this task, the computer must be supplied with three daily sales figures for each day of the week. Let's agree to use a separate input record for each day. Each of the three sales figures will occupy ten positions, with the Miami sales first, the Tampa sales second, and the Orlando sales last. Thus, the input record

```
        1         2         3
1234567890123456789012345678 90
   12615.57    9410.40  16750.05
```

specifies a single day's sales as follows:

Miami: $12,615.57
Tampa: $ 9,410.40
Orlando: $16,750.05

As specified in the problem statement, the output document must display

1. the week's sales for each store,
2. the total sales for the week, and
3. the amount and the day of the greatest combined daily sales.

Let's agree to print this information in the following form:

```
WEEKLY SALES REPORT
MIAMI      $-----.--
TAMPA      $-----.--
ORLANDO    $-----.--
TOTAL      $-----.--

GREATEST COMBINED DAILY SALES
(day of week)      $-----.--
```

Note that all of the sales data must be read before any of these output values can be determined. This suggests the following first attempt at an algorithm.

Algorithm:
a. Read the sales data for one week to determine all of the output values.
b. Print the weekly sales report.
c. Print a short report showing the amount and day of the greatest combined daily sales.

Let's consider step (a) more carefully. To obtain the weekly sales for the Miami store we must add the first entries in the five input records. The weekly sales for Tampa and Orlando are determined similarly. To obtain the greatest combined daily sales amount we must add the three amounts in each input record (they represent one day's sales for each of the stores) to obtain the combined sales for that day. As we pass from record to record we will "remember" only the largest of these five values. We must also determine the day of the week on which the greatest sales occurred. One way to do this is to assign the successive values 1, 2, 3, 4, and 5 (days of week) to a variable as we process the five input records. We can then keep track of the day corresponding to the greatest daily sales by "remembering" that number (1 through 5) that corresponds to the input record yielding this greatest amount. (Of course, the five input records must be ordered by day.)

To help us write down a concise description of the process just described for breaking down step (a) into simpler steps, let's choose variable names as follows:

MIA   = one day's sales—Miami
TAM   = one day's sales—Tampa
ORL   = one day's sales—Orlando
MIAWK = one week's sales—Miami
TAMWK = one week's sales—Tampa
ORLWK = one week's sales—Orlando
DAYTOT = one day's sales—total
WKTOT = one week's sales—total
BIG   = greatest combined daily sales
DAY   = day of the week (1,2,3,4, or 5) on which BIG occurred
N   = counts the input records

Algorithm (Refined):
a1. Initialize: N = 1, MIAWK = TAMWK = ORLWK = BIG = 0.
a2. Read values for MIA, TAM, and ORL.
a3. Add MIA, TAM, ORL to MIAWK, TAMWK, ORLWK, respectively.
a4. Calculate DAYTOT = MIA + TAM + ORL.
a5. If DAYTOT > BIG, assign DAYTOT to BIG and N to DAY.
a6. Add 1 to N and return to step (a2), if N ≤ 5.
a7. Calculate WKTOT = MIAWK + TAMWK + ORLWK.
b.   Print the weekly sales report.
c.   Print a short report showing the amount and day of the greatest combined daily sales.

Writing a program segment for step (b) is easy. After printing the report title we simply print the weekly sales figures MIAWK, TAMWK, and ORLWK, and their sum TOTWK, each labeled as previously agreed upon.

Producing the short report required in step (c) also is not difficult. The amount of the greatest combined daily sales (BIG) and the number (DAY) specifying the day of the week on which this sales amount occurred are known from step (a). Using five logical IF statements, we can compare the number DAY with the numbers 1, 2, 3, 4, and 5 to determine whether to print MONDAY, TUESDAY, . . . , or FRIDAY.

We are now ready to code the program. Clearly, N and DAY should be integer variables and since all others denote dollar amounts they should be declared as reals. Since this problem analysis contains a complete list of variable names with their meanings, we have not included their descriptions in the program. Note that the comment lines used correspond to the three steps in the first algorithm. The steps in the second algorithm assisted us in coding the program but are too detailed for comment lines.

The program is shown in Figure 6.3. Typical input data and the corresponding printout produced by the program are shown in Figure 6.4.

Remark 1: Although the program is rather long, it was easy to code. We simply coded the steps in the refined algorithm, referring back to the agreed upon form of the output for guidance in writing the WRITE and FORMAT statements.

Remark 2: It is possible to write a shorter program for this task. To do so, you will need string variables—that is, variables that store character strings instead of numbers. This topic is taken up in Chapter 12.

```
C*********WEEKLY SALES REPORT PROGRAM*********
       INTEGER DAY,N
       REAL BIG,DAYTOT,MIA,MIAWK,ORL,ORLWK,TAM,TAMWK,WKTOT
C READ SALES DATA FOR ONE WEEK TO DETERMINE THE WEEKLY
C SALES AMOUNTS MIAWK,TAMWK,ORLWK,TOTWK AND THE AMOUNT
C AND DAY (1,2,3,4,5) OF GREATEST COMBINED SALES
       MIAWK=0.
       TAMWK=0.
       ORLWK=0.
       BIG=0.
       N=1
     1 READ(5,10)MIA,TAM,ORL
          MIAWK=MIAWK+MIA
          TAMWK=TAMWK+TAM
          ORLWK=ORLWK+ORL
          DAYTOT=MIA+TAM+ORL
          IF(DAYTOT.GT.BIG) THEN
             BIG=DAYTOT
             DAY=N
          END IF
          N=N+1
       IF(N.LE.5) GO TO 1
       WKTOT=MIAWK+TAMWK+ORLWK
C PRINT THE WEEKLY SALES REPORT
       WRITE(6,11)
       WRITE(6,12)MIAWK
       WRITE(6,13)TAMWK
       WRITE(6,14)ORLWK
       WRITE(6,15)TOTWK
C PRINT AMOUNT AND DAY OF WEEK OF GREATEST COMBINED SALES
       WRITE(6,16)
       WRITE(6,17)
       IF(DAY.EQ.1) WRITE(6,18)BIG
       IF(DAY.EQ.2) WRITE(6,19)BIG
       IF(DAY.EQ.3) WRITE(6,20)BIG
       IF(DAY.EQ.4) WRITE(6,21)BIG
       IF(DAY.EQ.5) WRITE(6,22)BIG
       STOP
    10 FORMAT(F10.2,F10.2,F10.2)
    11 FORMAT(1X,'WEEKLY SALES REPORT')
    12 FORMAT(1X,'MIAMI   $',F9.2)
    13 FORMAT(1X,'TAMPA   $',F9.2)
    14 FORMAT(1X,'ORLANDO $',F9.2)
    15 FORMAT(1X,'TOTAL   $',F9.2)
    16 FORMAT(1X)
    17 FORMAT(1X,'GREATEST COMBINED DAILY SALES')
    18 FORMAT(1X,'MONDAY    $',F9.2)
    19 FORMAT(1X,'TUESDAY   $',F9.2)
    20 FORMAT(1X,'WEDNESDAY   $',F9.2)
    21 FORMAT(1X,'THURSDAY   $',F9.2)
    22 FORMAT(1X,'FRIDAY   $',F9.2)
       END
```

FIGURE 6.3. Program for Example 17.

Input Data:

```
         1          2          3
1234567890123456789012345678 90
  12615.57    9410.40   16750.05
   8505.00    8080.60   13520.37
  11520.40   13248.00   15200.50
  10450.25   18250.52   14526.25
  13524.04   12526.28   16007.42
```

Output:

```
WEEKLY SALES REPORT
MIAMI   $ 56615.26
TAMPA   $ 61515.80
ORLANDO $ 76004.59
TOTAL   $194135.65

GREATEST COMBINED DAILY SALES
THURSDAY   $ 43227.02
```

FIGURE 6.4. Typical input data and run for the program in Figure 6.3.

EXAMPLE 18. A perfect number N is an integer greater than 1 that is equal to the sum of its divisors, including 1 but not N. The task is to find all perfect numbers from 2 to 1,000.

Problem Analysis:
A first algorithm, with as little detail as possible, can be written as follows.

a. Let N = 2.
b. If N is perfect, print N.
c. Let N = N + 1, and go to step (b) if N ≤ 1,000.

Only step (b) is troublesome. To determine if N is perfect, we can sum its divisors and compare this sum with N. This subdivision of step (b) into two simpler tasks gives rise to the following refined algorithm.

a. Let N = 2.
b1. Sum the divisors of N, including 1 but not N.
b2. If this sum is N, print N.
c. Let N = N + 1, and go to step (b1) if N ≤ 1,000.

Although this four-step algorithm is correct, it could be more efficient. In particular, if during the process of carrying out step (b1) we obtain a sum that exceeds N, we know that N is not perfect so we can proceed immediately to step (c). We include this detail by using the following refinement of the original three-step algorithm:

a. Let N = 2.
b1. Sum the divisors of N, including 1 but not N. However, if during this process of summing, a sum exceeding N is obtained, go to step (c).
b2. If the sum obtained in step (b1) is N, print N.
c. Let N = N + 1, and go to step (b1) if N ≤ 1,000.

Note that the modified steps (b1) and (b2) also give a correct refinement of step (b). Although they are slightly more complicated than before, they will lead to a more efficient algorithm.

In this four-step algorithm, only step (b1) may be troublesome. To help us describe step (b1) in greater detail, let's introduce the variable name DIV to denote a possible divisor of N, and SUM to denote the sum of the divisors. With these variable names we can now write down the following more refined algorithm in which step (b1) is broken down into the four steps (b1.1), (b1.2), (b1.3), and (b1.4):

a.   Let N = 2.
b1.1. Let SUM = 1 and DIV = 2.
b1.2. If N is divisible by DIV, add DIV to SUM.
b1.3. If SUM > N, go to step (c).
b1.4. Let DIV = DIV + 1, and go to step (b1.2) until DIV > N/2.
b2.   If SUM = N, print N.
c.   Let N = N + 1, and go to step (b1.1) if N ≤ 1,000.

This algorithm has a harmless bug, but a bug nevertheless. An incorrect value of SUM will be obtained for N = 2. This bug did not exist in the first two algorithms—check and see. It was introduced when we broke down step (b1) into four simpler steps that were equivalent to step (b1) only for N ≥ 3. When using the method of step-wise refinement it is absolutely essential that you carefully check to see that each step that is broken down into simpler steps is broken down correctly. In this case, correcting our error is easy. We need only change step (b1.1) to

b1.1. Let SUM = 0 and DIV = 1.

The final six-step algorithm can easily be coded to give a correct program.

The Program:

```
C DETERMINE PERFECT NUMBERS FROM 2 TO 1000
      INTEGER SUM,DIV
      N=2
    1 SUM=0
      DIV=1
    2 IF((N/DIV)*DIV.EQ.N) SUM+SUM+DIV
      IF(SUM.LE.N) THEN
         DIV=DIV+1
         IF(DIV.LE.N/2) GO TO 2
         IF(SUM.EQ.N) WRITE(6,10)N
      END IF
      N=N+1
      IF(N.LE.1000) GO TO 1
      STOP
   10 FORMAT(I4)
      END
```

Output:

```
    6
   28
  496
```

Let's summarize some of the more relevant aspects of the method of top-down programming.

1. Each procedure (algorithm) is obtained from the preceding one by subdividing one or more of the individual tasks into simpler ones. At each step, or *level of refinement,* more details emerge to bring you closer to a solution—that is, to the desired program.
2. At the upper levels of refinement, dependence on the particular computer being used is avoided; procedures are expressed without regard to the computer language being employed.
3. At the lower levels of refinement, dependence on the computer language being used is unavoidable; the individual tasks in the final refinement correspond to actual program segments, and sometimes to single program statements.
4. At each level, the procedure obtained must be *debugged.* If the procedure at one level is

correct, it should be a simple matter to debug the procedure at the next lower level. You need only check to ensure that each task broken down into simpler tasks is broken down correctly. It is this aspect of the top-down approach that increases the likelihood that the final program will be correct.

We don't mean to imply that the method of top-down programming will always lead directly to a "good" program. It may be that a level of refinement is reached that, for some reason, is undesirable. When this happens, you may either start over at the top or back up one or more levels and continue from that point with a different refinement. Difficult problems may require backing up in this manner several times before a satisfactory procedure emerges.

The step-by-step process of segmenting complex tasks into simpler ones is not new; good programmers have always used such an approach. However, giving a name to the process has had two significant consequences. It has introduced the method of step-wise refinement to many people who previously programmed in a more or less haphazard fashion. As a result, better programs—that is, programs that are easier to read and more likely to be correct—are being written. The second consequence is that the method has been carefully studied and formulated into an orderly process, as illustrated in the worked-out examples. Since the way in which tasks are broken down into subtasks depends on who is carrying out this process, the method of top-down programming is not an algorithm that will always lead to the same program. Rather, it is a *process* that brings order to an otherwise disorderly human activity—namely, programming. We might say that some "structure" has been introduced into the process of designing programs.

As noted, one of the benefits of using a top-down approach is that the resulting programs are more likely to be correct. But *to know* that a program is correct is another matter. Any serious consideration of this topic must necessarily concern the structure of the program itself, not just the structure of the process that leads to the program. It is in this context that the expression **structured programming** has emerged. A complete discussion of what constitutes a structured program, and how this relates to the task of verifying its correctness, does not belong in an introductory text such as this. However, we can give you the following guidelines that will help you design good programs.

Guidelines for Writing Good (Structured) Programs

1. Use the method of top-down programming. If you follow the rules of top-down programming described in this section, you should obtain correct algorithms that are easily translated into correct and easy-to-read programs.
2. Code specific subtasks, using program segments with exactly one entry point and exactly one exit point. This means that the program segment should contain only one statement that initiates it and only one that gets you out. This is one of the basic rules of structured programming. Programs written in this way are said to be *block structured*.
3. Avoid statement labels and GO TO statements. In particular, use block IF statements to execute selectively one or more blocks of code. Programs written in this way are easier to understand than programs that use logical IF statements containing GO TO's to control the execution of these blocks of code.

Although we have barely introduced the topic of structured programming, we can state that the goal of structured programming is to produce programs that are easy to understand, easy to modify, and absolutely correct the first time they are written.

We conclude this chapter by quoting Edsger W. Dijkstra, who gave structured programming its name* and who remains a central figure in the effort to discover the true nature of programs and the programming process.

"We understand walls in terms of bricks, bricks in terms of crystals, crystals in terms of molecules, etc. . . .

"The only effective way to raise the confidence level of a program significantly is to give a convincing proof of its correctness. But one should not first make the program and then prove

___
*Structured Programming, Software Engineering Techniques, by E.W. Dijkstra (J.N. Buxton and B. Randell, Eds.), NATO Scientific Affairs Division, Brussels, Belgium, 1970, pp. 84–88.

its correctness, because then the requirement of providing the proof would only increase the poor programmer's burden. On the contrary: the programmer should let the correctness proof and program grow hand in hand."*

6.10 Problems

It is intentional that no problems are included here. The method of top-down programming is not an isolated topic. It is an approach to problem solving that should be used in all programming tasks. The experience you gain in using the top-down approach with simple problems will prepare you for the more challenging problems ahead.

6.11 Review True-or-False Quiz

1. The GO TO statement is called a conditional transfer statement because it initiates a transfer of control only if it is executed.   T F
2. A logical IF statement can be used to instruct the computer to execute a particular statement only if a certain condition, specified by the programmer, is satisfied.   T F
3. The condition in a logical IF statement must be a logical expression—that is, an expression that is either true or false.   T F
4. The statement

   IF((N.LT.52).OR.(N.GE.14)) K = K + 1

   is an admissible FORTRAN statement and will cause K to be increased by 1 if N satisfies the double inequality $14 \leq N < 52$.   T F
5. A flowchart is an excellent way to display the logic of a program, but flowcharting is of little value while writing the program.   T F
6. The condition shown in a decision diamond of a flowchart is the basis for the logical expression in an IF statement.   T F
7. The condition in a block IF statement can be any expression allowed as the condition in a logical IF statement.   T F
8. A block IF statement may contain either one or two blocks. A block IF statement with one block is called an IF–THEN statement, and one with two blocks is called an IF–THEN–ELSE statement.   T F
9. If the condition appearing in an IF–THEN statement is true, control passes to the first executable statement following the END IF statement.   T F
10. If the condition in an IF–THEN–ELSE statement is true, the THEN block is executed; otherwise, the ELSE block is executed.   T F
11. When nesting block IF statements, a single END IF statement can be used as the last statement for two block IF statements.   T F
12. When you are using the top-down approach, a good first step is to read the problem statement carefully to determine variable names to be used.   T F
13. The method of top-down programming is an advanced and difficult programming technique.   T F
14. In the top-down approach, debugging is simply the process of checking to see that individual tasks are correctly broken down into simpler tasks.   T F
15. Top-down programming is of little value in determining "how" to carry out a task. It is applicable only when the objective is to segment a task into subtasks.   T F
16. When using the top-down approach, the particular programming language being used is completely ignored until the coding stage.   T F
17. The second of the following two algorithms is a refinement of the first.   T F

---

*"The Humble Programmer" (1972 ACM Turing Award Lecture), by E.W. Dijkstra, *Communications of the ACM*, Vol. 15, No. 10, October 1972, pp. 859–866.

Algorithm 1
a. Read a list of numbers and print their sum.
b. Determine the average of all entries in the list and print this average.

Algorithm 2
a. Read a list of numbers.
b. Determine their sum and average.
c. Print both the sum and average.

Loops Made Easier—
The DO Statement

Loops occur in all but the most elementary programs. However, it is not always easy to construct loops by using only IF and GO TO statements, and programs written in this matter are often difficult to understand. Because of this, FORTRAN contains the DO statement which allows you to construct loops without using IF or GO TO statements. In this chapter we describe the **DO statement** and show how it can be used to simplify the process of writing loops and at the same time improve the readability of FORTRAN programs.

7.1 DO-Loops

Each of the following program segments calculates and prints the price of one, two, three, four, five, and six items selling at seven for $1.00.

Program Segment 1

```
      UNIT=1.00/7.
      I=1
100 IF(I.GT.6) GO TO 101
          PRICE=UNIT*FLOAT(I)
          WRITE(6,10)I,PRICE
          I=I+1
      GO TO 100
101 (next program statement)
```

Program Segment 2

```
      UNIT=1.00/7.
      I=0
100 I=I+1
          PRICE=UNIT*FLOAT(I)
          WRITE(6,10)I,PRICE
      IF(I.LT.6) GO TO 100
101 (next program statement)
```

The same thing can be accomplished as follows:

Program Segment 3

```
      UNIT=1.00/7.
      DO 100 I=1,6
         PRICE=UNIT*FLOAT(I)
100      WRITE(6,10)I,PRICE
101 (next program statement)
```

The statement

DO 100 I = 1,6

instructs the computer to execute all statements that follow the DO statement, up to and including the statement labeled 100, six times, once for each integer I from 1 to 6. These statements are called the **range** of the loop. Just how the computer will accomplish this depends on the particular implementation of FORTRAN on your system. Our assumption in this text is that Program Segment 3 is equivalent to Program Segment 1. This assumption conforms to the FORTRAN standard. Thus, the effect of the DO statement can be described as follows:

a. When the DO statement is executed, I is assigned the initial value 1.

b. I is compared with the terminal value 6.

   If $I > 6$, control passes to the statement following the statement labeled 100. *The loop has been satisfied.*

   If $I \leq 6$, control passes to the statement following the DO statement.

c. The range (the two statements PRICE = UNIT*FLOAT(I) and WRITE(6,10)I,PRICE) is executed. This calculates and prints the value of I and the price of I items.

d. I is increased by 1 and the comparison in step (b) is repeated.

Loops constructed by using DO statements are called DO-**loops.** Following are three examples illustrating other ways in which DO statements are used to construct loops. To clarify the meaning of the DO-loop, we've written each program in two ways, without and with the DO statement.

EXAMPLE 1. Here is a DO-loop to add the integers 2, 5, 8, 11, 14, 17, and 20:

```
      INTEGER SUM                         INTEGER SUM
      SUM=0                               SUM=0
      J=2                                 DO 1 J=2,20,3
  1 IF(J.GT.20) GO TO 2                 1    SUM=SUM+J
         SUM=SUM+J                          WRITE(6,10)SUM
         J=J+3                          10 FORMAT(1X,'SUM IS',I4)
      GO TO 1                              STOP
  2 WRITE(6,10)SUM                         END
 10 FORMAT(1X,'SUM IS',I4)
      STOP
      END
```

Output (for both programs):

```
SUM IS  77
```

The first program describes the action of the second as follows.

a. The DO statement assigns the initial value 2 to J. J is called the **DO-variable.**

b. J is compared with the terminal value 20.

   If J>20, control passes to the WRITE statement, the first executable statement following the statement labeled 1. The loop has been satisfied.

   If J≤20, control passes to the statement following the DO statement.

c. The range (the single statement SUM = SUM + J) is executed, adding J to SUM.

d. The DO-variable J is increased by the value 3 appearing in the DO statement and the comparison in step (b) is repeated.

The integers 2, 20, and 3 appearing in the DO statement are called the *initial, terminal,* and *increment values* or *parameters,* respectively. Together they are called *DO-parameters.*

Remark: The increment value 3 in the statement DO 1 J = 2,20,3 instructs the computer to increase the DO-variable J by 3 each time the range is executed. If this increment value is omitted, the increment value 1 is assumed. Thus, had we written DO 1 J = 2,20 we would have obtained the sum $2 + 3 + 4 + \cdots + 20$. The two statements DO 1 J = 2,20 and DO 1 J = 2,20,1 are equivalent.

EXAMPLE 2. Here are two programs to input integer values I and J and print all integers from I up to J, inclusive:

```
      READ(5,10)I,J
      WRITE(6,11)I,J
      N=I
    5 IF(N.GT.J) STOP
         WRITE(6,12)N
         N=N+1
      GO TO 5
   10 FORMAT(I3,2X,I3)
   11 FORMAT(1X,'INTEGERS BETWEEN',I4,' AND',I4,' :')
   12 FORMAT(1X,I3)
      END

      READ(5,10)I,J
      WRITE(6,11)I,J
      DO 5 N=I,J
    5    WRITE(6,12)N
      STOP
   10 FORMAT(I3,2X,I3)
   11 FORMAT(1X,'INTEGERS BETWEEN',I4,' AND',I4,' :')
   12 FORMAT(1X,I3)
      END
```

Input Data:

```
          1         2         3
1234567890123456789012345678 90
173  176
```

Output:

```
INTEGERS BETWEEN 173 AND 176:
173
174
175
176
```

The first program describes the action of the second as follows:

a. The READ statement reads the values 173 and 176 for I and J, respectively, and the WRITE statement prints the first line of output.

b. The DO statement then assigns the initial value 173 (value of I) to the DO-variable N.

c. N is compared to the terminal value 176 (value of J).

   If $N > 176$ control passes to the first executable statement following the range. Here, it is the STOP statement.

   If $N \leq 176$, control passes to the statement following the DO statement.

d. The range (the single statement WRITE(6,12)N) is executed, and the value of N is printed.

e. The DO-variable N is increased by the value 1 and the comparison in step (c) is repeated.

If the input values for the program in Example 2 are reversed, with 176 being assigned to I and 173 to J, the range will not be executed and nothing will be printed. This happens because the initial value 176 is greater than the terminal value 173. However, as noted previously, the precise action caused by a DO statement may differ on your system. Many FORTRAN systems are designed so that execution of a DO statement results in at least one pass through the loop. We restate this as a warning.

> *Warning:* On some FORTRAN systems, when the DO statement initializing a DO-loop is executed, at least one pass is made through the loop.

One way to avoid the difficulty cited in this warning is to precede the DO statement with an IF statement that transfers control around the loop whenever the initial parameter is greater than the terminal parameter. To write the program of Example 2 in this way, you can replace the three program statements

```
      DO 5 N=I,J
 5      WRITE(6,12)N
      STOP
```

with the statements

```
      IF(I.GT.J) GO TO 6
        DO 5 N=I,J
 5          WRITE(6,12)N
 6 STOP
```

or, better still, with

```
      IF(I.LE.J) THEN
        DO 5 N=I,J
 5          WRITE(6,12)N
      ENDIF
      STOP
```

EXAMPLE 3. Here is a DO-loop to print a 4-row by 6-column block of *'s.

```
      K=1
 10 IF(K.GT.4) STOP
        WRITE(6,11)
        K=K+1
      GO TO 10
 11 FORMAT(1X,'******')
      END
```

```
      DO 10 K=1,4
 10     WRITE(6,11)
 11 FORMAT(1X,'******')
      STOP
      END
```

Output:

```
******
******
******
******
```

The range of the DO-loop is simply the WRITE statement. The DO statement instructs the computer to execute this statement four times, once for each integer from 1 to 4. The following flowchart displays the effect of this program:

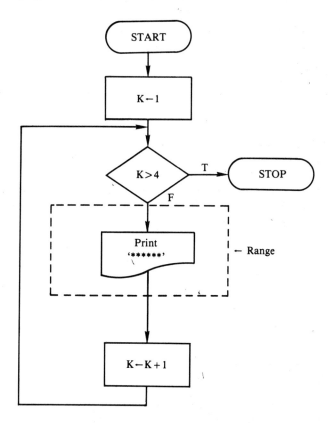

Remark: This example illustrates that the DO-variable (K) does not have to appear in the range of a DO-loop. Its purpose, in this case, is simply for loop control; it counts the number of passes made through the loop. In each of the preceding examples, the DO-variable did appear in the range.

The general form of a DO-loop is

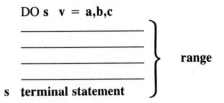

where:

s   denotes an unsigned integer used as the label of the **terminal statement.**

v   denotes an integer variable called the *DO-variable.**

a,b,c   denote integer constants or variables whose values are greater than zero. These values are the *initial, terminal,* and *incrementation parameters,* respectively. If **c** is omitted the value 1 is assumed.

range   denotes the sequence of all executable statements that follow the DO statement, up to and including the terminal statement. This sequence of statements must not contain statements that alter the value of **v.**

terminal statement   This can be any executable statement other than a control statement used to interrupt the normal sequential execution of the statements in a program. This rules out most of the control statements including the GO TO, arithmetic IF, STOP, DO, block IF, ELSE, END IF, and certain others yet to be considered. It does not rule out the logical IF statement unless the logical IF contains one of the listed control statements. For instance, the statements IF(A.LT.B)GO TO 5 and IF(A.LT.B)STOP are not allowed as terminal statements, whereas the statement IF(A.LT.B)N = N + 1 is allowed.

The action of a DO-loop is described in Figure 7.1.

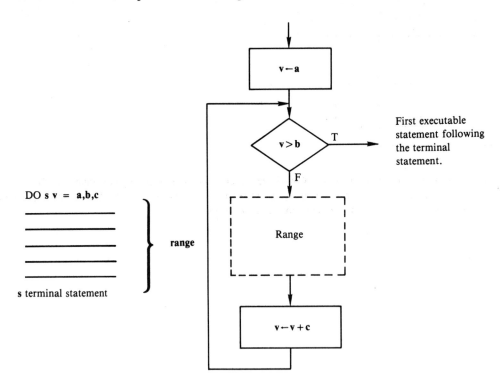

FIGURE 7.1. Action of a DO-loop.

*Some FORTRAN compilers allow real DO-variables, some allow negative DO-parameters, and some allow you to specify the DO-parameters by using numerical expressions other than variables. So that our programs will be as transportable as possible, we will take none of these liberties.

FORTRAN contains the **CONTINUE statement** that is often used in writing DO-loops. It is an executable statement that can be placed anywhere in a program without changing the effect of the program. When executed, control simply passes to the next executable statement. It can be used as the terminal statement of a DO-loop to avoid using one of the control statements that are not allowed as terminal statements. We illustrate this use of the CONTINUE statement in the following example.

EXAMPLE 4. Here is a program to find and print the first negative number appearing in any list of up to 1,000 input values:

```
    DO 1 N=1,1000
        READ(5,10)A
        IF(A.LT.0.) GO TO 2
  1 CONTINUE
  2 WRITE(6,11)A
    STOP
 10 FORMAT(F7.2)
 11 FORMAT(1X,'LAST VALUE READ IS',F8.2)
    END
```

The range of the DO-loop contains three statements, the READ, logical IF, and CONTINUE statements. The first two read a value and test if it is negative. The CONTINUE statement does nothing, but must be used because the logical IF statement

IF(A.LT.0) GO TO 2

is a transfer statement and as such cannot be used as the terminal statement of a DO-loop.

If a negative value is read for A, the IF statement transfers control out of the loop to the WRITE statement and this negative value is printed. However, if there are 1,000 nonnegative input values, the range is executed 1,000 times and control then passes to the statement following the CONTINUE statement. This happens to be the WRITE statement, so the thousandth value in the input list is printed, even though it is not negative.

Remark: Indenting the range of a DO-loop is an excellent programming practice that will enhance the readability of your programs. If a CONTINUE statement is used as the terminal statement it should not be indented, so that the DO statement initiating a loop and the CONTINUE statement terminating the loop will appear at the same level of indentation. From this point on we'll terminate all DO-loops with CONTINUE statements and indent them in this manner.

Example 4 illustrates the two ways in which an exit from a loop can occur: exit from a loop can be caused by a control statement appearing in the range; or, the loop can be satisfied. When transfer out of a loop is caused by a control statement in the range, the value of the DO-variable is retained and can be used in any subsequent statement. However, when an exit from a loop occurs because the loop is satisfied, the value of the DO-variable is not necessarily retained. On systems conforming to the FORTRAN standard, the DO-variable will have the first value not used. For instance, when the loop

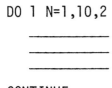

is satisfied, N will have the value 11 (the successive values of N are 1, 3, 5, 7, 9, and the first value not used is 11). On certain other systems the exit value of N will be 9 (the last value actually used). On still others, the exit value will be undefined. The safest policy, and the one we adopt, is to make no assumption about the value of a DO-variable when a DO-loop has been satisfied. We illustrate with a slight modification of the program shown in Example 4.

EXAMPLE 5. Here is a program to read up to 1,000 input values. The reading process stops as soon as a negative value is read. The last value read and also a count of how many values were read is printed.

```
      DO 1 N=1,1000
         READ(5,10)A
         IF(A.LT.0.) GO TO 2
    1 CONTINUE
      N=1000
    2 WRITE(6,11)A,N
      STOP
   10 FORMAT(F7.2)
   11 FORMAT(1X,'LAST VALUE',F7.2,5X,'NUMBER OF VALUES READ',I5)
      END
```

The initial value of N is 1 and it is increased by 1 on each pass through the loop, hence it counts how many values are read. When the first negative value is encountered, assuming there is one, the IF statement transfers control to the WRITE statement with the current value of N being retained. The WRITE statement then prints the last value read (it is negative) and the count N of how many values were read. If all 1,000 input values are nonnegative, the range is executed 1,000 times and control then passes to the assignment statement N = 1000 that follows the CONTINUE statement. This assignment statement replaces whatever value N had upon completion of the loop with 1,000, which is precisely the number of values read. The WRITE statement then prints the last value read (it is nonnegative) and the count N = 1000 of how many values were read.

The number of times the range must be executed to satisfy a DO-loop is called the **iteration count** of the DO statement. For instance, the iteration count for the statement DO 1 N = 1,1000 is 1000, and for DO 2 M = 1,20,3 it is 7 (the seven values taken on by M are 1, 4, 7, 10, 13, 16, and 19). There is a simple formula for determining the iteration count for any loop. If i, j, and k denote the initial, terminal, and increment values, the iteration count is the larger of the two numbers

$$\left(\frac{j - i + k}{k} \right) \quad \text{and} \quad 0$$

where the expression enclosed in parentheses is evaluated using integer arithmetic—that is, the fractional part of the value of $(j - i + k)/k$ is dropped to give an integer.

DO *Statement*	i,j,k	$(j-i+k)/k$	*Iteration count*
DO 1 N=1,20,3	1,20,3	$(20-1+3)/3 = 22/3 = 7\ 1/3$	7
DO 2 I=1,1000	1,1000,1	$(1000-1+1)/1 = 1000$	1000
DO 3 K=2,100,50	2,100,50	$(100-2+50)/50 = 148/50 = 2.96$	2
DO 4 L=10,1,3	10,1,3	$(1-10+3)/3 = -6/3 = -2$	0

As you progress in your study of programming you may be confronted with situations in which you must actually calculate iteration counts. In such situations, the formula given above can be used.

There is another reason we mention iteration counts. It is of general interest and concerns what actually happens when a FORTRAN compiler encounters a DO statement. The flowchart in Figure 7.1 explains the effect of a DO-loop but is not intended to describe exactly how the computer causes this effect. For instance, our description of the action caused by the statement

DO 1 N = 1,20,3

suggests that the computer first assigns 1 to N and then compares N with the terminal value 20. Although this helps us to understand the effect of the DO statement it does not necessarily correspond to what actually happens. Indeed, when a FORTRAN compiler encounters a DO statement, one of its first actions is to calculate the iteration count. It then determines machine instructions to decrease this count by 1 each time the range is executed and to exit the loop when the count is zero. Whenever the action of a FORTRAN statement is described in this text, only the effect of the statement is being described and not necessarily how the computer causes this effect.

We conclude this section by listing the more important rules concerning DO-loops. Although these may appear numerous, they are easily mastered with a little practice.

Rules for DO-Loops

1. The DO-parameters and the DO-variable must have integer values greater than zero. (Some systems relax this condition.)
2. The values of the DO-parameters are determined once, when the DO statement is executed, and cannot be altered during execution of the range.
3. Each time the range is executed, the increment value is added to the value of the DO-variable. This is the only way the value of the DO-variable can change during execution of a loop. It cannot be changed by a statement appearing in the range.
4. An exit from a DO-loop can be caused by a control statement appearing in the range. If this happens the current value of the DO-variable is retained. However, if an exit from a loop occurs because the loop has been satisfied, the value of the DO-variable is assumed to be undefined.
5. The only way that the range of a DO-loop can be entered is via the DO statement for that loop. In other words, a statement outside of a DO-loop must not transfer control to a statement in the range. For example, the following is not allowed:

```
      GO TO 5
      DO 1 N=1,10
         N1=N**2
 5       N2=N**3
         N3=N**4
 1 CONTINUE
```

Replacing GO TO 5 by the statement GO TO 1 is also not allowed; the statement labeled 1 is also in the range.
6. The terminal statement can be any executable statement other than a control statement used to interrupt the normal sequential execution of the statements in a program. However, the CONTINUE statement can be used to terminate every DO-loop and doing so is a good programming practice.
7. On some systems, execution of a DO statement causes the range to be executed at least once.
8. The range of one DO-loop may contain another DO-loop. This is the topic of Section 7.4.
9. The range of a DO-loop may contain a complete block IF statement, and a single block in a block IF statement may contain a complete DO-loop. (Block IF statements are described in Section 6.6.)

7.2 Flowcharting DO-Loops

DO-loops occur in most FORTRAN programs. For this reason, many flowchart symbols have been designed for representing such loops. The diagram we'll use has found wide acceptance and is one that can significantly improve the readability of flowcharts.

Using only the flowchart symbols given in Chapter 6, the loop

```
      DO 100 I = 1,10,3
      _____
      _____
      _____
100   terminal statement
```

may be flowcharted as follows:

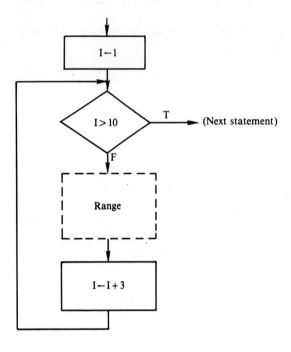

We'll represent this loop with the following diagram:

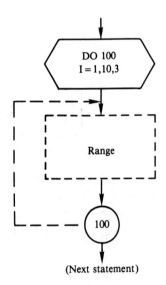

EXAMPLE 6. Here is a flowchart to read ten numbers and print their average:

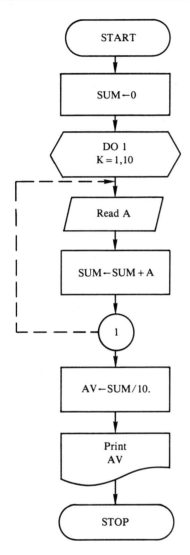

7.3 Problems

1. What will be printed when each program is run?

a.
```
      DO 1 J=2,2
      K=J+2
      WRITE(6,10)J,K
    1 CONTINUE
   10 FORMAT(1X,I2,I2)
      STOP
      END
```

b.
```
      N=0
      DO 2 K=4,30,3
      N=N+1
    2 CONTINUE
      WRITE(6,11)N
   11 FORMAT(1X,I3)
      STOP
      END
```

c.
```
      DO 3 M=1,10,2
         IF(M.EQ.6) STOP
         WRITE(6,12)M
    3 CONTINUE
   12 FORMAT(1X,I3)
      STOP
      END
```

d.
```
      INTEGER STEP
      SUM=0.
      STEP=2
      DO 4 N=2,7,STEP
         SUM=SUM+1./FLOAT(N)
    4 CONTINUE
      WRITE(6,13)SUM
   13 FORMAT(1X,F9.4)
      STOP
      END
```

2. Each of the following programs contains an error, either a compile-time error, a run-time error, or a programming error that the computer will not recognize but that will cause incorrect results. In each case find the error, tell which type it is, and correct the program so that it runs correctly.

a.
```
      S=0.
    1 DO 2 N=1,10
         READ(5,10)X
   10    FORMAT(F7.2)
         S=S+X
         GO TO 1
      WRITE(6,11)S
   11 FORMAT(1X,'SUM IS',F9.2)
      STOP
      END
```

b.
```
C SUM OF FRACTIONS PROGRAM
      SUM=0.
      DO 3 K=1,50
         SUM=SUM+FLOAT(1/K)
    3 CONTINUE
      WRITE(6,13)SUM
   13 FORMAT(1X,'SUM IS',F10.5)
      STOP
      END
```

c.
```
      SUM=0.
      N=10
      DO 4 J=1,10
         N=N-1
    4    SUM=FLOAT(J)+SUM
      AV=SUM/FLOAT(N)
      WRITE(6,14)AV
   14 FORMAT(1X,'AVERAGE IS',F9.1)
      STOP
      END
```

d.
```
C PRINT NUMBERS DIVISIBLE BY 3
      DO 5 M=1,100
         IF (M/3*3.NE.M) GO TO 5
         WRITE(6,5)M
    5    FORMAT(1X,I3)
      STOP
      END
```

e.
```
C READ UP TO 500 INTEGERS BUT
C STOP IF A MULTIPLE OF 29 IS READ
      DO 6 I=1,500
         READ(5,15)N
   15    FORMAT(I5)
    6    IF (N/29*29.EQ.N) STOP
      STOP
      END
```

Write the programs called for in Problems 3–15. In each case a single DO-loop is to be used.

3. Twenty real numbers are to be input. Determine the sum of those that are positive.

4. Twenty real numbers are to be input. Determine how many of these numbers are negative, how many are positive, and how many are zero.

5. Find the sum of the first K positive integers. A value for K is to be obtained with a READ statement.

6. Find the sum of all positive odd integers not exceeding K. A value for K is to be input.

7. A program is desired that will continually read input values (integers) until ten numbers have been read that lie in the range from 5 to 25 inclusive. The average of these ten numbers is then to be printed.

8. Two positive integers M and N, with M < N, are to be input. Find the sum of the odd integers between M and N, inclusive. If M $\geq$ N, or if either M or N is not positive, the program is to terminate.

9. Two positive integers M and N are to be input. Find the sum of all integers between M and N, inclusive. If either M or N is zero or negative, the program should terminate. However, the sum must be found in all other cases.

10. Two integers M and N are to be input. Find the sum of all integers between M and N, inclusive. The sum must be obtained even if M or N is not positive. (Use only positive DO-parameters.)

11. Print the integers M*I+N for I = 1,2,. . .,K. M, N, and K are to be input and the program run is to be terminated if K is not a positive integer.

12. Evaluate the following sums. If a value for N is required, it is to be input and you may assume it is positive.

   a. $1 + 2 + 3 + \cdots + N$
   b. $1 + 3 + 5 + 7 + \cdots + 51$
   c. $1 + 3 + 5 + 7 + \cdots + (2N - 1)$
   d. $2 + 5 + 8 + 11 + \cdots + K$, where $N - 3 < K \leq N$.
   e. $(.06) + (.06)^2 + (.06)^3 + \cdots + (.06)^N$
   f. $1 + 1/2 + 1/3 + 1/4 + \cdots + 1/N$
   g. $1 + 1/4 + 1/9 + 1/16 + \cdots + 1/N^2$
   h. $1 + 1/2 + 1/4 + 1/8 + \cdots + 1/2^N$
   i. $1 - 1/2 + 1/3 - 1/4 + \cdots - 1/100$
   j. $4[1 - 1/3 + 1/5 - 1/7 + \cdots + (-1)^{N+1}(2N - 1)]$

13. Produce the following printout. (The symbols $\times$ and $=$ must line up as shown.)

```
 1 × 7 =    7
 2 × 7 =   14
 3 × 7 =   21

       .
       .
       .

15 × 7 = 105
```

14. For any positive integer N, determine the product $1 \times 2 \times 3 \times 4 \times \cdots \times N$. This product is denoted by the symbol N! and is called N factorial. A value for N is to be input and the program is to terminate if N is not positive.

15. For positive integers N, N! is defined as in Problem 14. In addition, 0! is defined to be 1. (Thus, 0! = 1! = 1.) Find and print N! for any nonnegative input value N. If N < 0, the program should terminate. N! is not defined for negative integers.

7.4 Nested DO-Loops

It is permissible, and often desirable, to have one DO-loop contained in another. When nesting loops in this manner, there is one rule that must be observed.

> If the range of one DO-loop contains the DO statement of a second DO-loop, the first loop must also contain the entire range of the second loop.

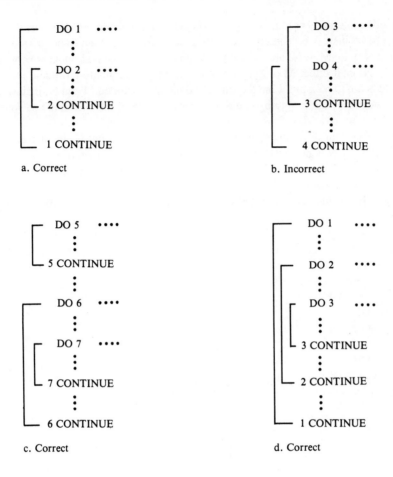

FIGURE 7.2. Correctly and incorrectly nested DO-loops.

EXAMPLE 7. Let's write a program to produce the following printout:

```
1ST    2ND    SUM
 1      1      2
 1      2      3
 1      3      4
 1      4      5
 2      1      3
 2      2      4
 2      3      5
 2      4      6
```

Problem Analysis:

In each line of output, the third column is the sum of the values in the first two columns. Thus, if we denote the values in columns 1, 2, and 3 by M, N, and SUM, respectively, we can write

SUM = M + N

The following algorithm shows one way to produce the required printout.

a. Print column headings.
b. Assign 1 to M.

c. Print M,N, and SUM for N = 1,2,3, and 4.

d. Add 1 to M and, if M≤2, repeat step (c).

e. Stop.

This algorithm says that M takes on the successive values 1 and 2, and for each of these values of M, N takes on the successive values 1, 2, 3, and 4. This assignment of values can be made as follows.

```
DO 2 M=1,2
    DO 1 N=1,4
        .
        .
        .
1    CONTINUE
2 CONTINUE
```

First, M = 1, and the inner loop (the N loop) is executed to give the successive values 1, 2, 3, and 4 for N. Then M = 2 and the inner loop is executed again. To complete the inner loop we need only include the statements that calculate SUM and print M, N, and SUM.

The Program:

```
    INTEGER SUM
    WRITE(6,10)
    DO 2 M=1,2
        DO 1 N=1,4
            SUM=M+N
            WRITE(6,11)M,N,SUM
1       CONTINUE
2   CONTINUE
    STOP
10  FORMAT(1X,'1ST   2ND   SUM')
11  FORMAT(1X,I2,4X,I2,4X,I2)
    END
```

The nested DO-loops appearing in the program of Example 7 can be written as follows:

```
DO 2 M=1,2
    DO 2 N=1,4
        SUM=M+N
        WRITE(6,11)M,N,SUM
2 CONTINUE
```

This program segment shows that a single statement can serve as the terminal statement for more than one DO-loop. The statement label appearing in a DO statement simply specifies the terminal statement for the loop, and it matters not if the statement specified is used as the terminal statement for another DO-loop.

Although this program segment is shorter than the equivalent form used in Example 7, it is not necessarily better. Indeed, using a separate CONTINUE statement for each loop, as was done in the program of Example 7, allowed us to indent the program so that the loop structure is clearly seen. In particular, not only is the range of each loop indented, but corresponding DO and CONTINUE statements appear at their own level of indentation with no intervening DO and CONTINUE statements appearing at this same level of indentation. We don't suggest that you always use CONTINUE statements in this manner. However, we do suggest that you write programs that are as easy to understand as possible.

EXAMPLE 8. Let's modify the program of Example 7 to produce the following printout:

1ST	2ND	SUM
1	1	2
1	2	3
1	3	4
1	4	5
2	2	4
2	3	5
2	4	6
3	3	6
3	4	7

Problem Analysis:

As in Example 7, let's denote the values in the columns 1, 2, and 3 by M, N, and SUM. Here, M takes on the successive values 1, 2, and 3, but the successive values of N depend on the current value of M. In particular the values of M and N are as follows:

When M = 1, N = 1,2,3,4.
When M = 2, N = 2,3,4.
When M = 3, N = 3,4.

This assignment of values can be made as follows:

```
DO 2 M=1,3
    DO 1 N=M,4
        .
        .
        .
1    CONTINUE
2 CONTINUE
```

The algorithm described by the following flowchart shows one way to produce the required printout. Since a decision has already been made to use DO-loops, we include them in the flowchart.

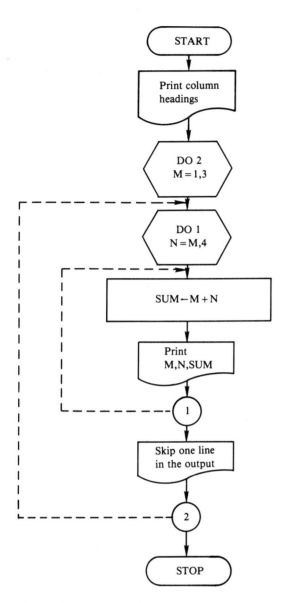

Remark: While constructing this flowchart, we had one eye on the required printout shown in the problem statement. Not only did this tell us that the flowchart had to contain an instruction to skip a line in the output, but it told us exactly where in the flowchart this instruction should appear—namely, just after the flowchart segment that prints the lines corresponding to a particular value of M. During the coding process, placement of the statement that skips a line will be no problem—we'll just follow the flowchart. Had we attempted to code the program without first constructing a flowchart, or an algorithm, the placement of this statement might not have been so obvious; indeed, it may even have been forgotten altogether.

The Program:

```
      INTEGER SUM
      WRITE(6,10)
      WRITE(6,11)
      DO 2 M=1,3
         DO 1 N=M,4
            SUM=M+N
            WRITE(6,12)M,N,SUM
 1       CONTINUE
         WRITE(6,13)
 2 CONTINUE
10 FORMAT(1X,' 1ST   2ND   SUM')
11 FORMAT(1X,'----- ----- -----')
12 FORMAT(1X,I3,3X,I3,3X,I3)
13 FORMAT(1X)
      STOP
      END
```

Remark: The statements

```
      WRITE(6,13)
13 FORMAT(1X)
```

cause nothing to be printed but have the effect of skipping one line in the output. In Chapter 8 you will see another way to do this.

As indicated in Figure 7.2d, more than two DO-loops may be nested. Examples 9 and 10 show two short programs illustrating this practice.

EXAMPLE 9. Loops nested to three levels:

```
      DO 1 I=1,2
         DO 2 J=1,2
            DO 3 K=1,2
               WRITE(6,10)I,J,K
 3          CONTINUE
 2       CONTINUE
 1 CONTINUE
10 FORMAT(1X,I3,I3,I3)
      STOP
      END
```

Output:

```
      1  1  1
      1  1  2
      1  2  1
      1  2  2
      2  1  1
      2  1  2
      2  2  1
      2  2  2
```

The following flowchart describes the action of this program:

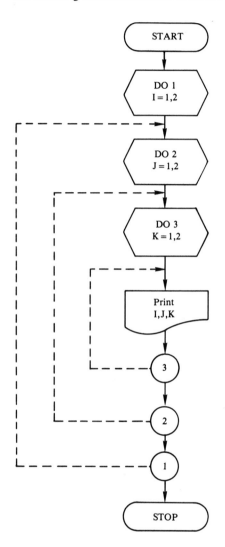

Remark: This program can be written more concisely as follows:

```
      DO 1 I=1,2
         DO 1 J=1,2
            DO 1 K=1,2
               WRITE(6,10)I,J,K
    1 CONTINUE
   10 FORMAT(1X,I3,I3,I3)
      STOP
      END
```

EXAMPLE 10. Loops nested to four levels:

```
      N=0
      DO 100 I=1,3
         DO 100 J=1,4
            DO 100 K=1,5
               DO 100 L=1,6
                  N=N+1
100   CONTINUE
      WRITE(6,10)N
 10   FORMAT(1X,'TIMES THROUGH LOOPS=',I4)
      STOP
      END
```

Output:

```
TIMES THROUGH LOOPS= 360
```

Each time the L-loop is executed, 6 is added to N. Each time the K-loop is executed, its range, the L-loop, is executed five times; hence, execution of the K-loop adds 30 ($= 5 \times 6$) to N. Similarly, each time the J-loop is executed, its range, the K-loop, is executed four times; hence, execution of the J-loop adds 120 ($= 4 \times 30 = 4 \times 5 \times 6$) to N. Finally, the range of the I-loop is executed three times. But this range is the J-loop which, as we have seen, adds 120 to N. Hence, execution of the I-loop adds 360 ($= 3 \times 120 = 3 \times 4 \times 5 \times 6$) to N.

Remark: We explained this program by considering the loops from the innermost loop to the outermost loop. It would be instructive to explain what this program does by considering the loops from the outermost to the innermost. You might begin as follows: "The range of the I-loop is executed three times. But this range is the J-loop, so the J-loop is executed a total of three times. . . ."

Nested DO-loops can be used to advantage in a great variety of programming tasks. Example 11 illustrates one such situation. Additional applications of nested DO-loops are indicated in the problem set following this section.

EXAMPLE 11. A business firm is contemplating a raise for all salaried employees. The raise is to consist of a flat across-the-board increase and a percentage increase of either 1%, 2%, or 3%. To give management some idea of the amounts involved, prepare a report showing the possible raises for the salary amounts $11,000, $12,000, . . . , $16,000.

Problem Analysis:
This problem calls for a single input value—namely, the amount of the flat across-the-board increase. The output will include many values. Indeed, for each of the percentages 1%, 2%, and 3%, a possible raise must be shown for each of the six salary amounts $11,000, $12,000, . . . , $16,000. Before attempting to write an algorithm for problems calling for many output values, it is important not only to identify the output values, but to describe the form in which these values will be printed.

Let's agree to print three separate tables, one for each of the percentages 1%, 2%, and 3%. The following form is appropriate for the 1% table. The others will be similar.

```
1 PERCENT TABLE
SALARY     RAISE
11000.00   _____
12000.00   _____
13000.00   _____
14000.00   _____
15000.00   _____
16000.00   _____
```

The second column is to show the raises corresponding to the amounts in the first column.

Having determined the form of the output document, we can return to the task of writing an algorithm to produce it. To assist in this task, let's choose variable names as follows:

SAL   = Present salary ($11,000, $12,000, . . . , $16,000).
INCR = Flat across-the-board increase (to be input).
PCT   = Percentage increase (1%, 2%, 3%).
RAISE = Amount of raise for a given SAL, INCR, and PCT.

The formula governing this situation is

$$RAISE = PCT/100*SAL + INCR$$

To produce the three tables we must first read a value for INCR. Then, for each percentage increase, we must display a two-column table, each line indicating a salary and the corresponding raise in salary. The following flowchart describes an algorithm for carrying out this task:

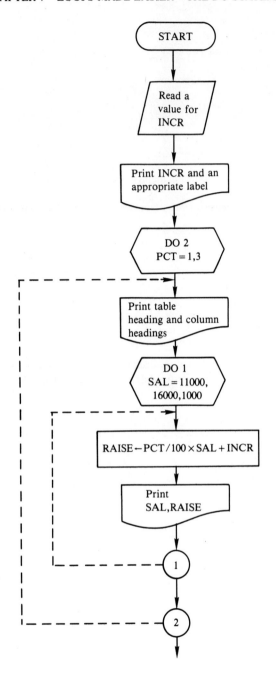

Before coding this algorithm, we must decide upon appropriate types for the variables. If we wish PCT and SAL to denote DO-variables, as indicated in the flowchart, they must be declared as integer variables. To avoid the risk of truncation errors that can occur when using integer arithmetic, we'll declare INCR and RAISE as reals and perform all calculations using real expressions.

Remark: While coding the following program we found it convenient to introduce the *real* variable RSAL so that the salary figures (SAL) could be printed in the standard real form used to print dollar amounts.

The Program:

```
C ********* SALARY INCREASE PROGRAM *********
      INTEGER PCT,SAL
      REAL INCR,RAISE,RSAL
C
C        SAL  = PRESENT SALARY
C        RSAL = PRESENT SALARY (REAL)
C        INCR = FLAT ACROSS-THE-BOARD INCREASE
C        PCT  = PERCENTAGE INCREASE
C        RAISE= AMOUNT OF RAISE
C
      READ(5,10)INCR
      WRITE(6,11)INCR
      WRITE(6,15)
      DO 2 PCT=1,3
         WRITE(6,12)PCT
         WRITE(6,13)
         DO 1 SAL=11000,16000,1000
            RSAL=FLOAT(SAL)
            RAISE=FLOAT(PCT)/100.*RSAL+INCR
            WRITE(6,14)RSAL,RAISE
    1    CONTINUE
         WRITE(6,15)
    2 CONTINUE
   10 FORMAT(F8.2)
   11 FORMAT(1X,'ACROSS-THE-BOARD INCREASE',F8.2)
   12 FORMAT(1X,I1,'PERCENT TABLE')
   13 FORMAT(1X,' SALARY',4X,'RAISE')
   14 FORMAT(1X,F8.2,2X,F7.2)
   15 FORMAT(1X)
      STOP
      END
```

Input Data:

```
          1         2         3
1234567890123456789012345678901234567890
 550.00
```

Output:

```
ACROSS-THE-BOARD INCREASE  550.00

1 PERCENT TABLE
 SALARY    RAISE
11000.00   660.00
12000.00   670.00
13000.00   680.00
14000.00   690.00
15000.00   700.00
16000.00   710.00
```

```
2 PERCENT TABLE
 SALARY    RAISE
11000.00   770.00
12000.00   790.00
13000.00   810.00
14000.00   830.00
15000.00   850.00
16000.00   870.00

3 PERCENT TABLE
 SALARY    RAISE
11000.00   880.00
12000.00   910.00
13000.00   940.00
14000.00   970.00
15000.00  1000.00
16000.00  1030.00
```

7.5 Problems

1. What will be printed when each program is run?

a.
```
      DO 1 I=1,3
         DO 1 J=2,3
            N=I+J
            WRITE(6,10)I,J,N
    1 CONTINUE
   10 FORMAT(1X,I2,I2,I3)
      STOP
      END
```

b.
```
      DO 1 I=1,3
         DO 2 J=I,3
            WRITE(6,11)I,J
    2    CONTINUE
    1 CONTINUE
   11 FORMAT(1X,I1,I1)
      STOP
      END
```

c.
```
      DO 3 M=3,6,2
         DO 3 N=1,3
            WRITE(6,12)M
    3 CONTINUE
   12 FORMAT(1X,I2)
      STOP
      END
```

d.
```
      N=0
      DO 4 I=1,6
         DO 4 J=2,7
            DO 4 K=2,4
               N=N+1
    4 CONTINUE
      WRITE(6,13)N
   13 FORMAT(1X,I4)
      STOP
      END
```

e.
```
      N=1
      DO 5 K=1,6
         DO 6 L=1,K
            N=N*L
    6    CONTINUE
         WRITE(6,14)K,N
         N=1
    5 CONTINUE
   14 FORMAT(1X,I2,'!=',I6)
      STOP
      END
```

f.
```
      DO 1 I=1,5
         IF(I/2*2.EQ.I) THEN
            DO 2 J=1,3
               WRITE(6,10)
    2       CONTINUE
         ELSE
            WRITE(6,11)
         ENDIF
    1 CONTINUE
   10 FORMAT(1X,'   XXX')
   11 FORMAT(1X,'XXXXXXX')
      STOP
      END
```

2. The following programs contain errors—either compilation errors (syntax errors) or programming errors that the computer will not recognize but that will cause incorrect results. Find all errors, tell which of the two types they are, and correct the programs so that they behave as indicated.

a.
```
C PRINT PRODUCTS
      INTEGER PROD
      DO 1 I=7,8
         DO 2 J=6,7
            PROD=I*J
            WRITE(6,10)I,J,PROD
10          FORMAT(1X,I1,' TIMES ',I1,' = ',I2)
1     CONTINUE
2 CONTINUE
      STOP
      END
```

b.
```
C PRINT SUMS
      INTEGER SUM
      DO 1 M=7,8
         DO 1 N=6,7
            SUM=M+N
            WRITE(6,10)M,N,SUM
1 FORMAT(1X,I1,'+',I1,'=',I3)
      STOP
      END
```

c. A program to print

```
12
13
14
23
24
34
```

```
   DO 1 I=1,4
      DO 1 J=2,4
         WRITE(6,10)I,J
1 CONTINUE
10 FORMAT(1X,I1,I1)
   STOP
   END
```

d. A program to print

```
XXXXX
X
X
X
XXXXX
```

```
   DO 1 I=1,3
      IF(I.NE.2) THEN
         DO 2 J=1,3
            WRITE(6,10)
2        CONTINUE
      ENDIF
      WRITE(6,11)
1 CONTINUE
10 FORMAT(1X,'XXXXX')
11 FORMAT(1X,'X')
   STOP
   END
```

Write a program to perform each task specified in Problems 3–15.

3. For each integer N from 1 to 20, determine the sum of all integers from 1 to N. The printout is to contain two columns with the following column headings:

```
    N          1+2+3+···+N
--------    -----------------------
```

4. For each integer N from 0 to 10, produce a two-column table with the following column headings:

     N   N FACTORIAL
    --------   --------------------

Recall that $0! = 1$, and for $N > 0$, $N! = 1 \times 2 \times 3 \times \cdots \times N$.

5. For each of the tax rates 5%, $5\frac{1}{8}$%, $5\frac{1}{4}$%, $5\frac{3}{8}$%, and $5\frac{1}{2}$%, produce a table showing the tax on the dollar amounts $1, $2, $3, . . . , $25. Each of the five tables is to have an appropriate title and is to contain two labeled columns, the first showing the dollar amounts $1, $2, $3, . . . , $25 and the second showing the corresponding tax amounts.

6. Five sets of numbers, with each set containing six integers, are to be input. The sum of the six numbers in each set is to be printed in the form

SUM FOR SET NUMBER _____ IS _____ .

Your program should contain only one READ statement and it should read only one number at a time.

7. Thirty nonnegative integers are to be input as described in Problem 6. After printing the sum of each of the five sets as shown in Problem 6, the computer is to print the message

THE LARGEST OF THESE SUMS IS _____ .

8. Modify the task described in Problem 7 so that the computer not only determines the largest of the five sums, but also the smallest.

9. The expression $4MN - M^3 - M^2 - 10M$ is to be examined for all integers M and N from 1 to 5 to determine those pairs (M, N) for which the expression is positive. All such pairs are to be printed with the corresponding positive value of the given expression.

10. Determine the largest value the expression $MN^2 - M^2N + M - N$ can assume if M and N are any integers from 1 to 5, inclusive.

11. Produce a listing of all three-digit numbers whose digits are 1, 2, or 3. Spaces are not to appear between the digits of the numbers. *Hint:* Use triple-nested loops with DO-variables I, J, and K ranging from 1 to 3.

12. Produce a listing of all three-digit numbers as described in Problem 11. However, if no digit is repeated in a number, it is to be preceded by an *. Thus, a portion of your printout should be as follows:

     .
     .
     .
   121
   122
 *123
   131
 *132
   133
     .
     .
     .

Hint: With I, J, and K as in Problem 11, print I, J, K by using FORMAT (1X,1X,I1,I1,I1) if I = J, I = K, or J = K. Otherwise, use FORMAT(1X,'*',I1,I1,I1).

13. Let SUM denote the sum of the digits in any four-digit number whose digits are 1, 2, 3, or 4. For example, SUM = 12 for the number 3243. Find the average of all possible sums SUM, one for each such four-digit number. (*Hint:* Use nested loops with DO-variables I, J, K, and L ranging from 1 to 4. Also include a counter N in the innermost loop to count how many such numbers there are.

14. Find all pairs of integers (I, J) that satisfy the following system of inequalities:

$$2I - J < 3$$
$$I + 3J \geq 1$$
$$-6 \leq I \leq 6$$
$$-10 \leq J \leq 10$$

The solutions are to be printed as individual ordered pairs (I,J).

15. Find the maximum and minimum values of the expression $3X^2 - 2XY + Y^2$ if X and Y are subject to the following constraints:

$$X = -4, -3.5, -3, \cdots, 4$$
$$Y = -3, -2.5, -2, \cdots, 5$$

7.6 Review True-or-False Quiz

1. If a group of instructions is to be executed several times in a program, it is always a good practice to use a DO-loop.   T F
2. The IF statement often provides a convenient way to transfer control out of a DO-loop.   T F
3. If an exit is made from a DO-loop via an IF statement, the current value of the DO-variable is retained.   T F
4. If an exit is made from a DO-loop because the loop is satisfied, the value of the DO-variable is reset to zero.   T F
5. If a loop begins with the statement DO 1 I = 1,35, the variable I must occur in some statement before the statement labeled 1 is encountered.   T F
6. The DO-variable in a DO-loop can be modified by a statement in the range of the loop.   T F
7. The initial, terminal, and increment parameters in a DO-loop cannot be modified in the range of the loop.   T F
8. The DO-variable of a loop containing a loop may be used as one or more of the DO-parameters of the inner loop.   T F
9. The statement GO TO 5 cannot appear in the range of a loop initiated by the statement DO 5 I = 1,10.   T F
10. An executable statement in the range of a loop initiated with DO 2 K = 5,9,2 will not necessarily be executed three times.   T F
11. During execution of a loop initiated with DO 2 K = 5,9,2, it may happen that a statement in the range is executed more than three times.   T F
12. The iteration count for the statement DO 1 N = 160,2290,13 is 164.   T F

8
More on Input-Output Programming

Our concern up to this point has been twofold: to present enough FORTRAN so that you can solve problems using the computer, and to stress the development of good programming habits. FORMAT statements have intentionally been kept as simple as possible so that you could concentrate on the programming process itself without becoming bogged down by the small details which often divert the attention of the beginning programmers. In this chapter we introduce some new edit descriptors to give you more control over both input and output.

In addition, we introduce the DATA statement that allows you to initialize variables during program compilation. Although the DATA statement is not used for I/O processing (the subject of this chapter) we'll show how it sometimes can be used to advantage in place of READ statements.

8.1 Carriage Control Characters

In every FORMAT statement used for output thus far, we have included a 1X edit descriptor to begin the format specification. On conversational systems this serves only to begin each line of output at the computer terminal with one blank space. However, if the output is to be printed by a line printer, as is usually the case on batch systems, the first character in the output has special significance. It is called a **carriage control character** because it controls the vertical movement of paper in the printer.

If the first character in the output is the blank character, it instructs the printer to advance one line before printing any subsequent output. Thus

```
    WRITE(6,10)
10  FORMAT(1X,'SALARY REPORT')
```

causes the character string SALARY REPORT to be printed on a new line at the left margin. A blank space does not begin this new line—carriage control characters are not printed.

FORTRAN provides four carriage control characters, as shown in Table 8.1.

TABLE 8.1. Carriage control characters for line printers.

Carriage control character	First entry in format specification	Purpose
Δ (blank)	1X or 'Δ' or 1HΔ	Advance one line (single spacing)
0 (zero)	'0' or 1H0	Advance two lines (double spacing)
1 (one)	'1' or 1H1	Advance to top of a new page
+	'+' or 1H+	Do not advance

If you forget to include a carriage control character as the first entry of an output format specification, the system will use the first character in the output record for this purpose. For instance, if NUM = 2, the formatted WRITE statement

```
      WRITE(6,10)NUM
   10 FORMAT(I2)
```

will transmit two output characters, a blank and a 2. The first will be used for carriage control so that the digit 2 will be printed at the left margin of the next print line. However, if NUM = 12, the character 1 will be used for carriage control so that the digit 2 will be printed at the left margin on the first line of a new page. If the first character in the output is not one of the four carriage control characters shown in Table 8.1, the results are unpredictable—what actually happens is system dependent. Because of this, you should always include a carriage control character as the first entry in each output format specification if your output is being directed to a line printer.

Remember that carriage control characters are not used if results are to be printed by any output device other than the line printer. If you are using a conversational system, beginning each output format specification with 1X will cause no harm. It simply means that the first print position of each new line is not used. However, the other three control characters (0, 1, and +) must not be used—they will be printed. We will continue to use 1X as the first entry in each output format specification. It is merely our way of indicating normal printing—that is, at the left margin of a new line. In Section 8.3 we discuss methods of vertical spacing that can be used on any system, whether it uses a line printer or not.

8.2 Edit Descriptors—Too Many or Too Few

As you know, FORMAT statements must contain I and F edit descriptors that match the types of any variables appearing in corresponding READ or WRITE statements. For instance,

```
      WRITE(6,10)A,N,B
   10 FORMAT(1X,F10.4,I5,F7.2)
```

describes a correct formatted WRITE statement since the types of the variables and of the edit descriptors are real, integer, and real, in that order. You have also seen that if there are more edit descriptors than variables, the extra edit descriptors are simply ignored. For instance,

```
      READ(5,11)A,B,N
   11 FORMAT(F10.4,I5,F7.2,I6,F8.0)
```

describes a correct formatted READ statement. The edit descriptors F10.4, I5, and F7.2 are used for A, N, and B, respectively; the last two are ignored. The following two examples show what happens when the number of variables exceeds the number of descriptors.

EXAMPLE 1. Here is a program segment to read four input values and print them two to a line:

```
    READ(5,10)A,M,B,N
10  FORMAT(F7.2,I3,F7.2,I3)
    WRITE(6,11)A,M,B,N
11  FORMAT(1X,'AMOUNT:',F7.2,5X,'COUNT:',I3)
```

Input Data:

```
          1         2
12345678901234567890
  15.23 25   23.49 72
```

The formatted READ statement reads the input record as usual to obtain the values

A = 15.23
M = 25
B = 23.49
N = 72

The WRITE statement says to print these four values according to the format specification in the statement labeled 11. But this format specification contains only the two descriptors F7.2 and I3 for editing numerical values. When this happens, the format specification is repeated. However, each time it is repeated, a new print line is used. Thus, in this example, the output will be

```
AMOUNT:  15.23    COUNT: 25
AMOUNT:  23.49    COUNT: 72
```

Remark: Note that when the edit descriptors F7.2 and I3 are repeated, their types match the types of the variables B and N whose values are to be printed. If this were not the case, an error would occur during program execution.

EXAMPLE 2. Here is a formatted READ statement to read one input value from each of three input records:

```
    READ(5,10)N1,N2,N3
10  FORMAT(I5)
```

Input Data:

```
          1
1234567890
   153   17
    27   27
  3005   37
```

Since the format specification contains only the one edit descriptor I5, it is repeated until values are read for all three variables N1, N2, and N3. However, each time the format specification is repeated, a new input record is used. Thus, in this example, the variable assignments are

N1 =   153
N2 =   27
N3 = 3005

(The other input values are not used.)

8.3 The / (Slash) Edit Descriptor

The slash (/) edit descriptor can be used in output format specifications to control the vertical spacing along a printed page. (Recall that the X descriptor is used to control the horizontal spacing along a print line.)

This use of the slash descriptor will now be described. Later in this section, we'll explain how the slash is used in format specifications that interpret input data being read by READ statements.

When a slash (/) is encountered in an output format specification it instructs the computer to terminate all printing on the current line. Unfortunately, this simple description leaves many questions unanswered. The following examples illustrate the use of the slash descriptor in several different situations:

EXAMPLE 3. Here are two equivalent program segments and the printout each produces:

```
LEFT
TURN
ONLY
```

Program Segment 1	Program Segment 2
``	```

```
      WRITE(6,10)                                WRITE(6,20)
10 FORMAT(1X,'LEFT')                        20 FORMAT(1X,'LEFT'/1X,'TURN'/1X,'ONLY')
      WRITE(6,11)
11 FORMAT(1X,'TURN')
      WRITE(6,12)
12 FORMAT(1X,'ONLY')
```

In Program Segment 1 we use three formatted WRITE statements to print the three lines. Up to now, this has been necessary. The conciseness of Program Segment 2 is apparent. It works this way: 1X,'LEFT' cause LEFT to be printed on a new line as usual. The slash (/) terminates printing on this line. The next descriptors 1X and 'TURN' are then used, causing TURN to be printed on a new line. The second slash (/) stops printing on this second line and then the descriptors 1X and 'ONLY' cause ONLY to be printed on a new (third) line.

Remark 1: If the output is to a line printer, the first character output after *each* slash (in this example, the blank given by 1X) is a carriage control character. A slash simply says to terminate output on the current line; it does not say to produce any subsequent output on a new line.

Remark 2: If the output is not to a line printer, output generated after a slash is encountered is automatically printed on a new line. For example, on a conversational system we can use the FORMAT statement

```
20 FORMAT('LEFT'/'TURN'/'ONLY')
```

to produce the indicated printout.

Remark 3: Edit descriptors are separated by commas in FORMAT statements. However, commas before or after the slash are optional and are usually omitted.

Consecutive slashes in FORMAT statements controlling output are also permitted, but their effect depends on their position in the FORMAT statement. In normal printing, if n consecutive slashes appear at the beginning or at the end of a FORMAT specification, n lines are skipped; otherwise $n-1$ lines are skipped.

EXAMPLE 4. Consecutive slashes:

```
      WRITE(6,15)
15 FORMAT(1X,'NONE'/1X,'ONE'//1X,'TWO'///1X,'THREE')
      STOP
      END
```

Output:

```
NONE
ONE
```
←— No line is skipped (single slash).

←— One line is skipped (double slash).

```
TWO
```

←— Two lines are skipped (triple slash).

```
THREE
```

Note: Since the slashes appear in the interior of the FORMAT specification, a single slash indicates single spacing, a double slash indicates double spacing, and so on.

EXAMPLE 5. Slashes at the end of a FORMAT statement:

```
      A=5.34
      B=97.465
      WRITE(6,25)A
   25 FORMAT(1X,'A=',F4.2//)
      WRITE(6,35)B
   35 FORMAT(1X,'B=',F6.3)
      STOP
      END
```

Output:

```
A=5.34
```

←— Two lines are skipped.

```
B=97.465
```

The two slashes at the end of the first FORMAT statement cause two blank lines to appear before normal printing continues. The two formatted WRITE statements in this program are equivalent to the following single formatted WRITE statement:

```
      WRITE(6,30)A,B
   30 FORMAT(1X,'A=',F4.2///1X,'B=',F6.3)
```

As shown in the next example, the slash can be employed to print titles and column headings for output documents with an economy of FORTRAN statements.

EXAMPLE 6. The formatted WRITE statement

```
      WRITE(6,10)
   10 FORMAT(1X,3X,'TABLE OF SQUARES'//1X,'NUMBER',10X,'SQUARE')
```

will produce the following printout:

```
   TABLE OF SQUARES
```

←— One line is skipped (double slash).

```
NUMBER          SQUARE
```

Without the slash, six FORTRAN statements would be needed to produce these three lines, one WRITE and one FORMAT statement for each line of output.

We now turn our attention to the slash descriptor as it applies to input specifications. Just as the X descriptor can be used to skip over unneeded portions of input records, the slash descriptor can be used to skip over entire input records. This use of the slash descriptor can be helpful if a program must be written to process an existing collection of input records such as a previously prepared deck of data cards or a data file that is stored on a magnetic disk or tape.

EXAMPLE 7. Here is a program segment to read and print the second, fourth, and sixth of six input records:

```
    DO 1 I=1,3
        READ(5,10)N
        WRITE(6,11)N
  1 CONTINUE
 10 FORMAT(/I5)
 11 FORMAT(1X,I5)
```

Input Data:

```
          1         2
12345678901234567890
 1259
   26
 4847
   31
 2668
   55
```

Output:

```
   26
   31
   55
```

When the READ statement is first encountered the current input record is the first record. The slash beginning the format specification says to stop reading from this record and to read any subsequent data from the next record; thus, 26 is assigned to N. After the READ instruction has been carried out, the next record (the third one) becomes the current record. On the second pass through the loop the format specification (/15) says to skip this third record and to read N from the next (fourth) record; thus, this time, 31 is assigned to N. Similarly, on the third pass through the loop, 55 is assigned to N.

Remark 1: As illustrated, a slash appearing at the beginning of a format specification causes one input record to be skipped. If n slashes appear at the beginning of a format specification, n records will be skipped.

Remark 2: If we change the FORMAT statement to

10 FORMAT(15/)

N will be assigned values from the first, third, and fifth input records. In general, n slashes encountered at the end of a format specification cause n records to be skipped.

A single slash encountered in the interior of a format specification instructs the computer to stop reading data from the current record and to read any subsequent data from the next record. Thus, a slash does not necessarily cause an entire record to be skipped: only the unused portion of the current record is skipped. For example, the formatted READ statement

```
    READ(5,10)M,N
 10 FORMAT(I3/I5)
```

reads a value for M from the current record by using the descriptor I3, and a value for N from the next record by using the descriptor I5. To skip an entire record, we would use

```
   READ(5,10)M,N
10 FORMAT(I3//I5)
```

This formatted READ statement reads M from the first record, skips over the remainder of the record (the first slash), skips the next record (the second slash), and finally reads N from the third record. Generally, n slashes encountered in the interior of format specifications cause $n-1$ records to be skipped.

EXAMPLE 8. A data-processing center produces the following short daily report (among many others):

```
PLANT OVERHEAD REPORT

  PLANT      OVERHEAD
 -------    ----------
   2401         -
   6002         -
```

The amounts in the overhead column are calculated as follows by using two cost figures supplied daily over the phone:

Overhead for Plant 2401: 22.875 percent of cost figure.
Overhead for Plant 6002: 28.625 percent of cost figure.

Here is the program the computer center uses to produce this report:

```
C*****PLANT OVERHEAD PROGRAM*****
      INTEGER PLANT1,PLANT2
      PLANT1=2401
      PLANT2=6002
      READ(5,10)RATE1,COST1,RATE2,COST2
      OVHD1=RATE1*COST1
      OVHD2=RATE2*COST2
C PRINT THE OVERHEAD REPORT
      WRITE(6,11)
      WRITE(6,12)PLANT1,OVHD1,PLANT2,OVHD2
      STOP
   10 FORMAT(F7.5/F10.2)
   11 FORMAT(1X,'PLANT OVERHEAD REPORT'//
     1       1X,' PLANT',6X,'OVERHEAD'/
     2       1X,'-------',4X,'----------'///)
   12 FORMAT(1X,I6,4X,F10.2)
      END
```

Note that the following READ statement is used for input:

```
   READ(5,10)RATE1,COST1,RATE2,COST2
10 FORMAT(F7.5/F10.2)
```

This means that each day the two percentage rates must be input along with the two daily cost amounts. When the READ statement is executed, a value from the first input record is assigned to RATE1 by using the descriptor F7.5; anything else on this first record is skipped (the /). A value from the second input record is then assigned to COST1 by using the descriptor F10.2.

At this point, the entire format specification must be repeated to obtain values for RATE2 and COST2. These are read from the third and fourth records just as RATE1 and COST1 were read from the first and second.

In light of this explanation of how the program reads input data, the cost amounts $57,535.00 for Plant 2401 and $110,560.00 for Plant 6002 can be entered by using four records as follows:

Input Data:

```
                1             2
     12345678901234567890
     0.22875
         57535.00
     0.28625
       110560.00
```

You should read this program to verify that it prints the report in the form specified.

We conclude this section with the following summary of the slash descriptor in input and output format specifications.

Summary: Slashes in Input and Output Format Specifications

1. When a slash is encountered in a format specification, it instructs the computer to terminate reading from the current record (input) or terminate printing on the current line (output).
2. Each slash encountered at the beginning or end of a format specification causes an entire record to be skipped (input) or a line to be skipped (output).
3. If n consecutive slashes are encountered in the interior of a format specification, $n-1$ complete records are skipped (input) or $n-1$ lines are skipped (output).

8.4 The DATA Statement—Initializing Variables

Every time the program shown in Example 8 is run, the same values, 0.22875 and 0.28625, must be input for the variables RATE1 and RATE2. Knowing that these rates will not change from day to day, it would be better to use assignment statements and avoid the requirement that they be included in the input data. If you do this, the program will contain the following four assignment statements:

```
        RATE1 = 0.22875
        RATE2 = 0.28625
        PLANT1 = 2401
        PLANT2 = 6002
```

The purpose of these statements is to initialize the four variables with the same values each time the program is run. The DATA statement provides an alternative method of specifying initial values for variables. The statement

```
    DATA RATE1,RATE2,PLANT1,PLANT2/0.22875,0.28625,2401,6002/
```

specifies the initial values 0.22875, 0.28625, 2401, and 6002 for the variables RATE1, RATE2, PLANT1, and PLANT2, respectively. (Remember that PLANT1 and PLANT2 were declared as integer variables.)

DATA statements are placed near the beginning of your program, after the type statements but before any executable statements. DATA statements are nonexecutable. The initial assignments are made during program compilation, not during program execution. Using DATA statements to initialize variables whose initial values are the same for each program run is an excellent programming practice. A person reading a program containing the statement

```
DATA C,E,G,PI/2.54,2.718,28.3495,3.1416/
```

will know immediately what the initial values of C, E, G, and PI are. The DATA statement will appear near the beginning of the program before any processing takes place, whereas assignment statements may be dispersed throughout the program. In addition, the program will be shorter, and hence easier to read. (We don't mean to imply that short programs are necessarily easier to read than long ones. However, we do claim that programs made shorter by the use of proper DATA statements will be easier to read.)

The following example illustrates two DATA statements and explains their meanings:

EXAMPLE 9. DATA statements:

a.
```
DATA N1,N2/1,2/
DATA SUM/0.0/
```

The first DATA statement specifies the initial values 1 and 2 for N1 and N2, respectively. The second initializes SUM to zero. These two DATA statements may be combined as follows:

```
DATA N1,N2/1,2/,SUM/0.0/
```

or, more simply, as

```
DATA N1,N2,SUM/1,2,0.0/
```

Note that integer constants are specified for integer variables and real constants for real variables. This is a requirement.

Note also that the number of constants between slashes is the same as the number of variables immediately preceding the slashes. This is also a requirement.

b.
```
INTEGER A,B,C,D
REAL U,V,W,X,Y,Z
DATA A,B,C,D/4*0/
DATA U,V,W,X,Y,Z/6*1./
```

The expression 4*0 is an abbreviation for 0,0,0,0; hence, the integer variables A,B,C, and D are initialized to zero.

Similarly, 6*1. is equivalent to 1.,1.,1.,1.,1.,1.; hence, the six real variables U,V,W,X,Y, and Z are initialized to 1.

These two DATA statements can be combined to give

```
DATA A,B,C,D/4*0/,U,V,W,X,Y,Z/6*1./
```

or

```
DATA A,B,C,D,U,V,W,X,Y,Z/4*0,6*1./
```

As we have mentioned, variables initialized by using DATA statements are initialized during program compilation. This means that if a program is compiled and, thereafter, only the object program is executed (this is often the case with heavily used programs), initial assignments made with DATA statements will be made only once, during program compilation. (Initial assignments using READ or assignment statements are made each time the object program is run.) For programs that initialize only a few variables, little is gained. However, as you'll see in the next chapter, there are programs that require initializing many hundreds of variables, and, in such cases, the best utilization of your computer resources will be made by using DATA statements. (As you'll see, this does not mean that you must write down hundreds of variable names.)

8.5 Problems

1. Exactly what will be printed by the following formatted WRITE statements? Assume that

    I = 24   X = 203.65
    J = 43   Y = −13.41
    K = −35   Z = 0.1234E + 02

    a.   ```
    WRITE(6,10)I,J,K
10 FORMAT(1X,I3,I3)
```

    b.     ```
    WRITE(6,10)X,I,Y,J,Z,K
10 FORMAT(1X,F6.2/1X,I6)
```

    c.   ```
    WRITE(6,10)I,X,J,Y
10 FORMAT(1X,'COUNT',4X,'VALUE'//1X,I4,F10.1/1X,I4,F10.1)
```

    d.     ```
    WRITE(6,11)X,Y,Z
11 FORMAT(1X,F8.0//)
```

    e.   ```
    WRITE(6,12)I,J,K
12 FORMAT(1X,I3//1X,I3///1X,I3)
```

    f.     ```
    WRITE(6,13)X,Y
13 FORMAT(1X,'X=',F8.3/1X,'Y=',F8.3)
```

2. Describe the effect of the following formatted READ statements if the input data consist of the following eight records:

```
          1         2
12345678901234567890
 1234567890123456789
 2345678901234567890
 3456789012345678901
 4567890123456789012
 5678901234567890123
 6789012345678901234
 7890123456789012345
 8901234567890123456
```

    a.   ```
    READ(5,10)N1,N2,N3
10 FORMAT(I6)
```

    b.     ```
    READ(5,10)JOB,MIN,LARGE,NUM
10 FORMAT(I2,3X,I3)
```

    c.   ```
    READ(5,10)A,B,C
    READ(5,10)D,E
10 FORMAT(F5.2,5X,F5.2/F5.3,F5.3)
```

    d.     ```
    READ(5,10)M,N
10 FORMAT(/17X,I3//17X,I3)
```

e.   ```
        READ(5,11)A,B,C,D
     11 FORMAT(F5.2,10X,F5.2//F5.2,10X,F5.2)
        ```

f.      ```
        READ(5,12)N1,N2,N3,N4
     12 FORMAT(/8X,I2,8X,I2//8X,I2,8X,I2)
        ```

g.   ```
        READ(5,13)N1,N2,N3,N4
     13 FORMAT(//17X,I3/17X,I3)
        ```

h.      ```
        READ(5,14)I,J,K
     14 FORMAT(I5//)
        ```

3. What will be printed when each program is run?

a.   ```
        WRITE(6,20)
        DO 1 I=1,5
           J=I*I
           WRITE(6,21)I,J
      1 CONTINUE
        STOP
     20 FORMAT(1X,' X ',5X,'X**2'/
      +   1X,'-----',5X,'----')
     21 FORMAT(1X,I3,5X,I3)
        END
        ```

b.      ```
        DATA P1,P2/.35,.65/
        DATA N1,N2/20,10/
        E=P1*FLOAT(N1)+P2*FLOAT(N2)
        WRITE(6,10)
        WRITE(6,11)P1,N1,P2,N2
        WRITE(6,12)E
        STOP
     10 FORMAT(1X,'PROBABILITY    COUNT'/)
     11 FORMAT(1X,F8.2,7X,I3)
     12 FORMAT(1X/1X,'EXPECTED VALUE IS',F7.2)
        END
        ```

c.   ```
        DATA X1,Y1,X2,Y2/1.5,2.5,3.5,4.5/
        U=X1+X2
        V=Y1+Y2
        WRITE(6,10)X1,Y1,X2,Y2
        WRITE(6,11)
        WRITE(6,10)U,V
     10 FORMAT(1X,'(',F3.1,',',F3.1,')')
     11 FORMAT(1X,'---------')
        STOP
        END
        ```
        ```

The following input data are for parts d, e, and f.

```
            1         2         3
12345678901234567890 1234567890
 1BRYANTVILLE    28     26589.43
 2  ITEM1924    500
 3  ITEM4326    450
 1SPRINGDALE    16      9207.75
 2  ITEM1924    480
 3  ITEM4326    200
 1CRANSTON      60     84516.93
 2  ITEM1924    500
 3  ITEM4326    350
```

d.
```
      INTEGER COUNT
      COUNT=0
      DO 1 N=1,3
          READ(5,10)M
          COUNT=COUNT+M
    1 CONTINUE
      WRITE(6,11)COUNT
      STOP
   10 FORMAT(16X,I3//)
   11 FORMAT(1X,'TOTAL EMPLOYEES',I5)
      END
```

e.
```
      I1=0
      I2=0
      DO 1 N=1,3
          READ(5,10)N1,K1,N2,K2
          I1=I1+K1
          I2=I2+K2
    1 CONTINUE
      WRITE(6,11)N1,I1,N2,I2
      STOP
   10 FORMAT(/8X,I4,4X,I3/8X,I4,4X,I3)
   11 FORMAT(1X,'ITEM',I4,3X,'INVENTORY',I5)
      END
```

f.
```
      GROSS=0.
      DO 1 N=1,3
          READ(5,10)SALES
          GROSS=GROSS+SALES
    1 CONTINUE
      WRITE(6,11)GROSS
      STOP
   10 FORMAT(20X,F10.0//)
   11 FORMAT(1X,'TOTAL SALES=$',F9.2)
      END
```

4. Write a single formatted WRITE statement to produce the indicated printout.

a.
```
 LINE1
    LINE2
       LINE3
```

b.
```
         ONE
     TWO    TWO
   THREE        THREE
```

c. Your name is to appear on the first line, street and number on the next, and city or town, state, and zip code on the third.

Write a program to perform each task specified in Problems 5–7.

5. Read four integers I, J, L, and M and print the product $(IX + J)(LX + M)$. For example, if $I = 2$, $J = 5$, $L = 3$ and $M = 4$, the output should be as follows:

$$(2X + 5)(3X + 4) = 6X**2 + 23X + 20$$

6. The sequence 1, 1, 2, 3, 5, 8, 13, . . . is called the Fibonacci sequence—each term is the sum of the two terms preceding it. Produce a two-column table as follows. The first column is to contain the integers $N = 1, 2, 3, . . . , 30$ and the second is to contain the first thirty numbers in the Fibonacci sequence. Use a single formatted WRITE or PRINT statement to print an appropriate title for the table and also to print underlined column headings. (N and FIB(N) are suitable column headings.)

7. Read three reals A, B, and C and print a two-column table as follows. The first column is to contain the values $X = 1, 1.1, 1.2, . . . , 2$ and the second column is to show the corresponding values of the expression $AX^2 + BX + C$. Use a single formatted WRITE statement to label the columns X and AX**2 + BX + C and also to underline these column headings.

8.6 Repeat Specifications

Many programming applications require that several variables be read or printed, each using the same edit descriptor. For instance, the programming lines

```
      READ(5,20)I,M,N
   20 FORMAT(I4,I4,I4)
```

read values for I, M, and N; the edit descriptor I4 is used in each case. FORTRAN allows the use of a **repeat specification** to simplify writing FORMAT statements containing repeated edit descriptors. The two statements

   20 FORMAT(I4,I4,I4)

and

   20 FORMAT(3I4)

are equivalent. The 3 in (3I4) is called the repeat specification. Similarly

   FORMAT(I6,I6,3X,F7.2,F7.2,F7.2)

is equivalent to

   FORMAT(2I6,3X,3F7.2).

An edit descriptor is called *repeatable* if it can be preceded by a nonzero unsigned integer constant indicating how many times it is to be repeated; otherwise, it is called *nonrepeatable*. Of the edit descriptors considered to this point only I and F are repeatable (see Table 8.2). Thus

   15F7.2   and   5I8

are admissible, but

   40'*'   and   5/

are not admissible.

TABLE 8.2. Repeatable and nonrepeatable edit descriptors.

Repeatable edit descriptors	*Nonrepeatable edit descriptors*
Iw	'...'
Fw.d	nH
Ew.d (Section 8.7)	nX
Dw.d (Section 16.1)	/
Lw (Section 16.1)	
Aw (Section 12.1)	

Note: Some FORTRAN compilers allow edit descriptors that are not described in this text. In general, an edit descriptor is repeatable if its application is to interpret (edit) values of variables being input or output.

Groups of edit descriptors can also be repeated. In the statement

45 FORMAT(I4,F6.3,I4,F6.3)

the third and fourth descriptors are merely a repeat of the first and second. This statement can be simplified to

45 FORMAT(2(I4,F6.3))

Note the parentheses around the group being repeated and the repeat specification (the number 2) immediately preceding the parentheses. Note also that 2(I4,F6.3) means that the group (I4,F6.3) is repeated twice and not that I4 is repeated twice followed by F6.3 repeated twice. As a further illustration

FORMAT(1X,2(I3,5X),3('*'))

is equivalent to

FORMAT(1X,I3,5X,I3,5X,'*','*','*').

Note that a group being repeated may contain nonrepeatable descriptors (5X and '*' in the previous illustration). Thus, the inadmissible form 40'*' may be written correctly as 40('*'). Similarly, 40(1H*) and 5(/) are admissible; the first is equivalent to 40('*') and the second to /////.

In general, any group of edit descriptors may be repeated whether it contains a single edit descriptor or several. Simply enclose the group in parentheses and precede this by a nonzero unsigned integer that specifies how many times the group is to be repeated.

EXAMPLE 10. A program to print

```
    *       *
    *       *
    *       *
****************
    *       *
    *       *
    *       *
****************
    *       *
    *       *
    *       *
```

is as follows:

```
      DO 1 N=1,11
         IF((N.EQ.4).OR.(N.EQ.8)) THEN
            WRITE(6,10)
         ELSE
            WRITE(6,11)
         END IF
    1 CONTINUE
   10 FORMAT(1X,17('*'))
   11 FORMAT(1X,2(5X,'*'))
      STOP
      END
```

8.7 The E Edit Descriptor

The descriptor E$w.d$ is used for input and output operations involving real data in exponential form. It provides an alternative to the descriptor F$w.d$ that is especially useful for input and output operations involving very large or very small numbers that cannot conveniently be expressed in decimal form.

On output, the descriptor E$w.d$ instructs the computer to use w positions to print a real datum in the form

$$\pm 0.x_1x_2\ldots x_d E \pm z_1z_2$$

where $x_1x_2 \ldots x_d$ represents the d most significant digits of the number being printed and E $\pm z_1z_2$ denotes the exponent. For example, if A = -123.45 is printed by using E12.5, the output will be

$$-0.12345E+02$$

The d most significant digits are obtained by rounding and the number is printed right-justified in the output field of w print positions. Thus, if B = 2.3481 is printed by using E12.3, the constant 2.3481 is first rounded to three significant digits to obtain 2.35. This number is then printed as

$$\Delta\Delta\Delta0.235E+01$$

Note that the leading + sign is not printed when the number being output is nonnegative.

The form E $\pm z_1z_2$ does not provide for exponents greater in magnitude than 99. Systems that allow three digit exponents print them in the form $\pm z_1z_2z_3$ (the E is not printed). For example, if A = 2.135×10^{150} is printed by using E12.4, the output will be

$$\Delta\Delta0.2135+151$$

When using E$w.d$ to specify the form of an output value, w must be large enough to accommodate the number being printed. Since the form of the output is

$$\pm 0.x_1x_2\ldots x_d E \pm z_1z_2$$

we see (by counting) that w must satisfy

$$w \geq d + 7$$

(7 positions are occupied by the characters $\pm 0.$ and E $\pm z_1z_2$). What happens if w is not large enough is system dependent. Although some systems will print the correct value with a special character indicating that enough space was not specified, others will print w asterisks in the allotted w positions instead of the number.

EXAMPLE 11. Printing real data by using E$w.d$

Value to be printed	Edit descriptor	Output
123456.	E14.4	$\Delta\Delta\Delta\Delta0.1235E+06$
$-123.$	E14.4	$\Delta\Delta\Delta-0.1230E+03$
.0005281	E10.3	$\Delta0.528E-03$
-7.23456	E10.6	*********

In the first example, E14.4 says to print 123456. by using four significant digits. Thus, 123456. is rounded to 123500. and 0.1235 is printed, followed by the exponent E + 06 needed to represent 123500.

In the second example, E14.4 says to print − 123. by using four significant digits. These are 1230; hence, − 0.1230 is printed, followed by the exponent E + 03 needed to represent − 123.0.

In the third example, E10.3 says to print .0005281 by using three significant digits. These are 528; so 0.528 is printed, followed by the exponent E − 03 needed to represent .000528.

In the last example, E10.6 says to print − 7.23456 by using six significant digits. This means that − 0.723456E + 01 must be printed. But this requires more than the ten positions specified in E10.6; hence the output field is filled with 10 asterisks.

EXAMPLE 12. A program to read and print real data:

```
      READ(5,10)A,B
10    FORMAT(2F10.0)
      C=A+B
      WRITE(6,20)A,B,C
20    FORMAT(1X,'A=',E14.6/1X,'B=',E14.6/1X'A+B=',E14.6)
      STOP
      END
```

Input Data:

```
         1         2         3         4
1234567890123456789012345678901234567890
 .001234 2.100003
```

Output:

```
A=  0.123400E-02
B=  0.210000E+01
A+B=  0.210124E+01
```

Since the value 2.100003 of B is to be printed by using six significant digits, it is first rounded to 2.10000. Similarly, A + B = 2.101237 is rounded to 2.10124 before being printed.

Remark 1: A + B is evaluated by using the values input for A and B, and not the rounded values. When a value is rounded to fit an output specification such as E14.6, the value of the variable is not affected.

Remark 2: Note that values for A and B are read by using F descriptors and printed by using E descriptors. This emphasizes that F and E descriptors are both used for I/O operations involving real-type data.

On input, the descriptor E$w.d$ instructs the computer to interpret the next w input characters (the input field) to obtain a real value for the variable being read. If the input field does not contain an exponent (the letter E followed by a positive or negative exponent), E$w.d$ is exactly equivalent to F$w.d$. In the next example we illustrate how the descriptor E$w.d$ interprets an input field containing an exponent.

EXAMPLE 13. We describe how the formatted READ statement

```
      READ(5,10)A,B
10    FORMAT(E10.2,E10.3)
```

interprets the following input record to obtain values for the real variables A and B:

```
        1         2
12345678901234567890
   1234E+03  -  64E  1
```

(Note that this input record contains no decimal point.)

The 10 in E10.2 says to use the first ten characters ΔΔ1234E + 03 to obtain a real value for A. The characters ΔΔ1234 preceding the letter E are interpreted as follows. The 2 in E10.2 indicates that 34, the two rightmost of these, are fractional digits. Thus, ΔΔ1234 is interpreted as 12.34. This value is then multiplied by 10^3 as specified by the exponent E + 03 to obtain A = 12.34E3 (equivalently, 12340.).

Similarly, the descriptor E10.3 says to use the next ten characters ΔΔ − Δ64EΔΔ1 to obtain a value for B. This time the 3 in E10.3 indicates that the three characters Δ64 immediately preceding the letter E are fractional digits; thus, ΔΔ − Δ64 becomes − .064 (recall that, on input, blanks are interpreted as zeros). The exponent EΔΔ1 is simply E001, hence − .064E1 (or − 0.64) is assigned to B.

Remark: If the first ten characters in the input record are changed to

```
        1
1234567890 12345
   1234E+3
```

A will be assigned the value 12.34E30. The blank in position ten is counted as a zero.

If the input field being read contains a decimal point, the *d* in E*w.d* is ignored and the value obtained is precisely what appears in the input field. For example, if the variable VAR is read from an input field containing ΔΔ − 1.23E − 5 by using the descriptor E10.0, VAR is assigned the value − 1.23E − 5 (equivalently, − .0000123.). The 0 in E10.0 is ignored—E10.1 or E10.2 could have been used with exactly the same result.

On many FORTRAN systems, the F and E descriptors are identical when used to interpret input data. Indeed, the FORTRAN standard describes the F descriptor on input to be equivalent to the E descriptor as described in this section.

8.8 Problems

1. What will be printed by the given formatted WRITE statements if I, J, X, and Y have the following values?

```
I = 27        X = 123.457
J = 216       Y = − 45.273
```

a.
```
      WRITE(6,10)I,X,J,Y
   10 FORMAT(1X,2(I3,2X,F7.2/1X))
```

b.
```
      WRITE(6,11)X,Y,I,J
   11 FORMAT(1X,2F8.3//1X,2(I6,2X))
```

c.
```
      WRITE(6,12)I,J
   12 FORMAT(1X,5('-'),'INTEGERS',5('-')/1X,2I9)
```

d.
```
      WRITE(6,13)
   13 FORMAT(1X,5X,5('X')/1X,6X,4('X')/1X,7X,3('X'))
```

e.
```
      WRITE(6,14)I,X,J,Y
   14 FORMAT(1X,'FIRST VALUE',I4,2X,'SECOND VALUE',F7.2//)
```

f.
```
      WRITE(6,15)
   15 FORMAT(1X,'*'/1X,2('X')/1X,3('X'))
```

2. Describe the effect of each formatted READ statement if the input data are as follows:

```
          1         2         3
12345678901234567890123456789 0
 1234E+3  5678E-03 1.234E004
```

a.
```
      READ(5,10)A,B
   10 FORMAT(E10.3,10X,E10.0)
```

b.
```
      READ(5,11)A,B,C
   11 FORMAT(3E10.2)
```

c.
```
      READ(5,12)A,B,C
   12 FORMAT(3(2X,E8.1))
```

d.
```
      READ(5,13)A,B,C
   13 FORMAT(E7.2,4X,E10.4,F5.0)
```

3. What will be printed when each program is run?

a.
```
      N=0
      DO 1 I=1,5
        N=10*N+I
        WRITE(6,10)I,N
    1 CONTINUE
      STOP
   10 FORMAT(1X,'TIME NO.',I2,5('*'),I5)
      END
```

b.
```
      DO 1 I=1,7
        IF(I.EQ.4) THEN
          WRITE(6,11)
        ELSE
          WRITE(6,12)
        END IF
    1 CONTINUE
   11 FORMAT(1X,7('H'))
   12 FORMAT(1X,'H',5X,'H')
      STOP
      END
```

Write a program to perform each task specified in Problems 4–6.

4. Print a rectangular array of A's with ten rows and eight columns. (Use a loop and repeat specifications.)

5. Print a row of fifteen A's beginning in print position 21 and a row of thirteen B's centered under the A's. (Use repeat specifications but only one FORMAT statement.)

6. Print the following design. Use only two FORMAT statements and, in each, use repeat specifications.

```
XXXXXXXXXXXX
X      X      X
X      X      X
X      X      X
XXXXXXXXXXXX
X      X      X
X      X      X
X      X      X
XXXXXXXXXXXX
```

8.9 Review True-or-False Quiz

1. The first character generated by a formatted WRITE statement is not necessarily a carriage control character.   T   F
2. If three consecutive slashes are encountered in an output format specification, three print lines will be skipped.   T   F
3. If all input data for a FORTRAN program are to be typed at a time-sharing terminal, it makes little sense to use slash edit descriptors in writing the formatted READ statements.   T   F
4. Using slash edit descriptors in FORMAT statements used to interpret input data can be useful if an existing collection of input records is to be processed.   T   F
5. The expression 6/ encountered in an output format specification will cause five print lines to be skipped.   T   F
6. The format specification (2(F7.2,F6.0)) is equivalent to (F7.2,F6.0,F7.2,F6.0).   T   F
7. The descriptor '*****' can be written as 5'*'.   T   F
8. To repeat a group of edit descriptors, you need only enclose the group in parentheses and precede this by a nonzero unsigned integer that specifies how many times the group is to be repeated.   T   F
9. If VAR = .00123 is printed by using the descriptor E12.4, the output will be $\Delta\Delta 0.0123E-01$.   T   F
10. If VAR = -1.5996 is printed by using the descriptor E8.4, the output will be $-0.1600E+01$.   T   F
11. If the input field $-\Delta\Delta\Delta 1235E+05$ is read by using E12.4, the value obtained will be equal to -12350.   T   F
12. The DATA statement is used to process input data.   T   F
13. READ statements whose purpose is to initialize variables are better replaced by DATA statements.   T   F

9 Arrays and Subscripted Variables

If we wish to examine all numbers in a list to count those less than 50 and those greater than 50, and then to perform some calculation on these counts, two variable names must be used to store the two counts. If more than two counts are involved, more than two variables must be used. This situation poses a real problem when only the FORTRAN variables considered to this point are available. (These variables henceforth will be called **simple variables.**) Imagine the complexity of a program using as many as 100 different simple variables. To be useful, a programming language must provide the means for handling such problems efficiently. FORTRAN meets this requirement with the inclusion of **subscripted variables.** These variables may be referenced simply by specifying their numerical subscripts. They not only resolve the difficulty cited but also greatly simplify numerous programming tasks involving large quantities of data. In this chapter the FORTRAN subscripted variables will be described and illustrated.

9.1 One-Dimensional Arrays

A **one-dimensional array** is an ordered collection of items in the sense that there is a first item, a second item, and so on. For example, if you have taken five quizzes during a semester and received grades of 71, 83, 96, 77, and 92, you have a one-dimensional array in which the first grade is 71, the second grade is 83, and so forth. In mathematics we might use the following subscripted notation:

$$n_1 = 71$$
$$n_2 = 83$$
$$n_3 = 96$$
$$n_4 = 77$$
$$n_5 = 92$$

However, since the FORTRAN character set does not include subscripts, the notation is changed:

$$N(1) = 71$$
$$N(2) = 83$$
$$N(3) = 96$$
$$N(4) = 77$$
$$N(5) = 92$$

We say that the *name* of the array is N, that N(1), N(2), N(3), N(4), and N(5) are *subscripted* variables, and that 1, 2, 3, 4, and 5 are the *subscripts* of N. N(1) is read **N sub 1** and in general N(I) is read **N sub I.** N(1) and N1 are different variables and can be used in the same program; the computer has no problem distinguishing between them.

The array N can be visualized as follows:

	1	2	3	4	5
N	71	83	96	77	92

The name of the array appears to the left, the subscripts above each entry, and the entries inside, just below their subscripts. Names that are acceptable for simple variables are also admissible array names.

An array has a type as well as a name. Like simple variables, an array can be declared in a type statement. (How to do this is explained in Section 9.2.) If not so declared, an array is of type *integer* when the first letter of its name is I, J, K, L, M, or N; otherwise its type is *real*. An integer array can contain only integer values and a real array can contain only reals.

The value of a subscripted variable—that is, an entry in an array—is referenced in a program just as values of simple variables are referenced. For example, the two assignment statements

$$N(1) = 71$$
$$N(6) = N(1) + 12$$

assign 71 to the subscripted variable N(1) and 83 to N(6); that is, 71 and 83 are assigned as the first and sixth entries of array N.

Arrays provide one significant advantage over simple variables—namely, the subscripts may be variables or other numerical expressions rather than just integer constants. We illustrate by example.

EXAMPLE 1. Here is a program segment to read five entries for an array N:

```
    DO 1 I=1,5
        READ(5,10)N(I)
  1 CONTINUE
 10 FORMAT(I3)
```

Input Data:

```
          1         2
 12345678901234567890
  71
  83
  96
  77
  92
```

On each pass through the loop, the DO-variable I serves as the subscript. The first time through the loop, I has the value 1; hence the statement READ(5,10)N(I) assigns the value 71 to N(1). Similarly, N(2) through N(5) are assigned their respective values during the remaining four passes through the loop.

EXAMPLE 2. Here is a program segment to calculate the sum SUM of the odd-numbered entries in an array N that contains five integers. This sum is then stored as the sixth entry of N.

```
    INTEGER SUM
    SUM=0
    DO 2 K=1,3
        SUM=SUM+N(2*K-1)
  2 CONTINUE
    N(6)=SUM
```

On the first pass through the loop the DO-variable K is 1, so the subscript $2*K - 1$ has the value $2*(1) - 1 = 1$. Thus, $N(2*K - 1)$ refers to $N(1)$, and this value is added to SUM. On the second pass, $2*K - 1$ has the value $2*(2) - 1 = 3$, so that $N(3)$ is added to SUM. Similarly, $N(5)$ is added to SUM on the third pass. After the loop has been satisfied, the value of SUM is assigned to $N(6)$. At this point both SUM and $N(6)$ have the same value.

The appearance of the same array name (N in the following example) in two DO-loops, each using a different DO-variable (I and J in the example), often causes some difficulty for the beginning programmer.

EXAMPLE 3. Here is a program segment that increases each entry of an array N by 2 and then stores the resulting values in a second array M, but in the reverse order:

```
    DO 3 I=1,5
        N(I)=N(I)+2
  3 CONTINUE
    DO 4 J=1,5
        M(J)=N(6-J)
  4 CONTINUE
```

Let's assume that prior to execution of this program segment, the array N is read as in Example 1. Pictorially,

	1	2	3	4	5
N	71	83	96	77	92

The first loop (the I loop) adds 2 to each entry in N.

	1	2	3	4	5
N	73	85	98	79	94

The second loop (the J loop) creates a new array M. For $J = 1$, the assignment statement is $M(1) = N(5)$; for $J = 2$, $M(2) = N(4)$; and so on. Thus, after execution of this second loop, M is as follows:

	1	2	3	4	5
M	94	79	98	85	73

Remark 1: Creating new arrays that are modifications of existing arrays is a common programming task. In this example, the entries in the array M are a rearrangement of the entries in array N. Note that the creation of array M by the J loop in no way modifies the existing array N.

Remark 2: Although it is common practice to refer to the symbols N(I) and M(J) as variables, remember that the actual variable names are N(1), N(2), N(3), and so on. Each time the assignment statements are executed, I and J have particular values indicating which of these variables is being referenced.

In the preceding three examples we have used integer constants, integer variables, and integer expressions as subscripts. In particular, I was used in Example 1, $2*K-1$ and 6 in Example 2, and in Example 3 we used I, J, and 6-J. The FORTRAN standard states that any integer expression is admissible as a subscript. However, many FORTRAN compilers are more restrictive in what forms are allowed as subscripts. Specifically, many compilers allow only subscripts in the five forms

$$m \qquad v \qquad v+m \qquad m*v \qquad m*v+n$$

where m and n denote integer constants and v denotes an integer variable. Each of the subscripts we have used is one of these five forms except the subscript 6-J used in Example 3. On systems that restrict subscripts in this manner, the DO-loop

```
      DO 4 J=1,5
         M(J)=N(6-J)
    4 CONTINUE
```

appearing in Example 3 can be written as follows:

```
      DO 4 J=1,5
         K=6-J
         M(J)=N(K)
    4 CONTINUE
```

This replaces the inadmissible subscript 6-J with the equivalent admissible subscript K.

9.2 The DIMENSION Statement

There is nothing in a symbolic name such as N, SUM, or VAR that tells whether it is a variable name or an array name. You must provide the FORTRAN compiler with this information. The DIMENSION statement is used for this purpose. The statement

DIMENSION N(10)

informs the compiler that N is the name of an array and that its size (the number of entries in the array) is ten. When the compiler encounters this statement, it reserves ten storage units in memory for the ten entries in N. These ten storage units correspond to the subscripted variables N(1), N(2), . . . , N(10).

DIMENSION statements must appear before the first executable statement in a program. DIMENSION statements themselves are nonexecutable. Their sole purpose is to provide certain information needed to compile the program; they cause nothing to happen during program execution.

EXAMPLE 4. Here is a program segment to read N values into an array SALES:

```
      DIMENSION SALES(50)
C READ THE COUNT N
      READ(5,10)N
C READ N ENTRIES INTO THE ARRAY SALES
      DO 1 K=1,N
         READ(5,11)SALES(K)
    1 CONTINUE
   10 FORMAT(I2)
   11 FORMAT(F10.2)
```

Input Data:

```
        1         2         3
123456789012345678901234567890
 6
     12.52
     47.90
    155.83
    180.00
    384.15
     85.50
```

This program segment works as follows:

1. The DIMENSION statement reserves fifty storage units in memory for the real array SALES. This allows us to use any of the fifty subscripted variables SALES(1), SALES(2), . . . , SALES(50).

2. The statement READ(5,10)N reads the first input record to obtain N = 6.

3. The DO-loop then reads input values for the first six entries SALES(1), SALES(2), . . . , SALES(6) of the array SALES.

Remark: For the segment shown, only the first six entries of SALES are used. The space reserved for SALES(7) through SALES(50), although available, is simply not used.

To declare INTRST as the name of a *real* one-dimensional array of size 40 you can write

REAL INTRST
DIMENSION INTRST(40)

or combine these into the equivalent type statement

REAL INTRST(40)

If you use this combined form, you must not include INTRST(40) in a separate DIMENSION statement. Thus, arrays can be declared in a DIMENSION statement or in a type statement, but not both.

When coding a program that will read input data into an array, you must see to it that the DIMENSION or type statement specifies an array large enough to accommodate all of the input values. Thus, if you know in advance that your program will never be required to read more than 1,000 values into an array A, the statement

DIMENSION A(1000)

or the equivalent

REAL A(1000)

will suffice. However, remember that this statement actually reserves 1,000 storage units in the computer's memory; that is, your program will tie up these 1,000 storage units whether or not a particular run of the program uses them. This means that you must not only ensure that your array is large enough, but you should keep it as small as possible.

The program segment in Example 4 shows how data can be read into an array when the number of values to be read is known in advance; in the example, this number is the first input value. Many programming applications require that data terminated with an EOD-tag be read into an array. The following example shows how this can be done.

EXAMPLE 5. Here is a program segment to read input data into an array K:

```
        DIMENSION K(100)
        I=0
C READ A VALUE AND COMPARE IT WITH THE EOD TAG 9999
      1 I=I+1
        READ(5,10)K(I)
        IF (K(I).NE.9999) GO TO 1
C N DENOTES THE ACTUAL SIZE OF ARRAY K
        N=I-1
```

The counter I keeps track of the subscript. Each time a value is read for K(I) it is compared with the EOD-tag 9999. If K(I) does not equal 9999, the subscript I is increased by 1 and another value is read. When the EOD-tag is read, we have K(I) = 9999; that is, the EOD-tag is in the Ith position of the array. Control then passes to the statement N = I − 1 so that N specifies the number of values, exclusive of the EOD-tag, read into the array. In any further processing of this array we would use N to specify its length.

More than one DIMENSION statement may appear in a program, and each DIMENSION statement may be used to dimension more than one array. The FORTRAN statement

DIMENSION A(100),X(50),ITEM(5)

is admissible and will reserve a sequence of 155 memory storage units: 100 for the real array A, 50 for the real array X, and 5 for the integer array ITEM.

When using arrays in programs, you must guard against subscripts not specified in your DIMENSION statements. If a program includes the above DIMENSION statement and incorrectly references A(101), the computer will normally use the 101st storage unit in the sequence of 155 storage units, counting from the 1st. If this happens to be X(1), the statement SUM = SUM + A(101) will simply add the value of X(1) to SUM and you may never detect the error. In light of this discussion, the following caution should be observed.

Caution:
Subscripts must remain in the range specified in DIMENSION statements. If a subscript exceeds this range, your computer may not detect an error and may simply produce incorrect results.

The following two examples illustrate programming situations that are easily handled if you use arrays, but that would pose serious difficulties if arrays were not included in the FORTRAN language.

EXAMPLE 6. Here is a program to reduce each of N input values by the average AV of all the input values:

```
        REAL LIST(100),VAL,SUM,AV
        INTEGER I,N
C READ ARRAY LIST AND FIND THE AVERAGE AV
        READ(5,10)N
        SUM=0.
        DO 1 I=1,N
           READ(5,11)LIST(I)
           SUM=SUM+LIST(I)
      1 CONTINUE
        AV=SUM/FLOAT(N)
C REDUCE ENTRIES IN LIST BY AV AND PRINT
        WRITE(6,12)AV
        DO 2 I=1,N
           VAL=LIST(I)-AV
           WRITE(6,13)VAL
      2 CONTINUE
```

```
10 FORMAT(I3)
11 FORMAT(F10.0)
12 FORMAT(1X,'INPUT VALUES REDUCED BY THEIR AVERAGE',F6.2)
13 FORMAT(1X,F10.2)
   STOP
   END
```

Input Data:

```
        1         2         3
123456789012345678901234567890
 5
     89.25
     45.50
     23.25
     74.60
     62.40
```

Output:

```
INPUT VALUES REDUCED BY THEIR AVERAGE 59.00
     30.25
    -13.50
    -35.75
     15.60
      3.40
```

The first type statement reserves 100 storage units in memory for the real array LIST. The rest of the program has two distinct parts as indicated by the two comment lines. In the first part the input values are read into the array LIST and the average AV is calculated. In the second part, the average AV is subtracted from each value in LIST and the difference is printed.

Remark 1: The second part of the program, subtracting AV from each input value, cannot be accomplished without first finding this average. This means that each input value must be used twice, first to determine AV and a second time to reduce it by AV. Reading all input values into the array LIST allowed us to reference each input value a second time as required.

Remark 2: The first line of the program shows that simple variables and arrays can be declared in the same type statement.

EXAMPLE 7. A list of integers, all between 1 and 100, is to be input. Let's write a program to determine how many of each integer are included. We assume that 9999 terminates the list.

Problem Analysis:
We must determine 100 counts: the number of 1's, the number of 2's, and so on. Let's use COUNT(1), COUNT(2), . . . , COUNT(100) to store these counts. Each input value must be read to determine which of the 100 integers it is. If it is 87, then COUNT(87) must be increased by 1; if it is 24, then COUNT(24) must be increased by 1. Using NUM to denote the number being read, we may write the following algorithm.

a. Initialize: COUNT(J) = 0 for J = 1 to 100.
b. Read a value for NUM.
c. If NUM = 9999, print the results and stop.
d. Add 1 to COUNT(NUM) and repeat step (b).

Let's conserve paper by printing two columns, containing NUM and COUNT(NUM), but suppressing the printout whenever COUNT(NUM) = 0 (that is, if NUM is not in the given list). The following flowchart segment shows how to do this.

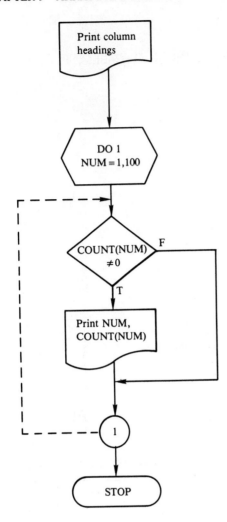

The Program:

```
C **************A COUNTING PROGRAM**************
      INTEGER COUNT(100),NUM
C INITIALIZE COUNTERS
      DO 2 J=1,100
         COUNT(J)=0
    2 CONTINUE
C READ NUM AND ADD 1 TO COUNT(NUM)
C UNTIL EOD TAB 9999 IS READ
    3 READ(5,10)NUM
         IF(NUM.EQ.9999) GO TO 4
            COUNT(NUM)=COUNT(NUM)+1
         GO TO 3
C PRINT FREQUENCY TABLE
    4 WRITE(6,11)
      DO 1 NUM=1,100
         IF(COUNT(NUM).NE.0) WRITE(6,12)NUM,COUNT(NUM)
    1 CONTINUE
      STOP
   10 FORMAT(I5)
```

```
 11 FORMAT(1X,'DATA VALUE',5X,'FREQUENCY'/)
 12 FORMAT(1X,I5,10X,I5)
    END
```

Input Data:

```
          1         2         3
12345678901234567890123456789O
    80
    80
    60
    50
    50
    50
    41
    32
    32
  9999
```

Output:

```
DATA VALUE       FREQUENCY

    32               2
    41               1
    50               3
    60               1
    80               2
```

The preceding program uses the loop

```
    DO 2 I=1,100
       COUNT(I)=0
  2 CONTINUE
```

to initialize each entry in the integer array COUNT to zero. This can be accomplished with a DATA statement by writing

    DATA COUNT/100*0/

As explained in Section 8.4, 100*0 is an abbreviation for a list of 100 0's. Since COUNT was dimensioned as an integer array of size 100, its 100 entries COUNT(1), COUNT(2), . . . , COUNT(100) are all initialized to zero. The following example illustrates the DATA statement as it is used with arrays.

EXAMPLE 8.

a.
```
    DIMENSION LIST(50),SLRY(25)
    DATA LIST,SLRY/50*0,25*0./
```

The 50 entries in the integer array LIST are initialized to the integer value 0 (50*0 specifies these 50 initial values) and the 25 entries in the real array SLRY are initialized to the real value 0 (25*0. specifies these 25 initial values).

b.
```
    REAL A(100),B(100)
    INTEGER C(50)
    DATA A,B,C/200*1.5,25*0,25*100/
```

The 100 entries in each of the arrays A and B are initialized to 1.5 (200*1.5 specifies these 200 initial values). Since C denotes an integer array of size 50, it is assigned the next 50 initial values. The first 25 are 0's, so C(1) through C(25) are initialized to 0. The next 25 are 100's, so C(26) through C(50) are initialized to 100.

```
c.  REAL LIST
    DIMENSION LIST(500)
    DATA X,LIST(1),LIST(500)/3*0./
```

The simple variable X and the subscripted variables LIST(1) and LIST(500) are all initialized to the real value 0. (3*0. specifies these three initial values.) The other 498 entries in LIST are not initialized.

The following form of the DATA statement was illustrated in Example 8:

DATA **vlist** / **clist** /

In this statement **vlist** denotes a list of variable (simple or subscripted) and array names; **clist** denotes a list of terms of the form c and $n*c$ where c denotes a constant and n denotes a nonzero, unsigned integer. The constants specified in **clist** are the initial values for the variables and array entries specified in **vlist**. The number of constants specified in **clist** must be the same as the number of variables and array entries specified in **vlist**. The assignment of values is determined by the order indicated in the two lists.

We conclude this section with an example illustrating again how the method of step-wise refinement leads finally to a program that is easy to read and, barring syntax errors, certain to be correct.

EXAMPLE 9. At the end of each month, a wholesale firm makes an inventory that shows, for each item in stock, the item code, the quantity on hand, and the average cost per unit. Following is a portion of the most recent inventory:

Item code	Units on hand	Average cost/unit
1015	844	1.63
1230	182	5.93
.	.	.
.	.	.
.	.	.

We are asked to prepare an inventory report that contains the given information and also the total cost of the inventory by item. In addition, a second short report is to be printed identifying the item (or items) whose inventory represents the greatest cost to the company. The report should have the form

WAREHOUSE INVENTORY REPORT

ITEM CODE	UNITS ON HAND	AV.COST/UNIT	TOTAL COST
1015	844	1.63	_____
1230	182	5.93	_____
.	.	.	.
.	.	.	.
.	.	.	.

ITEM _____ REPRESENTS MAXIMUM COST _____

Note that

Total cost = (Units on hand) × (Average cost per unit)

Problem Analysis:
Let's begin with the following simple algorithm:

a. Prepare the inventory report.
b. Determine the item (or items) whose inventory represents the greatest cost.

Although this two-step algorithm is simply a restatement of the problem statement, it serves to segment the given task into two slightly more manageable subtasks.

Writing a program segment to produce a printed report such as the one required in step (a) is not new to you. After printing a report title and appropriate column headings for the values to be printed, you can process the data, item by item, to determine and print these values.

To carry out step (b), you must find the greatest total cost of all items in stock and then compare the total cost for each item with this largest value. Thus, step (b) can be broken down into the two simpler tasks (b1) and (b2) shown in the following refined algorithm:

a.   Prepare the inventory report.
b1. Determine the greatest total cost of all items in stock.
b2. Print a report identifying each item whose inventory represents this greatest cost figure.

The task of finding the largest number in a set of numbers is likewise not new to you. You simply go through the list of total cost amounts one at a time, always keeping track of the largest of the amounts encountered. To carry out step (b2) you must again go through the list of total cost amounts, item by item, and compare each with the largest amount found in step (b1).

There are three subtasks to be performed and, having considered briefly how each can be carried out, we now consider how to carry them out in the FORTRAN language. Let's agree to present each line of the inventory data in a separate input record. Thus, each record will contain the three values associated with a single stock item. The first record in the following typical input data shows an item code of 1015, 844 units on hand, and an average cost per unit of \$1.63. Three 0's are used to denote the end of the data.

Input Data:

```
          1         2         3         4
1234567890123456789012345678901234567890
1015      844       1.63
1230      182       5.93
   :         :         :
   :         :         :
   0         0         0
```

The next task is to choose variable names. Since the input data must be used more than once (for instance, in step (b2) the list of item codes must be available for printing), we'll use three one-dimensional arrays to store these data. A fourth array will be used to store the total cost amounts for the individual inventory items—they are needed in each of the three steps. In addition, we need a variable for the largest amount to be found in step (b1). Let's use the following names for these arrays and variables:

ITEM   = Array of item codes.
QUANT = Array containing units on hand for each item.
COST   = Array containing average cost per unit for each item.
TOTAL = Array containing total cost for each item.
GREAT = Largest value in the array TOTAL.

Since all input data are to be stored in arrays, step (a) can be broken down into the two simpler steps, (a1) and (a2), shown in the following algorithm.

Algorithm (final refined form):
a1. Read the input data into the arrays ITEM, QUANT, and COST.
a2. Determine values for the array TOTAL and print the inventory report.
b1. Determine the greatest total cost of all items in stock. (This is the largest value in the array TOTAL.)
b2. Print a report identifying each item whose inventory represents this greatest cost figure.

Coding this algorithm is not difficult if it is done one step at a time. While coding steps (a2) and (b2), we must of course refer to the form of the output specified in the problem statement.

The Program:

```
C*******************INVENTORY PROGRAM*******************
C
      INTEGER ITEM(50),QUANT(50)
      REAL COST(50),TOTAL(50),GREAT
C ITEM  = ITEM CODE NUMBERS
C QUANT = QUANTITIES ON HAND
C COST  = AVERAGE COSTS PER UNIT
C TOTAL = TOTAL COSTS OF INDIVIDUAL ITEMS
C GREAT = LARGEST VALUE IN ARRAY TOTAL
C
C READ INPUT DATA INTO ARRAY
      DO 1 I=1,50
          READ(5,10)ITEM(I),QUANT(I),COST(I)
          IF(ITEM(I).EQ.0) GO TO 2
    1 CONTINUE
C     ***INADEQUATE ARRAY DIMENSIONS***
      STOP
    2 N=I-1
C     ***THERE ARE N INVENTORY ITEMS***
C
C DETERMINE TOTAL COST AMOUNTS AND
C PRINT THE INVENTORY REPORT
C     ***PRINT REPORT TITLE AND COLUMN HEADINGS***
      WRITE(6,11)
      WRITE(6,12)
C     ***CALCULATE AND PRINT TABLE VALUES***
      DO 3 I=1,N
          TOTAL(I)=QUANT(I)*COST(I)
          WRITE(6,13)ITEM(I),QUANT(I),COST(I),TOTAL(I)
    3 CONTINUE
C
C DETERMINE THE GREATEST TOTAL COST AMOUNT
      GREAT=TOTAL(1)
      DO 4 I=2,N
          IF(TOTAL(I).GT.GREAT) GREAT=TOTAL(I)
    4 CONTINUE
C
C PRINT REPORT OF ITEM (ITEMS) WHOSE
C INVENTORY REPRESENTS THE GREATEST COST
      DO 5 I=1 TO N
          IF(TOTAL(I).EQ.GREAT) WRITE(6,14)ITEM(I),GREAT
    5 CONTINUE
      STOP
   10 FORMAT(I4,3X,I4,3X,F6.2)
   11 FORMAT(1X,15X,'WAREHOUSE INVENTORY REPORT'/)
   12 FORMAT(1X,'ITEM CODE',4X,'UNITS ON HAND',4X,
      +      'AV.COST/UNIT',4X,'TOTAL COST'/)
   13 FORMAT(1X,2X,I4,10X,I5,10X,F7.2,8X,F8.2)
   14 FORMAT(1X/1X,'ITEM',I5,' REPRESENTS MAXIMUM COST',F8.2)
      END
```

Input Data:

```
         1              2          3           4
12345678901234567890123456789012345678901234567890
1015      844      1.63
1230      182      5.93
2561      467      4.37
9856      764      5.62
3756      875      4.73
3321      636      2.64
1437      292      9.63
5738     1067      3.78
2364      532      7.41
7576      103     11.53
   0        0        0
```

Output:

```
              WAREHOUSE INVENTORY REPORT


ITEM CODE     UNITS ON HAND     AV.COST/UNIT     TOTAL COST

   1015           844               1.63          1375.72
   1230           182               5.93          1079.26
   2561           467               4.37          2040.79
   9856           764               5.62          4293.68
   3756           877               4.73          4148.21
   3321           636               2.64          1679.04
   1437           292               9.63          2811.96
   5738          1067               3.78          4033.26
   2364           532               7.41          3942.12
   7576           103              11.53          1187.59
```

ITEM 9856 REPRESENTS MAXIMUM COST 4293.68

Remark: The job of finding the greatest cost GREAT (step (b1)) could have been accomplished by modifying the program segment written for step (a2). The resulting program would have been slightly shorter, but not necessarily better. Indeed, combining tasks during the coding process can easily lead to serious programming errors. The problem analysis we carried out led us to consider four separate tasks. The program is segmented into four parts corresponding to these tasks. They are identified in the comment statements. As a result, the program is easy to read and understand, even though it may be slightly longer than necessary. In addition, because of the systematic way in which tasks were broken down into simpler tasks, we can be confident that, barring syntax errors, the program is absolutely correct.

The problem analysis carried out in the preceding example can be displayed in a diagram as follows:

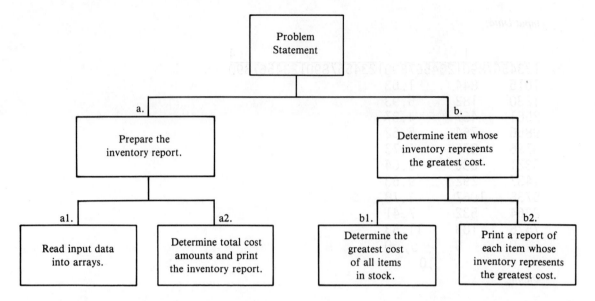

At the "top" is the problem statement. It contains a complete description of what is to be done. The two tasks at the next "lower" level show how the problem was broken down into two slightly simpler tasks (the first algorithm). While carrying out the problem analysis, each of these two tasks was again broken into slightly simpler subtasks as shown at the bottom level. It was then found that each of the terminal tasks, steps (a1), (a2), (b1), and (b2), could easily be translated into a FORTRAN program segment. Hence, no further subdivision was carried out.

9.3 Problems

1. What will be printed when each program is run?

a.
```
      DIMENSION M(2)
      K=2
      READ(5,10)M(K),M(1)
      DO 1 I=1,2
         WRITE(6,20)M(I)
    1 CONTINUE
   10 FORMAT(I2,2X,I2)
   20 FORMAT(1X,I2)
      STOP
      END
```

b.
```
      DIMENSION K(5)
      J=1
      READ(5,10)K(J)
      DO 1 I=1,3
         READ(5,10)K(I+1)
         WRITE(6,20)K(I)
    1 CONTINUE
   10 FORMAT(I3)
   20 FORMAT(1X,I3)
      STOP
      END
```

Input Data:

a.
```
            1         2
 12345678901234567890
    4    5
    7    3
```

Input Data:

b.
```
            1         2
 12345678901234567890
    3
    1
    5
    6
    8
```

2. Explain what is wrong with each of the following.

a.
```
        SUM=0.
        DIMENSION A(10)
        DO 1 I=1,10
            READ(5,10)A(I)
            SUM=SUM+A(I)
      1 CONTINUE
        WRITE(6,11)SUM
     10 FORMAT(F10.2)
     11 FORMAT(1X,F12.2)
        STOP
        END
```

b.
```
        READ(5,10)N
        INTEGER LIST(N),SUM
        DO 1 I=1,N
            READ(5,10)LIST(I)
            SUM=SUM+LIST(I)
      1 CONTINUE
        WRITE(6,11)SUM
     10 FORMAT(I3)
     11 FORMAT(1X,'SUM IS',I5)
        STOP
        END
```

c.
```
        INTEGER M(10),N(10)
        DO 1 I=1,10
            M(I)=I
      1 CONTINUE
        DO 2 J=1,10
            N(2*J)=M(J)
      2 CONTINUE
        DO 3 K=1,10
            WRITE(6,10)M(K),N(K)
      3 CONTINUE
     10 FORMAT(1X,2I5)
        STOP
        END
```

d.
```
C PROGRAM SEGMENT TO REVERSE
C THE ORDER IN AN ARRAY L
C PREVIOUSLY DIMENSIONED
C TO BE OF LENGTH 10
        DO 1 K=1,10
            N=11-K
            L(N)=L(K)
      1 CONTINUE
```

Write a program to perform each task specified in Problems 3–16.

3. Input a list of data values of undetermined length and print the values in reverse order. Use an EOD-tag to terminate the data list.

4. Five data values are to be read into an array B as follows. The first value is to be assigned to B(1) and B(10), the second to B(2) and B(9), and so on. The array B is then to be printed, and five more values are to be read in the same manner. This process is to continue until all data values have been processed. Your program is to come to an orderly halt.

5. Ten values are to be read into an array Y. Then a new array X containing 20 values is to be created so that the odd-numbered entries in X contain zeros and the even-numbered entries are the entries of Y in the same order. Print both arrays.

6. Read 20 values into an array A, and print three columns as follows. Column 1 contains the 20 values in the original order; column 2 contains the 20 values in reverse order; column 3 contains the average of the corresponding elements in columns 1 and 2.

7. An undetermined number of integers is to be read into an array LIST. A new array NEWLIS is to be created so that its entries are those entries of LIST which are divisible by 3 or 5 and which are also less than the last value in LIST. The array NEWLIS is then to be printed.

8. An undetermined number of values are to be input. Two arrays POS and NEG are to be created and printed. POS is to contain all positive values and NEG is to contain all negative values. Zeros are to be ignored. Use the number 1E25 as the EOD-tag.

9. Let any three consecutive entries of an integer array L be related to each other by the equation

$$L(J+2) = L(J+1)+L(J).$$

Input two integer values for L(1) and L(2) and generate L(J) for J = 3, . . . , 100, but print L(J) only for J = 10, 20, 30, . . . , 100. (Be sure the values printed by your program are correct.)

10. The following input data show the annual salaries of all the employees in Division 72 of the Manley Corporation. The last value (72) is an EOD-tag.

Input Data:

```
          1         2         3
 1234567890123456789012345 67890
  14000.00
  16200.00
  10195.00
  18432.00
  13360.00
  19300.00
  16450.00
  12180.00
  25640.00
   8420.00
   8900.00
   9270.00
   9620.00
   9940.00
  11200.00
 72
```

Calculate and print the average salary of all employees in Division 72, and then print a list of those salaries exceeding this average.

11. Read the salary data shown in Problem 10 into an array SLRY. Then create a new array DEV as follows. DEV(I) is to be obtained by subtracting SLRY(I) from the average of all the salaries. The arrays SLRY and DEV are then to be printed as a two-column table with column headings SALARY and DEVIATION FROM MEAN.

12. Use the salary data shown in Problem 10 to create two arrays as follows. SALLO is to contain all salaries less than $14,000, and SALHI is to contain the rest. Lists SALLO and SALHI are then to be printed as columns with appropriate column headings.

13. The mean MEAN and standard deviation S of a set of input values are desired. The following method should be used to compute S.
If the numbers are $x_1, x_2, x_3, \ldots, x_n$, then $S = \sqrt{S2/(n-1)}$ where
$$S2 = (x_1 - MEAN)^2 + (x_2 - MEAN)^2 + \cdots + (x_n - MEAN)^2.$$

14. A number of scores, each lying in the range from 0 to 100, are given. These scores are to be used to create an integer array COUNT as follows:

COUNT(1) = a count of those scores S satisfying $S \leq 20$;
COUNT(2) = a count of those scores S satisfying $20 < S \leq 40$;
COUNT(3) = a count of those scores S satisfying $40 < S \leq 60$;
COUNT(4) = a count of those scores S satisfying $60 < S \leq 80$;
COUNT(5) = a count of those scores S satisfying $80 < S \leq 100$.

The results should be printed in tabular form as follows:

INTERVAL	FREQUENCY
0–20	COUNT(1) (actually the value of (COUNT(1))
20–40	COUNT(2)
40–60	COUNT(3)
60–80	COUNT(4)
80–100	COUNT(5)

15. Problem 14 asked for a count of the number of scores in each of five equal-length intervals between 0 and 100. Instead of using five intervals, produce a similar frequency table using N equal-length intervals. The positive integer N is to be read after all of the scores have been read.

16. (Electric Bill Problem.) Given the customer number, the previous month's reading, and the current reading in kilowatt hours (KWH), print a report showing the customer number, the total number of KWH's used, and the total monthly bill. The charges are computed according to the following schedule: $1.41 for the first 14 KWH; the next 85 KWH at $.0389/KWH; the next 200 at $.0214/KWH; the next 300 at $.0134/KWH; and the excess at $.0099/KWH. In addition, there is a fuel adjustment charge of $.0322/KWH for all KWH's used.

Customer number	Previous month's reading	Current reading
2516	25,346	25,973
2634	47,947	48,851
2917	21,342	21,652
2853	893,462	894,258
3576	347,643	348,748
3943	41,241	41,783
3465	887,531	888,165

9.4 Array Input and Output

We have been greatly restricted in the ways in which we can read and print array values. For example, consider the simple task of reading eight input values into an array. If the input data are

```
         1
1234567890
 71
 83
 90
 77
 92
 45
 53
 62
```

we can use the loop

```
   DO 1 I=1,8
      READ(5,10)N(I)
 1 CONTINUE
10 FORMAT(I3)
```

However, if we wish to include all eight input values on one input record, as follows

```
        1         2         3
1234567890123456789012345678 90
 71 83 90 77 92 45 53 62
```

this DO-loop is not appropriate. Changing the format specification (I3) to (8I3) doesn't help; each time the READ statement is executed, a value for N(I) is read from the next input record. Of course, we could use the formatted READ statement

```
   READ(5,10)N(1),N(2),N(3),N(4),N(5),N(6),N(7),N(8)
10 FORMAT(8I3)
```

but this is rather awkward. FORTRAN provides two alternative ways to write such READ statements in a simpler and more compact form. We illustrate these two forms in Examples 10 and 11.

EXAMPLE 10. This example shows that an entire array can be read by including only its name in a READ statement.

```
      DIMENSION N(8)
      READ(5,10)N
10 FORMAT(8I3)
```

Input Data:

```
          1         2         3
12345678901234567890123456789 0
 71 83 90 77 92 45 53 62
```

N is dimensioned to allow subscripts from 1 to 8. The appearance of the array name N in the READ statement causes the computer to read eight values according to the format specification and assign them in order to $N(1)$, $N(2)$, $N(3)$, . . . , $N(8)$. Thus, when an array name appears in a READ statement without any subscript following it, values are read for the *entire* array; the first value read is assigned to position 1, the second to position 2, and so on, until the last position specified in the DIMENSION statement is assigned.

Remark: The eight values in the above record could appear on eight distinct records, if that is desired. You would simply change the edit descriptor (8I3) in the FORMAT statement to (I3) to read one integer from each record. Remember, a READ statement simply indicates the variables being assigned values; the actual input data are interpreted to obtain these values according to the edit descriptors appearing in FORMAT statements.

The preceding example illustrates that the following two program segments are equivalent:

```
DIMENSION N(8)                                           DIMENSION N(8)
   READ(5,10),N(1),N(2),N(3),N(4),N(5),N(6),N(7),N(8)       READ(5,10)N
10 FORMAT(8I3)                                           10 FORMAT(8I3)
```

The second form is not only easier to write, but it can be used to read values for much larger arrays. For example,

```
      DIMENSION N(30)
      READ(5,11)N
11 FORMAT(30I2)
```

will read thirty input fields, of two characters each, from a single input record to obtain thirty values for the array N. If the thirty input values are written ten to a record, you can simply change the format specification (30I2) to (10I2). Similarly,

```
      DIMENSION A(100)
      READ(5,12)A
12 FORMAT(F10.2)
```

will read the first ten characters of each of the "next" 100 input records to obtain one hundred real values for the array A. If the 100 input values are written five to a record, you can simply change the format specification (F10.2) to (5F10.2).

If an array A has been dimensioned to be of size 100 and you wish to read values only for the first five positions A(1), A(2), A(3), A(4), and A(5), you cannot use the array name A in a READ statement since that would indicate that values are to be read for all 100 positions. Rather than using the somewhat awkward statement

READ(5,10)A(1),A(2),A(3),A(4),A(5)

FORTRAN allows you to write

READ(5,10)(A(I),I = 1,5)

The expression (A(I),I = 1,5) is called an **implied-DO list.** It specifies that the input variables for the READ statement are A(1), A(2), A(3), A(4), and A(5), in that order. Thus, the two statements

READ(5,10)A(1),A(2),A(3),A(4),A(5)

and

READ(5,10)(A(I),I = 1,5)

are equivalent.

Similarly, if N has been assigned a positive integer value, the statement

READ(5,10)(A(I),I = 1,N)

is equivalent to a READ statement with the N input variables A(1) through A(N), in that order. Of course, since N is a variable, you cannot write such a statement. Its length depends on N.

The similarity between implied-DO lists and DO-loops should be evident. Indeed, if you wish to read values only for A(1), A(3), A(5), and A(7), you can write

READ(5,10)(A(I),I = 1,7,2)

The implied-DO list (A(I),I = 1,7,2) specifies the input variables A(I), for I = 1 to 7 in increments of 2.

EXAMPLE 11. Here is a program to determine the largest of up to 100 input values:

```
      DIMENSION A(100)
C READ THE COUNT N
      READ(5,10)N
C READ N VALUES INTO ARRAY A
      READ(5,11)(A(K),K=1,N)
C FIND THE LARGEST VALUE BIG
      BIG=A(1)
      DO 1 I=2,N
         IF(BIG.LT.A(I)) BIG=A(I)
    1 CONTINUE
      WRITE(6,12)BIG
      STOP
   10 FORMAT(I3)
   11 FORMAT(3F10.0)
   12 FORMAT(1X,'LARGEST VALUE IS',F10.2)
      END
```

Input Data:

```
          1         2         3         4         5
1234567890123456789012345678901234567890123456789 0
  8
   1726.50    2046.25    1950.00
   2025.36     998.35     872.43
   1968.40    1988.22
```

Output:

```
LARGEST VALUE IS    2046.25
```

This program has three parts as described by the three comment lines. When executed with the given input data, the first part assigns the value 8 to N. In the second part, the input variables for the READ statement are specified by the implied-DO list

(A(K),K = 1,N)

Since N = 8, the input variables are

A(1),A(2),A(3),A(4),A(5),A(6),A(7), and A(8).

The format specification (3F10.0) says to read three input fields of ten characters each from each record until all eight values have been assigned. The third part of the program simply examines the first N entries of A, using the variable BIG to keep track of the largest value.

Remark: If you do not wish to include three input values in each record, you can simply change the format specification (3F10.0). For instance, if the input values appear on distinct records, use (F10.0); if five input values appear on each record, use (5F10.0).

Implied-DO lists can also be used with WRITE and PRINT statements. Remember, an implied-DO list simply indicates a list of variables. Thus,

WRITE(6,10)(N(J),J = 1,5)

is equivalent to

WRITE(6,10)N(1),N(2),N(3),N(4),N(5)

The conciseness of the implied-DO list is apparent. Its usefulness in both input and output statements will be seen in many programs throughout the text. The next example illustrates several implied-DO lists and explains their meanings.

EXAMPLE 12. Implied-DO lists.

  a. (N(K),A(K),K = 1,3) is equivalent to N(1),A(1),N(2),A(2),N(3),A(3).
  b. (N(I),I = 1,2),(A(J),J = 1,3) is equivalent to N(1),N(2),A(1),A(2),A(3).
  c. If I = 2, J = 8, and K = 3, (B(N),N = I,J,K) is equivalent to B(2),B(5),B(8).
  d. (I,A(I),I = 1,3) is an abbreviation for 1,A(1),2,A(2),3,A(3).

  Remark: The implied-DO list in Part (d) must not be used in a READ statement. The variable I acts like a DO-variable; that is, it takes on the successive values 1, 2, and 3 during execution of the READ statement. Reading an input value for I is tantamount to reading an input value for a DO-variable during execution of a DO-loop, and that is not allowed. If this implied-DO list is used to specify an output list, the successive values 1, 2, and 3 of I will be printed. (See Example 13.)

The general form of the implied-DO list as it applies when using one-dimensional arrays is

(list, v = a, b, c)

where **list** denotes a list of variables (simple or subscripted) separated by commas, and **v, a, b,** and **c** are the same as for DO-statements (Chapter 7, page 122). Note that the entire implied-DO list is enclosed in parentheses and that a comma terminates the list of variables.

In Examples 13 and 14 we illustrate the use of implied-DO lists in output statements.

EXAMPLE 13.

```
      DIMENSION A(8)
      READ(5,10)A
   10 FORMAT(4F10.0)
      WRITE(6,11)(I,A(I),I=1,8,2)
   11 FORMAT(1X,I3,3X,F8.2)
      STOP
      END
```

Input Data:

```
          1         2         3         4         5         6
1234567890123456789012345678901234567890123456789012345678901234567890
    21.386    817.534    26.998    643.312
    55.000    761.125    67.372    940.450
```

Output:

```
1      21.39
3      27.00
5      55.00
7      67.37
```

The READ statement reads input values for the eight entries of A. The input format specification (4F10.0) says to read four real values from each input record, using ten character positions to obtain each of these values.

The implied-DO list (I,A(I),I=1,8,2) in the WRITE statement says to print the values of I and A(I) for the successive values I = 1, 3, 5, and 7. The output format specification (1X,I3,3X,F8.2) contains edit descriptors specifying how to print only one of the four pairs I,A(I). This means that this format specification will be repeated four times, each time causing the values of I and A(I) to be printed on a new line as shown in the output.

Using implied-DO lists in output statements not only simplifies the coding process, but, in addition, allows you almost total control in determining the precise form of your output. For instance, suppose the first thirty entries in an array M are to be printed six to a line. The formatted WRITE statement

```
      WRITE(6,10)(M(I),I=1,30)
   10 FORMAT(1X,6I5)
```

accomplishes this. If they are to be printed ten to a line, simply change the format specification (1X,6I5) to (1X,10I5). If each of these lines is to be followed by a row of dashes, use the format specification (1X,6I5/1X,30(' − ')). Although this can all be accomplished without using implied-DO lists, it is not so simple. (Try it.)

Just as an entire array can be read by including its name in a READ statement, it can be printed by including its name in a WRITE or PRINT statement.

EXAMPLE 14. Copper connectors are selling at the special price of $3.19/dozen. Let's write a program to print a table in two rows; the first gives the number of connectors 1, 2, 3, . . . , 12, and the second the corresponding price for each number.

Problem Analysis:
The problem statement calls for a table of the form

```
NUMBER      1  2  3  4  5  6  7  8  9  10  11  12
PRICE       -  -  -  -  -  -  -  -  -  -   -   -
```

To produce this output without the use of subscripted variables would require, at best, a rather cluttered program. (Try it!) But, with subscripted variables the task is straightforward. The first row can be printed by using the implied-DO list (I,I=1,12). To print the second row, you can store the twelve values in the array PRICE. Since the sale price is $3.19 a dozen, the price of each connector is $3.19 ÷ 12, and the price of I connectors is (3.19 ÷ 12) × I. So, let PRICE(I)=(3.19/12.)*FLOAT(I), for I = 1, 2, . . . , 12, and all array values are assigned.

The statement

WRITE(6,11)PRICE

will print all twelve amounts contained in the array PRICE. To print them on one line with the identifier to the left, you can use

11 FORMAT(1X,'PRICE',2X,12F5.2)

The Program:

```
      DIMENSION PRICE(12)
C PRINT THE FIRST LINE OF TABLE
      WRITE(6,10)(I,I=1,12)
   10 FORMAT(1X,'NUMBER',12I5)
C ASSIGN THE INDIVIDUAL PRICES TO THE ARRAY PRICE
      DO 1 I=1,12
          PRICE(I)=(3.19/12.)*FLOAT(I)
    1 CONTINUE
C PRINT THE SECOND LINE OF THE TABLE
      WRITE(6,11)PRICE
   11 FORMAT(1X,'PRICE',2X,12F5.2)
      STOP
      END
```

Output:

```
NUMBER     1    2    3    4    5    6    7    8    9   10   11   12
PRICE    0.27 0.53 0.80 1.06 1.33 1.59 1.86 2.13 2.39 2.66 2.92 3.19
```

Remark: Normally, the Ith entry in an array does not in any way depend on the value of I; that is, there is no relationship between the value stored in a particular position in an array and the position number. However, here the value in the Ith position of the array PRICE is (3.19/12.)*FLOAT(I).

Conversational system users have found it impossible in many instances to have their output printed in the form of a table. When the input device is the terminal keyboard, each input record is printed as it is typed and interrupts the flow of output. Let's write a program for a relatively simple problem to show how the use of arrays alleviates this difficulty and allows output in tabular form.

EXAMPLE 15. Given five pairs of integers, write a program to find the sum of each pair and print the results in the form of a three-column table with the headings 1ST INTEGER, 2ND INTEGER, and SUM.

Problem Analysis:
Rather than reading the first pair of integers into simple variables, finding their sum, and printing the first row of the table as we might be tempted to do (this approach does not eliminate the difficulty cited above), let's use three arrays, I, J, and SUM. We'll read the first pair of integers into I(1) and J(1) and let SUM(1) = I(1) + J(1); then read the next pair into I(2) and J(2) and let SUM(2) = I(2) + J(2), and so on, until all five pairs have been processed. At this point all 15 values to be printed are stored in arrays I, J, and SUM. We need only print them.

The Algorithm:
a. Read I(K) and J(K), and let SUM(K) = I(K) + J(K), for K = 1 to 5.
b. Print I(K), J(K), and SUM(K), for K = 1 to 5.
c. Stop.

The Program:

```
      INTEGER I(5),J(5),SUM(5)
C READ THE ARRAYS I AND J, AND
C CALCULATE VALUES FOR THE ARRAY SUM
      DO 1 K=1,5
         READ(5,10)I(K),J(K)
         SUM(K)=I(K)+J(K)
    1 CONTINUE
C PRINT COLUMN HEADINGS
      WRITE(6,11)
C PRINT THE TABLE VALUES
      WRITE(6,12)(I(K),J(K),SUM(K),K=1,5)
      STOP
   10 FORMAT(I3,2X,I3)
   11 FORMAT(1X,'1ST INTEGER',3X,'2ND INTEGER',3X,'SUM')
   12 FORMAT(1X,4X,I3,10X,I3,6X,I4)
      END
```

Input Data:

```
          1         2         3
12345678901234567890123456789 0
  41    22
  37     5
   6    32
  12    91
  63    13
```

Output:

```
1ST INTEGER  2ND INTEGER   SUM
        41           22     63
        37            5     42
         6           32     38
        12           91    103
        63           13     76
```

If this program is run in a conversational mode, the input values will be printed as you type them. However, since all input values are stored in an array before any output is produced by the program, these input values will appear before the output shown above and, hence, will not clutter it. Of course, if operating in a conversational mode, you must precede the READ statement by an appropriate WRITE or PRINT statement.

9.5 Problems

1. What will be printed when each program is run? Assume the input data are as follows.

```
            1         2         3         4
12345678901234567890123456789012345678890
    3     135.00  100
   18     140.25  101
  275     150.50  102
 3500     160.75  103
 5000     170.00  104
```

a.
```
      DIMENSION N(5)
      READ(5,10)N
   10 FORMAT(15X,I5)
      WRITE(6,11)N
   11 FORMAT(1X,5I5)
      STOP
      END
```

b.
```
      DIMENSION A(4)
      READ(5,12)A
   12 FORMAT(5X,F10.0)
      WRITE(6,13)A
   13 FORMAT(1X,F10.1)
      STOP
      END
```

c.
```
      INTEGER L(4)
      READ(5,14)(L(K),K=1,4)
      DO 1 I=1,3
         L(I)=L(I+1)
         L(I+1)=L(I)
         WRITE(6,15)L(I),L(I+1)
    1 CONTINUE
      STOP
   14 FORMAT(I5,10X,I5)
   15 FORMAT(1X,2I5)
      END
```

d.
```
      DIMENSION NUM(4)
      READ(5,16)K
   16 FORMAT(I5)
      READ(5,16)(NUM(I),I=1,K)
      READ(5,17)NUM(4)
   17 FORMAT(17X,I3)
      WRITE(6,18)NUM
   18 FORMAT(1X,8I5)
      STOP
      END
```

e.
```
      DIMENSION M(12),N(7)
      READ(5,19)M,N
   19 FORMAT(12I1,1X,7I1)
      WRITE(6,20)M,N
   20 FORMAT(1X,12I2)
      STOP
      END
```

f.
```
      DIMENSION N(5)
      DATA N/1,2,3,4,5/
      K=5
    1 WRITE(6,21)(N(I),I=1,K)
      K=K-1
      IF(K.GT.0) GO TO 1
      STOP
   21 FORMAT(1X,5I1)
      END
```

g.
```
      DIMENSION M(5),N(5)
      DATA M,N/5*1,5*0/
      DO 1 K=1,5
         DO 1 L=1,K
            N(K)=N(K)+M(L)
    1 CONTINUE
      WRITE(6,23)(M(I),N(I),I=1,5)
      STOP
   23 FORMAT(1X,2I3)
      END
```

h.
```
      DIMENSION M(6)
      DATA M/6*1/
      DO 1 I=1,6
         WRITE(6,22)(M(J),J=1,I)
    1 CONTINUE
      STOP
   22 FORMAT(1X,6I2)
      END
```

Write a program to perform each task specified in Problems 2–8.

2. Print the integers from 10 to 99, nine to a line.

3. Print the first fifty multiples of seven, five to a line, but in decreasing order.

4. Print all positive integer factors of N, three to a line. N is to be input and must be a positive integer. For example, for N = 30 the output should be

```
 1   2   3
 5   6  10
15  30
```

5. The following input data show the annual salaries of all the employees of the Minot Company. The first value (9) is a count of the number of employees.

```
          1         2         3         4
1234567890123456789012345678901234567890
  9
  19865.00  15222.00
  28462.00  13525.00
  11250.00   9765.00
  10350.00  17500.00
  17750.00
```

Your program is simply to read the salary figures and print them in a single column. Use implied-DO lists on both input and output.

6. Each employee of the Minot Company (see Problem 5) is to receive a salary increase of $400.00 plus four percent of the current salary. Produce a two-column report, with the first column showing the current salaries and the second showing the new salaries. Use implied-DO lists on both input and output. (The report is to be printed with a report title centered on the page and with appropriate column headings.)

7. Print a list of the salary figures for all employees of the Minot Company (see Problem 5) in the order of their appearance, but only up to and including the smallest salary. (For the input data shown, the output will be a list of the salaries up to $9,765. The last three will not be printed.) Use implied-DO lists on both input and output. (Your program will have to determine the subscript corresponding to the smallest salary.)

8. I.M. Good, a candidate for political office, conducted a preelection poll. Each voter polled was assigned a number from 1 to 5 as follows.

1. Will vote for Good.
2. Leaning toward Good but still undecided.
3. Will vote for Shepherd, Good's only opponent.
4. Leaning toward Shepherd but still undecided.
5. All other cases.

The results of the poll are included in input records as follows. (The last input value 0 is the EOD-tag.)

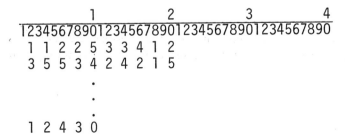

```
          1         2         3         4
1234567890123456789012345678901234567890
  1 1 2 2 5 3 3 4 1 2
  3 5 5 3 4 2 4 2 1 5
              .
              .
              .
  1 2 4 3 0
```

Write a program to print two tables as follows:

TABLE 1

```
             FOR    LEANING

GOOD          -        -
SHEPHERD      -        -
```

TABLE 2

```
            FOR OR    PERCENTAGE OF TOTAL
            LEANING   NUMBER OF PEOPLE POLLED

GOOD          -              -
SHEPHERD      -              -
OTHERS        -              -
```

9.6 Sorting

Many programming tasks require sorting (arranging) arrays according to some specified order. When lists of numbers are involved, this usually means arranging them according to size, from smallest to largest or from largest to smallest. For example, you may be required to produce a salary schedule in which salaries are printed from largest to smallest. When lists of names are involved, you may wish to arrange them in alphabetical order. In this section we'll describe the **bubble sort,** an algorithm that will take any array A(1), A(2), . . . , A(N) of numbers and rearrange them so that they are in ascending order—that is, so that

$$A(1) \leq A(2) \leq \cdots \leq A(N).$$

In Chapter 12 we'll show how algorithms used to sort arrays of numbers can be modified to sort arrays whose entries are strings.

The bubble sort is not a very efficient sorting algorithm. However, it is reasonably easy to understand and for this reason serves as an excellent introduction to the topic of sorting. A more comprehensive treatment of this topic is included in Chapter 15. We demonstrate the bubble sort with a short array A containing only four values:

4 3 5 1

First, we compare the values in positions 1 and 2. If they are in the proper order (the first is less than or equal to the second), we leave them alone. If not, we interchange them:

4 3 5 1   becomes   **3 4** 5 1.

Next we compare the values in positions 2 and 3 in the same manner:

3 **4 5** 1   remains   3 **4 5** 1.

Then we compare the values in positions 3 and 4:

3 4 **5 1**   becomes   3 4 **1 5**.

The effect of these three comparisons was to move the largest value to the last position. This process is now repeated, except that this time the final comparison is omitted because the largest value is already in the last position:

3 4 1 5   remains   **3 4** 1 5.
3 **4 1** 5   becomes   3 **1 4** 5.

We repeat the process once more, this time noting that the final two comparisons are unnecessary because the correct numbers are already in the last two positions:

3 1 4 5   becomes   **1 3** 4 5.

The array is now in the proper order.

To summarize, the array A contains four values, and we make three passes through the array.

On pass number 1, we compare A(I) with A(I + 1) for I = 1, 2, 3.
On pass number 2, we compare A(I) with A(I + 1) for I = 1, 2.
On pass number 3, we compare A(I) with A(I + 1) for I = 1.

If an array contains N values instead of 4, we make N − 1 passes through the array. In this case the following comparisons are made:

On pass number 1, compare A(I) with A(I + 1) for I = 1, 2, . . . , N − 1.
On pass number 2, compare A(I) with A(I + 1) for I = 1, 2, . . . , N − 2.
On pass number 3, compare A(I) with A(I + 1) for I = 1, 2, . . . , N − 3.

.
.
.

On pass number N − 2, compare A(I) with A(I + 1) for I = 1, 2.
On pass number N − 1, compare A(I) with A(I + 1) for I = 1.

Note that on each pass through the array, one fewer comparison is made. N − 1 comparisons are made the first time (I = 1, 2, . . . , N − 1), N − 2 the second, N − 3 the third, and so on.

In general, on the Jth pass through the array, N − J comparisons are made, one for each I = 1, 2, 3, . . . , N − J. All necessary comparisons can thus be accomplished with the nested DO-loops:

```
      NM1=N-1
      DO 1 J=1,NM1
         NMJ=N-J
         DO 2 I=1,NMJ
            .
            .
            .
2        CONTINUE
1     CONTINUE
```

The actual method of comparison is as follows: if A(I) is greater than A(I + 1), we must interchange them. Using the *temporary* variable TEMP, the three instructions

```
TEMP = A(I)
A(I) = A(I + 1)
A(I + 1) = TEMP
```

accomplish this. If A(I) is not greater than A(I + 1), these three lines must be skipped. The flowchart in Figure 9.1 displays the process just described. The corresponding program segment, shown in Figure 9.2, can be used in any program to sort, in ascending order, any array A of N numbers.

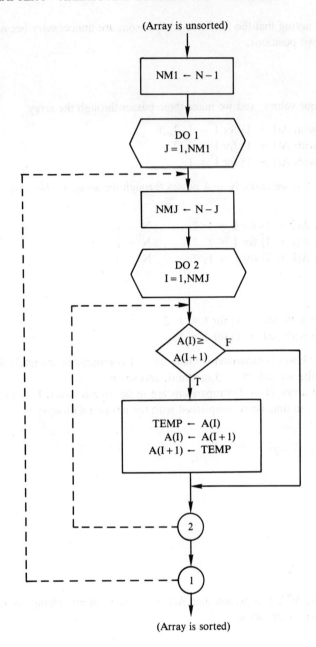

FIGURE 9.1. Flowchart to perform a bubble sort.

```
C BUBBLE SORT TO ARRANGE THE N TERMS
C OF ARRAY A IN ASCENDING ORDER
      NM1=N-1
      DO 1 J=1,NM1
         NMJ=N-J
         DO 2 I=1,NMJ
            IF(A(I).GT.A(I+1)) THEN
               TEMP=A(I)
               A(I)=A(I+1)
               A(I+1)=TEMP
            END IF
    2    CONTINUE
    1 CONTINUE
C ARRAY A IS SORTED
```

FIGURE 9.2. Program segment to perform a bubble sort.

If the comparisons are reversed, that is, if the statement

IF(A(I).GT.A(I + 1)) THEN

is replaced by

IF(A(I).LT.A(I + 1)) THEN

the program segment in Figure 9.2 will sort the array A in descending rather than ascending order. This accounts for the name *bubble sort*—the smaller or lighter values are "bubbled" to the top.

Many applications requiring arrays to be sorted involve more than one array. For example, suppose CODE and PRICE denote one-dimensional arrays with each pair CODE(I),PRICE(I) giving an item code number and the price of the item. If the contents of these two arrays must be printed in a two-column report of item codes and prices, with the item codes appearing from smallest to largest, the list of pairs CODE(I),PRICE(I) must be sorted so that the entries in CODE are in increasing order. This can be accomplished by modifying a bubble sort that sorts the array CODE. Simply insert lines that interchange PRICE(I) and PRICE(I + 1) whenever CODE(I) and CODE(I + 1) are interchanged. We illustrate with an example.

EXAMPLE 16. Several pairs of numbers are to be read. The first of each pair is a quality point average (QPA), and the second gives the number of students with this QPA. Write a program to produce a table with the two column headings QPA and FREQUENCY. The frequency counts in the second column are to appear in descending order.

Problem Analysis:
Let's agree to include a single QPA and the corresponding count of students with this QPA in each input record as follows:

Input Data:

```
         1          2          3
12345678901234567890 1234567890
4.00      3
3.75     16
3.40     41
3.20     38
3.00     92
2.75    162
2.30    352
2.00    280
1.70     81
1.50     27
0.        0
```

Note that we have included the pair 0.,0 as an EOD-tag.

Two lists are given in the input data. Since they must be sorted before being printed we should read them into arrays where the sorting can be carried out. Let's use QPA to denote the list of QPAs and COUNT to denote the frequency counts. The following procedure shows the three subtasks that must be performed:

a. Read arrays QPA and COUNT.
b. Sort the two arrays so that the frequencies appear in descending order.
c. Print the two arrays as a two-column table.

To code step (a), we must remember that the arrays are presented in input records as pairs of numbers. Thus, we will read values for QPA(I) and COUNT(I) for I = 1, 2, and so on, until all pairs have been read.

To code step (b), we will use a bubble sort to sort the array COUNT in descending order. However, since a pair QPA(I),COUNT(I) must not be separated, we will interchange QPA values whenever the corresponding COUNT values are interchanged.

The Program:

```
      INTEGER COUNT(50),ITEMP
      REAL QPA(50),TEMP
C READ ARRAYS QPA AND COUNT
      DO 1 I=1,50
         READ(5,10)QPA(I),COUNT(I)
         IF(QPA(I).EQ.0.) GO TO 2
    1 CONTINUE
      WRITE(6,11)
      STOP
    2 N=I-1
C THERE ARE N ENTRIES IN THE ARRAYS
C SORT THE ARRAYS QPA AND COUNT
C ACCORDING TO DECREASING COUNT VALUES
      NM1=N-1
      DO 3 J=1,NM1
         NMJ=N-J
         DO 3 I=1,NMJ
            IF(COUNT(I).LT.COUNT(I+1)) THEN
```

```
                  ITEMP=COUNT(I)
                  COUNT(I)=COUNT(I+1)
                  COUNT(I+1)=ITEMP
                  TEMP=QPA(I)
                  QPA(I)=QPA(I+1)
                  QPA(I+1)=TEMP
               END IF
     3      CONTINUE
C PRINT COLUMN HEADINGS AND TABLE VALUES
        WRITE(6,12)
        WRITE(6,13)(QPA(I),COUNT(I),I=1,N)
        STOP
    10 FORMAT(F4.2,2X,I3)
    11 FORMAT(1X,'I CAN ONLY HANDLE 49 PAIRS')
    12 FORMAT(1X,'QPA',2X,'FREQUENCY'/)
    13 FORMAT(1X,F4.2,5X,I3)
        END
```

Output (for the given input values):

```
QPA   FREQUENCY

2.30      352
2.00      280
2.75      162
3.00       92
1.70       81
3.40       41
3.20       38
1.50       27
3.75       16
4.00        3
```

The statements

TEMP = QPA(I)
QPA(I) = QPA(I + 1)
QPA(I + 1) = TEMP

were inserted in the bubble sort to interchange QPA values whenever the corresponding COUNT values were interchanged.

Remark: Notice that a DO-loop is used to read the data values even though the number of values to be read is unknown (an EOD-tag terminates the input list). Since QPA and COUNT were dimensioned to have length 50, there is no point in attempting to read more than 50 pairs with the READ statement. If a user includes too many pairs in the input list, the program will print the message "I CAN ONLY HANDLE 49 PAIRS" and the user will know what went wrong.

9.7 Problems

Write a program to perform each task specified in Problems 1–12.

1. Print, in ascending order, any five input values L(1), L(2), L(3), L(4), and L(5). Your program should process many such sets of five integers during a single run. Test your program with the following input data.

```
         1          2
12345678901234567890
   5    4    3    2    1
   5    1    2    3    4
  -1   -2   -3   -4   -5
   2    1    4    3    5
  15   19   14   18   10
   1    2    3    4    5
```

2. Modify your program for Problem 1 so that each group of five integers is printed in descending order. (Only one line needs to be changed.)

3. Print a single list of all thirty input values given in Problem 1. The numbers are to be printed from smallest to largest, five numbers per line.

4. Modify your program for Problem 3 so that the thirty numbers are printed in descending order, three numbers per line. (Only two lines need changing.)

5. A list of numbers is to be read to obtain a two-column printout with the column headings ORIGINAL LIST and SORTED LIST. The first column is to contain the list values in the order in which they are read, and the second column is to contain the same values printed from largest to smallest. Use the following algorithm.
   a. Input the list values into identical arrays A and B.
   b. Sort array A into descending order.
   c. Print the table as described.
   Test your program with the following input data. (0.0 is an EOD-tag.)

```
       1          2
12345678901234567890
   64.43
   34.25
   89.50
   88.40
   60.77
   42.35
   39.33
   25.65
   22.43
    0.0
```

6. Several numbers, ranging from 0 to 100, are to be read and stored in two arrays A and B. A is to contain those numbers that are less than 50, and the others are to be stored in array B. Arrays A and B are then to be sorted in descending order and printed side by side with the column headings LESS THAN 50 and 50 OR MORE. Test your program, using the input data shown in Problem 5.

7. Read a list of integers into an array NUM and sort it in ascending order. Then create a new array M containing the same values as NUM but with no repetitions. For example, if NUM(1) = 7, NUM(2) = NUM(3) = 8, and NUM(4) = NUM(5) = NUM(6) = 9, then the array M is to have M(1) = 7, M(2) = 8, and M(3) = 9. Print both arrays.

8. Read a list of integers into an array NUM and sort it in ascending order. Then modify NUM by deleting all values appearing more than once. For example, if NUM(1) = 7, NUM(2) = NUM(3) = 8, and NUM(4) = NUM(5) = NUM(6) = 9, then the modified array NUM is to have NUM(1) = 7, NUM(2) = 8, and NUM(3) = 9.

9. In carrying out a bubble sort to sort an array A, several passes are made through A and on each pass several comparisons of A(I) and A(I + 1) are made to determine whether the values of A(I) and A(I + 1) should be swapped. If, on any one pass, no swaps are made—that is, if all of the pairs A(I), A(I + 1) are already in the desired order—you can be sure that the sorting is complete. Use this fact to write an improved version of the bubble sort. You will need a counter K that counts the number of swaps made

on any one pass through the array. After each pass is complete, simply check to see if K = 0. If it is, the sort is complete. If not, set K = 0 and continue.

10. A study of the Tidy Corporation's annual reports for the years 1970–1980 yielded the following statistics:

Year	Gross sales (in thousands)	Earnings per share
1970	19,500	.27
1971	18,350	− .40
1972	18,400	− .12
1973	18,000	− .84
1974	18,900	.65
1975	20,350	.78
1976	24,850	1.05
1977	24,300	.68
1978	27,250	.88
1979	28,500	.80
1980	23,250	− .05

Include the second and third columns of this table in input records for a program to print two columns with the same headings as those shown. However, the earnings-per-share figures are to appear in ascending order. (Use the method described in Example 16.)

11. Include all three columns given for the Tidy Corporation (Problem 10) in input records for a program to produce a three-column table with the same headings. However, the gross sales figures are to appear in descending order.

12. N pairs of numbers are to be read so that the first of each pair is in array A and the second in array B. Sort the pairs A(I), B(I) so that $A(1) \leq A(2) \leq \cdots \leq A(N)$ and also so that $B(I) \leq B(I + 1)$ wherever $A(I) = A(I + 1)$. Print the modified arrays in two adjacent columns with the headings LIST A and LIST B. (*Hint:* If $A(I) > A(I + 1)$, a swap is necessary; if $A(I) < A(I + 1)$, no swap is necessary; otherwise, that is, if $A(I) = A(I + 1)$, swap only if $B(I) > B(I + 1)$.)

9.8 Two-Dimensional Arrays

Data to be processed by the computer are often presented in tabular form. For example, you may wish to write a program to analyze the following data, which summarize the responses of college students to a hypothetical opinion poll concerning the abolition of grades.

Class	In favor of abolishing grades	Not in favor of abolishing grades	No opinion
Freshmen	207	93	41
Sophomores	165	110	33
Juniors	93	87	15
Seniors	51	65	8

If you wanted to determine the number of sophomores who were polled, you would add the three entries in the second row; to determine the percentage of sophomores polled who are not in favor of abolishing grades, the entry 110 would be divided by this sum. Many such calculations may be desired, and the computer is ideally suited for such tasks. What is needed is a convenient way to present these data to the computer. First, we will introduce some terminology to make it easier to refer to such tables of values.

A **two-dimensional array** is a collection of items arranged in a rectangular fashion. That is, there is a first (horizontal) row, a second row, and so on, and a first (vertical) column, a second column, and so on. An array with *m* rows and *n* columns is called an *m-by-n array* (also written *m* × *n array*). Thus the opinion-poll data are presented as a 4-by-3 array.

A particular item in an array is specified simply by giving its row number and column number. For example, the item in the third row and second column of the opinion-poll table is 87. By convention, when specifying an item in an array, we give the row number first. Hence, in the opinion-poll table, 33 is in the 2,3 position and 51 is in the 4,1 position. In mathematical notation we could write

$$N_{1,1} = 207, N_{1,2} = 93, N_{1,3} = 41$$

to indicate the values in the first row of our table. Since the FORTRAN character set does not include subscripts, this notation is changed as it was for one-dimensional arrays. Thus, the values in the opinion-poll table would be written as follows:

N(1,1) = 207	N(1,2) = 93	N(1,3) = 41
N(2,1) = 165	N(2,2) = 110	N(2,3) = 33
N(3,1) = 93	N(3,2) = 87	N(3,3) = 15
N(4,1) = 51	N(4,2) = 65	N(4,3) = 8

We say that N is the *name* of the array, that N(1,1), N(1,2), . . . are *doubly subscripted* variables, and that the numbers enclosed in parentheses are the *subscripts* of N. The symbol N(I,J) is read "N sub I comma J" or simply "N sub IJ."

The 4-by-3 array N can be visualized as follows:

	(Column)		
N	1	2	3
1	207	93	41
2	165	110	33
3	93	87	15
4	51	65	8

(Row)

This schematic displays the array name N, the row number for each item, and the column numbers.

The statements about name, type, and dimensioning made in the section on *one-dimensional arrays* also apply here. Thus, either of the statements

DIMENSION N(4,3)   or   INTEGER N(4,3)

instructs the compiler to reserve twelve storage units in memory for the 4-by-3 integer array N. These twelve storage units correspond to the twelve doubly-subscripted variables N(1,1), N(1,2), . . . , N(4,3). The value of a doubly-subscripted variable—that is, an array entry—is referenced in a program just as values of singly-subscripted variables are referenced. The subscripts can be integer constants, variables, or expressions. For example, the DO-loop

```
    DO 1 J=1,3
        N(1,J)=5*J
  1 CONTINUE
```

assigns the values 5, 10, and 15 to the first row N(1,1), N(1,2), N(1,3) of N. Similarly,

```
    K=1
    DO 2 I=1,4
        N(I,K)=N(I,K)+6
  2 CONTINUE
```

adds 6 to each entry in the first column N(1,1), N(2,1), N(3,1), N(4,1) of N.

More than one array can be dimensioned in a single DIMENSION or type statement. For instance,

DIMENSION N(4,3),A(20),B(5,5)

reserves 57 memory storage units: 12 for the 4-by-3 integer array N, 20 for the one-dimensional real array A, and 25 for the 5-by-5 real array B.

The next four examples illustrate the most common methods for reading values into two-dimensional arrays.

EXAMPLE 17. Here is a program segment to read the opinion-poll data shown at the outset of this section into a 4-by-3 array N:

```
      DIMENSION N(4,3)
      DO 1 I=1,4
C         READ VALUES FOR THE ITH ROW OF N
          DO 2 J=1,3
              READ(5,10)N(I,J)
   2      CONTINUE
   1 CONTINUE
  10 FORMAT(I4)
```

Input Data:

```
          1         2
12345678901234567890
 207
  93
  41
 165
 110
  33
  93
  87
  15
  51
  65
   8
```

When the first DO statement is encountered, I is assigned the initial value 1. The J-loop then reads the first three input values 207, 93, and 41 for the variables N(1,1), N(1,2), and N(1,3), respectively. That is, when I = 1, values are read into the first row of N. Similarly, when I = 2, values are read into the second row of N, and so on until all twelve input values have been assigned to the array N.

In the preceding example, each time the READ statement is encountered, a single input value is read from the "next" record. This necessitates including a separate input record for each of the twelve input values. Suppose now that our input data are as follows:

```
          1         2
12345678901234567890
 207  93   41
 165 110   33
  93  87   15
  51  65    8
```

The three entries in the first record are the three values to be read into the first row of N. Similarly, the second, third, and fourth records contain the values for the second, third, and fourth rows of N. The formatted READ statement

```
      READ(5,11)N(I,1),N(I,2),N(I,3)
   11 FORMAT(3I4)
```

can be used to read one of these records to obtain the three values for the Ith row of N. The input list

N(I,1),N(I,2),N(I,3)

can be written as an implied-DO list as follows:

(N(I,J),J = 1,3)

EXAMPLE 18. Here is a program segment that uses an implied-DO list to read the opinion poll data into a 4-by-3 array N:

```
     DIMENSION N(4,3)
     DO 1 I=1,4
          READ(5,11)(N(I,J),J=1,3)
   1 CONTINUE
  11 FORMAT(3I4)
```

Input Data:

```
          1         2
12345678901234567890
 207  93  41
 165 110  33
  93  87  15
  51  65   8
```

FORTRAN allows implied-DO lists to be nested in much the same way that DO-loops are nested. For instance, the DO-loop of the previous example

```
     DO 1 I=1,4
          READ(5,11)(N(I,J),J=1,3)
   1 CONTINUE
```

can be replaced by

READ(5,11)((N(I,J),J = 1,3),I = 1,4).

The meaning of this statement is that the implied-DO list

(N(I,J),J = 1,3)

is to be repeated for I = 1, 2, 3, and 4. Thus the statement is equivalent to

```
     READ(5,10)N(1,1),N(1,2), N(1,3),N(2,1),N(2,2),N(2,3),
    +N(3,1),N(3,2),N(3,3),N(4,1),N(4,2),N(4,3)
```

(This latter statement actually requires a continuation line. It is too long for a single line.) Note that the inner variable J in the implied-DO list changes more rapidly than the outer variable I. This is always true when nesting implied-DO lists.

Because the statement

READ(5,11)((N(I,J),J = 1,3),I = 1,4)

is equivalent to a statement in which all twelve variable names appear in one READ statement, all twelve values can appear in one input record if we use an appropriate edit descriptor, say 12I4. However, we can still have the three values for each row appear on a separate record and use the 3I4 descriptor as before.

EXAMPLE 19. Here is a program segment that uses nested implied-DO lists to read the opinion poll data into a 4-by-3 array N:

```
   DIMENSION N(4,3)
   READ(5,11)((N(I,J),J=1,3),I=1,4)
11 FORMAT(12I4)
```

Input Data:

```
            1         2         3         4         5         6
   1234567890123456789012345678901234567890123456789012345678901234567890
    207  93  41 165 110  33  93  87  15  51  65   8
```

If the input data are presented to the computer as shown in Example 18, simply change the format specification (12I4) to (3I4).

Following are some nested implied-DO lists and their meanings.

Nested implied-DO list	Equivalent list of variables
((A(I,J),I=1,2),J=4,5)	A(1,4),A(2,4),A(1,5),A(2,5)
((B(K,L),L=1,2),K=4,6)	B(4,1),B(4,2),B(5,1),B(5,2),B(6,1),B(6,2)
((N(I,J),I=1,3,2),J=1,3,2)	N(1,1),N(3,1),N(1,3),N(3,3)
((M(I,J),J=1,1),I=1,5)	(M(I,1),I=1,5)

Values for an *entire* array can be read by placing the array name, with no subscripts, in a READ statement. For example,

DIMENSION N(4,3)
READ(5,10)N

can be used to read values for all twelve entries of N. However, the input values will not be assigned to N by rows as was done in Examples 17, 18, and 19. When a FORTRAN compiler encounters the statement

DIMENSION N(4,3)

it reserves a sequence of twelve storage units for the entries N(1,1), N(1,2), . . . , N(4,3) in the following order.

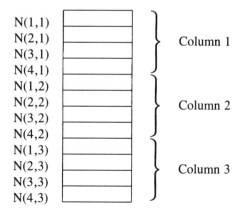

It is in this order that input values are assigned to N when only the array name N appears in a READ statement. As indicated in the diagram, the first four of these storage units correspond to the first column

N(1,1), N(2,1), N(3,1), N(4,1) of the rectangular array N, the next four to the second column, and the last four to the third column. Hence, FORTRAN stores the values from a rectangular array sequentially, column by column.

Although we, as programmers, visualize the two-dimensional array as a rectangular array with rows and columns, the computer stores array entries as a list. The terms row and column have no physical meaning inside the computer.

EXAMPLE 20. Here is a program segment to read the opinion poll data into an array by placing the array name in a read statement:

```
      DIMENSION N(4,3)
      READ(5,10)N
   10 FORMAT(4I4)
```

Input Data:

```
         1         2         3         4
1234567890123456789012345678901234567890
 207 165  93  51
  93 110  87  65
  41  33  15   8
```

Since the first column entries N(1,1), N(2,1), N(3,1) and N(4,1) of N will be read first, the first-column entries 207, 165, 93, and 51 appear in the first input record. Similarly, input values for the second column of N appear in the second record, followed by the four input values for the third and final column of N in the last record.

Remark: If the twelve input values are presented on one input record as follows,

```
         1         2         3         4         5         6         7
1234567890123456789012345678901234567890123456789012345678901234567890
 207 165  93  51  93 110  87  65  41  33  15   8
```

we would simply change the format specification (4I4) to (12I4).

Once the array N

		(Column)		
	N	1	2	3
(Row)	1	207	93	41
	2	165	110	33
	3	93	87	15
	4	51	65	8

has been assigned, the entire array or any part of it can be printed by WRITE or PRINT statements. For instance,

```
      WRITE(6,10)N(2,3),N(4,1)
   10 FORMAT(1X,2I4)
```

will print the values of N(2,3) and N(4,1) on one line as

```
  33  51
```

Similarly,

```
   WRITE(6,11)(N(2,J),J=1,3)
11 FORMAT(1X,3I4)
```

will print the entries N(2,1),N(2,2),N(2,3) of the second row of N on one line as

```
165 110  33
```

The formatted WRITE statement

```
   WRITE(6,12)N
12 FORMAT(1X,12I4)
```

will print the entire array on one line in the column-by-column order in which the entries of N are stored to give

```
207 165  93  51  93 110  87  65  41  33  15   8
```

This printing is not particularly helpful in visualizing the original two-dimensional array, since it separates neither the rows nor the columns of N. By changing the FORMAT statement to

```
12 FORMAT(1X,4I4)
```

we get the output

```
207 165  93  51
 93 110  87  65
 41  33  15   8
```

Here, the columns of N are printed as rows, but are at least distinguished one from the other.

Just as in the input process, to print a two-dimensional array by row, you must specify the order in which the entries are to be printed. Either of the following program segments will print the entries in the 4-by-3 array N, row by row, to obtain the output

```
207  93  41
165 110  33
 93  87  15
 51  65   8
```

```
   DO 1 I=1,4                         WRITE(6,12)((N(I,J),J=1,3),I=1,4)
      WRITE(6,12)(N(I,J),J=1,3)     12 FORMAT(1X,3I4)
 1 CONTINUE
12 FORMAT(1X,3I4)
```

EXAMPLE 21. Let's write a program to count the number of students in each class who participated in the opinion poll given at the outset of this section. The printout should display the opinion poll results followed by these counts. Each of the four counts should be printed with an identifying label.

Problem Analysis:
Since all three entries in any one row correspond to students in one of the four classes, our task is to add the three entries in each row. Let's use COUNT(1) to denote the sum of the entries in the first row, and similarly COUNT(2), COUNT(3), and COUNT(4) for the other three rows. As in Example 17, we'll use the 4-by-3 array N to store the opinion poll data. Thus, we are using a *one*-dimensional array COUNT to sum the entries in the rows of a *two*-dimensional array N.

The specified counts are determined as follows:

COUNT(1) = N(1,1) + N(1,2) + N(1,3)
COUNT(2) = N(2,1) + N(2,2) + N(2,3)
COUNT(3) = N(3,1) + N(3,2) + N(3,3)
COUNT(4) = N(4,1) + N(4,2) + N(4,3)

Note that COUNT(1) is obtained by summing N(I,J) for I = 1 and J = 1, 2, and 3. Similarly COUNT(2) is obtained by summing N(I,J) for I = 2 and J = 1, 2, and 3. Since the order in which the subscripts of N are considered is the same as described in Example 17, the same nested DO-loops are applicable to this problem.

Of course, COUNT(1), COUNT(2), COUNT(3), and COUNT(4) should all be initialized to zero. An algorithm describing the process follows.

Algorithm:
a. Initialize the array COUNT.
b. Read the opinion poll data into array N.
c. Print the opinion poll results.
d. For each I = 1, 2, 3, 4, determine the count COUNT(I) and print this count with an identifying label.
e. Stop.

The Program:

```
      INTEGER N(4,3),COUNT(4)
C INITIALIZE THE ARRAY COUNT
      DATA COUNT/4*0/
C READ THE OPINION POLL DATA INTO ARRAY N
      READ(5,10)((N(I,J),J=1,3),I=1,4)
C PRINT THE OPINION POLL RESULTS
      WRITE(6,11)
      WRITE(6,12)((N(I,J),J=1,3),I=1,4)
      WRITE(6,13)
C DETERMINE AND PRINT THE ROW SUMS
      DO 2 I=1,4
        DO 1 J=1,3
          COUNT(I)=COUNT(I)+N(I,J)
    1   CONTINUE
        WRITE(6,14)I,COUNT(I)
    2 CONTINUE
      STOP
   10 FORMAT(3I4)
   11 FORMAT(/1X,'OPINION POLL RESULTS'/)
   12 FORMAT(1X,3I6)
   13 FORMAT(/1X,20('*')/)
   14 FORMAT(1X,'SUM OF VALUES IN ROW',I2,' IS',I5)
      END
```

Input Data:

```
         1         2         3
123456789012345678901234567890
 207  93  41
 165 110  33
  93  87  15
  51  65   8
```

Output:

```
OPINION POLL RESULTS

   207    93    41
   165   110    33
    93    87    15
    51    65     8


********************

SUM OF VALUES IN ROW 1 IS 341
SUM OF VALUES IN ROW 2 IS 308
SUM OF VALUES IN ROW 3 IS 195
SUM OF VALUES IN ROW 4 IS 124
```

Remark: The blank lines before and after the row of *'s are caused by the slashes in the output FORMAT statement labeled 13.

In the preceding example, we used the DATA statement

DATA COUNT/4*0/

to initialize COUNT(1), COUNT(2), COUNT(3), and COUNT(4). Two-dimensional arrays can also be initialized by using the DATA statement. For instance,

```
DIMENSION K(2,3)
DATA K/4,3,1,6,7,2/
```

will cause the 2-by-3 integer array K to be assigned initial values as follows.

K	1	2	3
1	4	1	7
2	3	6	2

Note that the variables are assigned values in the order in which they are stored—that is, by columns. Similarly,

```
DIMENSION A(5,5),B(100),N(500)
DATA A,B,N/125*0.,500*0/
```

will initialize all 625 storage units reserved for the arrays A, B, and N to zero. Remember, DATA statements are nonexecutable—the initialization takes place during compilation and not during program execution.

Many programming applications involve rearranging the entries in arrays. We saw one such situation in Section 9.6 where the entries in a one-dimensional array were rearranged to yield an array whose entries were in increasing or decreasing order. We conclude this chapter with two examples illustrating the rearrangement of entries in two-dimensional arrays.

EXAMPLE 22. Here is a program segment to interchange rows K and L of an N-by-N array A:

```
    DO 1 J=1,N
       T=A(K,J)
       A(K,J)=A(L,J)
       A(L,J)=T
  1 CONTINUE
```

When J = 1, the three statements in the range of the loop interchange A(K,1) and A(L,1), the first entries in the Kth and Lth rows of A. When J = 2, the second entries A(K,2) and A(L,2) are interchanged. Similar statements apply for J = 3, 4, . . . , N.

EXAMPLE 23. A self-explanatory program:

```
      DIMENSION A(4,4)
C READ VALUES FOR ARRAY A, ROW BY ROW
      DO 1 I=1,4
          READ(5,10)(A(I,J),J=1,4)
    1 CONTINUE
   10 FORMAT(4F7.2)
C FIND THE ROW NUMBER K OF THE ROW OF A WITH
C THE LARGEST FIRST VALUE A(K,1)
      K=1
      DO 2 I=2,4
          IF(A(I,1).GT.A(K,1)) K=I
    2 CONTINUE
C INTERCHANGE ROWS K AND 1.
      DO 3 J=1,4
          T=A(K,J)
          A(K,J)=A(1,J)
          A(1,J)=T
    3 CONTINUE
C PRINT THE MODIFIED ARRAY A, ROW BY ROW
      DO 4 I=1,4
          WRITE(6,11)(A(I,J),J=1,4)
    4 CONTINUE
   11 FORMAT(1X,4F7.2)
      STOP
      END
```

Input Data:

```
          1         2         3         4         5
1234567890123456789012345678901234567890123456789
    22.25  21.75  28.63  29.84
    61.20  55.40  59.55  62.33
    33.35  42.78  39.25  48.62
    44.45  43.25  27.62  39.00
```

Output:

```
    61.20  55.40  59.55  62.33
    22.25  21.75  28.63  29.84
    33.35  42.78  39.25  48.62
    44.45  43.25  27.62  39.00
```

9.9 Problems

1. What will be printed when each program is run?

a.
```
      DIMENSION M(4,4)
      DO 2 I=1,4
         DO 1 J=1,4
            M(I,J)=I*J
 1       CONTINUE
 2    CONTINUE
      WRITE(6,10)(M(K,K),K=1,4)
10    FORMAT(1X,4I3)
      STOP
      END
```

b.
```
      DIMENSION M(4,4)
      DATA M/16*0/
      DO 1 I=1,4
         DO 2 J=1,4
            IF(I.LE.J)M(I,J)=1
 2       CONTINUE
 1    CONTINUE
      WRITE(6,11)((M(I,J),J=1,4),I=1,4)
11    FORMAT(1X,4I2)
      STOP
      END
```

c.
```
      DIMENSION A(2,3)
      DATA A/1.,2.,3.,4.,5.,6./
      WRITE(6,12)((A(I,J),J=1,3),I=1,2)
12    FORMAT(1X,6F4.1)
      STOP
      END
```

d.
```
      DIMENSION A(2,3)
      DATA A/1.,2.,3.,4.,5.,6./
      WRITE(6,13)A
13    FORMAT(1X,3F4.1)
      STOP
      END
```

e.
```
      DIMENSION M(2,2)
      READ(5,14)M
14    FORMAT(4I3)
      WRITE(6,15)((M(I,J),J=1,2),I=1,2)
15    FORMAT(1X,2I3)
      STOP
      END
```

Input Data:

```
          1         2         3
1234567890123456789012345678 90
 10 20 30 40
```

f.
```
      INTEGER NUMA(3,2),NUMB(2,3)
      READ(5,16)NUMA
16    FORMAT(9I2)
      DO 1 I=1,3
         DO 1 J=1,2
            NUMB(J,I)=NUMA(I,J)
 1    CONTINUE
      WRITE(6,17)(NUMB(2,K),K=1,3)
17    FORMAT(1X,3I2)
      STOP
      END
```

Input Data:

```
          1         2         3
1234567890123456789012345678 90
 1 2 3 4 5 6 7 8 9
```

2. Find and correct the errors in the following program segments. You are to assume that values have already been assigned to the 5-by-5 array A.

a.
```
C PRINT THE SUM S
C OF EACH ROW OF A
      S=0
      DO 2 I=1,5
         DO 1 J=1,5
            S=S+A(I,J)
 1       CONTINUE
         WRITE(6,10)I,S
 2    CONTINUE
10    FORMAT(1X,'ROW',I2,' SUM',F10.2)
```

b.
```
C INTERCHANGE THE ROWS
C AND COLUMNS OF A
      DO 2 I=1,5
         DO 1 J=1,5
            N=A(I,J)
            A(I,J)=A(J,I)
            A(J,I)=N
 1       CONTINUE
 2    CONTINUE
```

c.
```
C PRINT ARRAY A, ROW BY ROW
      DO 1 I=1,5
        DO 2 J=1,5
          WRITE(6,11)A(I,J)
    2     CONTINUE
    1 CONTINUE
   11 FORMAT(1X,5F10.2)
```

d.
```
C PRINT THE 5TH ROW OF A
C AND THEN ASSIGN THE VALUE
C ZERO TO EACH ENTRY OF A
      WRITE(6,12)(A(I,5),I=1,5)
   12 FORMAT(1X,5F10.2)
      DATA A/25*0./
```

Write a program to perform each task specified in Problems 3–16.

3. Read 16 values into the 4×4 array M. The array M is then to be printed. In addition, the four column sums are to be printed below their respective columns.

4. Read 16 values into the 4×4 array M. Then print the array. Row sums are to be printed to the right of their respective rows and column sums below their respective columns.

5. Values are to be read into an $N \times N$ array A. Then the sum of the entries in the upper-left to lower-right diagonal of A is to be printed. This sum is called the *trace* of the array (matrix) A. (N is to be input before the array values are read. You may assume that N will never exceed ten.)

6. Values are to be read into an $N \times N$ array A. The product of the entries in the upper-left to lower-right diagonal of A is to be printed. (Assume $N \le 10$.)

7. Read values into a 3×6 array B. The computer is then to perform the following tasks:
   a. Create and print a one-dimensional array whose Ith position contains the average of the 6 elements in the Ith row of B.
   b. Create and print another 3×6 array Z whose values are the values of B reduced by the average of all elements in B.

8. Create the following 5×5 array N:

$$\begin{array}{rrrrr} 0 & 1 & 1 & 1 & 1 \\ -1 & 0 & 1 & 1 & 1 \\ -1 & -1 & 0 & 0 & 0 \\ -1 & -1 & -1 & 0 & 1 \\ -1 & -1 & -1 & -1 & 0 \end{array}$$

   The values N(I,J) are to be determined during program execution without using READ statements. The array N should be printed as it appears above. (*Hint:* the value to be assigned to N(I,J) can be determined by comparing I with J.)

9. Read values into a 5-by-3 array N. Then print the subscripts corresponding to the largest entry in N. If this largest value appears in N more than once, more than one pair of subscripts must be printed. Use the following algorithm.
   a. Read values for array N.
   b. Determine M, the largest number in array N.
   c. Print those subscripts I,J for which N(I,J) = M.

10. Read values into a 5-by-3 array N. Print the row of N with the smallest first entry. If this smallest value is the first entry in more than one row, print only the first of these rows. Then, interchange this row with the first row and print the modified array N. Use the following algorithm.
    a. Read values for array N.
    b. Find the first K such that row K has the smallest first entry.
    c. Print row K.
    d. Interchange rows 1 and K.
    e. Print the modified array N.

11. Read values into a 5-by-3 array A. Rearrange the rows of A so that their first entries are in ascending order. Print the modified array, row by row. (Use a bubble sort to place the first-column entries A(1,1), A(2,1), A(3,1), A(4,1), A(5,1) in ascending order. However, instead of swapping A(I,1) and A(I+1,1) whenever they are out of order, you must interchange all of row I with row I+1.)

12. Modify your program for Problem 11 to handle M-by-N arrays rather than just 5-by-3 arrays.

13. Read N pairs of numbers into an N-by-2 array A. Sort these pairs (that is, the rows of A) so that the first column entries are in ascending order and also so that $A(I,2) \le A(I+1,2)$ whenever $A(I,1) =$

A(I+1,1). (Use a bubble sort that will place the first-column entries A(1,1), A(2,1), . . . , A(N,1) in ascending order with the following modification. If A(I,1) > A(I+1,1), swap rows I and I+1; if A(I,1) < A(I+1,1), no swap is necessary; otherwise, that is, if A(I,1) = A(I+1,1), swap only if A(I,2) > A(I+1,2).)

14. An N × N array of numbers is called a *magic square* if the sums of each row, each column, and each diagonal are all equal. Test any N × N array in which N will never exceed 10. Values for N and array values should be input. Be sure to print out and identify all row, column, and diagonal sums, the array itself, and a message indicating whether or not the array is a magic square. Try your program on the following arrays.

a. 11 10   4 23 17
     18 12   6   5 24
     25 19 13   7   1
       2 21 20 14   8
       9   3 22 16 15

b.   4 139 161   26 174 147
     85 166 107 188   93   12
     98 152 138   3 103 157
    179   17   84 165 184   22
    183   21   13 175   89 170
    102 156 148   94   8 143

15. Five numbers are to be input to produce a five-column table as follows. The first column is to contain the five numbers in the order they are input. The second column is to contain the four differences of successive values in the first column. For example, if the first column contains 2 4 8 9 3, the second column will contain 2 4 1 −6. In the same way, each of columns 3 through 5 is to contain the differences of successive values in the column before it. Thus, if the values 1, 5, 9, 6, 12 are input, the output should be

   1   4   0   −7   23
   5   4   −7   16
   9   −3   9
   6   6
  12

In the following suggested algorithm, K denotes a 5-by-5 array.
a. Read the first column of K.
b. Generate the remaining four columns of K as specified in the problem statement.
c. Print the table as specified.

16. N numbers are to be input to produce a table of differences as described in Problem 15. Assume that N is an integer from 2 to 10.

9.10 Review True-or-False Quiz

1. DIMENSION statements may appear anywhere in a program as long as they appear before the arrays being dimensioned are used.   T **F**

2. Placing an array name, without subscripts, in a WRITE or PRINT statement will cause the entire array to be printed.   **T** F

3. A DO-loop should be used to read input data only if a count of how many values are to be read is included as the first input value.   T **F**

4. Implied-DO lists offer little advantage over DO-loops in input and output of arrays.   T **F**

5. Implied-DO lists are especially useful when only part of an array is to be read or printed. However, they are of little value when all entries in an array are to be read or printed.   T **F**

6. The bubble sort is always used to arrange the terms of a list in ascending order.   T **F**

7. The bubble sort is one of the most efficient sorting algorithms.   T **F**

8. The statement DIMENSION A(20), B(5,5), C(2,3) is an admissible FORTRAN statement. It instructs the compiler to reserve a sequence of 51 storage units in the computer's memory.   **T** F

9. If the statement DIMENSION L(5,4) appears in a program, all 20 storage units must be assigned values.   T **F**

10. If the statement DIMENSION L(5,4) appears in a program, we can use the statement DATA L/20*0/at any point in the program where we wish to reset the array L entries to zero.   T F

11. If M is a 2-by-3 array, the statement DATA M/1,2,1,2,1,2/ can be used to initialize M so that its first row consists entirely of 1's and its second row consists of 2's.   T F

12. If the statements

    REAL ALPHA(5)
    DIMENSION ALPHA(5)

appear in a program, ALPHA is declared to be a real one-dimensional array of size 5.   T F

10

Functions

Since FORTRAN is a problem-solving language and since problems are often formulated in mathematical terms, three types of functions are included in the language. In Section 10.1 the *intrinsic* functions, those functions supplied with your FORTRAN system, are described. Then, in Section 10.3, you will learn how to define other functions, ones that you may need but that are not included in your system. The third type of function, the *function subprogram*, is discussed in Chapter 11.

10.1 Intrinsic Functions

The **intrinsic functions** (also called **built-in functions** or **library functions**) are an integral part of the FORTRAN language and may be used in any program. The function FLOAT, described in Chapter 3, is an intrinsic function. Its purpose is to convert integer values into real values, and, principally, it is used to avoid mixed-mode expressions. On some systems you may use the name REAL instead of FLOAT. For instance, to average N real numbers whose sum is SUM, you can write SUM/FLOAT(N) or, equivalently, SUM/REAL(N).

Another frequently used intrinsic function is the **square root function** SQRT. Instead of writing A**.5 to evaluate the square root of A, you can write SQRT(A). There are two advantages in doing this. First, your programs will be easier to read since SQRT(A) is *English-like,* and A**.5 is not. The second advantage is that computers generally calculate SQRT(A) in such a way that, if A is the square of a positive integer, then SQRT(A) will equal this positive integer, *exactly*. Thus, SQRT(9.0) has the value 3.0 and is not an approximation to 3 as is the case with 9.0**.5. Thus, on most computers, the condition

(9.0**.5.EQ.3.0)

will be false, whereas the condition

(SQRT(9.0).EQ.3.0)

will be true, as it should be.

The value supplied to an intrinsic function is called the *argument* of the function. Thus, N is the argument in FLOAT(N) and 9.0 is the argument in SQRT(9.0). The function FLOAT must have an *integer* argument and SQRT must have a *real* argument. In what follows we'll use the letters *i* and *r* to indicate the argument types for the functions being described; *i* and *r* denote, respectively, integer and real constants, variables, or expressions.

We now describe some of the most commonly used intrinsic functions. A more complete list is provided in Appendix B.

The Functions **IFIX**, **INT**, and **AINT**

IFIX(r) determines an integer value by dropping the fractional part of r. Thus, IFIX(7.34) = 7 and if A = -3.46, IFIX(A) = -3. INT(r) is equivalent to IFIX(r).

AINT(r) drops the fractional part of r, but leaves the result a real number. Thus, AINT(7.356) = 7., and if B = -13.45, AINT(B) = -13. In general, AINT(r) = FLOAT(IFIX(r))—r itself is not changed.

Each intrinsic function has a *type* indicated by the first letter of its name, just as for variables and arrays. Thus, IFIX (equivalently INT) is an integer-valued function, whereas FLOAT, REAL, SQRT, and AINT are real-valued functions.

The Functions **ABS** and **IABS**

If ABS(r) appears in a FORTRAN program, its value is the absolute value of r. Similarly, IABS(i) is the absolute value of i. For example, ABS(3.4) = 3.4, ABS(-4.7) = 4.7, IABS(-2) = 2, and IABS($4-9$) = 5. For this reason, ABS and IABS are called the *absolute value functions*.

EXAMPLE 1. Here is a program to find the absolute value of the sum of two integers:

```
      READ(5,10)J,K
      M=IABS(J+K)
      WRITE(6,20)J,K,M
   10 FORMAT(I4,I4)
   20 FORMAT(1X,3I4)
      STOP
      END
```

Input Data:

```
        1         2         3
12345678901234567890123456  7890
    5  -9
```

Output:

```
    5  -9   4
```

This program could have been written without using the IABS function. For example, if the statement

$$M = IABS(J + K)$$

were replaced by the two statements

$$M = J + K$$
$$IF(M.LT.0) \ M = -M$$

the resulting program would behave just as the original. Clearly the first version is more desirable. Its logic is transparent, whereas the logic of the second version is somewhat obscure. As a general rule you should use the intrinsic functions supplied with your system. Your programs will not only be easier to write but will also be easier to understand and, hence, easier to debug or modify.

The appearance of IABS(J + K) in the second line of the preceding program is called a **function reference.** It causes the function to be evaluated for the given argument and its value (4, for the given input data) is made available to the program. A function can be referenced in any FORTRAN expression. Thus, the following are admissible expressions:

IABS(J + K)
ABS(X) + ABS(Y)
5.23*AINT(SUM)
SQRT(ABS(X) + ABS(Y))
SQRT(FLOAT(N))

The last two of these show that an expression used as the argument of an intrinsic function can itself include function references.

EXAMPLE 2. Let's write a program to read a list of real values and count how many of these are within 2.5 units of 7.

Problem Analysis:
We choose variable names as follows:

VAL   = value being read.
COUNT = number of values within 2.5 units of 7.

To find how close a number VAL is to 7, we subtract VAL from 7 or 7 from VAL, depending on whether 7 is larger or smaller than VAL. Since we are not interested in which is larger, only in how close VAL is to 7, we simply examine the absolute value of VAL − 7. VAL will be within 2.5 units of 7 if ABS(VAL − 7.) is less than or equal to 2.5. The following flowchart describes the required procedure. The value 9999.0 is used as an EOD-tag.

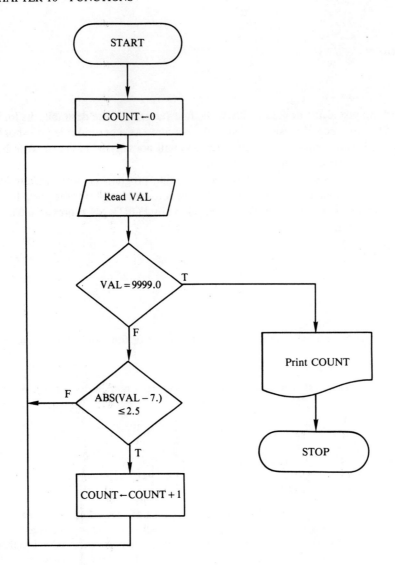

The Program:

```
    INTEGER COUNT
    COUNT=0
  1 READ(5,10)VAL
        IF(VAL.EQ.9999.0) GO TO 2
        IF(ABS(VAL-7.).LE.2.5) COUNT=COUNT+1
    GO TO 1
  2 WRITE(6,20)COUNT
 10 FORMAT(F7.2)
 20 FORMAT(1X,I5)
    STOP
    END
```

The Functions **NINT** and **ANINT**

NINT(r) *rounds* the real number r to the nearest integer. Thus, NINT(5.73) = 6, NINT(7.23) = 7, and NINT (-6.75) = -7. To find the number N of 2½ in. lengths that can be cut from a 7 ft. length of tape, use N = NINT(7.*12./2.5).

ANINT(r) = FLOAT(NINT(r)); that is, ANINT(r) rounds r to the nearest integer but leaves the result a real value. ANINT(5.34) and ANINT(7.84) have the real values 5. and 8., respectively. To round the real number r to the nearest hundredth, use ANINT(100.*r)/100. For example, if r = 41.3564, ANINT(100.*r) = 4136. and ANINT(100.*r)/100. = 41.36, as desired.

The Function **MOD**

If you divide 19 by 5, you obtain the quotient 3 and the remainder 4. MOD(19,5) gives this remainder. In general, for any integers i_1 and i_2, with $i_2 \neq 0$, MOD(i_1,i_2) equals the remainder when i_1 is divided by i_2. In the following examples, you should check that the quotients are simply i_1/i_2 (integer arithmetic).

i_1	i_2	i_1/i_2 (quotient)	$MOD(i_1,i_2)$ (remainder)
14	4	3	2
9	-4	-2	1
-19	5	-3	-4
-8	-3	2	-2
4	7	0	4
12	6	2	0

Note that the function MOD must have exactly two integer arguments. You should verify that the value MOD(i_1,i_2) is as follows:

$$MOD(i_1,i_2) = i_1 - (i_1/i_2)*i_2 \text{ (integer arithmetic).}$$

EXAMPLE 3. Here is a program segment to print all factors of the positive integer N, other than N itself:

```
1 K=1
    IF(MOD(N,K).EQ.0) WRITE(6,10)K
    K=K+1
  IF(K.LE.N/2) GO TO 1
```

K a factor of N means that division of N by K leaves a remainder of zero. Thus, the condition (MOD(N,K).EQ.0) is true precisely when K is a factor of N. (Note that an exit is made from the loop as soon as K exceeds N/2. The only factor of N that is greater than N/2 is N itself.)

The **MAX** and **MIN** Functions

FORTRAN contains several intrinsic functions for determining the largest or smallest number in a collection of numbers. Following are four such functions:

Function	Value
MAX0($i_1, i_2, \ldots, i_n$)	largest of the integers $i_1, i_2, \ldots, i_n$
MIN0($i_1, i_2, \ldots, i_n$)	smallest of the integers $i_1, i_2, \ldots, i_n$
AMAX1($r_1, r_2, \ldots, r_n$)	largest of the reals $r_1, r_2, \ldots, r_n$
AMIN1($r_1, r_2, \ldots, r_n$)	smallest of the reals $r_1, r_2, \ldots, r_n$

The number of arguments that may appear in a MAX or MIN function is system dependent but is usually very large:

```
MAX0(3,-7,5,-1,4)=5

AMAX1(2.3,-4.7,5.8)=5.8

MIN0(-3,4,-6,4)=-6

AMIN1(1.2,3.7)=1.2
```

EXAMPLE 4. Each dive in a diving meet is rated by five judges. Each rating is a number from 1.0 to 6.0. The score for an individual dive is found by eliminating the highest and lowest of the five ratings and averaging the remaining three. Let's write a program to compute the scores, given the five ratings.

Problem Analysis:
Rather than actually finding the highest and lowest rating so that we can add the other three ratings to get the average, let's add all five ratings and subtract the highest and lowest from the sum. This is easily accomplished using the AMAX1 and AMIN1 functions.

The Program:

```
      READ(5,10)R1,R2,R3,R4,R5
      SUM=R1+R2+R3+R4+R5
     +     -AMAX1(R1,R2,R3,R4,R5)
     +     -AMIN1(R1,R2,R3,R4,R5)
      SCORE=SUM/3.0
      WRITE(6,20)SCORE
   10 FORMAT(5F4.1)
   20 FORMAT(1X,'THE SCORE IS',F4.1)
      STOP
      END
```

Input Data:

```
          1         2         3         4
1234567890123456789012345678901234567890
 4.8 5.1 4.8 4.7 4.3
```

Output:

```
THE SCORE IS 4.8
```

Remark: Note that we have used two continuation lines for the assignment statement that evaluates SUM. If an error is found in any one of these lines, only that line needs to be changed.

The Trigonometric Functions SIN, COS, and TAN

$SIN(r)$, $COS(r)$, and $TAN(r)$ evaluate the sine, cosine, and tangent of the values of r. r must be in radian measure.

EXAMPLE 5. Here is a program to print DEGREE and SIN(DEGREE) for DEGREE $= 0°, 5°, \ldots, 45°$.

Problem Analysis:
Since DEGREE denotes an angle in degrees, it must be changed to radian measure. Recalling the correspondence

1 degree $= \pi/180$ radians

we must multiply DEGREE by $\pi/180$ to convert to radian measure.

The Program:

```
C PRINT COLUMN HEADINGS
      WRITE(6,10)
      WRITE(6,11)
C CALCULATE AND PRINT TABLE VALUES
      DEGREE=0.
    1 S=SIN(3.14159/180.*DEGREE)
      WRITE(6,12)DEGREE,S
      DEGREE=DEGREE+5.
      IF(DEGREE.LE.45) GO TO 1
      STOP
   10 FORMAT(1X,'DEGREES   SINE')
   11 FORMAT(1X,'-------   -------')
   12 FORMAT(1X,F5.0,3X,F8.5)
      END
```

Output:

```
DEGREES   SINE
-------   -------
    0.    0.00000
    5.    0.08716
   10.    0.17365
   15.    0.25882
   20.    0.34202
   25.    0.42262
   30.    0.50000
   35.    0.57358
   40.    0.64279
   45.    0.70711
```

10.2 Problems

1. Evaluate the following FORTRAN expressions.

a. FLOAT(3*(4–2))	**b.** REAL (3*(4–2))	**c.** IFIX(7.3/4.1)
d. IFIX((3. + 5.)/3.)	**e.** INT((3. + 5.)/3.)	**f.** NINT((3. + 5.)/3.)
g. ANINT((3. + 5.)/3.)	**h.** ANINT(10.*42.384)/10.	**i.** ANINT(1000.*3.56477)/1000.
j. ABS(− 3.0 + 2.1)	**k.** IABS(5*(− 3 + 2))	**l.** IABS(IFIX(− 3.75))
m. MOD(19,8)	**n.** MOD(− 25,3)	**o.** MAX0(3,5,7) + MIN0(3,5,7)

2. Evaluate the following with A = − 4.32, B = 5.93, I = 15, and J = 7.

a. FLOAT(I/J)	**b.** REAL(I/J)	**c.** IFIX(A + B)
d. INT(A + B)	**e.** NINT(A + B)	**f.** IABS(IFIX(A + 0.4))
g. IFIX(ABS(A + 0.4))	**h.** MOD(I + J,I − J)	**i.** MAX0(I + J,I − J,I,J)
j. AMIN1(AINT(B),AINT(A),FLOAT(I))		**k.** ANINT(10.*A)/10.
l. ANINT(10.*B)/10.		

3. What will be printed when each program is run?

a.
```
      N=1
    1 IF(N.GT.4) STOP
         J=N*(N-1)
         I=IABS(J-8)
         WRITE(6,10)N,I
         N=N+1
      GO TO 1
   10 FORMAT(1X,I3,I4)
      END
```

b.
```
      N=30
      RN=REAL(N)
      K=1
    1 IF(K.GT.INT(SQRT(RN))) STOP
         IF(MOD(N,K).EQ.0) THEN
            L=N/K
            WRITE(6,10)K,L
         END IF
         K=K+1
      GO TO 1
      STOP
   10 FORMAT(1X,I3,I3)
      END
```

c.
```
      S=13.92738
      D=1.
      K=1
    1 IF(K.GT.5) STOP
         R=ANINT(D*S)/D
         WRITE(6,10)R
         D=10.*D
         K=K+1
      GO TO 1
   10 FORMAT(1X,F8.4)
      END
```

d.
```
      VAL=5274.0
    1 DVAL=VAL/10.
         IF(IFIX( VAL).EQ.0) STOP
         N=NINT(VAL)-10*IFIX(DVAL)
         WRITE(6,10)N
         VAL=AINT(DVAL)
      GO TO 1
      STOP
   10 FORMAT(1X,I1)
      END
```

4. Using the ANINT function, write the programming line that will round off the value of X:
 a. to the nearest tenth.
 b. to the nearest hundredth.
 c. to the nearest thousandth.
 d. to the nearest hundred.
 e. to the nearest thousand.

Write programs to perform the tasks specified in Problems 5–8. In each, a list of numbers, terminated by an EOD-tag, is to be input.

5. Find the sum and the sum of the absolute values of any list of integers. Print the number of values in the list as well as the two sums.

6. The deviation of a number N from a number M is defined to be the absolute value of M − N. Find the sum of the deviations of the numbers 2, 5, 3, 7, 12, −8, 43, −16, from M = 6.

7. For any list of real numbers, two sums SUM and INTSUM are to be found. SUM is the sum of the numbers and INTSUM is the sum of the numbers, each rounded to the nearest integer. Print both sums and also the number of values in the list.

8. A list of positive integers is to be input. For each, print a column showing its digits with the units digit shown first and the most significant digit shown last. For example, the printout for the input value 257 should be

DIGITS OF 257
```
        7
        5
        2
```

(*Hint:* MOD(257, 10) = 7.)

Write programs to perform the tasks specified in Problems 9–16.

9. In plane analytic geometry, it is demonstrated that the distance d from the point (x,y) to the line $ax + by + c = 0$ is given by

$$d = \frac{|\, ax + by + c\,|}{\sqrt{a^2 + b^2}}$$

Write a program to input the coefficients a, b, and c and compute the distance d for any number of points (x,y) whose coordinates are input.

10. If a, b, and c are any three numbers with $a \neq 0$, the quadratic equation

$$ax^2 + bx + c = 0$$

can be solved for x by using the formula

$$x = \frac{-b \pm \sqrt{b^2 - 4ac}}{2a}$$

If $b^2 - 4ac > 0$, the formula gives two solutions; if $b^2 - 4ac = 0$, it gives one solution. However, if $b^2 - 4ac < 0$, there are no real solutions. Your program is to solve the quadratic equation for any input values a, b, and c, with $a \neq 0$. (Use the SQRT function.)

11. Produce a four-column table showing the values x, $\sin x$, $\cos x$, and $\tan x$, for all values of x from 0 to π in increments of 0.1 (x is in radian measure).

12. Produce a table of values for the sine, cosine, and tangent for the values 0° to 45° in increments of 1°.

13. An object moves so that its distance d from a fixed point P at time t is

$$d = \frac{1}{1 + .5 \cos t}$$

Produce a table (with column headings) of the d values for t between 0 and 2π in increments of 0.1. The d-column values should be printed with four fractional digits.

14. Determine side b of the triangle

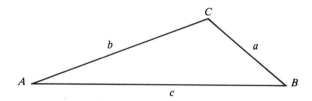

given side a and angles A and B in degrees. Use the Law of Sines

$$\frac{a}{\sin A} = \frac{b}{\sin B}$$

15. Referring to the figure in Problem 14, write a program to determine side c if sides a and b and angle C are given. (Use the Law of Cosines: $c^2 = a^2 + b^2 - 2ab\cos(C)$.)

16. Let's define an operation whose symbol is $\odot$ on the set A = $\{0, 1, 2, 3, 4, 5\}$ as follows: The "product" of two integers i and j is given by

$$i \odot j = \text{the remainder when } i \times j \text{ is divided by 6.}$$

Write a program to print all possible "products" of numbers in the set A.

10.3 Statement Functions

In addition to providing the intrinsic functions, FORTRAN allows you to define and name your own functions. In this section we'll show how a name can be given to any numerical expression so that the value of the expression can be referenced simply by giving its name. We illustrate with an example.

EXAMPLE 6. The statement

IRS(N) = N*(N + 1)/2

defines a function whose name is IRS and whose value for any integer N is N*(N + 1)/2. If the expression IRS(5) is used in the program its value will be 5*6/2 = 15. Similarly, if the variable K has been assigned the value 5, then the expression IRS(K) will also have the value 15. The following short program uses this function to produce a table of values for the expression N(N + 1)/2:

```
    IRS(N)=N*(N+1)/2
    DO 1 K=1,5
        M=IRS(K)
        WRITE(6,10)K,M
  1 CONTINUE
 10 FORMAT(2I4)
    STOP
    END
```

Output:

```
1    1
2    3
3    6
4    10
5    15
```

The occurrence of IRS(K) in the assignment statement M = IRS(K) represents a *function reference*. On the first pass through the loop, K = 1, and IRS(K) has the value IRS(1) = 1*(1 + 1)/2 = 1. On the second pass, K = 2, and IRS(K) has the value IRS(2) = 2*(2 + 1)/2 = 3. Similar remarks apply when K = 3, 4, and 5.

Remark: It can be shown that

N(N + 1)/2 = 1 + 2 + 3 + ··· + N

This formula is sometimes called the IRS formula because it is encountered in carrying out certain tax computations.

The variable name N used in the definition of the function IRS (line 1 of the preceding program) could have been any integer variable name. It is called a **dummy variable** or **dummy argument,** for it serves only to define the function and to give the *type* of the argument for the function. If it is used later in the program it is treated like any other variable. For example, if the statement

IRS(N) = N*(N + 1)/2

in the program were changed to

IRS(K) = K*(K + 1)/2

the program would function as before. No conflict would arise because of the appearance of the variable K elsewhere in the program.

In contrast, the variable K appearing in the assignment statement

M = IRS(K)

actually supplies values to the function: 1 on the first pass through the loop, 2 on the second pass, and so on. For this reason, it is called the **actual argument.**

The function IRS is called a **statement function** because it is defined with a *single* FORTRAN statement. The statement

IRS(N) = N*(N + 1)/2

is called a **statement function statement.** It is *nonexecutable*; it simply instructs the compiler to set up the machine code that will evaluate the expression $N*(N+1)/2$ whenever the function IRS is referenced in the program.

You may have noted that there is nothing in either the statement function statement

$$IRS(N) = N*(N+1)/2$$

or the assignment statement

$$M = IRS(K)$$

that tells us that IRS is the name of a *function* and not the name of an integer *array*. A FORTRAN compiler determines that IRS is a function name since it is not declared as an array in a DIMENSION or type statement.

Any name that is admissible as a variable name is also admissible as a function name. Unless the function name is declared in a type statement its type is determined by the first letter of its name, just as for variables and arrays. The statements

    INTEGER CUBE
    CUBE(N) = N**3

define CUBE as an integer function whose value for any integer N is N^3.

EXAMPLE 7. If SALES represents the total sales, RATE the commission rate, and SALARY the base monthly salary of a salesperson, the total monthly income TMI is RATE × SALES + SALARY. Here is a program that uses a statement function TMI to compute the total monthly income for sales of $1000, $1500, . . . , $5000. Values for RATE and SALARY are input.

```
      TMI(SALES)=RATE*SALES+SALARY
      READ(5,10)RATE,SALARY
      WRITE(6,11)
      DO 1 I=1000,5000,500
         SALES=FLOAT(I)
         TOTAL=TMI(SALES)
         WRITE(6,12)SALES,TOTAL
    1 CONTINUE
      STOP
   10 FORMAT(F5.0,F10.2)
   11 FORMAT(1X,' SALES',6X,'INCOME')
   12 FORMAT(1X,F8.2,F10.2)
      END
```

Input Data:

```
         1         2
1234567890123456789 0
0.125    1100.00
```

Output:

```
SALES      INCOME
1000.00    1225.00
1500.00    1287.50
2000.00    1350.00
2500.00    1412.50
3000.00    1475.00
3500.00    1537.50
4000.00    1600.00
4500.00    1662.50
5000.00    1725.00
```

The first line defines a real function whose name is TMI and whose value for any sales amount SALES is RATE × SALES + SALARY. As noted in Example 6, the variable SALES appearing in the statement function statement (line 1) is a dummy variable and is in no way related to the variable SALES occurring in the rest of the program. In the assignment statement TOTAL = TMI(SALES) the symbol SALES is the name of the actual argument. On the nine passes through the loop, this variable SALES supplies the successive values 1000., 1500., . . . , 5000. to the function.

Note that the numerical expression RATE*SALES+SALARY contains not only the dummy argument SALES, but also contains references to the variables RATE and SALARY. For the given input data the values 0.125 and 1100.00 are read for RATE and SALARY in the second line of the program and are not changed again. Thus, each time the assignment statement TOTAL=TMI(SALES) is executed it evaluates TMI(SALES)=0.125*SALES+1100.00 for the current value of the actual argument SALES.

FORTRAN allows you to define functions of more than one variable. For example, the statement

ISUMSQ(I,J) = I**2 + J**2

defines an integer function whose name is ISUMSQ and whose value for any integers I and J is $I^2 + J^2$. If the function reference ISUMSQ(2,3) is used in a program its value will be $2^2 + 3^2 = 13$. Similarly, if the variables M and N have the values 2 and 3 respectively, then ISUMSQ(M,N) will also have the value 13.

EXAMPLE 8. Here is a program segment to read four values A, B, C, D and print the larger of $\sqrt{A^2 + B^2}$ and $\sqrt{C^2 + D^2}$:

```
      F(X,Y)=SQRT(X**2+Y**2)
      READ(5,10)A,B,C,D
      IF(F(A,B).GE.F(C,D)) THEN
         X=F(A,B)
         WRITE(6,20)A,B,X
      ELSE
         X=F(C,D)
         WRITE(6,20)C,D,X
      END IF
      STOP
   10 FORMAT(4F4.0)
   20 FORMAT(1X,'THE INPUT VALUES',2F6.2/
     +          'GIVE THE MAXIMUM VALUE',F10.5)
```

Input Data:

```
         1         2         3
123456789012345678901234567890
  2.  6.  3.  5.
```

Output:

```
THE INPUT VALUES  2.00  6.00
GIVE THE MAXIMUM VALUE   6.32456
```

In the preceding example, the expression used to define the statement function F contains a reference to the intrinsic function SQRT. In general, the expression used in a function definition can contain references to any intrinsic function and also to any statement function that has been defined in an earlier line of the program. For example, if a program contains the statement function statements

```
F(X)=3.*X+5.
G(Y)=10.*F(Y)
```

two functions F and G are defined. The reference F(1.5) will be evaluated as 3.*1.5+5. = 9.5, as usual. The reference G(1.5) is evaluated as 10.*F(1.5) = 10.*9.5 = 95. Since X and Y in these function definitions are dummy variables, they can be replaced by any other real variable names. We can even write

```
F(X)=3.*X+5.
G(X)=10.*F(X)
```

with no conflict occurring because of the appearance of X in both function definitions.

The general form of the statement function statement is

fun(a,b,c,. . .) = e

where

fun   denotes a function name
a,b,c,. . .   denote variable names which serve as dummy arguments
e   denotes an arithmetic expression

The following rules govern the use of the statement function statement and of the statement functions.

1. All function definitions must appear before the first executable statement and after any *specification* statements. (The *specification* statements considered to this point are the DIMENSION and type statements.)
2. The arithmetic expression used in the function definition may contain references to intrinsic functions, and to statement functions that have been defined in earlier lines of the program.
3. A function may not be defined in terms of itself. Statements such as F(Y) = 2 + F(Y) are not admissible function statements.
4. The *actual arguments* in a statement function reference may be constants, variables, or expressions. Such expressions may involve intrinsic functions and statement functions.
5. *Actual arguments* must agree in order, number, and type with the *dummy arguments* that appear in the function definition.
6. Names that are declared as array names in DIMENSION or type statements must not be used as function names. Also, do not use the names of intrinsic functions as names of the functions you define.

10.4 Problems

1. What will be printed when each program is run?

a.
```
    INTEGER FUN
    FUN(M,N)=M/N
    DO 2 I=1,2
        DO 2 J=1,3
            K=FUN(J,I)
            WRITE(6,10)K
  2 CONTINUE
 10 FORMAT(1X,I4)
    STOP
    END
```

b.
```
    INTEGER FUN1,FUN2
    FUN1(I)=I+1
    FUN2(I)=I+2
    DO 1 M=1,3
        K=FUN2(FUN1(M))
        WRITE(6,11)M,K
  1 CONTINUE
 11 FORMAT(1X,2I4)
    STOP
    END
```

c.
```
   RINTST(P,R,T)=P*R/100.*T
   T=1./2.
   P=1000.
   DO 1 J=2,5
      DUE=RINTST(P,FLOAT(J),T)
      WRITE(6,12)J,DUE
 1 CONTINUE
12 FORMAT(1X,I2,1X,F6.2)
   STOP
   END
```

d.
```
   X(T)=2.*T+1.
   Y(T)=10.-4.*T
   DSQ(T)=X(T)**2+Y(T)**2
   DO 1 K=1,4
      D=DSQ(FLOAT(K))
      WRITE(6,13)K,D
 1 CONTINUE
13 FORMAT(1X,I4,F8.1)
   STOP
   END
```

2. Find all errors in the following programs.

a.
```
C PRINT SIX PERCENT
C OF ANY REAL NUMBER
      F(V)=.06*U
      READ(5,10)Y
      V=F(U)
      WRITE(6,20)V
10 FORMAT(F7.2)
20 FORMAT(1X,F9.2)
   STOP
   END
```

b.
```
C PRINT TABLE OF SQUARES
      INTEGER SQ,SQUAR
      SQ(I)=N**2
      DO 5 I=1,9
         SQUAR=SQ(I)
         WRITE(6,10)I,SQUAR
 5 CONTINUE
10 FORMAT(1X,2I6)
   STOP
   END
```

c.
```
C PRINT RECIPROCALS OF THE
C NUMBERS 1,2,3,···,10.
      RECIP(N)=FLOAT(N)/FLOAT(I)
      N=1
      DO 5 I=1,10
         R=RECIP(I)
         WRITE(6,10)R
 5 CONTINUE
10 FORMAT(1X,F10.5)
   STOP
   END
```

d.
```
   FN1(X,Y)=X+Y
   FN2(X)=X**2
   READ(5,10)R
   Z=FN2(FN1(R),R)
   WRITE(6,20)R,Z
10 FORMAT(F7.2)
20 FORMAT(1X,2F9.2)
   STOP
   END
```

3. Write a statement function that:
   a. Rounds a decimal to the nearest tenth.
   b. Gives the average speed for a trip of D miles which takes T hours.
   c. Gives the selling price if an article whose list price is X dollars is selling at a discount of Y percent.
   d. Gives the cost of a trip of X miles in a car which averages 15 miles per gallon if gasoline costs Y cents per gallon.
   e. Converts feet to miles.
   f. Converts square inches to square feet.
   g. Converts degrees Celsius to degrees Fahrenheit (F = 9/5C + 32).
   h. Converts degrees Fahrenheit to degrees Celsius.
   i. Converts miles to kilometers (1 mile = 1609.3 meters).
   j. Converts kilometers to miles.
   k. Gives the hypotenuse of a right triangle whose legs are A and B.
   l. Gives the area of a circle whose diameter is D.
   m. Gives the radius of a circle whose area is A.
   n. Converts degrees to radians.
   o. Gives the tangent of an angle of A degrees.

Write programs to perform the tasks specified in Problems 4–12.

4. Following is the weekly inventory report of a sewing-supply wholesaler.

Item code	Item	Batches on hand Monday	Batches sold during week	Cost per batch	Sales price per batch
1210	Bobbins	220	105	8.20	10.98
1211	Buttons	550	320	5.50	6.95
1311	Needles-1	450	295	2.74	3.55
1312	Needles-2	200	102	7.25	9.49
1410	Pins	720	375	4.29	5.89
1510	Thimbles	178	82	6.22	7.59
1611	Thread-A	980	525	4.71	5.99
1612	Thread-B	1424	718	7.42	9.89

Produce a three-column report showing the item codes, the number on hand at the end of the week, and the week's income for each item. Denoting the markup by UP and the quantity sold by N, use a function F(UP,N) to calculate the income figures.

5. Using the inventory report shown in Problem 4, produce a five-column report showing the item codes, the cost per batch, the sales price per batch, the dollar markup per batch, and the percent markup per batch. Denoting the markup by UP and the sales price by S, use a statement function PERCNT(UP,S) to calculate the percent figures in the fifth column. (UP/S times 100 gives the required percentage.)

6. Produce a three-column report as in Problem 4. However, the income column is to appear in decreasing order. (You will need subscripted variables.)

7. Produce a three-column table showing the conversions from grams G to ounces and then to pounds (1 oz. = 28.3495 g) for G = 20, 40, 60, . . . , 400. All output values are to be rounded to three decimal places. Use statement functions to do the converting.

8. Produce a three-column table showing the values of t, x, and y for $t = 0, 1, 2, \ldots , 10$ where $x = 5/(1 + t)$ and $y = \sqrt{x^2 + 1}$. Determine x and y with statement functions.

9. Determine the area in square centimeters of any rectangle whose length and width in inches are input. Use a function to convert inches to centimeters.

10. Write a statement function CAREA whose value CAREA(C) is the area of a circle with circumference C. Also, write a function SAREA whose value SAREA(P) is the area of a square with perimeter P. Use these two functions in a program to produce a table of values of CAREA(X) and SAREA(X) for X = 1, 2, 3, . . . , 10.

11. A thin wire of length X is cut into two pieces of lengths X1 and X2. One piece is bent into the shape of a circle and the other into a square. Decide how the wire should be cut if the sum of the two enclosed areas is to be as small as possible. (Use the functions CAREA and SAREA of Problem 10.) How should the wire be cut if the sum of the areas is to be as large as possible?

12. Produce a four-column table as follows. The first column is to contain the mileage figures 10 miles, 20 miles, . . . , 200 miles. The second, third, and fourth columns are to give the time in minutes required to travel these distances at the respective speeds 45 mph, 50 mph, and 55 mph. All output values are to be rounded to the nearest minute. Use a statement function to calculate the times.

10.5 Review True-or-False Quiz

1. If there is an intrinsic function that performs a needed task, you should use it unless it is a simple matter to write your own programming lines to perform this task.   T F

2. To determine whether or not the positive integer M is divisible by the positive integer N, you should use a logical IF statement with the condition (MOD(M,N).EQ.0) and not the condition (MOD(M,N).NE.0).   T F

3. The expressions *intrinsic function, library function,* and *built-in function* are used synonymously.   T F

4. Statement functions are referenced in exactly the same way as the intrinsic functions are referenced.   T F

5. All variables appearing in a statement function statement are called dummy variables.   T F

6. If FN(X) is defined in a function statement, the expression FN(SQRT(A)) is a valid
   function reference but SQRT(FN(A)) is not.   T F

7. If a function F with one real argument is defined in a program, we may also define
   a function G with the statement G(X) = X + F(X).   T F

8. There is nothing wrong with the function statement

   F(Y) = SQRT(ABS(Y)) + F(Y).   T F

9. There is nothing wrong with the function statement

   F(X,Y) = A*X + B*Y.   T F

10. If functions FN1 and FN2 have been defined, the assignment statement
    X = FN1(A,FN2(A)) will necessarily result in an error when the program is run.   T F

11. Function statements are nonexecutable; they represent instructions to the compiler.   T F

11
Subprograms

The *statement function statement* described in Chapter 10 allows you to define a function (*statement function*) by assigning a name to any arithmetic expression. Having done this, the function can be referenced anywhere in the program simply by giving its name and supplying values for its arguments. FORTRAN also allows you to assign a name to any *program segment,* however long or complex it may be, so that the entire program segment can be referenced by name. This is accomplished by writing the program segment as a **function subprogram** or as a **subroutine subprogram,** as described in this chapter.

11.1 Function Subprograms

Here is a program segment to calculate the sum of the integers from 1 to any positive integer N:

```
      INTEGER SUM
          .
          .
          .
      SUM=0
      DO 1 K=1,N
         SUM=SUM+K
    1 CONTINUE
```

Here is the same program segment written as a function subprogram:

```
      FUNCTION SUM(N)
      INTEGER SUM
      DO 1 K=1,N
         SUM=SUM+K
    1 CONTINUE
      RETURN
      END
```

This subprogram defines a function whose value for any positive integer N is the sum of the integers from 1 to N. The name SUM and the *dummy argument* N of the function are specified in the **FUNCTION statement** (the first line).

Function subprograms are referenced just as the intrinsic and statement functions are referenced. For example, if the assignment statement

$$M = 5 + SUM(4)$$

is encountered during program execution, the reference SUM(4) causes a transfer of control to the subprogram with N = 4. The subprogram is then executed to obtain SUM = 10 (1 + 2 + 3 + 4 = 10). The **RETURN statement** transfers control back from the subprogram, with SUM supplying the integer value 10 (recall that SUM is declared in an INTEGER type statement) for the expression SUM(4). This value is then added to 5 to obtain M = 15. The argument 4 in the function reference SUM(4) is called the *actual argument*—it supplies a value for the dummy variable N.

EXAMPLE 1.

```
C ***** A PROGRAM THAT USES THE SUBPROGRAM SUM *****
      INTEGER SUM
      DO 100 I=1,5
         M=SUM(I)
         WRITE(6,10)I,M
  100 CONTINUE
   10 FORMAT(1X,2I5)
      STOP
      END
C ********** FUNCTION SUBPROGRAM SUM **********
C CALCULATES THE SUM OF THE INTEGERS FROM 1 to N
      FUNCTION SUM(N)
      INTEGER SUM
      SUM=0
      DO 1 K=1,N
         SUM=SUM+K
    1 CONTINUE
      RETURN
      END
```

Output:

```
1     1
2     3
3     6
4    10
5    15
```

Each time the assignment statement M = SUM(I) is executed, control passes to the subprogram to obtain a value for the expression SUM(I). The variable I is the actual argument; it supplies the successive values 1, 2, 3, 4, and 5 for the dummy variable N.

Remark 1: Note that the name SUM is declared in an INTEGER statement at the beginning of the program and also in the subprogram. The reason for this is explained following this example.

Remark 2: The first two lines in the subprogram

FUNCTION SUM(N)
INTEGER SUM

specify SUM as the name of an integer function with the dummy argument N. These two statements can be combined into the equivalent statement

INTEGER FUNCTION SUM(N)

Although either form is correct, the second is preferred. It more clearly displays the type of the function being defined.

The complete program shown in Example 1 has two parts, each terminated with an END statement. These parts are called program units. The second program unit is a function subprogram, as indicated by the FUNCTION statement; the first is called the main program. A FORTRAN program can contain many subprograms or none; it must contain exactly one main program.

Program units are compiled separately. For this reason, each program unit must contain any type statements, DIMENSION statements, DATA statements, and so on, needed to compile it. It must also contain an END statement to tell the compiler that the end of a program unit has been reached. A function subprogram must contain at least one RETURN statement to return control from the subprogram.

This explains why the program in Example 1 contains two type statements for the name SUM. During compilation of the main program, the compiler needs to know that SUM has the type integer. When the subprogram is being compiled, the computer knows nothing at all about the main program; hence, a type statement for SUM is also required in the subprogram.

Since program units are compiled separately, variable names and statement labels used in one program unit can be used in any other program unit with no conflict occurring. We illustrate with an example.

EXAMPLE 2.

```
C *************** THE MAIN PROGRAM ***************
C THIS PROGRAM READS A COUNT N AND PRINTS
C THE SUM OF THE NEXT N INPUT VALUES.
C ALL INPUT DATA IS UNFORMATTED
      READ(5)N
      SUM=ADD(N)
      WRITE(6,10)N,SUM
      STOP
   10 FORMAT(1X,'NUMBER OF VALUES:',I3/
     +       1X,'SUM OF THE VALUES:',F7.2)
      END
C *********** FUNCTION SUBPROGRAM ADD ***********
C DETERMINES THE SUM OF THE NEXT NUM INPUT VALUES
      REAL FUNCTION ADD(NUM)
      ADD=0.
      DO 10 N=1,NUM
         READ(5)VAL
         ADD=ADD+VAL
   10 CONTINUE
      RETURN
      END
```

Input Data (unformatted):

```
         1         2
12345678901234567890
4
2.50
30.00
6.50
1.25
```

Output:

```
NUMBER OF VALUES:  4
SUM OF THE VALUES:  40.25
```

This program works as follows:

1. The main program reads a value for N and then transfers control to the subprogram when the assignment statement SUM = ADD(N) is encountered. The actual argument N supplies a value for the dummy argument NUM. (For the given input data, this value is 4.)
2. The variable N in the subprogram bears no relationship to the variable N in the main program. It is simply the DO variable and takes on the successive values of 1, 2, 3, and 4. The subprogram calculates a value for ADD by adding the four numbers it reads from the input data. This value is returned to the main program as the value of the expression ADD(N). For the given input data, ADD = 2.50 + 30.00 + 6.50 + 1.25 = 40.25.
3. The main program prints N and SUM. Note that the value printed for N is the same as the value input for N. The main program contains no statement that changes N.

Remark 1: The statement number 10 is used to label a FORMAT statement in the main program and a CONTINUE statement in the subprogram. This is perfectly acceptable—since program units are compiled separately, the computer is not "aware" that we did this. As we have noted, the computer is not even aware that we used the variable name N in both the main program and the subprogram. Assigning a value to N in one program unit does not change its value in the other. For this reason, the names of variables and arrays appearing in a single program unit are said to be local to that program unit. They can be used in any other program unit for any purpose whatsoever.

Remark 2: Although we specified the type of the function ADD to be real by writing

REAL FUNCTION ADD(N)

we could have written

FUNCTION ADD(N)

If you do not specify a type for a function, the computer assumes the normal I through N type convention.

The function subprogram ADD shown in Example 2 is correct, but it violates a fundamental programming principle. As explained, the occurrence of the single statement

SUM = ADD(N)

in the main program causes N input values to be read and added. But there is nothing in this statement that indicates that input data will be read. We had to explain this in comment lines. Things could be even worse. Given the function ADD, the following is a correct statement that compares the sum of the next ten input values with the sum of the ten that follow these:

IF(ADD(10).EQ.ADD(10))K = K + 1

How could you convincingly explain this absurd statement? The programming principle that was violated when we wrote the function ADD is as follows:

Functions are written to determine a single value. They should do nothing else. In particular, they should not read input data and they should not print output data.

Each of the subprograms shown in Examples 1 and 2 contains one dummy variable. Also, each function reference uses a variable as the actual argument. As illustrated in the next example, subprograms can have many dummy variables and the actual arguments that supply values for these dummy variables can be numerical expressions other than variables.

EXAMPLE 3. The Ace Tool Company offers a discount of LARGE% if the list price LIST exceeds $150; otherwise the discount is SMALL%. Here is a function subprogram DISC to find the amount of the discount:

```
REAL FUNCTION DISC(LIST,LARGE,SMALL)
REAL LIST,LARGE,SMALL
DISC=LIST*SMALL/100.
IF(LIST.GT.150.) DISC=LIST*LARGE/100.
RETURN
END
```

Values for the dummy arguments LIST, LARGE, and SMALL must be supplied by any program using this subprogram. Each of the following FORTRAN statements represents a correct way to reference this function:

a. AMT = DISC(200.,10.,5.)
b. CHARGE = AMT + DISC(AMT,PCT + 2.,PCT)
c. IF(DISC(AMT,PCT + 2.,PCT).LT.10.) N = N + 1
d. DSCT = DISC(AMAX1(AMTOLD,AMTNEW),10.,5.)

In (a), the values 200., 10., and 5. are supplied for the dummy arguments LIST, LARGE, and SMALL, respectively. Since 200. > 150., DISC = LIST*LARGE/100. = 200. × 10./100. = 20., and the subprogram returns the value DISC(200., 10., 5.) = 20. This value is assigned to AMT.

If AMT = 100. and PCT = 4., the actual arguments AMT, PCT + 2., and PCT in parts (b) and (c) supply the values 100., 6., and 4. for the dummy arguments LIST, LARGE, and SMALL. Since 100. is not greater than 150., DISC = LIST*SMALL/100. = 100. × 4./100. = 4. Thus, DISC(AMT, PCT+2., PCT) = 4. In part (b) this value is added to obtain CHARGE = 104. In part (c) the statement N = N + 1 is executed since 4. < 10.

In (d), the actual arguments 10. and 5. supply values for the dummy arguments LARGE and SMALL. If AMTOLD = 155. and AMTNEW = 148., the computer evaluates AMAX1(AMTOLD,AMTNEW) to obtain the value 155. for the dummy variable LIST. Since LIST = 155. > 150., DISC = LIST*LARGE/100. = 155.*10./100. = 15.5. This value is returned and assigned to DSCT.

Remark 1: Each function reference contains three real actual arguments since three real dummy variables are specified in the FUNCTION statement. In general, a list of dummy variables and a list of actual arguments supplying values for the dummy variables must agree in number and types. The first actual argument supplies a value for the first dummy variable, and so on.

Remark 2: Part (d) illustrates that numerical expressions used as actual arguments in a function reference can contain references to the intrinsic functions. More generally, any expression whose value has the type required in an actual argument can be used as this actual argument. For instance, if FUNC is the name of a function subprogram such that FUNC(AMT) returns a real value, the statement

CHARGE = DISC(FUNC(AMT),10.,5.)

is perfectly acceptable. If AMT = 500., the computer will supply the value of FUNC(500.) to the dummy argument LIST.

When preparing a FORTRAN program that contains more than one program unit, the subprograms are placed after the main program. Figure 11.1 shows the arrangement of cards in a FORTRAN package that contains two subprograms. On conversational systems, subprograms can be typed immediately following the main program. However, a common practice is to "save" your subprograms and later "append" them to any program you wish. How this is done must be gleaned from your time-sharing user's guide—the procedure varies from system to system.

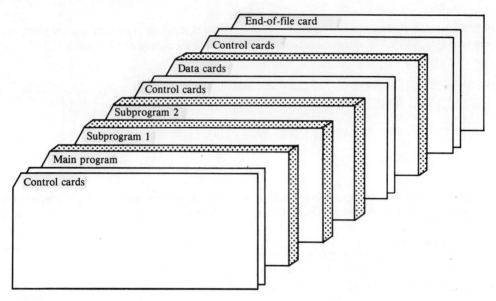

FIGURE 11.1. Arrangement of cards in a FORTRAN deck containing two subprograms.

11.2 Dummy Arrays

In each subprogram shown in Section 11.1, the dummy arguments appearing in FUNCTION statements represent variables. Here is a function subprogram with a dummy argument A that represents a one-dimensional array:

```
REAL FUNCTION SUM(A,M)
DIMENSION A(100)
SUM=0
DO 1 I=1,M
    SUM=SUM+A(I)
1 CONTINUE
RETURN
END
```

This subprogram defines a function whose value for any one-dimensional array A of size 100 is the sum of its first M entries. As always, the name SUM and the dummy arguments A and M of the function are specified in the FUNCTION statement.

EXAMPLE 4. Here is a program that uses the function subprogram SUM:

```
C ************* THE MAIN PROGRAM *************
      REAL LIST
      DIMENSION LIST(100)
C READ N VALUES INTO THE ARRAY LIST
      READ(5,10)N
      IF(N.GT.100) STOP
      DO 1 I=1,N
         READ(5,11)LIST(I)
    1 CONTINUE
C FIND AND PRINT THE AVERAGE OF THESE N VALUES
      AVER=SUM(LIST,N)/FLOAT(N)
      WRITE(6,12)(LIST(J),J=1,N)
      WRITE(6,13)AVER
      STOP
```

```
     10 FORMAT(I3)
     11 FORMAT(F7.2)
     12 FORMAT(1X,'INPUT VALUES:'/1X,20(5F7.2/))
     13 FORMAT(1X,'AVERAGE:',F7.2)
        END
C
C ******** FUNCTION SUBPROGRAM SUM ********
C DETERMINE SUM OF FIRST M ENTRIES IN ARRAY A
        REAL FUNCTION SUM(A,M)
        DIMENSION A(100)
        SUM=0
        DO 1 I=1,M
           SUM=SUM+A(I)
      1 CONTINUE
        RETURN
        END
```

Input Data:

```
            1         2         3
12345678901234567890123456789 0
   3
    5.00
   10.75
    3.00
```

Output:

```
INPUT VALUES:
    5.00  10.75    3.00
AVERAGE:    6.25
```

The comment lines in the main program and the subprogram tell what these two program units do.

When the assignment statement

AVER = SUM(LIST,N)/FLOAT(N)

is encountered, control passes to the subprogram to obtain a value for the expression SUM(LIST,N). The names LIST and N in this function reference represent the actual arguments; they supply values for the dummy arguments A and M. For the given input data,

LIST(1) supplies the value 5.00 for A(1),
LIST(2) supplies the value 10.75 for A(2),
LIST(3) supplies the value 3.00 for A(3), and
N   supplies the value 3 for M.

Remark 1: Note that the formatted WRITE statement

```
   WRITE(6,12)(LIST(J),J=1,N)
12 FORMAT(1X,'INPUT VALUES:'/1X,20(5F7.2/))
```

echoes all input values. This WRITE statement will print the values read into LIST, five to a line. Since the given input data contain only three values, they are printed on one line as shown in the output.

Remark 2: In the main program, LIST is dimensioned to be of length 100; hence, this program will handle only up to 100 input values. The statement

IF(N.GT.100) STOP

causes an orderly exit from the program should the count N (first input value) exceed N.

FORTRAN allows you to use integer variables as well as integer constants to specify dimensions for dummy arrays appearing in subprograms. For example, it is perfectly acceptable to begin a FUNCTION subprogram with the following two statements:

```
FUNCTION SUM(A,M)
DIMENSION A(M)
```

If such a function is referenced with the expression SUM(B,5), the first 5 entries in the actual array B will supply values for the first 5 entries in the dummy array A. In Section 11.4 we'll describe in greater detail how values are passed between actual arguments and dummy arguments. The following example illustrates how the use of integer variables to dimension dummy arrays allows you to write subprograms that will have wide application.

EXAMPLE 5. Here is a subprogram to search the one-dimensional integer array LIST of size N for the entry ITEM. If ITEM is found, the subscript K such that LIST(K) = ITEM is returned. Otherwise, the value zero is returned.

```
      INTEGER FIND(LIST,N,ITEM)
      DIMENSION LIST(N)
      DO 1 K=1,N
         IF(LIST(K).EQ.ITEM) GO TO 2
    1 CONTINUE
C     ITEM NOT FOUND IN LIST
      FIND=0
      RETURN
C     ITEM IS THE KTH LIST ENTRY
    2 FIND=K
      RETURN
      END
```

This subprogram can be used in any programming task that involves searching an integer array for a specific value. For example, if ID is an integer array and both M and VAL are integer variables, FIND(ID,M,VAL) will return the subscript of ID corresponding to the entry VAL if VAL is one of the first M entries of ID. Otherwise, the value 0 is returned. Note that we have said nothing of how ID is dimensioned. The subprogram doesn't care if M is 5 or 5,000.

When arrays are used as actual arguments in a function subprogram reference, care must be taken that the subprogram does not alter these array values. Altering array values in a subprogram causes the corresponding actual array values in the main program to be changed in the same way. (How this happens is explained in Section 11.5.) Indeed, as specified in the FORTRAN standard, and as implemented in many (but not all) FORTRAN compilers, this is true for variables as well. That is, the value of a variable used as an actual argument will be changed if the value of the corresponding dummy variable is changed in the subprogram. We mention this not to alert you to the possibility of writing "clever" function subprograms that do more than return a single value to the main program. Indeed, you should never do this; that's what the subroutines described in Section 11.4 are for. Rather, we mention it so that you will write function subprograms that return a single value and do nothing else. This means that your subprograms must not alter the values of dummy arrays or dummy variables. Not only will this keep you out of trouble, but your programs will be easier to read, debug, and modify at a later date, should that be required.

Our objective in this section was to show how function subprograms can be used in programming situations for which the statement functions, described in Chapter 10, are inadequate. Recall that a statement function must be defined in a single program statement, whereas a function subprogram can be as long and as complex as you wish. Our objective was not to give a complete description of function subprograms and their use. As you'll see, function subprograms are very similar to the subroutine subprograms described in Section 11.4. Because of this, advanced aspects of both are best considered together.

We conclude this section by restating the following programming principle.

Function subprograms are written to return a single value and to do nothing else. They should not read or print anything. In addition, care must be taken that values of dummy variables and dummy arrays are not altered in function subprograms. If they are, your programs may not behave as they should.

11.3 Problems

1. What value is assigned to NUM by each assignment statement? The functions NEG and DIFF are as follows:

```
FUNCTION NEG(I,J)              FUNCTION DIFF(M,N)
NEG=0                          INTEGER DIFF
IF(I.LT.0) NEG=NEG+1           DIFF=0
IF(J.LT.0) NEG=NEG+1           I=M+N-M*N
RETURN                         IF(I.LT.0) DIFF=-1
END                            IF(I.GT.0) DIFF=+1
                               RETURN
                               END
```

   a. NUM = NEG(2, − 3)   b. NUM = NEG(5,4)
   c. NUM = DIFF(5,2)   d. NUM = DIFF(2,5)
   e. NUM = DIFF(− 2,5)   f. NUM = NEG(DIFF(5,2),DIFF(2,1))

2. What, if anything, is wrong with the following FUNCTION statements?
   a. FUNCTION EVAL(X,X + Y,F)   b. FUNCTION DENT(A,B)
   c. FUNCTION(N1,N2,X)   d. FUNCTION AVERAGES(A,B,(A + B)/2.,(A − B)/2.)

3. What is wrong with each of the following subprograms?

   a.
```
FUNCTION EVAL(A,B,Z)
Z=A
IF(Z.LT.B) Z=B
RETURN
END
```
   b.
```
C FIND THE MIDDLE ENTRY
C IN AN ARRAY LIST
      FUNCTION MID(LIST,N)
M=N/2
MID=LIST(M)
RETURN
END
```

   c.
```
C CALCULATE THE SUM OF THE
C FIRST N ENTRIES OF ARRAY A
      FUNCTION SUM(A,N)
      DIMENSION A(N)
      DO 1 I=1,N
        SUM=SUM+A(I)
    1 CONTINUE
      RETURN
      END
```

Write a function subprogram for each task specified in Problems 4–19. Each subprogram should return a single value as specified, and do nothing else. In each case, write a short main program that can be used to debug the subprogram.

4. For any reals A, B, and C, determine the average of the sums A + B, B + C, and A + C.

5. For any integers, I, J, and K, determine the average of the sums I + J, J + K, K + I.

6. For any integer N, POINT(N) is to be 2 for N = 1 or 5, 3 for N = 3 or 4, 4 for N = 2, and 0 for any other value of N.

7. Determine the cube root $\sqrt[3]{X}$ for any real number X. (Recall that X**(1./3.) will result in an error if X is negative.)

8. Calculate the average of the first N entries in any one-dimensional array A.

9. The *range* of a list of numbers is defined as the largest minus the smallest. Determine the range for any list of numbers stored in a one-dimensional array.

10. Determine the new balance BAL for a checking account given the old balance OLDBAL, an array DEPST containing the amounts of all deposits since OLDBAL was calculated, and an array CHKS containing the amounts of all checks drawn since OLDBAL was calculated. (The name of your function must be BAL and you must use five dummy arguments (OLDBAL, DEPST, CHKS, and two others that denote the sizes of the two arrays).)

11. Determine the *median* of the N entries in a one-dimensional array A. You are to assume that the entries of A appear in ascending order. (The median is the middle term if N is odd, and is the average of the two "middle" terms if N is even.)

12. For any two arrays A and B of size N, determine the following sum of products:

$$DOT = A(1) \times B(1) + A(2) \times B(2) + \cdots + A(N) \times B(N)$$

13. Evaluate the polynomial

$$1 + x + x^2 + x^3 + \cdots + x^n$$

for any real number x and positive integer n.

14. Evelute the polynomial

$$1 + x + 2x^2 + 3x^3 + \cdots + nx^n$$

for any real number x and positive integer n.

15. Evaluate the polynomial

$$A(1) + A(2)x + A(3)x^2 + \cdots + A(n)x^{n-1}$$

for any real number x and real coefficients A(1), A(2), . . . , A(n).

16. For any positive integer N, determine the sum of all factors of N, including 1 but not N. If N ≤ 1, return the value 0.

17. Determine the least common multiple (LCM) of any two positive integers M and N. (If K denotes the larger of M and N, and L denotes the smaller, LCM is the first multiple of K that is divisible by L.)

18. Determine the greatest common divisor (GCD) of any two positive integers M and N. (If L denotes the smaller of M and N, GCD is the first number in the sequence L, L − 1, L − 2, . . . , 1 that is a divisor (factor) of both M and N.)

19. For any nonnegative integer N, N factorial (written N!) is defined as follows. 0! = 1! = 1, and N! = 1 × 2 × 3 × · · · × N for N ≥ 2. Your function is to be named FACT and is to return the integer value FACT(N) = N!.

11.4 Subroutine Subprograms

Any program segment can be written as a subprogram. If it calculates a single value, but does nothing more, the customary practice is to write it as a *function* subprogram; otherwise, it is written as a *subroutine* subprogram. Here is a subroutine subprogram designed to interchange the values of two variables:

```
SUBROUTINE SWAP(X,Y)
TEMP=X
X=Y
Y=TEMP
RETURN
END
```

The **SUBROUTINE statement** (first line) specifies the name SWAP and the dummy arguments X and Y of this subroutine. (The expressions *subroutine* and *subroutine subprogram* are synonymous.)

Program control is transferred to a subroutine with a **CALL statement.** If you wish to interchange the values of the variables A and B, simply write

CALL SWAP(A,B)

This statement transfers control from the main, or *calling,* program to the subroutine SWAP with the following correspondence between the actual and dummy arguments:

A ↔ X
B ↔ Y

By this correspondence we mean that the actual arguments A and B supply values to the dummy arguments X and Y, and also that any changes to X and Y in the subroutine are reflected as changes to A and B. The RETURN statement returns control back to the first executable statement following the CALL statement. The subroutine SWAP can be "called" as often as you wish. For instance, if later in the program you must interchange the array entries A(I) and A(I + 1), write

CALL SWAP(A(I),A(I + 1))

The subroutine will interchange the values of these two subscripted variables and return control to the first executable statement following *this* CALL statement.

Subroutines may contain many dummy arguments, or none. Example 6 shows a subroutine with six dummy arguments and Example 7 shows a subroutine with none.

EXAMPLE 6. Here is a subroutine to return two values as follows:

MAX = the larger of I and J
MIN = the smaller of K and L

```
      SUBROUTINE HILOW(I,J,K,L,MAX,MIN)
C FIRST FIND MAX OF I AND J
      MAX=I
      IF(MAX.LT.J) MAX=J
C NOW FIND MIN OF K AND L
      MIN=K
      IF(MIN.GT.L) MIN=L
      RETURN
      END
```

If during program execution the computer encounters the statement

CALL HILOW(N1,N2,M1,M2,IBIG,ITINY)

control will transfer to the subroutine HILOW with the following correspondence between actual and dummy variables:

N1   ↔ I
N2   ↔ J
M1   ↔ K
M2   ↔ L
IBIG ↔ MAX
ITINY ↔ MIN

The subroutine assigns the larger of I and J to MAX and the smaller of K and L to MIN. These two values are returned to the calling program as the values of IBIG and ITINY.

Remark 1: The actual arguments IBIG and ITINY are used only to obtain values from the subroutine. Whatever values they may have had prior to execution of the CALL statement are not used in the subroutine. For this reason, values do not have to be assigned to IBIG and ITINY before the CALL statement is executed. On the other hand, the values passed to the subroutine by the actual arguments N1, N2, M1, and M2 are needed in the subroutine. Hence, these four variables must be assigned values prior to execution of the CALL statement.

Remark 2: Actual arguments that supply values to dummy variables can be numerical expressions other than variables (just as for function subprograms). For instance, if N1 = 85 and N2 = 20, the statement

CALL HILOW(N1+N2,100,N1−N2,50,IBIG,ITINY)

will cause the expressions N1 + N2 and N1 − N2 to be evaluated as N1 + N2 = 105 and N1 − N2 = 65, and will then make the following assignments.

105 →I
100 →J
 65 →K
 50 →L

The subroutine will then calculate MAX = 105 and MIN = 50 and return these values as the values of IBIG and ITINY. Note that it makes no sense for the actual arguments corresponding to MAX and MIN to be anything but variables. For instance, if M = 100 and N = 25, the statement

CALL HILOW(N1,N2,M1,M2,M+N,M−N)

will calculate M + N = 125 and M − N = 75 and set up the following correspondence between the actual and dummy arguments:

N1 ←→ I
N2 ←→ J
M1 ←→ K
M2 ←→ L
125 →→ MAX
 75 →→ MIN

The subroutine will then calculate values for MAX and MIN as before; but these values will not be returned to the main program. There are no variables to accept them—the arguments for MAX and MIN are 125 and 75, and not M and N.

EXAMPLE 7. Here is a subroutine with no dummy arguments:

```
SUBROUTINE DASHES
WRITE(6,10)
RETURN
10 FORMAT(1X,40('-'))
END
```

Each time the statement

CALL DASHES

is encountered during program execution a row of forty dashes will be printed.

11.5 Variable Dimensioning of Dummy Arrays

The dummy arguments in subroutines can denote arrays as well as variables (just as in function subprograms). Here is a subroutine to read up to 100 unformatted real values into an array.

```
SUBROUTINE GET(A,M)
DIMENSION A(100)
READ(5)(A(I),I=1,M)
RETURN
END
```

The DIMENSION statement informs the compiler that A denotes a one-dimensional array. Precisely what happens when this subroutine is called is explained in the next example.

EXAMPLE 8. Here is a program that uses the subroutine GET:

```
C ****** THE MAIN PROGRAM ******
      REAL LIST
      DIMENSION LIST(100)
C READ N VALUES INTO THE ARRAY LIST
      READ(5)N
      IF(N.GT.100) STOP
      CALL GET(LIST,N)
C PRINT THE ARRAY ENTRIES 4 TO A LINE
      WRITE(6,10)(LIST(I),I=1,N)
      STOP
10    FORMAT(1X,'INPUT VALUES:'/1X,25(4F10.2/))
      END
C
C          SUBROUTINE GET
C READ M UNFORMATTED INPUT VALUES INTO ARRAY A
      SUBROUTINE GET(A,M)
      DIMENSION A(100)
      READ(5)(A(I),I=1,M)
      RETURN
      END
```

Input Data (unformatted):

```
         1         2         3
12345678901234567890123456789 0
13
7214.40,6319.55,6000.00
5722.29,4811.45,4024.15
2005.00,1825.25,1225.37
1056.60,925.32,726.49,502.46
```

Output:

```
INPUT VALUES:
   7214.40    6319.55    6000.00    5722.29
   4811.45    4024.15    2005.00    1825.25
   1225.37    1056.60     925.32     726.49
    502.46
```

The comment lines in the main program and the subroutine tell what these two program units do.

This program contains two DIMENSION statements: DIMENSION LIST(100) in the main program and DIMENSION A(100) in the subprogram. When the main program is compiled, a sequence of 100 memory storage units is reserved for the 100 entries of LIST. However, when the subprogram is compiled, no memory space is reserved for the dummy array A. Rather, the compiler sets up machine code to cause the following to happen during program execution. When the statement CALL GET(LIST,N) is executed, the subprogram is instructed to use the memory location containing the first entry LIST(1) of the actual array LIST as the first entry A(1) of the dummy array A. The sequence of 100 storage units reserved for LIST by its DIMENSION statement is then used to supply values for array A just as for array LIST. In particular, since the dummy array A is dimensioned as a one-dimensional array in the subprogram, A(I) refers to the Ith entry in this sequence of storage units. But so does LIST(I); hence, A(I) and LIST(I) share the same memory storage unit. As a consequence, any change to A(I) in the subprogram causes the same change to LIST(I) in the main program; since they share the same memory location, they always have the same value. This explains how one-dimensional arrays are passed from one program unit to another. Two-dimensional arrays are passed in the same way (see Example 10).

Dummy arrays appearing in subroutines can be dimensioned with integer variables as well as integer constants (just as in function subprograms). For example, we could have written the subroutine GET as follows:

```
SUBROUTINE GET(A,M)
DIMENSION A(M)
READ(5)(A(I),I=1,M)
RETURN
END
```

Since no memory space is reserved for dummy arrays, a value for M is not required during compilation. The sole purpose of the DIMENSION statement is to specify that A is a one-dimensional array. The computer then "knows" that A(I) refers to the Ith entry in a sequence of memory locations counting from A(1). The memory address to be used by A(1) is supplied by a CALL statement. For instance, CALL GET(ARRAY,N) specifies that the address of ARRAY(1) is to be used as the address of A(1). (If we had dimensioned the dummy array A as a two-dimensional array, the sequence of memory locations beginning with A(1,1) would supply values for A in the usual column-by-column order. (See Example 10.))

We illustrate the variable dimensioning of arrays in the following example.

EXAMPLE 9. We write a program to find the average of all values in an input list other than the largest and the smallest. The input values are unformatted real numbers and a first input record contains a count of how many values are included. In addition, no two input values are the same.

Problem Analysis:
Programs of this type are not new to us. First we should observe that the input list must be examined twice: once to find the largest and smallest values, and a second time to determine the average of all numbers other than the largest and smallest. Following is one way to carry out this task.

Algorithm:
a. Read the input data into an array.
b. Find the largest and smallest entries in the array.
c. Determine and print the average of all numbers in the array other than the largest and smallest.

Step (a) is easy. We simply read the count and then use the subroutine GET to get the array values. Let's also agree to use a subprogram for the task in step (b). The code for the final step can be included in the main program. (The problem of deciding when to use a subprogram is discussed later in this chapter.) Since a subprogram for step (b) must return two values, we should use a subroutine subprogram rather than a function subprogram. The following subroutine to carry out step (b) is almost immediate:

```
C *********** SUBROUTINE MAXMIN ***********
C DETERMINES THE LARGEST (B) AND SMALLEST (S)
C ENTRIES IN ARRAY A OF SIZE N
      SUBROUTINE MAXMIN(A,N,B,S)
      DIMENSION A(N)
      B=A(1)
      S=A(1)
      DO 1 I=2,N
         IF(B.LT.A(I)) B=A(I)
         IF(S.GT.A(I)) S=A(I)
```

```
    1 CONTINUE
      RETURN
      END
```

With the subroutines GET and MAXMIN at your disposal, it should now be a simple matter to code the main program. Following is one way to do this:

```
C ****** THE MAIN PROGRAM ******
      REAL LIST(1000)
C READ THE COUNT N OF THE NUMBER OF INPUT VALUES
      READ(5)N
      IF(N.GT.1000) STOP
C READ N VALUES FOR THE ARRAY LIST
      CALL GET(LIST,N)
C FIND BIG AND SMALL,THE MAX AND MIN OF THE N ENTRIES OF LIST
      CAL MAXMIN(LIST,N,BIG,SMALL)
C FIND AND PRINT THE AVERAGE(AVG) OF ALL
C ARRAY ENTRIES OTHER THAN BIG AND SMALL.
      SUM=0.
      DO 1 I=1,N
         IF(LIST(I).EQ.BIG) GO TO 1
         IF(LIST(I).EQ.SMALL) GO TO 1
         SUM=SUM+LIST(I)
    1 CONTINUE
      AVG=SUM/FLOAT(N-2)
      WRITE(6,10)N,BIG,SMALL,AVG
      STOP
   10 FORMAT(1X,'VALUES READ:',I5/
     +       1X,'LARGEST VALUE:',F8.2/
     +       1X,'SMALLEST VALUE:',F8.2/
     +       1X,'AVERAGE(EXCLUDING EXTREMES):',F8.2)
      END
```

Input Data (unformatted):

```
          1         2         3
12345678901234567890123456 7890
13
7214.40,6319.55,6000.00
5722.29,4811.45,4024.15
2005.00,1825.25,1225.37
1056.60,925.32,726.49.502.46
```

Output:

```
VALUES READ:   13
LARGEST VALUE: 7214.40
SMALLEST VALUE:  502.46
AVERAGE(EXCLUDING EXTREMES): 3149.22
```

Remark 1: When the statement CALL MAXMIN(LIST,N,BIG,SMALL) is encountered, the actual arguments LIST, N, BIG, and SMALL supply values for the dummy arguments A, N, B, and S. That BIG and SMALL are not assigned values prior to the subroutine call doesn't matter. Their sole purpose is to receive information (the values of B and S) from the subroutine.

Remark 2: In the subroutine MAXMIN, note that neither the array entries in the dummy array A nor the dummy variable N are changed in the subroutine. Any such changes would be reflected as changes to the corresponding actual arguments LIST and N. As indicated in the comment lines describing the subroutine MAXMIN, the subroutine is to determine the largest and smallest values in an array of size N. It does that, and nothing more. Of course, the subroutine GET does change the dummy array A and dummy variable N. That's what it's meant to do.

At this point, a word concerning how computers pass information between program units is in order. We have already explained how arrays are passed: the storage unit reserved for the first entry of the actual array is also used as the first entry of the corresponding dummy array. Thus, it is the address of a memory location that is passed to a subprogram and not the value stored in that location. This is referred to as **call by address** or **call by location.** It is essentially this method that is used by all FORTRAN systems to pass *arrays* between program units.

Normally, a different method, referred to as **call by value,** is used for variables. This expression is used to indicate that the value of an actual argument is actually copied into a storage unit reserved (during compilation) for the corresponding dummy variable. Then, when a RETURN statement is encountered, one of two things will happen depending on the form of the actual argument. If it is a variable name, the current value of the dummy variable is copied back into the storage unit reserved for this variable. However, if the actual argument is any expression other than a variable, the final value of the dummy argument is not returned to the main program. Thus, if a subroutine whose first line is

SUBROUTINE SUBR(A,B,N)

is called by either of the statements

CALL SUBR(X,Y,10)   or   CALL SUBR(X,Y,I+J−5)

the value of the dummy variable N is not returned. However, if SUBR is called with the statement

CALL SUBR(X,Y, I)

the final value of the variable N is returned as the value of I.

This brief discussion of *call by address* and *call by value* is not intended to be complete. Our reasons for introducing these terms are as follows.

1. After being told how arrays are passed between program units (call by address), beginners often assume that variable values are passed in the same way. As noted, this may or may not be the case, but most often it is not.

2. Understanding how *call by value* works, a beginner will understand how it is that an actual argument can be a variable in one CALL statement and a numerical expression other than a variable in another.

3. Some FORTRAN systems treat dummy variables in function subprograms differently than dummy variables in subroutine subprograms. In particular, when control is returned to a calling program after a function subprogram reference, the values of any dummy variables are not copied back into the storage units reserved for the actual arguments. This means that you cannot return values by means of variable names appearing in argument lists of function subprograms. But then, you shouldn't. Remember, function subprograms should be written to do only one thing—namely, return a single value to the calling program.

4. Some FORTRAN systems allow you to specify whether *call by value* or *call by address* is to be used for variables. For example, the WATFOR (WATerloo FORtran) and WATFIV (WATerloo Fortran IV) compilers allow you to place slashes on either side of a dummy variable to indicate that call by address is to be used. Thus, if you begin a subroutine with the statement

SUBROUTINE SUBR(X,Y,/Z/)

call by value is used for X and Y and call by address for Z.

We conclude this section with an example illustrating an error often made by beginners, and show how it is easily avoided.

EXAMPLE 10. Here is a function subprogram to sum the entries in the main diagonal of any N-by-N array MAT. (The main diagonal entries are MAT(1,1), MAT(2,2), MAT(3,3), . . . , MAT(N,N). Their sum is called the *trace* of MAT.)

```
      INTEGER FUNCTION TRACE(MAT,N)
      DIMENSION MAT(N,N)
      TRACE=0
      DO 1 J=1,N
         TRACE=TRACE+MAT(J,J)
    1 CONTINUE
      RETURN
      END
```

Let's see what happens if we reference this subprogram as follows:

```
C A MAIN PROGRAM THAT USES THE FUNCTION SUBPROGRAM TRACE
      INTEGER TR
      DIMENSION M(3,3)
      DATA M/9*0/
C READ VALUES INTO ARRAY M
      READ(5,10)K
      DO 1 I=1,K
         READ(5,11)(M(I,J),J=1,K)
    1 CONTINUE
C CALCULATE AND PRINT THE TRACE OF M
      TR=TRACE(M,K)
      WRITE(6,12)TR
      STOP
   10 FORMAT(I2)
   11 FORMAT(3I4)
   12 FORMAT(1X,'TRACE=',I4)
      END
```

Input Data:

```
         1         2         3
12345678901234567890123456789 0
 2
    3    5
    7    6
```

For the given input data, K is assigned the value 2 and the remaining four input values are assigned to M as follows. (Notice that M is first initialized to contain all zeros.)

(Column)

M	1	2	3
1	3	5	0
2	7	6	0
3	0	0	0

(Row)

Since M is dimensioned as a 3-by-3 array, the entries of M are stored in memory in the following column-by-column order:

M(1,1)	3
M(2,1)	7
M(3,1)	0
M(1,2)	5
M(2,2)	6
M(3,2)	0
M(1,3)	0
M(2,3)	0
M(3,3)	0

Column 1 } M(1,1), M(2,1), M(3,1)
Column 2 } M(1,2), M(2,2), M(3,2)
Column 3 } M(1,3), M(2,3), M(3,3)

When the assignment statement

TR = TRACE(M,K)

is encountered, control passes to the subprogram with the following correspondence being set up.

$$M(1,1) \longleftrightarrow MAT(1,1)$$
$$K \longleftrightarrow N$$

Since $N = 2$, the statement DIMENSION MAT(N,N) informs the subprogram that MAT is to be treated as a 2-by-2 array. This means the four values for MAT are obtained in the column-by-column order starting from the storage unit corresponding to MAT(1,1). Since MAT(1,1) and M(1,1) share the same storage unit, we obtain the following correspondence between MAT and M:

Column 1	M(1,1)	3	MAT(1,1)	Column 1
	M(2,1)	7	MAT(2,1)	
	M(3,1)	0	MAT(1,2)	Column 2
Column 2	M(1,2)	5	MAT(2,2)	
	M(2,2)	6		
	M(3,2)	0		
Column 3	M(1,3)	0		
	M(2,3)	0		
	M(3,3)	0		

The remaining five entries of M are simply not used. This gives

(Column)

MAT	1	2
(Row) 1	3	0
2	7	5

so we can see that the subprogram calculates TRACE $= 3 + 5 = 8$, and not $3 + 6 = 9$ as it should be.

The difficulty in this program is that the actual array M and the dummy array MAT may be assigned different dimensions. M is always a 3-by-3 array, but, for the given input data, MAT is dimensioned as a 2-by-2 array. To avoid this difficulty you *must* dimension the dummy array MAT just as the actual array M is dimensioned in the main program. One way to do this is to use the statement DIMENSION MAT(3,3); indeed, if the subprogram will never be used with a different main program, this is the best and safest thing to do. Another way to accomplish the same thing is to replace the first two lines of the subprogram with the following:

FUNCTION TRACE(MAT,N,ID)
DIMENSION MAT(ID,ID)

The reference TRACE(M,K,3) then causes the dummy array MAT to be dimensioned as a 3-by-3 array, just as the actual array M is dimensioned in the main program. If M had been dimensioned as a 50-by-50 array, you would simply reference the subprogram with TRACE(M,K,50). Using this technique, you can write subprograms that can be used, without modification, for many different programming tasks.

11.6 Subprograms That Call Other Subprograms

A function or subroutine subprogram can reference any of the intrinsic functions supplied with your system. For example, the following subroutine references the intrinsic function MOD:

```
C SUBROUTINE TO PERFORM INTEGER DIVISION. DETERMINES AND PRINTS
C THE QUOTIENT Q AND THE REMAINDER R WHEN N IS DIVIDED BY D.
      SUBROUTINE DIVIDE(N,D)
      INTEGER N,D,Q,R
      Q=N/D
      R=MOD(N,D)
      WRITE(6,10)Q,R
      RETURN
   10 FORMAT(1X,'QUOTIENT:',I4/1X,'REMAINDER:',I4/)
      END
```

The statement

        CALL DIVIDE (2950,100)

will cause the printout

        QUOTIENT: 29
        REMAINDER: 50

A subprogram can also reference another subprogram (but not itself). For example, the following subroutine calls the subroutine DIVIDE.

```
C A SUBROUTINE WITH NO DUMMY ARGUMENTS
C THAT USES THE SUBROUTINE DIVIDE.
      SUBROUTINE EUCLID
    1 READ(5)K,L
        IF(K.LE.0.OR.L.LE.0) RETURN
        WRITE(6,10)K,L
        CALL DIVIDE(K,L)
      GO TO 1
   10 FORMAT(1X,'DIVIDEND:',I5/1X,'DIVISOR:',I5)
      END
```

The following input data and printout show the effect of the statement

        CALL EUCLID

Input Data (unformatted):

```
            1               2
12345678901234567890
2950,100
425,7
0,0
```

Output:

```
DIVIDEND: 2950
DIVISOR:  100
QUOTIENT:  29
REMAINDER:  50

DIVIDEND:  425
DIVISOR:    7
QUOTIENT:  60
REMAINDER:   5
```

The following diagram displays how control passes from the main program to the subroutine EUCLID, then from EUCLID to the subroutine DIVIDE, several times, and finally back to the main program.

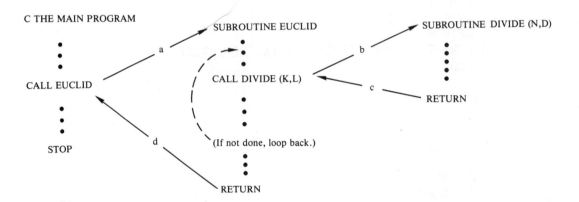

The statement CALL EUCLID in the main program transfers control (arrow a) to the subroutine EUCLID. Since EUCLID contains no dummy arguments, no actual arguments can be included in the CALL statement. The statements in EUCLID are executed until the statement CALL DIVIDE(K,L) is encountered. This statement transfers controi (arrow b) to the subroutine DIVIDE. Since DIVIDE contains two dummy arguments, two (K and L) must be included in the CALL statement. The statements in DIVIDE are executed until a RETURN statement is encountered. This transfers control back to EUCLID (arrow c). Since this particular subroutine DIVIDE does not change the values of its dummy variables N and D, the values of K and L are not changed. EUCLID may now loop back and execute the statement CALL DIVIDE(K,L) several times. Each time the action is as just described. Finally when EUCLID is finished looping back, the RETURN statement in EUCLID is encountered. This transfers control (arrow d) back to the main program.

A subprogram cannot reference a statement function defined in another program unit. Statement function definitions are local to the program unit in which they are made. Thus, to use a statement function in a subprogram, you must define it in the subprogram, even if it is defined in the main program.

Programming applications calling for long printed reports are not uncommon. If confronted with such a programming task you will do well to examine the requirements carefully to see if the long report really consists of several short reports that are each repeated many times. Such short reports are often ideal candidates for subroutines. The following example shows a simple subroutine that may be of value for producing a repetitive portion of a payroll.

EXAMPLE 11. Here is a subroutine to print a short payroll report:

```
C ********* SUBROUTINE PAY **********
      SUBROUTINE PAY(ID,HOURS,RATE)
C CALCULATE THE GROSS PAY
      IF(HOURS.LE.32.) THEN
          OT=0.
          BASE=HOURS*RATE
      ELSE
          OT=(HOURS-32.)*(1.5)*RATE
          BASE=32.*RATE
      END IF
      GROSS=BASE+OT
C PRINT REPORT FOR ONE EMPLOYEE
      CALL DASHES
      WRITE(6,10)ID,HOURS,RATE,OT,GROSS
   10 FORMAT(1X,'EMPLOYEE NUMBER:',I6/1X,'HOURS WORKED:',F6.2/
     +1X,'HOURLY RATE:',F6.2/1X,'OVERTIME:',F7.2/1X,'GROSS PAY:',F7.2)
      CALL DASHES
      RETURN
      END
C
C ********* SUBROUTINE DASHES **********
      SUBROUTINE DASHES
      WRITE(6,10)
      RETURN
   10 FORMAT(1X,40('-'))
      END
```

Each time the statement

CALL PAY(EMP,HRS,RATE)

is executed, the subroutine will print a short report in the following form.

```
------------------------------------------
EMPLOYEE NUMBER: 62013
HOURS WORKED: 47.50
HOURLY RATE:  8.00
OVERTIME: 186.00
GROSS PAY: 442.00
------------------------------------------
```

For the report shown, the values passed to the subroutine are EMP = 62013, HRS = 47.5, and RATE = 8.00.

Remark: Note that the subroutine returns no new information to the calling program. The overtime OT and gross pay GROSS are printed, but not returned. The purpose of the subroutine is to print a document. It does that, and nothing more.

In each subprogram considered to this point, the dummy arguments represented either variables or arrays. The next example illustrates that dummy arguments can also represent subprogram names.

EXAMPLE 12. Here is a subroutine to print a table of values for any function of one variable:

```
      SUBROUTINE TABLE(A,B,D,FUNCT)
C THIS SUBROUTINE PRINTS A TABLE OF VALUES FOR ANY FUNCTION FUNCT
C THE OUTPUT IS A TWO-COLUMN TABLE SHOWING X AND FUNCT(X)
C AS X RANGES FROM A TO B IN INCREMENTS OF D UNITS.
      WRITE(6,10)
      X=A
    1 IF(X.GT.B) RETURN
        Y=FUNCT(X)
        WRITE(6,11)X,Y
        X=X+D
      GO TO 1
   10 FORMAT(1X,3X,'X VALUE',4X,'FUNCTION VALUE')
   11 FORMAT(1X,F10.4,6X,F10.4)
      END
```

The statement

SUBROUTINE TABLE(A,B,D,FUNCT)

defines a subroutine with the name TABLE and the dummy arguments A, B, D, and FUNCT, as usual. Observing that A, B, and D are used as variables in the subroutine, they are dummy variables. However, the assignment statement

Y = FUNCT(X)

tells us that FUNCT is not a variable—variables aren't used this way. It must denote either an array or a function. Since it isn't dimensioned as an array, it is a function. This means that the actual argument that corresponds to the dummy argument FUNCT must supply FUNCT with a function name.

IF FCN denotes a function subprogram to evaluate the expression

FCN(X) = (X − 0.5)**2 − 0.14

the statement

CALL TABLE(0.,1.,0.1,FCN)

will produce the following output.

```
X VALUE      FUNCTION VALUE
 0.0000          0.1100
 0.1000          0.0200
 0.2000         -0.0500
 0.3000         -0.1000
 0.4000         -0.1300
 0.5000         -0.1400
 0.6000         -0.1300
 0.7000         -0.1000
 0.8000         -0.0500
 0.9000          0.0200
 1.0000          0.1100
```

Every reference to the function FUNCT in the subroutine TABLE becomes, in fact, a reference to the function FCN.

The name of any function (other than a statement function) can be passed to the subroutine in this manner. Thus, the subroutine TABLE has wide application: it can be used to produce a table of values for any intrinsic function or any function subprogram simply by including the name of the function as an actual argument.

If you include a function name such as FCN in a CALL statement (we did this when we wrote CALL TABLE(0., 1., 0.1, FCN)), you must place the statement

EXTERNAL FCN

in your main program. This tells the computer that the actual argument FCN is a subprogram name and not a variable name. The general form of the EXTERNAL statement is

EXTERNAL **a, b, c,** . . .

where **a, b, c,** . . . denote names of subprograms that will appear as actual arguments in subprogram references. EXTERNAL statements are nonexecutable. Their placement in a program is shown in Appendix A.

11.7 Summary

Function subprograms and subroutine subprograms are very similar in construction, but quite different in how they are used. Following is a summary of the important differences between these two types of subprograms.

1. A subroutine subprogram begins with a SUBROUTINE statement

    SUBROUTINE name (list of dummy arguments)

    and a function subprogram begins with a FUNCTION statement

    type FUNCTION name (list of dummy arguments).

    In either, the dummy arguments can represent names of variables, arrays, or subprograms. The dummy argument list is optional in subroutines, whereas functions must have at least one dummy argument.

2. A subroutine is called by including its name with a list of actual arguments in a CALL statement. A function is referenced (called) by including its name with a list of actual arguments in a FORTRAN expression.

3. The name of a subroutine has no value associated with it. For this reason it makes no sense to talk about the type of a subroutine; the first letter of its name has no special significance. The name of a function must be assigned a value in the subprogram. This value is returned as the value of any function reference. If the type of the function is not declared, its type is determined by the normal I through N convention.

4. A function subprogram is used only when a single value is to be returned to a calling program. Other than returning this value, it should do nothing else. A subroutine is used in any other situation calling for a subprogram.

The examples in this chapter show several situations where subroutines can be useful. In general, subroutines are written for one or both of the following two reasons.

1. If a particular program segment is of such a general nature that it can be used in many different programming situations, it should be written as a subroutine. Once written, it can be used at any time simply by appending it to any program that needs it. Having debugged the subroutine when it was written, you can be sure that errors in a program that use it will be found elsewhere. Typical examples of useful subroutines are subroutines that sort arrays, search arrays for specific values, print specially formatted output documents, print header lines on multiple page documents, and so on.

2. When writing a program for a somewhat lengthy programming task, it is natural to segment the given task into simpler, more manageable subtasks. Having done this, you may wish to use subroutines to perform these subtasks, even if these subroutines would not be written for the reasons cited in (1). There are three major advantages in doing this.

a. The subroutines can be debugged separately by writing short calling programs that use them. Then, when they are combined into a single program, you can be confident that the subroutines perform their subtasks correctly.

b. The main program will be much shorter than one in which subroutines are not used. For this reason, the program should be easier to maintain (modify to meet current needs). Of course, adequate documentation must be provided. This means including comment lines to explain the purpose of each CALL statement and possibly documentation that is not part of the program (*external documentation*) to explain what each program unit does and how it does it.

c. The subroutines can be written by different programmers (possibly at different locations). Since program units are compiled separately, no conflicts will arise if two or more programmers happen to use the same symbolic names for variables and arrays.

11.8 Problems

1. Each of parts (a) through (d) contains a program segment that calls one or more of the following subprograms. In each case, show the values of the indicated variables upon return from the subroutine.

```
SUBROUTINE SUB(I,J,K,M,N)
M=I
IF(M.LT.J) M=J
N=J
IF(N.GT.K) N=K
RETURN
END
```

```
FUNCTION FCN(I,J,K)
INTEGER FCN
FCN=0
DO 1 N=I,J,K
    FCN=FCN+N
1 CONTINUE
RETURN
END
```

a.
```
I=5
J=I-2
K=I+2
CALL SUB(I,J,K,N1,N2)
```

I = _____
J = _____
K = _____
N1 = _____
N2 = _____

b.
```
N1=3
N2=2*N1
N3=N1+1
CALL SUB(N1,N2,N3,M,N)
```

N1 = _____
N2 = _____
N3 = _____
M = _____
N = _____

c.
```
I=1
J=2
K=3
CALL SUB(I,J,FCN(1,5,K),N1,N2)
```

I = _____
J = _____
K = _____
N1 = _____
N2 = _____

d.
```
K=5
L=FCN(1,K,3)
CALL SUB(L,K,K-L,M,N)
```

K = _____
L = _____
M = _____
N = _____

2. Each of parts (a) and (b) contains a main program segment that calls the following subroutine named SUBAV. The subprograms SUB and FCN are as in Problem 1. In each case, show the values of the indicated variables upon return from the subroutine.

```
SUBROUTINE SUBAV(N,AV)
I=N+3
J=N*N
K=5*J-7
CALL SUB(I,J,K,M,N)
AV=FLOAT(M+N)/2.
RETURN
END
```

a. K = 2
CALL SUBAV(K,AV)

K = _____
AV = _____

b. N = FCN(1,4,3)
CALL SUBAV(N,ANS)

N = _____
ANS = _____

3. What, if anything, is wrong with the following SUBROUTINE statements?
   a. SUBROUTINE SUB1(A,AB,ABC)   **b.** SUBROUTINE SUB2(X,X + 1.,NAME)
   c. SUBROUTINE(A,B,C,SUB3)   **d.** SUBROUTINE COUNTERS(I,J,((I + J)/2,(I*J)/2))

4. What is wrong with the following subroutines?

a.
```
C EVALUATE AX+BY
      SUBROUTINE EVAL(A,B,X,Y)
      EVAL=A*X+B*Y
      RETURN
      END
```

b.
```
C FIND LARGEST VALUE IN ARRAY A
      SUBROUTINE LARGE(A,N,BIG)
      BIG=A(1)
      DO 1 I=2,10
         IF(BIG.LT.A(I)) BIG=A(I)
    1 CONTINUE
      RETURN
      END
```

c.
```
C CALCUALTE SUM AND PRODUCT
C OF N ENTRIES IN ARRAY A
      SUBROUTINE SUMPRD(A,N,SUM,PROD)
      DIMENSION A(N)
      PROD=1.
      DO 1 I=1,N
         PROD=PROD*A(I)
         SUM=SUM+A(I)
    1 CONTINUE
      RETURN
      END
```

Write a subroutine for each task specified in Problems 5–28. In each case write a short main program to debug the subroutine.

5. For any reals A, B, and C, return the sums A + B, B + C, and A + C, and also the average of these sums.

6. For any integers I, J, and K, return the sums I + J, J + K, and I + K, and also the average of these sums.

7. For any one-dimensional array A of size N and any real value VAL, print a list of all entries in A that exceed VAL. The number of entries exceeding VAL is to be returned to the calling program.

8. Given last month's checking account balance (BAL), a list of current deposits (array DEPS), and a list of checks drawn (array CHKS), print a report showing the old balance, the total amount of the deposits, the total amount of the checks drawn, and the new balance. In addition, the new balance is to be returned to the calling program by way of BAL. (No service charges or interest are involved.)

9. Array ID contains employee numbers for N salaried employees, array YRCUMM contains the year-to-date earnings of the N employees, and WKPAY contains this week's gross salary amounts. Your subroutine is to update the array YRCUMM to reflect the current week's salaries and then print a two-column report, complete with column headings, displaying the information contained in ID and YRCUMM.

10. A capital item costing COST dollars is estimated to have a salvage value of SALVAL dollars after a useful life of LIFE years. Using the straight-line method of depreciation, the depreciation allowance for each year is (COST − SALVAL)/LIFE. Your subroutine is to produce a four-column depreciation schedule complete with column headings. The first column is to show the year number (1, 2, 3, . . . , LIFE), the second is to show the depreciation amount for the current year, the third is to show the cumulative depreciation, and the fourth is to show the book value at the end of the year. (The initial book value is COST.) Use the dummy arguments COST, SALVAL, and LIFE and return to the calling program with these three values unchanged. That is, the subroutine is to print the depreciation schedule and do nothing more.

11. An apple orchard occupying one acre of land now contains NTREES apple trees and each tree yields NYLD apples per season. For each new tree planted, the yield per tree will be reduced by NRED apples per season. Produce a three-column table, complete with column headings, showing the yield per tree and the total yield if N = 1, 2, 3, . . . , 25 additional trees are planted.

12. A merchant must pay a fixed price of COST dollars a yard for a certain fabric. From experience it is known that N yards will be sold each month if the material is sold at cost and also that a ten-cent increase in price will mean that FWR fewer yards will be sold each month. Your subroutine is to produce a two-column table, complete with column headings, showing the merchant's profit for each selling price from COST dollars to COST + $2.00 in increments of 10¢. Use the dummy arguments COST, N, and FWR as described. In addition, use a fourth dummy argument BEST that will return the selling price yielding the maximum profit.

13. Array A containing N reals is to be sorted into ascending order. (Any sorting algorithm is acceptable.)

14. For any array A of size N, print a list of all entries that do not exceed the average of the largest and smallest values in A.

15. Determine the larger of X and F(X) where X denotes a real and F denotes any function subprogram with one dummy variable.

16. Find the smallest value taken on by ABS(F(X)) as X ranges from A to B in increments of D units. F denotes an arbitrary function subprogram and A, B, and D denote reals with A < B and D > 0.

17. Write a subroutine beginning with the line SUBROUTINE MAXTBL(A,B,D,F,G). F and G denote functions of one argument, and A, B, and D are reals with A < B and D > 0. The subroutine is to produce a two-column table showing X and the larger of F(X) and G(X), for all values of X from A to B in increments of D units.

The subroutines for Problems 18–28 involve dummy arguments representing two-dimensional arrays. In each case, you should use an extra dummy argument (or two) so that information concerning how an actual array is dimensioned in the main program can be passed to the subprogram. (This practice was discussed in Example 10 of Section 11.5.)

18. Determine the sum of all entries in an N-by-N array A.

19. Determine the sum of all entries in an M-by-N array.

20. Determine the product of the main diagonal entries in an N-by-N array A. Recall that the main diagonal entries are A(1,1), A(2,2), A(3,3), . . . , and A(N,N).

21. Determine the largest entry in the first column of an N-by-N array A.

22. Determine that entry in an N-by-N array whose value is closest to zero.

23. Modify any N-by-N array A by reducing each entry by the average of all N^2 entries in the array.

24. Interchange rows I and J of an M-by-N array A.

25. Rearrange the rows of an N-by-2 array A so that the entries in the first column are in ascending order.

26. Rearrange the rows of an M-by-N array A so that the entries in the first column are in ascending order. (Your subroutine may call the subroutine described in Problem 24.)

27. For any M-by-N array A, return two one-dimensional arrays R and C such that R(I) gives the sum of the entries in the Ith row of A and C(J) gives the sum of the entries in the Jth column of A.

28. This one is more difficult. Modify an M-by-N array A so that it will include an (M + 1)st row and (N + 1)st column as follows. For J = 1, 2, . . . , N, A(M + 1,J) is to contain the sum of the M entries in column J and for I = 1, 2, . . . , M, A(I,N + 1) is to contain the sum of the entries in row I. In addition, A(M + 1,N + 1) is to contain the sum of all entries in the original array.

11.9 Review True-or-False Quiz

1. All of the variables appearing in a subprogram are called dummy variables.

    T F

2. The symbolic names used as dummy arguments in FUNCTION and SUBROUTINE statements can represent variables, arrays, or subprograms.

    T F

3. An actual argument that is used to pass information to a subprogram can be a numerical expression, an array name, or a subprogram name. However, it cannot be a statement function name.

    T F

4. The correspondence between actual and dummy arguments is always a two-way correspondence.

    T F

5. A subprogram can call another subprogram only if the name of the subprogram being called appears in an EXTERNAL statement.

    T F

6. A careless programmer could write a program in which the following statement will result in 1 being added to K:

   IF(FN(M).NE.FN(M)) K = K + 1

    T F

7. The expressions *program unit* and *subprogram* have the same meaning.

    T F

8. All variable and array names appearing in a single program unit are "local" to that program unit.

    T F

9. Any symbolic name used in one program unit can be used in any other program unit for any purpose whatever. (Recall that a symbolic name is any string of 1 to 6 letters and digits whose first character is a letter.)

    T F

10. Statement labels are "local" to the program unit containing them. This is true for main programs as well as subprograms.

    T F

11. Suppose that A is dimensioned in the main program as a 3-by-2 array. If A is used as an actual argument supplying values to a one-dimensional dummy array B, any change to B(5) in the subprogram will be reflected as a change to A(2,2) in the main program.

    T F

12. A subroutine that is designed to produce output, but not to return any values to a calling program, will have no dummy arguments.

    T F

13. The dummy argument A in the following subroutine must necessarily represent a function:

    T F

```
SUBROUTINE EVAL(A,N,B)
B=A(N)
RETURN
END
```

12
Processing Character Data

Several of the examples considered to this point have involved processing input records containing character data as well as numerical data. However, in each case, only the numerical values were used—nX edit descriptors were used to skip over the character data. For instance, the formatted READ statement

```
    READ(5,20)I,J
 20 FORMAT(16X,I4,I4)
```

interprets the input record

```
        1         2         3
12345678901234567890234567890
MCCARTHY,JOHN J.  24    2
```

to obtain the values $I = 24$ and $J = 2$; the descriptor 16X instructs the computer to skip over the first 16 positions. Many programming applications require that character data be processed, not ignored. In this chapter we describe how FORTRAN allows you to assign character data to variables, to process these data, and to print the results of this processing, be it numerical data or character data.

12.1 Storing Character Data

You will recall that a *string* is any sequence of FORTRAN characters. Following are eight examples of strings.

A	PRICE-EARNINGS-RATIO
Z13	HAPPY DAYS
ADAM	6 PLUS SIGNS + + + + + +
1239	WASHINGTON, GEORGE

FORTRAN allows you to assign strings to variables (simple and subscripted) using DATA statements and READ statements. However, the lengths of these strings cannot be arbitrary. The statement

DATA NAME/'MARY ELLEN'/

may or may not assign the ten-character string MARY ELLEN to the variable NAME. What actually happens depends on how many characters the variable NAME can store.

EXAMPLE 1. In Parts (a) and (b) we describe two possible effects of the statement

DATA NAME1,NAME2,NAME3/'MARY ELLEN','VI','SUSAN'/

a. If each of the variables NAME1, NAME2, and NAME3 can store up to ten characters, the DATA statement initializes these variables as follows. (Δ denotes the nonprinting blank character.)

NAME1 | M | A | R | Y | Δ | E | L | L | E | N |

NAME2 | V | I | Δ | Δ | Δ | Δ | Δ | Δ | Δ | Δ |

NAME3 | S | U | S | A | N | Δ | Δ | Δ | Δ | Δ |

Since 'MARY ELLEN' contains exactly ten characters, they are all stored in NAME1. 'VI' specifies a string with only two characters, so these two characters are stored *left-justified* in the ten character positions allowed for NAME2; the rightmost eight positions are filled with blanks. Similarly, SUSAN is stored left-justified in NAME3 with the rightmost five positions being blank-filled.

b. If each of the variables NAME1, NAME2, and NAME3 can store up to four characters, the DATA statement initializes them as follows:

NAME1 | M | A | R | Y |

NAME2 | V | I | Δ | Δ |

NAME3 | S | U | S | A |

The ten-character string MARY ELLEN does not fit into the four character positions allowed for NAME1 so only the *first* four characters are stored. The other six (ΔELLEN) are lost. Similarly, only the first four characters of SUSAN are stored in NAME3. As explained in Part (a), VI is stored left-justified with the rightmost two positions being filled with blanks.

The number of characters that can be stored in one computer memory location is system dependent. For example, the CDC series 6000 and 7000 computers can store ten characters in each memory location, and for this reason, many CDC-based FORTRAN systems always store ten characters whenever a string (whatever its length) is assigned to a variable. Similarly, the IBM 360 and 370 series computers can store four characters in each memory location; hence, many IBM-based FORTRAN systems store exactly four characters for each variable. Many FORTRAN compilers provide the CHARACTER statement that allows you to specify separate string lengths for any variables used to store character data.

If your compiler allows the CHARACTER statement, you can write

CHARACTER NAME1*10,NAME2*10,NAME3*10

to declare NAME1, NAME2, and NAME3 as character variables and to specify that each of these variables is to store ten characters. The situation described in Example 1.a will then hold. If you write

CHARACTER NAME1*10,NAME2*4,NAME3*4

ten characters are specified for NAME1 and four characters are specified for each of the other two variables. The effect of the DATA statement shown in Example 1 will then be as follows:

NAME1 | M | A | R | Y | Δ | E | L | L | E | N |

NAME2 | V | I | Δ | Δ |

NAME3 | S | U | S | A |

The CHARACTER statement is included in the FORTRAN standard. However, it has yet to be implemented in all FORTRAN compilers. If your compiler does not allow the CHARACTER statement, any variables can be used to store character data, and the number of characters stored is the same for each variable. This number can be found in your FORTRAN manual. The common practice is to use only integer variables for character data; this avoids problems that can arise because of the difference in how computers store integer and real data.

Our objective in this section is to show how character data can be assigned to variables, and not to explain how systems differ. This is most easily accomplished if we assume that all variables used to store character data contain the same number C of characters. In each example we will use C = 4 and also explain what happens for the case C = 10. These are two of the most common situations. If your system allows the CHARACTER statement, simply assume that each variable used to store character data has been declared a character variable with C characters.

EXAMPLE 2. If C = 4 characters are stored for each variable, the statement

```
DATA N1,N2,N3,INAUG/'WASH','INGT','ON','1789'/
```

will initialize the variables N1,N2,N3, and INAUG as follows:

N1 | W | A | S | H |

N2 | I | N | G | T |

N3 | O | N | Δ | Δ |

INAUG | 1 | 7 | 8 | 9 |

Since we are assuming that only C = 4 characters can be stored for a single variable, the name WASHINGTON requires three variables.

The compiler stores the string 1789 as a sequence of four separate characters 1, 7, 8, and 9. That is, it stores a sequence of 0's and 1's for the character 1, another sequence of 0's and 1's for the character 7, and so on. In contrast, DATA NUM/1789/ will store 1789 as the single binary representation of the number 1789. There is a difference.

If C = 10, the assignment of values is as follows:

N1 | W | A | S | H | Δ | Δ | Δ | Δ | Δ | Δ |

N2 | I | N | G | T | Δ | Δ | Δ | Δ | Δ | Δ |

N3 | O | N | Δ | Δ | Δ | Δ | Δ | Δ | Δ | Δ |

INAUG | 1 | 7 | 8 | 9 | Δ | Δ | Δ | Δ | Δ | Δ |

However, one variable can, and should, replace N1, N2, and N3. If you use the statement

DATA NAME,INAUG/'WASHINGTON','1789'/

the assignments will be

NAME

W	A	S	H	I	N	G	T	O	N

INAUG

1	7	8	9	Δ	Δ	Δ	Δ	Δ	Δ

Character data appearing in input records can be read by using the Aw edit descriptor. The computer uses this descriptor to interpret the next w input characters to obtain a string value for the input variable.

EXAMPLE 3. Each of parts (a) and (b) shows a formatted READ statement, and describes how it reads values from the following input record.

```
         1         2
12345678901234567890
MARY JANE SAL
```

a.   READ(5,10)N1,N2,N3
     10 FORMAT(A4,1X,A4,1X,A4)

Case C = 4. The variable assignments are

N1

M	A	R	Y

N2

J	A	N	E

N3

S	A	L	Δ

The first edit descriptor A4 is used to interpret the first four input characters MARY to obtain a character string for N1. The 1X descriptor skips over the next character (the blank in position 5). Similarly the next three descriptors A4, 1X, and A4 interpret the next nine input characters to obtain the values shown for N2 and N3.

Case C = 10. The assignments are

N1

M	A	R	Y	Δ	Δ	Δ	Δ	Δ	Δ

N2

J	A	N	E	Δ	Δ	Δ	Δ	Δ	Δ

N3

S	A	L	Δ	Δ	Δ	Δ	Δ	Δ	Δ

The first edit descriptor A4 interprets the first four input characters MARY to obtain a string value for N1. Since N1 stores ten characters, MARY is stored left-justified, with six trailing blanks as shown. The 1X descriptor skips the next input character. Similarly the next three descriptors A4, 1X, and A4 interpret the next nine input characters to obtain the values shown for N2 and N3.

b.   READ(5,11)M1,M2
     11 FORMAT(A10,A10)

Case C = 4. The variable assignments are

M1

A	N	E	Δ

M2

Δ	Δ	Δ

The first descriptor A10 interprets the first ten input characters (MARY JANEΔ) to obtain a string value for M1. Since only C = 4 characters can be stored in M1, the last four (ANEΔ) are used. The first six are lost.

Similarly, the second descriptor A10 interprets the next ten input characters (SALΔΔΔΔΔΔΔ) and uses the last four (ΔΔΔΔ) for M2.

Remark: It seldom, if ever, makes sense to read input data by using a descriptor Aw with $w >$ C. (In this example, $w = 10$ and C $= 4$.) Since only the last C characters in an input field of width w are used, you must see to it that the input string appears right-justified in these w positions. This is awkward to do, whether you are typing or keypunching the input data. For instance, to type a 15-character input field containing EASY you must type (and count) eleven leading blanks; to type AWKWARDLY, you must start with six blanks (or is it 5?).

Case C $= 10$. The variable assignments are as follows:

M1 | M | A | R | Y | Δ | J | A | N | E | Δ |

M2 | S | A | L | Δ | Δ | Δ | Δ | Δ | Δ | Δ |

Since both C $= 10$ and Aw = A10, the first ten input characters are assigned to M1 and the next ten to M2.

Remark: If MARY JANE is meant to denote one person's name, A10 is appropriate. However, if MARY and JANE denote two names, they should be stored by using two variable names.

12.2 Printing Character Data

The edit descriptor Aw is also used to print the contents of variables containing character data. The letter A in Aw specifies that the contents of the variable are to be interpreted as a sequence of characters, and w specifies the number of print positions to be used.

EXAMPLE 4. Each of parts (a) through (c) shows a formatted WRITE statement and gives a description of its effect. We assume that the variables appearing in these WRITE statements have previously been assigned values as follows. (Note that we are assuming that C $= 4$.)

NAME1 | S | A | L | Δ |

NAME2 | M | A | R | Y |

a.
```
    WRITE(6,10)NAME1,NAME2
 10 FORMAT(1X,A4,A4)
```

Output: SAL MARY

The first A4 descriptor specifies that four print positions are to be used to print the string contents of NAME1. Since C $= 4$ characters are stored for each variable, the entire string SALΔ is printed. Similarly, the second A4 descriptor causes all four characters stored in NAME2 (MARY) to be printed.

b.
```
    WRITE(6,11)NAME1,NAME2
 11 FORMAT(1X,A2,A1)
```

Output: SAM

The descriptor A2 specifies that two print positions are to be used to print the string contents of NAME1. The *first* two (SA) of these are printed. Similarly, the A1 descriptor causes the *first* character (M) stored in NAME2 to be printed.

```
c.    WRITE(6,12)NAME1,NAME2
   12 FORMAT(1X,A10)
```

Output: ΔΔΔΔΔΔSALΔ
             ΔΔΔΔΔΔMARY

A10 specifies that ten print positions are to be used to print the contents (SALΔ) of NAME1. Since the variables contain only four characters, they are printed *right-justified* in the output field of width 10 with six leading blanks.

The format specification (1X,A10) is repeated for NAME2 to give the second line shown in the output.

Remark: An output descriptor Aw with w > C is sometimes used for spacing. For example, using A10 when C = 4, as in this example, produces six blank spaces. This practice is not recommended. If six blank spaces are wanted, use 6X. Thus, the formatted WRITE statement shown in part (c) is better written with the format specification (1X,6X,A4). In general, you should keep w ≤ C on both input and output.

EXAMPLE 5. The program in this example reads input records such as

```
          1         2
12345678901234567890
ELISON    3.35 36
```

to produce short payroll reports in the following form:

```
 NAME: ELISON
 HOURS: 36
 GROSS PAY:_____
```

The name appears in the first eight positions of an input record, the hourly rate in positions 9 through 15, and the hours worked in positions 16 through 18. (There is no overtime.) The program halts when an hourly rate of zero is encountered.

```
C PAYROLL PROGRAM
C NAMES ARE STORED USING N1 AND N2
      INTEGER HOURS
    1 READ(5,10)N1,N2,RATE,HOURS
      IF(RATE.EQ.0.) STOP
      GROSS=RATE*FLOAT(HOURS)
      WRITE(6,11)N1,N2,HOURS,GROSS
      GO TO 1
   10 FORMAT(2A4,F7.2,I3)
   11 FORMAT(/ 1X,'NAME:',1X,2A4/1X,'HOURS:',I3/1X,'GROSS PAY:',F7.2/)
      END
```

Input Data:

```
          1         2
12345678901234567890
ELISON    3.35 36
BRANDEN   6.50 40
XXXX      0.    0
```

Output:

```
NAME: ELISON
HOURS: 36
GROSS PAY: 120.60


NAME: BRANDEN
HOURS: 40
GROSS PAY: 260.00
```

Remark 1: This program reads and prints character and numerical data, but otherwise processes only numerical data. In Section 12.4 you will see how character data can be processed by using statements other than input and output statements.

Remark 2: This program will behave as described on any system that can store at least four characters in each variable. However, if your system can store as many as eight characters in a variable (for instance if the CHARACTER statement is allowed), you can improve the program by using a single variable to store names in place of the two (N1 and N2) used in the program. The only other change required is to change each of the two descriptors 2A4 to the single descriptor A8. The output will be exactly the same.

Remark 3: If this program is run in a conversational mode, the input values will also be displayed as they are typed. As always, a user will need instructions concerning what should be typed.

As shown in Examples 3 and 4 the effect of an input or output operation involving character data depends not only on the field width w specified in the descriptor Aw, but also on the number C of characters that are stored in variables. Precisely what happens can be summarized as follows.
On input:

1. If w = C, the w input characters are stored.
2. If w < C, the w input characters are stored left-justified with nonprinting blank characters filling the rightmost C-w character positions.
3. If w > C, only the rightmost C characters of the input field are stored. (This case should be avoided entirely; see Example 3.b.)

On output:

1. If w = C, the contents (C characters) of the output variable are printed.
2. If w < C, only the leftmost w characters are printed.
3. If w > C, the contents (C characters) of the output variable are printed right-justified, with leading blanks, in an output field of w print positions. (This case is not recommended; see Example 4.c.)

12.3 Manipulating Character Data

Character data that are stored in variables can be processed by using FORTRAN statements other than input and output statements. For instance, suppose that the variables N1 and N2 are used for storing character data and that each stores the same number of characters. The assignment statement

N1 = N2

will cause the contents of N2 to be copied into N1. Also, the logical expression N1.EQ.N2 can be used as the condition in an IF statement. It is true if the contents of N1 and N2 are identical; otherwise, it is false. The following short program uses such a logical expression to print the first word in an input list that begins with the letter J. We assume that C = 4 characters are stored in each variable:

```
        DATA JAY/'J'/
    1   READ(5,10)N1,N2,N3
            IF(N1.NE.JAY) GO TO 1
        WRITE(6,11)N1,N2,N3
        STOP
   10   FORMAT(A1,A4,A4)
   11   FORMAT(1X,A1,A4,A4)
        END
```

Input Data:

```
            1           2
12345678901234567890
DECEMBER
AND
JANUARY
ARE
COLD
MONTHS
```

Output:

JANUARY

During compilation we obtain

JAY | J | Δ | Δ | Δ |

Each time the READ statement is executed, one input record is used to obtain values for N1, N2, and N3. Since the edit descriptors are A1, A4, and A4, the first nine input characters are interpreted to obtain string values for these variables. Then the IF statement compares N1 with JAY, and repeats the READ statement if their contents are not identical. If they are, the WRITE statement is executed and the program stops. For the given input data, the first three passes through the loop yield the following values:

	Pass 1	Pass 2	Pass 3
N1	D Δ Δ Δ	A Δ Δ Δ	J Δ Δ Δ
N2	E C E M	N D Δ Δ	A N U A
N3	B E R Δ	Δ Δ Δ Δ	R Y Δ Δ

On the first two passes N1.NE.JAY is true, so control returns to the READ statement. On the third pass N1 and JAY are identical; that is, N1.NE.JAY is false, so control passes to the WRITE statement to produce the indicated output. Recall that when N1 = JΔΔΔ is printed by using the edit descriptor A1, the first character is printed.

FORTRAN also allows you to compare variables containing character data by using any of the relational operators .EQ., .LT., .LE., .GT., .GE., and .NE..

To understand when one string is less than another string, you should have some knowledge of how computers store character data. When a string is stored in memory, each character is assigned a numerical value called its **numeric code.** It is these numerical values that are compared. As one would expect, the numeric code for the letter A is smaller than that for B, the numeric code for B is smaller than that for C, and so on. But it is not only letters that can be compared; each FORTRAN character has its own unique numeric code so that any two characters can be compared. One FORTRAN character is less than a second character if the numeric code of the first is less than the numeric code of the second.

Unfortunately, computer systems differ in their numeric codes. The ordering sequence of the FORTRAN character set as given by the American Standard Code of Information Interchange (ASCII) is presented in Table 12.1.

TABLE 12.1. ASCII numeric codes for the FORTRAN character set.

Character	Numeric code	Character	Numeric code	Character	Numeric code
(blank)	32	5	53	J	74
!	33	6	54	K	75
"	34	7	55	L	76
#	35	8	56	M	77
$	36	9	57	N	78
%	37	:	58	O	79
&	38	;	59	P	80
'	39	<	60	Q	81
(	40	=	61	R	82
)	41	>	62	S	83
*	42	?	63	T	84
+	43	@	64	U	85
,	44	A	65	V	86
—	45	B	66	W	87
.	46	C	67	X	88
/	47	D	68	Y	89
0	48	E	69	Z	90
1	49	F	70	[	91
2	50	G	71	\	92
3	51	H	72	]	93
4	52	I	73	∧	94

Using these ASCII numeric codes, we can write the following:

'G' .LT. 'P' since 71 < 80
'4' .LT. 'A' since 52 < 65
'$' .LT. '1' since 36 < 49
'8' .LT. '?' since 56 < 63

If strings containing more than one character are to be compared, they are compared character by character beginning at the left. Strings consisting only of letters of the alphabet are ordered just as they would appear in a dictionary:

'ACHE' .LT. 'ACT'
'ELBOW' .EQ. 'ELBOW'
'FINGERS' .GT. 'FINGER'
'SAL' .LT. 'SALLY'

Note that the ASCII numeric code for the blank character is smaller than each of the others. Thus, if

M = | A | L | Δ | Δ | and   N = | A | L | E | Δ |

then M.LT.N. Note also that the code for a comma is smaller than the code for each of the letters. Thus,

'SMITH,ZACHARY' .LT. 'SMITHSON,ANDREW'

as it should be if names in this form are to be alphabetized.

EXAMPLE 6. Let's write a program to read a list of names and print only those that begin with a letter from G to L.

Problem Analysis:
Since a decision concerning whether to print a particular name can be made as soon as it is read, we will read a name, print it if it begins with a letter from G to L, and repeat this process for each name.

Before proceeding with this problem analysis we should know how the input data are formatted. Let's assume that column positions 1 through 20 of each record contain a name in the form "last,first", and that the last input record contains the EOD-tag END. We can now prepare a test set of input records as follows:

Input:

```
          1         2         3
12345678901234567890123456789
LINCOLN,ABRAHAM
JOHNSON,ANDREW
GRANT,ULYSSES
HAYES,RUTHERFORD
GARFIELD,JAMES
ARTHUR,CHESTER
CLEVELAND,GROVER
HARRISON,BENJAMIN
MCKINLEY,WILLIAM
ROOSEVELT,THEODORE
END
```

That the following algorithm is appropriate for the task at hand should now be evident.

Algorithm:
a. Read a name.
b. If the name read is END, stop.
c. If the first letter of the name read is one of the letters G to L, print the name.
d. Go to step (a).

Before coding this algorithm we must decide how to read the input data. Let's assume that our system allows at most C = 4 characters to be assigned to any variable. Since up to 20 characters must be read for each name, we can use the five variables N1, N2, N3, N4, and N5. In particular, the first four characters will be read into N1, the next four into N2, and so on.

We now know how to code step (a). Step (b) involves comparing N1 with the string END and step (c) involves examining N1 to see if its first character is one of the letters from G to L. In the program, this latter test is accomplished by making two comparisons: (N1.LT.'M') and (N1.GE.'G').

The Program:

```
C PROGRAM TO READ A LIST OF NAMES AND PRINT THOSE
C WHOSE FIRST LETTER IS BETWEEN G AND M INCLUSIVE.
      INTEGER END,GEE,EM
      DATA END,GEE,EM/'END','G','M'
    1 READ(5,10)N1,N2,N3,N4,N5
      IF(N1.EQ.END) STOP
      IF(N1.GE.GEE).AND.(N1.LT.EM) WRITE(6,20)N1,N2,N3,N4,N5
      GO TO 1
   10 FORMAT(5A4)
   20 FORMAT(1X,5A4)
      END
```

Output:

```
LINCOLN,ABRAHAM
JOHNSON,ANDREW
GRANT,ULYSSES
HAYES,RUTHERFORD
GARFIELD,JAMES
HARRISON,BENJAMIN
```

12.4 Problems

1. Tell first what values are assigned to each variable and then what is printed by each program segment. Use the following three input records for each part:

```
          1         2         3
1234567890123456789012345 67890
ABCDEFGHIJKLMNOP
1234567890123456
A1B2C3D4E5F6G7H8
```

a. (Assume that C = 4.)

```
   READ(5,10)I,J,K
10 FORMAT(A4,A2,A6)
   WRITE(6,20)I,J,K
20 FORMAT(1X,3A4)
```

b. (Assume that C = 10.)

```
   READ(5,16)I,J,K
16 FORMAT(A4,A8,A2)
   WRITE(6,26)(I,J,K)
26 FORMAT(1X,A6,A6,A4)
```

c. (Assume that C = 1.)

```
   READ(5,12)I,J,K
12 FORMAT(A1)
   WRITE(6,22)I,J,K
22 FORMAT(1X,A1)
```

d. (Assume that C = 4.)

```
   READ(5,14)I,J,K
14 FORMAT(A4)
   WRITE(6,24)I,J,K
24 FORMAT(1X,A8)
```

e. (Assume that C = 6.)

```
   READ(5,11)I,J,K
11 FORMAT(A4/A2/A6)
   WRITE(6,21)I,J,K
21 FORMAT(1X,A4)
```

f. (Assume that C = 10.)

```
   READ(5,13)I,J,K
13 FORMAT(A5/A15/A10)
   WRITE(6,23)I,J,K
23 FORMAT(1X,A10)
```

2. What will be printed when each program is run?

a. (Assume that C = 4.)

```
   DATA N/'BOAT'/
   WRITE(6,10)N,N
10 FORMAT(1X,'RIVER',A4/1X,9X,A4,
  + 'SWAIN')
   STOP
   END
```

b. (Assume that C = 4.)

```
   DATA M/'*'/
   WRITE(6,11)M,M,M,M,M,M
11 FORMAT(1X,A1/1X,2A1/1X,3A1)
   STOP
   END
```

Write a program for each task described in Problems 3–9. In each case use whatever value of C is correct for your FORTRAN system. If the CHARACTER statement is allowed, you should use it. (If you are operating in a batch environment, Problems 3–12 in Section 12.7 are appropriate at this time.)

3. Each of several input records contains a five-character string (no blanks) in positions 1 through 5. The first string whose first character is $ indicates that there are no more input strings. Your program is to print each of these five-character strings backwards. Use only one READ statement and one WRITE or PRINT statement.
4. A string is called a palindrome if it reads the same forwards and backwards. With input data as described in Problem 3, print each string followed by a label telling whether it is or isn't a palindrome.
5. Each of several input records contains 1, 2, 3, 4, or 5 characters in positions 1 through 5. (Any blanks are trailing blanks.) After reading a string, print its characters one under the other and then print a message telling how many characters it contained. The first input string containing one character should serve as an end-of-data tag.
6. For input data as described in Problem 5, print each string followed by a label telling whether it is or isn't a palindrome.
7. Given the employee name and monthly sales, print an individual report for each employee showing the employee name, monthly sales, and commission if the commission rate for each person is 6%.

Employee name	Monthly sales
Geroux	$4,050
Erickson	6,500
LaFreniere	3,750
Maxwell	3,640
Cohen	7,150

8. Given the monthly sales and commission rate, print an individual report for each employee showing the employee name, the monthly sales, the commission rate, and the total commission.

Name	Monthly sales	Commission rate
Lyons	$28,400	2%
Madden	34,550	2.5%
Gliniewicz	19,600	3%
Russell	14,500	2%
Marcotte	22,300	3.25%
Edwards	31,350	1.5%

9. Given the employee name, base salary, monthly sales, and commission rate, print an individual report for each employee showing the employee name, base salary, commission, and total monthly earnings.

Name	Base salary	Monthly sales	Commission rate
Malinowski	$400	$6,900	3%
Johnson	445	8,400	2.5%
Machna	430	9,250	3%
Gentile	465	8,920	4%
Constantino	425	9,725	3.5%

12.5 Character Arrays

FORTRAN allows the processing of character data by means of arrays. The next three examples show how character data can be assigned to arrays and how these arrays can be printed. (Note that these examples assume that C = 4 characters are stored for each variable.)

EXAMPLE 7. The statements

```
DIMENSION I(3)
DATA I/'PROG','RAMM',"ING'/
```

will initialize the variables I(1), I(2), and I(3) as follows:

I(1) | P | R | O | G |

I(2) | R | A | M | M |

I(3) | I | N | G | Δ |

Since we are assuming that only C = 4 characters can be stored for a single variable, the word PROGRAMMING requires three variables. Storing "long" strings in an array as is done here is a common programming practice.

EXAMPLE 8. Either of the following two equivalent program statements

```
     DIMENSION LEFT(26)                    DIMENSION LEFT(26)
     READ(5,10)(LEFT(I),I=1,26)            READ(5,10)LEFT
10   FORMAT(26A1)                      10  FORMAT(26A1)
```

interprets the input record

```
          1         2         3
 12345678901234567890123456789 0
 ABCDEFGHIJKLMNOPQRSTUVWXYZ
```

to assign the variables as follows:

LEFT(1) | A | Δ | Δ | Δ |

LEFT(2) | B | Δ | Δ | Δ |

LEFT(3) | C | Δ | Δ | Δ |
   ⋮
   ⋮
LEFT(26) | Z | Δ | Δ | Δ |

The format specification (26A1) is equivalent to a sequence of 26 A1 descriptors. Hence, for each I from 1 to 26, a one-character string is stored left-justified in A(I).

Remark: If the format specification (26A1) were changed to (A1), 26 input records would be needed, each containing a single letter of the alphabet in its first character position.

EXAMPLE 9. Assuming that the variables have previously been assigned as follows,

J(1) | A | L | L | Δ |

J(2) | O | N | Δ | O |

J(3) | N | E | Δ | L |

J(4) | I | N | E | . |

the formatted WRITE statement

```
    WRITE(6,11)(J(I),I=1,4)
11 FORMAT(1X,4A4)
```

will print

ALL ON ONE LINE.

The edit descriptor 4A4 causes the contents of the four variables $(N(I), I = 1,4)$, each of which contains four characters, to be printed on one line as shown.

Remark: If J were dimensioned to be of length 4, the statement WRITE(6,11)J could have been used.

Programs that process character data can often be simplified by using the CHARACTER statement to specify lengths for character variables. As explained in Section 12.1, the statement

CHARACTER NAME*20,DEPT*5

declares NAME as a character variable containing 20 characters and DEPT as another containing 5 characters. Without the CHARACTER statement, the two variables NAME and DEPT may not be adequate. For instance, if your system stores $C = 4$ characters in each variable, five variables are needed to store the twenty characters NAME can handle, and two are needed in place of DEPT. Systems that allow the CHARACTER statement allow you to declare character arrays as well as character variables. On systems conforming to the FORTRAN standard, the statement

```
CHARACTER LIST(100)*20,MAT(10,10)*5
```

declares two character arrays: LIST, as a one-dimensional array of size 100, each of whose entries contains 20 characters, and MAT as a 10-by-10 array each of whose entries contains 5 characters.

EXAMPLE 10. Here are two program segments to read the words and abbreviations contained in the following input records into arrays. (Program segment 2 is for systems that store $C = 4$ characters for each variable.)

```
        1         2
12345678901234567890
ALUMINUM  AL
GOLD      AU
SILVER    AG
BORON     B
BROMINE   BR
CARBON    C
COPPER    CU
CALCIUM   CA
COBALT    CO
CHROMIUM  CR
CHLORINE  CL
HYDROGEN  H
```

```
(Program Segment 1)        CHARACTER ELEM(12)*10,ABBR(12)*2
                           DO 1 I=1,12
                              READ(5,10)ELEM(I),ABBR(I)
                         1 CONTINUE
                        10 FORMAT(A8,2X,A2)
```

(Program Segment 2)

```
INTEGER ABBR(12),ELEM1(12),ELEM2(12)
DO 1 I=1,12
    READ(5,10)ELEM1(I),ELEM2(I),ABBR(I)
 1 CONTINUE
10 FORMAT(2A4,2X,A2)
```

Note the simplicity of program segment 1. Each element is stored using a single array entry ELEM(I) and the corresponding abbreviation is stored in a two-character array entry ABBR(I). Thus, the information in the first input record is stored as follows:

ELEM(1) | A | L | U | M | I | N | U | M |

ABBR(1) | A | L |

The second program segment is not so clear; two array entries ELEM1(I) and ELEM2(I) are needed to store the name of a single element. This program segment stores the information in the first input record as follows.

ELEM1(1) | A | L | U | M |

ELEM2(1) | I | N | U | M |

ABBR(1) | A | L | Δ | Δ |

Question:

In Example 8, we used an array name without subscripts in a READ statement to read values for all array entries. Assuming the input data for the present example are as shown, why can't the DO-loop in program segment 1 be replaced by the single statement

READ(5,10)ELEM,ABBR

and why can't the DO-loop in program segment 2 be replaced by the following READ statement?

READ(5,20)ELEM1,ELEM2,ABBR

Explain how the input records should be changed to allow you to do this.

In Chapter 9 (on arrays), several of the worked-out examples illustrated programming situations that required the use of arrays containing numerical values. For instance, the task of sorting a list of numerical values into ascending order is almost impossible without the use of arrays. The same is true for many programming tasks that involve processing character data. The next two examples in this section, and the sorting example in the following section, illustrate the use of arrays containing character data in programming situations that would be awkward, if not impossible, were arrays not used. In each case, we make the assumption that variables store $C = 4$ characters. Because of this restriction, we will be required to use more than one array to store a single list of strings, as was illustrated in Example 9. This will necessarily complicate the coding process. However, it is unavoidable on systems that do not allow the CHARACTER statement (and many don't). (If the CHARACTER statement is implemented on your system, you can simply assume that each array used to store character data has been declared in a CHARACTER statement specifying that each array entry contains $C = 4$ characters. It would also be instructive to show how each program can be simplified by using appropriate CHARACTER statements.)

EXAMPLE 11. Here is a program segment to count the number of A's in a single input record:

```
      INTEGER A,CHAR(72),COUNT
      DATA A/'A'/
      READ(5,10)(CHAR(K),K=1,72)
   10 FORMAT(72A1)
      COUNT=0
      DO 1 K=1,72
         IF(CHAR(K).EQ.A) COUNT=COUNT+1
    1 CONTINUE
```

The DATA statement assigns the one-character string A to the variable A. The READ statement stores the characters appearing in the next input record in the array CHAR, one character being assigned to each entry of the array. The DO-loop then examines each character stored in CHAR and adds 1 to COUNT if the character is the letter A.

Remark 1: Since the READ statement reads values for all 72 entries of CHAR, it can be replaced by the statement

READ (5,10) CHAR

Remark 2: Since C = 4 characters are stored in each variable, a typical entry in CHAR is as follows.

CHAR(I) | Q | Δ | Δ | Δ |

Thus, three-fourths of the memory space reserved for the array CHAR is wasted space. If the CHARACTER statement is allowed, you should use

CHARACTER CHAR(72)*1

Then, no memory space is wasted.

EXAMPLE 12. Here is a program to read and print a list of up to 100 strings. Each string is presented in a separate input record and contains no more than 48 characters.

```
      INTEGER STR(100,12)
C NUM DENOTES THE NUMBER OF STRINGS
C THE ITH STRING IS STORED IN (STR(I,K),K=1,12)
      READ(5,10)NUM
      IF(NUM.GT.100) STOP
C READ AND STORE ALL INPUT DATA
      DO 1 I=1,NUM
         READ(5,11)(STR(I,K),K=1,12)
    1 CONTINUE
C PRINT THE NUM STRINGS
      DO 2 I=1,NUM
         WRITE(6,12)(STR(I,K),K=1,12)
    2 CONTINUE
      STOP
   10 FORMAT(I5)
   11 FORMAT(12A4)
   12 FORMAT(1X,12A4)
      END
```

Input Data:

```
THIS PROGRAM WORKS ON SYSTEMS THAT STORE AT
LEAST 4 CHARACTERS FOR EACH VARIABLE. THE
PROGRAM CAN BE MODIFIED SO THAT IT WILL WORK ON
```

ANY FORTRAN SYSTEM. TO DO THIS, DIMENSION STR WITH
        DIMENSION STR(100,48)
AND CHANGE THE TWO 12A4 DESCRIPTORS TO 48A1.

Output:

THIS PROGRAM WORKS ON SYSTEMS THAT STORE AT
LEAST 4 CHARACTERS FOR EACH VARIABLE. THE
PROGRAM CAN BE MODIFIED SO THAT IT WILL WORK ON
ANY FORTRAN SYSTEM. TO DO THIS, DIMENSION STR WITH
        DIMENSION STR(100,48)
AND CHANGE THE TWO 12A4 DESCRIPTORS TO 48A1.

Remark 1: It was necessary to use a two-dimensional array STR so that all input data could be read before any printing took place. If all input data are submitted at one time (for instance, in a card operation), STR can be dimensioned as a one-dimensional array of size 12 and each string can be printed as it is read. This would not be appropriate in a conversational mode; each string would be echoed as you typed it and immediately printed again by the WRITE statement.

Remark 2: If your system allows the CHARACTER statement, you can use a one-dimensional array by declaring STR as follows

CHARACTER STR(100)*48

Then, each string can be stored as one entry in the character array STR.

12.6 Sorting Character Data

It is often necessary to arrange lists of strings in some specified order (for example, lists of names in alphabetical order). Any algorithm that sorts lists of numbers can also be used for lists of strings. For example, in Section 8.7 we coded the bubble sort algorithm to sort an array A of numbers in ascending order as follows:

```
C BUBBLE SORT TO ARRANGE THE N TERMS
C OF ARRAY A IN ASCENDING ORDER.
      NM1=N-1
      DO 1 J=1,NM1
        NMJ=N-J
        DO 2 I=1,NMJ
          IF (A(I).LE.A(I+1)) GO TO 2
          TEMP=A(I)
          A(I)=A(I+1)
          A(I+1)=TEMP
  2     CONTINUE
  1 CONTINUE
C ARRAY A IS SORTED
```

If the number C of characters that can be assigned to a single variable is large enough to accommodate each name in the list to be alphabetized, exactly the same program segment can be used—of course, as mentioned in Section 12.1, you should declare A as an integer array. (If your system allows the CHARACTER statement, you can always specify C to be large enough for this purpose.) However, it often happens that strings to be sorted contain more characters than can be stored in a single variable. In such cases, special considerations must be taken during the coding process. To illustrate what's involved, let's consider the task of reading a list of names and printing them in alphabetical order. To be specific, we'll use the following input data and assume that at most C = 4 characters can be stored in a single variable.

Input Data:

```
            1              2              3
12345678901234567890123456789 0
LINCOLN,ABRAHAM
JOHNSON,ANDREW
GRANT,ULYSSES
HAYES,RUTHERFORD
GARFIELD,JAMES
ARTHUR,CHESTER
CLEVELAND,GROVER
HARRISON,BENJAMIN
MCKINLEY,WILLIAM
ROOSEVELT,THEODORE
END
```

Since each name in this input list contains at most 20 characters, we will use

```
NAMES(I,1),NAMES(I,2),NAMES(I,3),NAMES(I,4),NAMES(I,5)
```

to store 20 characters for the Ith name. The given input data can be read into the two-dimensional array NAMES as follows:

```
      DIMENSION NAMES(200,5)
      DATA LAST/'END'/
      DO 1 N=1,200
        READ(5,10)(NAMES(N,K),K=1,5)
        IF(NAMES(N,1).EQ.LAST) GO TO 2
    1 CONTINUE
      WRITE(6,20)
   20 FORMAT(1X,'INADEQUATE ARRAY DIMENSION')
      STOP
    2 N=N-1
```

The only part of the bubble sort program that is no longer appropriate is the range of the inner loop that swaps A(1) with A(I + 1) whenever they are out of order. We must replace these lines with a program segment that compares the name stored in the Ith row

```
NAMES(I,1),NAMES(I,2),NAMES(I,3),NAMES(I,4),NAMES(I,5)
```

with the name stored in the (I + 1)st row

```
NAMES(I+1,1),NAMES(I+1,2),NAMES(I+1,3),NAMES(I+1,4),NAMES(I+1,5)
```

and interchanges these two names if they are not in alphabetical order. The following subroutine COMP can be used for this purpose. So that the subroutine can be used in other situations, integer variables K and L are used to denote the dimensions 200 and 5 of the array NAMES.

```
C ***************** SUBROUTINE COMP *****************
C THIS SUBROUTINE COMPARES THE NAMES STORED IN THE ITH
C AND JTH ROWS OF THE ARRAY NAM. IF THEY ARE NOT IN
C ALPHABETICAL ORDER, THEY ARE SWAPPED.
      SUBROUTINE COMP(NAM,K,L,I,J)
      DIMENSION NAM(K,L)
```

```
      INTEGER TEMP
C COMPARE ENTRIES IN ITH AND JTH ROWS OF NAM
      DO 1 M=1,L
         IF(NAM(I,M).GT.NAM(J,M)) GO TO 3
         IF(NAM(I,M).LT.NAM(J,M)) GO TO 2
    1 CONTINUE
C ROWS ARE IN ORDER-DON'T SWAP
    2 RETURN
C ROWS ARE OUT OF ORDER, SWAP THEM
    3 DO 4 M1=M,L
         TEMP=NAM(I,M1)
         NAM(I,M1)=NAM(J,M1)
         NAM(J,M1)=TEMP
    4 CONTINUE
      RETURN
      END
```

If this subroutine is called with the statement

```
CALL COMP(NAMES,200,5,I,I+1)
```

the Ith and (I + 1)st names stored in NAMES will be compared, and swapped if they are not in alphabetical order.

We can now write the following program segment to alphabetize a list of names:

```
C BUBBLE SORT TO ARRANGE THE N NAMES
C STORED IN THE ROWS OF THE 200-BY-5 ARRAY
C NAMES IN ALPHABETICAL ORDER.
      NM1=N-1
      DO 1 J=1,NM1
         NMJ=N-J
         DO 2 I=1,NMJ
            CALL COMP(NAMES,200,5,I,I+1)
    2    CONTINUE
    1 CONTINUE
C THE LIST OF NAMES IS ALPHABETIZED.
```

12.7 Problems

1. Tell first what values are assigned to each variable and then what is printed by each program segment. Use the following as input records:

```
         1         2
12345678901234567890
ABCDEFGHIJKLMNOP
1234567890123456
A1B2C3D4E5F6G7H8
```

a. (Assume C = 4.)

```
      DIMENSION N(6)
      READ(5,10)N
   10 FORMAT(A1,9X,A1)
      WRITE(5,20)N
   20 FORMAT(1X,4A4)
```

b. (Assume C = 4.)

```
      DIMENSION N(4)
      READ(5,11)N
   11 FORMAT(4A4)
      WRITE(6,21)N
   21 FORMAT(1X,A4)
```

c.   (Assume C = 4.)

```
       DIMENSION N(5)
       READ(5,12)(N(J),I=1,5)
12 FORMAT(10X,3A2/)
       WRITE(6,22)(N(I),I=1,5)
22 FORMAT(1X,A4)
```

d.   (Assume C = 1.)

```
       DIMENSION N(12)
       READ(5,13)(N(I),I=1,12)
13 FORMAT(12A1)
       WRITE(6,23)N
23 FORMAT(1X,12(1X,A1))
```

2. What will be printed when each program is run?

a.   (Assume C = 4.)

```
       DIMENSION N(5)
       DATA LAST/'END'/
       READ(5,12)N
       DO 1 I=1,5
          IF(N(I).EQ.LAST) STOP
          WRITE(6,13)N(I)
 1 CONTINUE
12 FORMAT(5A3)
13 FORMAT(1X,A3)
       END
```

Input Data:

```
          1         2         3
 12345678901234567890123456789 0
 S ENDBENDLENDMENDTEND
```

b.   (Assume C = 10.)

```
       DIMENSION N(5)
       DATA LAST/'END'/
       READ(5,12)N
       DO 1 I=1,5
          IF(N(I).EQ.LAST) STOP
          WRITE(6,13)N(I)
 1 CONTINUE
12 FORMAT(5A3)
13 FORMAT(1X,A3)
       END
```

Input Data:

```
          1         2         3
 12345678901234567890123456789 0
 S ENDBENDLENDMENDTEND
```

c.

```
       CHARACTER N(5)*1
       READ(5,10)N
       J=5
 1 WRITE(6,20)(N(I),I=1,J)
          J=J-1
       IF(J.GT.0) GO TO 1
       STOP
10 FORMAT(5A1)
20 FORMAT(1X,5A1)
       END
```

Input Data:

```
          1         2
 12345678901234567890
 *****
```

d.

```
       CHARACTER L(4)*1
       DATA L/'A','B','C','D'/
       DO 1 J=1,4
          WRITE(6,20)(L(I),I=J,4)
 1 CONTINUE
20 FORMAT(1X,4A1)
       STOP
       END
```

Write a program to print each report described in Problems 3–9. Make sure that each report has a title, centered on the page, and that each column has an appropriate heading.

Batch mode: Prepare input records containing the given information. Arrays are not necessary and should not be used.

Conversational mode: You will have to use arrays to store all input data before producing any output. Unformatted READ statements are most appropriate for reading the input data.

3. Given the base salary, commission rate, and monthly sales for each person, print a four-column report

showing the employee name, the base salary, the commission, and the total earnings. A salesperson receives a commission only on those sales that exceed the quota.

Name	Base salary	Quota	Commission rate	Sales
Crompton	$350	$7,000	5%	$10,900
Maitland	400	9,000	5.5%	7,600
Khavilz	390	6,500	6%	9,700
Glidden	425	3,500	5%	10,200
MacBarron	450	7,500	4.7%	7,100

4. Given the item code, the quantity, and the unit value of each item, print a four-column report showing the item code, the quantity, the unit value, and the total value of each item. The total value of the entire inventory should be printed below the report.

Item code	Quantity	Unit value
X3047A	198	$ 2.43
Y3055B	457	3.97
X3068B	237	1.96
Y3093A	1047	5.47
Y3247B	593	10.93
X3346A	1159	12.41
X3469B	243	.83
Y3947B	2042	8.37

5. Given the item code, the item type, the number of units on hand, the average cost per unit, and the selling price per unit, produce a printed report displaying precisely the information in the table.

Item code	Item type	Units on hand	Average cost/unit	Selling price/unit
XZ14A	A	20500	1.55	1.95
XZ13B	A	54000	0.59	0.74
XZ12A	B	8250	3.40	4.10
MN17A	B	4000	5.23	6.75
AA43C	A	15000	0.60	0.75
AB97D	B	10500	1.05	1.35
KY23M	A	6000	7.45	9.89

6. Using the input data from Problem 5, print a report displaying the given information for type A items only.

7. Using the input data from Problem 5, produce a printed five-column report showing the item code, the number of units on hand, and the total cost, total sales price, and total income these units represent (income = sales − cost). The report is to be concluded with a message showing the total cost, total sales price, and total income represented by the entire inventory.

8. The following table describes an investor's stock portfolio. Print a report displaying precisely the information that is given.

Company	Shares owned	Closing cost last week	Closing cost this week
STERLING DRUG	800	16.50	16.125
DATA GENERAL	500	56.25	57.50
OWENS ILLINOIS	1200	22.50	21.50
MATTEL INC.	1000	10.375	11.625
ABBOTT LAB	2000	33.75	34.75
FED NATL MTG	2500	17.75	17.25

9. Using the input data for Problem 8, prepare a four-column report showing the company name, the equity at last week's closing, the equity this week, and the dollar change in equity. The report should be concluded with a message showing the total net gain or loss during the week.

Write a program to produce each report described in Problems 10–16. These reports all require data to be sorted. As always, each report must have a title, columns must have headings, and any other output values must be labeled.

10. Given the name, hourly rate, and hours worked, print a four-column report showing the name, hourly rate, hours worked, and gross pay for each person. Time-and-a-half is applied to all hours over 32. The amounts in the gross pay column are to be printed from largest to smallest.

Name	Hourly rate	Hours worked
Horton	$4.25	42
Elison	5.95	32
Sonners	3.35	32
Bellows	6.50	50
Hobson	5.00	40
Janson	4.75	32
Kraft	6.30	44

11. Produce the four-column report described in Problem 10 with the names being printed in alphabetical order.

12. Using the following table, determine the batting average and slugging percentage for each player. In the table, 1B indicates a single, 2B a double, 3B a triple, HR a homerun, and AB the number of times a player has been at bat. (Batting averages and slugging percentages should be rounded to the nearest thousandth.) Use these formulas:

$$\text{Batting average} = \frac{\text{Number of hits}}{\text{AB}} \qquad \text{Slugging percentage} = \frac{\text{Total bases}}{\text{AB}}$$

Player	1B	2B	3B	HR	AB
Gomes	100	22	1	14	444
Ryan	25	1	1	0	104
Jackson	83	15	8	7	395
O'Neil	68	22	1	8	365
Struik	65	11	3	5	310
McDuffy	54	11	4	0	256
Vertullo	78	18	1	15	418
Boyd	68	20	0	3	301
Torgeson	49	15	0	11	301
Johnson	54	5	2	0	246

Print a table listing the players with their batting averages and slugging percentages in two adjacent columns, with the slugging percentages in decreasing order.

13. Using the batting information of Problem 12, produce a similar table but with the players' names in alphabetical order.

14. Compute the semester averages for all students in a psychology class. Averages should be rounded to the nearest integer. A separate input record should be used for each student and should include the student's name and five grades. A letter grade should be given according to the following table:

Average	Grade
90–100	A
80–89	B
70–79	C
60–69	D
Below 60	E

The five one-character strings A, B, C, D, and E should be assigned to an array MARK in a DATA statement. The output should be in tabular form with these headings:

STUDENT   AVERAGE   LETTER GRADE

The student names are to be in alphabetical order.

15. Each of N input records contains an English word, left-justified in column positions 1 through 10. A first input record contains (in its first three positions) an integer value for N. Read the words and store them in three arrays ATOK, LTOQ, and RTOZ. ATOK is to contain all words A through K, LTOQ is to contain all words L through Q, and the rest are to be stored in RTOZ. Next, sort each of the three lists in alphabetical order and print them as three separate lists, one under the other, with the headings A–K, L–Q, and R–Z. (Use a subroutine to do all of the sorting.)

16. Print the three alphabetized lists described in Problem 15, side by side.

12.8 Review True-or-False Quiz

1. The statement DATA N/'*'/ can be placed at any point in a program to assign the one character string * to N.   T F

2. If the statement DATA L/'ABCDEFGHIJKLMN'/ is placed before the first executable statement in a program, the string of characters from A to N will always be assigned to L.   T F

3. Suppose that the statement DATA LAST/'9999'/ is used to initialize the variable LAST. It is then inappropriate to use the statement

   IF(NUM.EQ.LAST) GO TO 5

   to transfer control out of a loop used to process many input integers NUM.   T F

4. The I, F, A, and X edit descriptors can be used in the same format specification.   T F

5. If a variable N that can store four characters (C = 4) is printed by using the descriptor A1, the first character stored in N will be printed and followed by three blanks.   T F

6. If the variable NAME stores C characters, it is the common practice to read values for NAME using a descriptor Aw with $w \geq C$.   T F

7. The format specification (A26) is equivalent to the format specification (26A1).   T F

8. The ASCII codes given in Table 12.1 are used by all FORTRAN systems as the numeric codes for the FORTRAN character set.   T F

13
Random Numbers and Their Application

If a coin is tossed several times, a sequence such as HTTHTHHHTTH, where H denotes a head and T a tail, is obtained. We call this a **randomly generated sequence** because each letter is the result of an experiment (tossing a coin) and could not have been determined without actually performing the experiment. Similarly, if a die (a cube with faces numbered 1 through 6) is rolled several times, a randomly generated sequence such as 5315264342 is obtained. The numbers in such a randomly generated sequence are called **random numbers.**

Modern computing machines have the ability to generate sequences of numbers that have the appearance of being randomly generated. Although these numbers are called random numbers, they are more accurately referred to as **pseudo-random numbers** because the computer does not perform an experiment such as tossing a coin to produce a number; rather, it uses an algorithm carefully designed to generate sequences of numbers that emulate random sequences. The ability to generate such sequences makes it possible for us to use the computer in many new and interesting ways. Using "random-number generators," people have written computer programs to simulate the growth of a forest, to determine the best location for elevators in a proposed skyscraper, to assist social scientists in their statistical studies, to simulate game playing, and to perform many other tasks.

Some FORTRAN systems include a random-number generator in the form of an intrinsic function RANF. (The names RAN, RAND, and RND are also used.) In Section 13.1 we describe this function and explain its use. In Section 13.2 we present a method for generating sequences of random numbers without using the RANF function. In particular, we will describe a function subprogram, also called RANF, that can be used exactly the way the intrinsic function RANF is used. Thus, if your system does not implement the built-in function RANF (it is not included in the FORTRAN standard), you may simply attach this function subprogram to the programs presented in the text and they will behave as outlined. The remainder of the chapter is devoted to a variety of applications involving random numbers.

13.1 The RANF Function

The RANF function is used somewhat differently than the other intrinsic functions. If the expression RANF(X) appears in a program, its value will be a number from 0 up to, but not including, 1:

$$0 \leq RANF(X) < 1.$$

The particular value assumed by RANF(X) is unpredictable. It will appear to have been selected randomly from the numbers between 0 and 1.

EXAMPLE 1. Here is a program to generate and print eight random numbers lying between 0 and 1:

```
      DO 1 I=1,8
         Y=RANF(X)
         WRITE(6,10)Y
    1 CONTINUE
   10 FORMAT(1X,F8.6)
      STOP
      END
```

Output:

```
 .017831
 .597702
 .986238
 .526585
 .302629
 .619982
 .899148
 .184081
```

Observe that each time the WRITE statement is executed a different number is printed even though the same expression RANF(X) is used to obtain each Y value.

The value of X in RANF(X) has different meanings on different systems. We will use the RANF function in the form RANF(0). Your system may allow or even require you to use RANF(1), RANF(-1), or some other form of the RANF function.

EXAMPLE 2. Here is a program to generate 1,000 random numbers between 0 and 1 and determine how many are in the interval from 0.3 to 0.4, inclusive.

```
      INTEGER COUNT
      COUNT=0
      DO 1 I=1,1000
         X=RANF(0)
         IF((X.GE.0.3).AND.(X.LE.0.4)) COUNT=COUNT+1
    1 CONTINUE
      WRITE(6,10)COUNT
   10 FORMAT(1X,I4)
      STOP
      END
```

Output:

104

Each time the assignment statement X = RANF(0) is executed, RANF(0) takes on a different value, which is then assigned to X. The IF statement adds 1 to COUNT whenever X lies in the specified interval. In this example it was necessary to assign the value of RANF(0) to a temporary variable X so that the comparisons could be made. If we had written

IF((RANF(0).GE.0.3).AND.(RANF(0).LE.0.4)) COUNT = COUNT + 1

the two occurrences of RANF(0) would have different values, which is not what was wanted in this situation.

The numbers generated by the RANF function are nearly uniformly distributed between 0 and 1. For example, if many numbers are generated, approximately as many will be less than .5 as greater than .5, approximately twice as many will be between 0 and ⅔ as between ⅔ and 1, approximately 1/100th of the numbers will be between .37 and .38, and so on. The examples throughout the rest of this chapter illustrate how this property of random-number sequences can be put to use by a programmer.

EXAMPLE 3. Write a program to simulate tossing a coin 20 times, and print the total number of heads and tails that occur.

Problem Analysis:
Since RANF(0) will be less than .5 approximately half the time, let's say that a head is tossed whenever RANF(0) is less than .5. The following program is then immediate.

```
   INTEGER HEAD,TAIL
   HEAD=0
   DO 1 I=1,20
       IF(RANF(0).LT.0.5) HEAD=HEAD+1
 1 CONTINUE
   TAIL=20-HEAD
   WRITE(6,10)HEAD,TAIL
10 FORMAT(1X,'HEADS',I3/1X,'TAILS',I3)
   STOP
   END
```

Output:

```
HEADS 11
TAILS  9
```

Remark: If you wish to simulate tossing a bent coin that produces a head twice as often as a tail, you could say that a head occurs whenever RANF(0)<.66667. Thus, one change in the IF statement allows the same program to work in this case.

We conclude this section with an example of how the RANF function can be used to simulate a real-life situation.

EXAMPLE 4. A professional softball player has a lifetime batting average of .365. Assuming she will come to bat four times in each of her next 100 games, estimate in how many games she will go hitless, have one hit, have two hits, have three hits, and have four hits.

Problem Analysis:
To simulate one time at bat, we will generate a number RANF(0) and concede a hit if RANF(0) < 0.365. For any one game we will compare four such numbers with 0.365. If in a particular game HIT hits are made ($0 \le$ HIT ≤ 4), we will record this by adding 1 to the counter COUNT(HIT + 1). Thus, COUNT(1) counts the number of hitless games, COUNT(2) the games in which one hit is made, and so on.

The Flowchart:

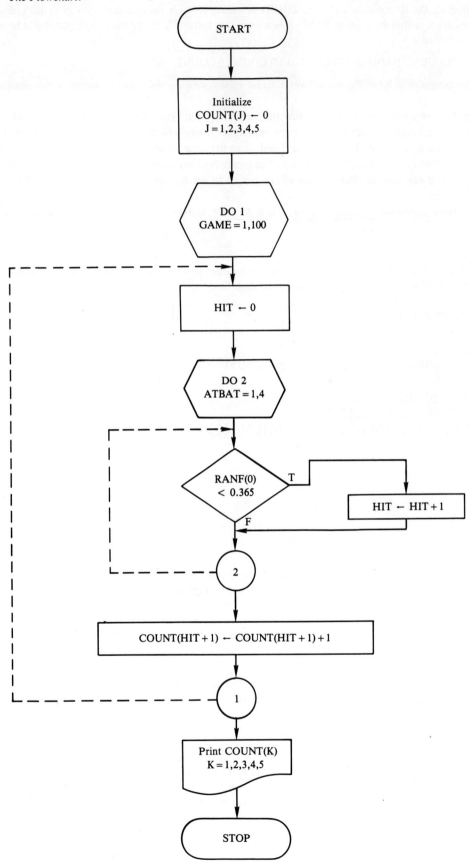

The Program:

```
C ****** SOFTBALL SIMULATION PROBLEM ******
C   GAME  = NUMBER OF GAMES
C   HIT   = NUMBER OF HITS IN A GIVEN GAME
C   ATBAT = NUMBER OF AT BATS IN A GIVEN GAME
C   COUNT = AN ARRAY THAT COUNTS THE NUMBER OF GAMES
C           IN WHICH 0,1,2,3, OR 4 HITS ARE MADE
      INTEGER GAME,HIT,ATBAT,COUNT(5)
C INITIALIZE COUNTERS TO ZERO
      DATA COUNT/5*0/
C THE GAME LOOP COUNTS THE NUMBER OF GAMES
      DO 2 GAME=1,100
C        THE BAT LOOP DETERMINES THE NUMBER (HIT) OF HITS IN EACH GAME
         HIT=0
         DO 1 ATBAT=1,4
            IF(RANF(0).LT.0.365) HIT=HIT+1
    1    CONTINUE
         COUNT(HIT+1)=COUNT(HIT+1)+1
    2 CONTINUE
      WRITE(6,10)
      DO 3 K=1,5
         J=K-1
         WRITE(6,11)J,COUNT(K)
    3 CONTINUE
   10 FORMAT(1X,'HITS PER GAME','  FREQUENCY'/)
   11 FORMAT(1X,6X,I1,12X,I2)
      STOP
      END
```

Output:

```
HITS PER GAME  FREQUENCY

      0            16
      1            39
      2            35
      3            9
      4            1
```

13.2 Modular Arithmetic and Random Numbers

The realization that the use of random numbers in computer programs makes possible new and promising applications of the computer brought about an intensive search for ways to generate sequences of numbers possessing the attributes of random sequences. In this section, we describe a method for generating such sequences that has its basis in modular arithmetic. The method is one of the very first tried and is probably still the most widely used.

To illustrate, let us start with 33 as the first number in a sequence to be generated. To obtain the second number in the sequence, we multiply the first by 33 to obtain 33*33 = 1089; however, we will keep only the last two digits, 89, of this product. To obtain the third number, multiply the second by 33 to obtain 89*33 = 2937 and again keep only the 37. (To keep the last two digits of any product, divide the product by 100 to obtain a quotient and a remainder; the remainder will be the last two digits. Thus, if 89*33 = 2937 is divided by 100 the quotient is 29 and the remainder is 37 as desired. When we divide the product by 100 and keep only the remainder we say we are multiplying modulo 100; 100 is called the modulus.) Continuing to multiply each new number obtained by 33 modulo 100, we get

$$33*33 = 89 \bmod 100$$
$$89*33 = 37 \bmod 100$$
$$37*33 = 21 \bmod 100$$
$$\vdots$$

The first 20 integers in the sequence so generated are

33, 89, 37, 21, 93, 69, 77, 41, 53, 49, 17, 61, 13, 29, 57, 81, 73, 9, 97, 1.

Although these numbers were not randomly generated (we know exactly how they were produced), they are rather uniformly distributed between 0 and 100. For example, the interval 0 to 25 contains five integers as do the intervals 25 to 50, 50 to 75, and 75 to 100. If we want numbers between 0 and 1, we can simply divide each of these twenty numbers by 100, the modulus, to obtain

.33, .89, .37, .21, .93, .69, .77, .41, .53, .49, .17, .61, .13, .29, .57, .81, .73, .09, .97, .01.

The process just described may be generalized by using numbers other than 33 and 100. In the following description of this procedure, START is used to denote the starting value, VAL to denote the successive integers in the sequence, and M to denote that multiplication is to be done modulo M. The product of two integers A and B modulo M is the remainder R obtained upon division of the product A*B by M. If we use the intrinsic function MOD, R can be evaluated as follows:

R = MOD(A*B,M)

Algorithm to Generate Sequences of Numbers between 0 and 1

a. Assign values to M and START; VAL is initially equal to START.
b. Replace VAL by VAL*START modulo M.
c. Float(VAL)/FLOAT(M) is the next number in the sequence.
d. Go to step (b) if another number is desired.

If M and START are chosen appropriately, the numbers generated will have many of the attributes of random numbers. The function subprogram RANF shown in Figure 13.1 implements this algorithm with the values $M = 2^{27} = 134{,}217{,}728$ and $START = 5^9 = 1{,}953{,}125$. Note that the dummy argument X in RANF(X) is not used. This means that the actual argument in any function reference can be any value whatever—it will be ignored.

```
FUNCTION RANF(X)
INTEGER START,VAL,M
DATA START,VAL,M/2*1953125,134217728/
VAL=MOD(VAL*START,M)
RANF=FLOAT(VAL)/FLOAT(M)
RETURN
END
```

FIGURE 13.1. Function subprogram RANF to return
a pseudo-random number between 0 and 1.

EXAMPLE 5. Here is a program to print the first 100 pseudo-random numbers generated by the function subprogram
RANF:

```
      DIMENSION R(100)
      DO 1 I=1,100
         R(I)=RANF(0)
    1 CONTINUE
      WRITE(6,10)R
   10 FORMAT(1X,5F12.8)
      STOP
      END
C THE FUNCTION SUBPROGRAM RANF GENERATES PSEUDO RANDOM NUMBERS
      FUNCTION RANF(X)
      INTEGER START,VAL,M
      DATA START,VAL,M/2*1953125,134217728/
      VAL=MOD(VAL*START,M)
      RANF=FLOAT(VAL)/FLOAT(M)
      RETURN
      END
```

Output:

```
.70943040    .25782702    .40074528    .62516991    .98142678
.18536339    .87021805    .62111238    .12480874    .06278417
.33709873    .94753925    .59291489    .88822780    .91805602
.16142682    .75754089    .04899285    .15993441    .89250533
.46362693    .34497557    .40694166    .92919639    .70894522
.63710735    .29283632    .92955057    .44878752    .12079225
.35811520    .75718478    .52565259    .22434447    .79220093
.44221989    .72393376    .13242588    .30062938    .76721815
.94960637    .93448351    .09723724    .47812072    .53491528
.39818702    .02134944    .12018517    .66806240    .36786626
.77996672    .49892298    .94789416    .78794871    .31495310
.76603702    .06358904    .35139702    .29522336    .13035909
.59934504    .77314649    .73393060    .19378737    .96406717
.68854258    .73065365    .91222397    .44605500    .17677841
.33858467    .18151239    .39269013    .90933225    .55671657
.04837505    .51512367    .92340503    .44703055    .54635075
.31796379    .02035782    .37668360    .15673224    .65396316
.78914938    .38519598    .89450363    .40370650    .25477359
.67663873    .01927797    .28029806    .15169702    .23682118
.37123469    .75904913    .82229636    .57547844    .33205716
```

Remark: If you run this program on a FORTRAN system that contains an intrinsic function named RANF, your computer will probably use the intrinsic function RANF and ignore the function subprogram. If you wish to use your own random-number generator, you should use a function name different from any of the intrinsic functions supplied with your system.

Whether the numbers generated by using these values for M and START do emulate random numbers is of course a very relevant question. Problem 7 of Section 13.3 describes one of the statistical tests used for making this evaluation.*

To assist you in making promising choices for M and START, we state the following guidelines which experience has shown increase the likelihood that "good" random sequences will be obtained.

1. M should be large. (For a variety of reasons, powers of 2 are popular.)
2. M and START should have no common factors. (We used 2^{27} and 5^9 for these values.)
3. START should not be too small in comparison to M.

The method described in this section is called the **power residual method:** "power" because successive powers of a single number START are used, "residual" because the numbers used are residues (remainders) upon division by a fixed number M. In all likelihood, if a RANF function is provided with your FORTRAN system, it generates random numbers by using a method not unlike the power residual method.

13.3 Problems

Write a program to perform each task specified in Problems 1–7. If yor system contains a built-in function to generate sequences of random numbers you may use it in writing these programs; otherwise include the function subprogram of Figure 13.1 as a program unit.

1. Print approximately 1% of all integers from 1,000 to 9,999, inclusive. They are to be selected randomly.
2. Simulate tossing two coins 100 times. The output should be a count of the number of times each of the possible outcomes HH, HT, TH, and TT occurs.
3. A game between players A and B is played as follows. A coin is tossed three times or until a head comes up, whichever occurs first. As soon as a head comes up, player A collects $1 from player B. If no head comes up on any of the three tosses, player B collects $6 from player A. In either case, the game is over. Your program is to simulate this game 1,000 times to help decide whether A or B has the advantage, or if it is a fair game.
4. Generate a one-dimensional array A of 1,000 random numbers between 0 and 1. Using the array A, determine an array COUNT as follows: COUNT(1) is a count of how many entries of A are between 0 and .1, COUNT(2) a count of those between .1 and .2, and so on. The array COUNT should then be printed.
5. Create an array L of approximately 20 different integers from 1 to 100. The integers are to be chosen randomly. The array L should be printed, but only after it has been completely determined.
6. The first three hitters in the Bears' batting order have lifetime batting averages of .257, .289, and .324, respectively. Simulate their first trip to the plate for the next 100 games, and tabulate the number of games in which they produce zero, 1, 2, and 3 hits.
7. Let A be an array of N numbers between 0 and 1 and let COUNT be as in Problem 4. If A emulates a random sequence, we can expect each COUNT(J) to be approximately E = N/10. In statistics, the value

$$X = \frac{(COUNT(1) - E)^2}{E} + \frac{(COUNT(2) - E)^2}{E} + \cdots + \frac{(COUNT(10) - E)^2}{E}$$

is called the Chi-Square Statistic for COUNT. If it is small, it means that the COUNT(J) do not differ drastically from the expected value E. For the present situation, statistics tells us that if $X \geq 16.92$ we can be 95% confident that A does not emulate a random sequence. Thus, unless $X < 16.92$, we should reject A as a potential random sequence.

Random Numbers, by Robert E. Smith, is an excellent and inexpensive monograph on random-number generators and the statistical tests used for measuring their goodness. It is available from Control Data Corporation, Minneapolis, Minnesota.

a. Assuming that N and the array COUNT are known, write a subroutine to compute and print the Chi-Square Statistic X.

b. Modify the program of Problem 4 so that X is printed as well as the ten entries in the array COUNT. (*Note:* If COUNT gives a count of numbers in intervals other than (0,.1), (.1,.2), and so on, a critical value other than 16.92 must be used. The test described here is called a Chi-Square Goodness-of-Fit Test and is described in most introductory statistics books.)

13.4 Random Integers

Many computer applications require generating random *integers* rather than just random numbers between 0 and 1. For example, suppose a manufacturer estimates that a proposed new product will sell at the rate of 10 to 20 units each week and wants a program to simulate sales figures over an extended period of time. To write such a program, you must be able to generate random integers from 10 to 20 to represent the estimated weekly sales. To do this, you can multiply RANF(0), which is between 0 and 1, by 11 (the number of integers from 10 to 20) to obtain

$$0 \leq 11.*RANF(0) < 11.$$

If many numbers are obtained by using 11.*RANF(0), they will be nearly uniformly distributed between 0 and 11. This means that the value of IFIX(11.*RANF(0)) will be one of the *integers* 0, 1, 2, . . . , 10. Thus, if you add 10 to this expression, you will get an integer from 10 to 20.

$$10 \leq IFIX(11.*RANF(0)) + 10 \leq 20.$$

The important thing here is that integers generated in this manner will appear to have been chosen randomly from the set of integers {10, 11, 12, . . . , 20}.

In general, if M and N are integers with M < N,

$$IFIX(FLOAT(N - M + 1)*RANF(0))$$

will generate an integer from 0 to N − M. (Note that N − M + 1 gives the number of integers between M and N, inclusive.) Thus, adding M to this expression, we obtain

$$IFIX(FLOAT(N - M + 1)*RANF(0)) + M$$

whose value is an integer chosen randomly from the set {M, M + 1, M + 2, . . . , N}.

EXAMPLE 6. Write a program to generate 20 numbers randomly from the set {1, 2, 3, 4, 5}.

Problem Analysis:
From the preceding discussion we know that the expression IFIX(5.*RANF(0)) will be an integer from 0 to 4. Thus, IFIX(5.*RANF(0)) + 1 will be an integer from 1 to 5, as required.

The Program:

```
      DIMENSION LIST(20)
      DO 1 I=1,20
         LIST(I)=IFIX(5.*RANF(0))+1
    1 CONTINUE
      WRITE(6,10)(LIST(I),I=1,20)
   10 FORMAT(1X,20I3)
      STOP
      END
```

Output:

```
   1  2  5  1  5  5  4  3  5  3  3  4  2  4  2  2  1  5  4  1
```

EXAMPLE 7. Write a program to generate 20 numbers randomly from the set {100, 101, 102, . . . , 199}.

Problem Analysis:
The technique used in Example 6 is also applicable here. Since IFIX(100.*RANF(0)) is an integer from 0 to 99, we must add 100 to obtain an integer from the specified set. Thus, the program required is that of Example 6 with the statement in the third line changed to

```
LIST(I)=IFIX(100.*RANF(0))+100
```

13.5 Simulation

The simulation of future events, based on data obtained by observing the results of similar or related previous events, is now a common computer application. Example 4 of Section 13.1, concerning the estimation of a ballplayer's future performance, is one illustration of the simulation of a real-life situation. In this section we give two examples showing how this technique may be used in a business setting.

EXAMPLE 8. A retail store will soon handle a new product. A preliminary market survey indicates that between 500 and 1,000 units will be sold each month. (The survey is no more specific than this.) Write a program to simulate sales for the first six months. The retail store management is to be allowed to experiment by specifying the periodic (monthly) inventory purchase.

Problem Analysis:
The problem statement does not specify the nature of the output. Let's agree to print a table showing the following items.

PRCH   = monthly inventory purchase (to be input).
MONTH   = the month (1,2, . . . ,6).
BEGQTY = quantity on hand at the beginning of the month.
SALES   = estimated sales (500-1000) for one month.
ENDQTY = quantity on hand at the end of the month.

For each month we must generate a random integer SALES from 500 to 1,000. There are 501 integers to choose from (501 = 1,000 − 500 + 1). Thus, we can use the expression

IFIX(501.*RANF(0)) + 500

to select an integer randomly from 500 to 1,000.

As soon as the monthly inventory purchase PRCH is input, we can calculate BEGQTY, SALES, and ENDQTY as follows:

BEGQTY = ENDQTY + PRCH (ENDQTY will initially be 0).
SALES   = IFIX(501.*RANF(0)) + 500.
ENDQTY = BEGQTY − SALES if BEGQTY ≥ SALES. Otherwise, ENDQTY = 0.

The Program:

```
C NEW PRODUCT SIMULATION
C    PRCH   = MONTHLY INVENTORY PURCHASE
C    MONTH  = MONTH(1,2,···,6)
C    BEGQTY = ON HAND-BEGINNING OF MONTH
C    SALES  = SALES FOR ONE MONTH (500-1000)
C    ENDQTY = ON HAND-END OF MONTH
      READ(5,10)PRCH
      INTEGER PRCH,MONTH,BEGQTY,ENDQTY,SALES
      WRITE(6,11)PRCH
      WRITE(6,12)
```

```
      BEGQTY=0
      DO 1 MONTH=1,6
         BEGQTY=ENDQTY+PRCH
         SALES=IFIX(501.*RANF(0))+500.)
         IF(SALES.GT.BEGQTY) THEN
            ENDQTY=0
         ELSE
            ENDQTY=BEGQTY-SALES
         END IF
         WRITE(6,13)MONTH,BEGQTY,SALES,ENDQTY
    1 CONTINUE
      STOP
   10 FORMAT(I5)
   11 FORMAT(1X,'MONTHLY INVENTORY PURCHASE',I6/)
   12 FORMAT(1X,'MONTH',3X,'ON HAND',3X,'EST.SALES',3X,'ON HAND AT END OF MONTH')
      END
```

Input Data:

```
          1         2
 12345678901234567890
  1000
```

Output:

```
MONTHLY INVENTORY PURCHASE  1000

MONTH    ON HAND    EST. SALES    ON HAND AT END OF MONTH
  1       1000        642             358
  2       1358        923             435
  3       1435        784             651
  4       1651        531            1120
  5       2120        807            1313
  6       2313        789            1524
```

Remark: The large values in the last column suggest that this program should be run again wtih something less than 1,000 as the monthly inventory purchase figure.

EXAMPLE 9. The owner of a drive-in theater is planning a $5.00 per car special for Tuesday nights. Previous experience indicates that between 150 and 200 cars enter the theater on Tuesdays and that the number of people arriving in each car varies from 1 to 5. Approximately one-half of the cars have two passengers, approximately one-fourth have four, and the remaining one-fourth have either 1, 3, or 5 passengers, with each of these last three counts being equally likely. Experience also indicates that a special of the type being planned will result in a 30% to 50% increase in the number of cars arriving on any one night. Assuming that the regular admission price is $2.50 per person, simulate the admissions for the next five Tuesdays to compare the revenue under the special price with what would be taken in at the regular price.

Problem Analysis:

The problem statement does not specify the precise form of the output. Let's agree to produce a five-column printout showing the following values for each of the five Tuesdays.

CARREG = the number of cars under the regular admission price.

PASS   = the total number of passengers in the CARREG cars.

REVREG = the total revenue represented by these PASS people (REVREG = PASS × 2.50).

CARSPC = the number of cars under the special admission price.

REVSPC = the total revenue represented by these CARSPC cars (REVSPC = CARSPC × 5.00).

The specification of "what" is to be printed leads us directly to the following algorithm.

The Algorithm:

a. Choose CARREG (a random integer from 150 to 200).

b. Determine the total number PASS of passengers in the CARREG cars.

c. Multiply 2.50 by PASS to obtain the revenue REVREG.

d. Increase CARREG by from 30% to 50% to obtain CARSPC.

e. Multiply 5.00 by CARSPC to obtain the revenue REVSPC.

f. Print the values CARREG, PASS, REVREG, CARSPC, REVSPC on one line.

g. Go to step (a) until five lines have been printed.

Steps (a), (c), (e), and (f) can each be accomplished with one programming line, whereas step (g) simply involves setting up a DO-loop.

Step (b) is more complicated. To determine the count PASS, we must determine the number of people in each of the CARREG cars and add these CARREG numbers together. Since approximately one-half of the cars have two passengers, we will generate a random number R between 0 and 1 and add 2 to PASS if $R < .5$. Similarly, since approximately one-fourth of the cars have four passengers, we will add 4 to PASS if $1/2 \le R < 3/4$. However, if $R \ge 3/4$, we must select a number from the set $\{1, 3, 5\}$ and add it to PASS. You may check that the FORTRAN expression

2*IFIX(3.*RANF(0)) + 1

has a value from the set $\{1, 3, 5\}$ and that each of these three numbers is equally likely to occur. The partial flowchart shown in Figure 13.2 displays the method just described for finding the count PASS. Since the number PASS of passengers can be determined by knowing only what value CARREG has (this is evident both in the algorithm and in the flowchart), we can write a function subprogram with one argument CARREG to obtain a value for PASS. Since PASS is needed in more than one place (steps (c) and (f)) we will name the function NUMPAS so that its value NUMPAS(CARREG) can be assigned to PASS. With the flowchart before us, coding the subprogram is easy. Here is one way to do it:

```
FUNCTION NUMPAS(CARREG)
INTEGER CARREG
NUMPAS=0
DO 1 J=1,CARREG
   R=RANF(0)
   IF(R.LT.0.5) THEN
      NUMPAS=NUMPAS+2
   ELSE
      IF(R.LT.0.75) THEN
         NUMPAS=NUMPAS+4
      ELSE
         NUMPAS=NUMPAS+IFIX(3*RANF(0))+1
      END IF
   END IF
1 CONTINUE
RETURN
END
```

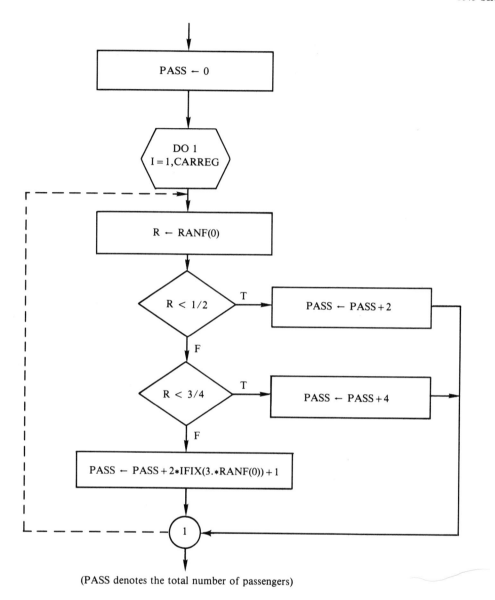

FIGURE 13.2. Partial flowchart for Example 9.

Step (d) requires that we generate a number from 30 to 50 to represent the percentage by which CARREG must be increased to obtain CARSPC. Letting PCT denote this percentage, step (d) can be accomplished as follows. (INCR denotes the additional cars.)

```
PCT    = 21.*RANF(0) + 30.
INCR   = NINT((PCT/100.)*FLOAT(CARREG))
CARSPC = CARREG + INCR
```

The intrinsic function NINT rounds a real value to the nearest integer. The main program with the printout for a typical run follows.

The Program:

```
      INTEGER CARREG,PASS,CARSPC,INCR
      REAL REVREG REVSPC,PCT
      WRITE(6,10)
   10 FORMAT(1X,25X,'DRIVE-IN SIMULATION'//
     +   1X,'REGULAR ADMISSION-$2.50 PER PERSON'/
     +   1X,'SPECIAL ADMISSION-$5.00 PER CAR'//
     +   1X,10X,'REGULAR ADMISSION',20X,'SPECIAL ADMISSION'/
     +   1X,37('-'),8X,22('-')/
     +   1X,'NO.OF CARS',4X,'NO.OF PEOPLE',2X,'REVENUE',
     +   8X,'NO.OF CARS',4X,'REVENUE'/)
C     SIMULATE ADMISSIONS FOR 5 TUESDAYS
      DO 2 I=1,5
C        FIND CARREG,THE NUMBER OF CARS AT REGULAR ADMISSION PRICE
         CARREG=IFIX(51.*RANF(0))+150
C        FIND PASS,THE NUMBER OF PASSENGERS IN THE CARREG CARS
         PASS=NUMPAS(CARREG)
C        FIND REVREG,THE REVENUE REPRESENTED BY THE PASS CUSTOMERS
         REVREG=FLOAT(PASS)*2.50
C        FIND CARSPC,THE NUMBER OF CARS AT SPECIAL ADMISSION PRICE
         PCT=21.*RANF(0)+30.
         INCR=NINT((PCT/100.)*FLOAT(CARREG))
         CARSPC=CARREG+INCR
C        FIND REVSPC,THE REVENUE REPRESENTED BY THE CARSPC CARS
         REVSPC=FLOAT(CARSPC)*5.00
C        NOW PRINT ONE ROW OF THE REPORT
         WRITE(6,11)CARREG,PASS,REVREG,CARSPC,REVSPC
    2 CONTINUE
      STOP
   11 FORMAT(1X,4X,I3,12X,I3,8X,F7.2,11X,I3,9X,F7.2)
      END
```

Output:

```
                      DRIVE-IN SIMULATION

REGULAR ADMISSION = $2.50 PER PERSON
SPECIAL ADMISSION - $5.00 PER CAR

          REGULAR ADMISSION                  SPECIAL ADMISSION
----------------------------------       -----------------------
NO. OF CARS    NO. OF PEOPLE  REVENUE     NO. OF CARS    REVENUE

      153           395        987.50         211        1055.00
      197           538       1345.00         288        1440.00
      197           539       1347.50         292        1460.00
      167           450       1125.00         235        1175.00
      196           554       1385.00         257        1285.00
```

13.6 A Statistical Application

Programmers are often confronted with tasks which simply cannot be programmed to run within a specified time limit. When this happens, it is not always necessary to abandon the task. It may be that satisfactory results can be obtained by doing only a part of the job. The following example, which illustrates one such situation, makes use of the statistical fact that the average of a large collection of numbers can be estimated by taking the average of only a fraction of the numbers, provided that the numbers chosen are chosen randomly.

EXAMPLE 10. A researcher has compiled two lists A and B of 1,000 measurements each. For each pair of measurements, one from list A and one from list B, a lengthy series of calculations which is known to take 0.1 seconds of computer time must be performed to determine a value VAL. In addition, the average of all such numbers VAL is to be found. Write a program to assist the researcher in this task. The program must take no longer than 30 minutes of computer time. (Computer time is very valuable.)

Problem Analysis:
On the surface this appears to be a simple programming task. For each pair A(I), B(J), we simply determine VAL, add it to a sum accumulator SUM (SUM = SUM + VAL), and finally divide SUM by the number of VAL's added. However, let us estimate how long such a program would take. Since each list contains 1,000 entries, there are 1,000 times 1,000 or 1,000,000 (one million) pairs A(I), B(J) to be treated. For each pair we must determine VAL, which takes 0.1 second. Thus, it will take 1,000,000/10 = 100,000 (one hundred thousand) seconds, or nearly 28 hours, to determine all such VAL's—which is considerably more than the 30 minutes allowed.

About the only way out of this dilemma is to treat only a fraction of the million pairs A(I), B(J) and use their average as an estimate of the actual average desired. Determining VAL for 1 out of every 100 pairs will take approximately .28 hours which is under 17 minutes. So that the average obtained will be a reliable estimate of the average of all VAL's, we must choose these pairs randomly. To do this, we will generate I,J in a nested DO-loop and determine VAL for the pair A(I),B(J) only if RANF(0) < .01.

In the following flowchart, which describes the program, NUM is a count of how many pairs were "chosen."

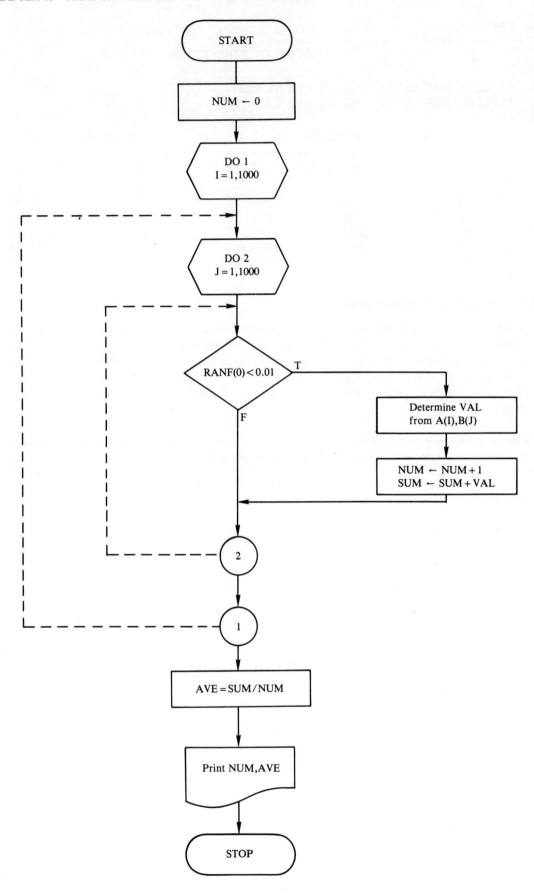

13.7 Monte Carlo

The speed of modern computing machines, together with their ability to generate rather good random sequences, allows us to approach many problems in ways not previously possible. The following example illustrates one such method, called the **Monte Carlo Method.** When you complete the example, you should have little difficulty in explaining why this name is applied to the technique involved.

EXAMPLE 11. Consider the following figure of a circle inscribed in a square.

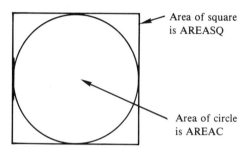

If darts are randomly tossed at this figure and tosses landing outside the square are ignored, we can expect the number falling within the circle to be related to the number falling on the entire square as the area AREAC of the circle is to the area AREASQ of the square. We will use this observation to approximate the area AREAC of a circle of radius 1.

Problem Analysis:
Let's suppose that N darts have landed on the square and that M of these are in the circle. Then, as noted in the problem statement, we will have the approximation

M/N $\doteq$ AREAC/AREASQ

or, solving for AREAC,

AREAC $\doteq$ M $\times$ AREASQ/N.

The more darts thrown (randomly), the better we can expect this approximation to be. The problem, then, is to simulate this activity, keeping an accurate count of M and N. To simplify this task, let's place our figure on a coordinate system with its origin at the center of the circle as shown in the following diagram.

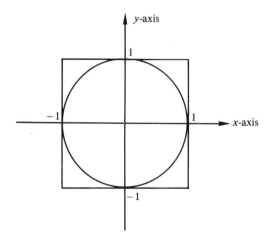

A point (x,y) will lie in the square if both x and y lie between -1 and $+1$. Such a point will lie within the circle if

$x^2 + y^2 < 1$.

To simulate tossing a single dart, we randomly generate two numbers x and y between -1 and $+1$. The following algorithm describes the procedure for N = 10,000 tosses.

a. Let M = 0 and N = 1.

b. Generate x and y between −1 and +1.

c. If $x^2 + y^2 < 1$, add 1 to M (counts those falling within circle).

d. Let N = N + 1, and go to step (b) until N exceeds 10,000.

e. Print M × AREASQ/N (approximate area of circle).

f. Stop.

Since 2.*RANF(0)−1. is between −1 and +1, and since the area AREASQ of the square is 4, the following program is immediate:

```
      M=0
      DO 1 N=1,10000
          X=2.*RANF(0)-1.
          Y=2.*RANF(0)-1.
          IF (X**2+Y**2.LT.1.) M=M+1
    1 CONTINUE
      AREAC=4.*FLOAT(M)/10000.
      WRITE(6,10)AREAC
   10 FORMAT(1X,'AREA IS',F7.2)
      STOP
      END
```

Output:

```
AREA IS   3.132
```

Remark: Since we know that the area of a circle of radius 1 is π (approximately 3.1416), we see that the result is accurate to one decimal place. To obtain greater accuracy, we would take more than 10,000 points. For N = 20,000, we obtained an area of 3.147, which is slightly better. If RANF were a true random-number generator, that is, if it actually performed an experiment such as tossing coins to generate numbers, we could expect to obtain any degree of accuracy desired by taking N large enough. The fact that it is not a true random-number generator places a limit on the accuracy obtainable.

13.8 Problems

1. Write FORTRAN statements to generate the following.
    a. A nonnegative random number (not necessarily an integer) less than 4.
    b. A random number less than 11 but not less than 5.
    c. A random number less than 3 but not less than −5.
    d. A random integer between 6 and 12, inclusive.
    e. A random number from the set {0, 2, 4, 6, 8}.
    f. A random number from the set {1, 3, 5, 7, 9}.

2. Which of these relational expressions are always true? Which are always false? Which may be true or false?
    a. RANF(0)<=0.
    b. 4.*RANF(0)>=4.
    c. IFIX(7.*RANF(0))<=6
    d. IFIX(2.*RANF(0)+4)<6
    e. RANF(0)<=RANF(0)
    f. RANF(0)=RANF(0)
    g. RANF(0)+1.>RANF(0)
    h. RANF(0)+RANF(0)=2.*RANF(0)

3. What values can be assumed by each of the following expressions? For each expression, tell whether the possible values are all equally likely to occur.
    a. IFIX(2.*RANF(0)+1.)
    b. 3*IFIX(RANF(0))
    c. IFIX(5.*RANF(0))−2
    d. IFIX(2.*RANF(0)+1.)+IFIX(2.*RANF(0)+1.)
    e. IFIX(6.*RANF(0)+1.)+IFIX(6.*RANF(0)+1.)
    f. IFIX(3.*RANF(0)+1.)*(IFIX(3.*RANF(0))+1.)

4. If two coins are tossed, two heads, two tails, or one of each may result. The following program was written to simulate tossing two coins a total of 10 times. If it is run, the output will not reflect what would happen if the coins were actually tossed. Explain why, and then write a correct program.

```
    DO 1 I=1,10
        J=IFIX(3*RANF(0))
        IF(J.EQ.0) WRITE(6,10)
        IF(J.EQ.1) WRITE(6,11)
        IF(J.EQ.2) WRITE(6,12)
  1 CONTINUE
 10 FORMAT(1X,'ONE OF EACH')
 11 FORMAT(1X,'TWO OF EACH')
 12 FORMAT(1X,'THREE OF EACH')
    STOP
    END
```

Write a program to perform each task specified in Problems 5–17. If your system contains a built-in function to generate sequences of random numbers, you may use it in writing these programs; otherwise include the function subprogram of Figure 13.1 as a program unit.

5. Simulate tossing a single die 500 times, and count the number of 1's, 2's, . . . , 6's.

6. Simulate tossing a pair of dice 1,000 times, and count the number of 2's, 3's, 4's, . . . , 12's.

7. Randomly select and print an integer from 1 to 100 and then another from the remaining 99 integers.

8. Create a one-dimensional array L containing *exactly* 20 different integers from 1 to 100. The integers are to be chosen randomly. The list should be printed but only after it is completely determined.

9. A retail store will soon carry a new product. A preliminary market analysis indicates that between 300 and 500 units will be sold each week. (The survey is no more specific than this.) Assuming that each unit costs the store $1.89, write a program to simulate sales for the next 16 weeks. The selling price is to be input. The printout is to show the week, the estimated sales in number of units, the total revenue, the income (revenue minus cost), and the cumulative income.

10. Juanita Fernandes is offered the opportunity to transfer to another sales territory. She is informed that, for each month of the past year, sales in the territory were between $18,000 and $30,000, with sales of $25,000 or more being twice as likely as sales under $25,000. A 4% commission is paid on all sales up to $25,000 and 8% on all sales above that figure. Simulate the next six months' sales and print the monthly sales and commission to give Juanita some information on which to base her decision to accept or reject the transfer.

11. The IDA Production Company will employ 185 people to work on the production of a new product. It is estimated that each person can complete between 85 and 95 units each working day. Previous experience shows that the absentee rate is between 0% and 15% on Mondays and Fridays and between 0% and 7% on the other days. Simulate the production for one week. The results of this simulation are to be printed in four columns showing the day of the week, the number of workers present, the number of units produced, and the average number produced per worker.

12. If 30 numbers are randomly selected from any list of numbers, a principle of statistics tells us that the mean of the 30 numbers can be used as an estimate of the mean MEAN of all numbers in the list. Generate a long one-dimensional array LIST and randomly select approximately 30 numbers from LIST for the purpose of checking this result of statistics. Use a DO-loop to repeat this process at least 20 times. The 20 means obtained should cluster about MEAN. (LIST can be any list of numbers. If you wish, you may generate it by using the RANF function.)

13. Jones and Kelley are to have a duel at 20 paces. At this distance Jones will hit the target on the average of two shots in every five and Kelley will hit one in every three. Kelley shoots first. Who has the better chance of surviving? Use a DO-loop to simulate at least 20 duels and print the results.

14. (Drunkard's Walk.) A poor soul, considerably intoxicated, stands in the middle of a ten-foot-long bridge that spans a river. The inebriate staggers along, either toward the left bank or toward the right, but fortunately cannot fall off the bridge. Assuming that each step taken is exactly one foot long, how many steps will be taken before the drunkard reaches either bank of the river?

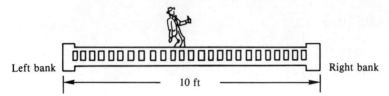

It must be assumed that it is just as likely that a step will be toward the left bank as toward the right. You must do three things.

  a. Find how many steps are taken in getting off the bridge.
  b. Tell which bank is reached.
  c. Let the drunkard go out for several nights and arrive at the same point (the center) on the bridge. Find, on the average, how many steps it takes to get off the bridge.

15. Two knights begin at diagonally opposite corners of a chessboard and travel randomly about the board but always make legitimate knight moves. (The knight moves either one step forward or backward and then two steps to the right or left or else two steps forward or backward and one step to the right or left.) Calculate the number of moves before one knight captures the other (that is, lands in the other knight's square). However you number the squares, each knight's move should be printed as it is taken.

16. A single trip for a knight is defined as follows. The knight starts in one corner of a chessboard and randomly makes N knight moves to arrive at one of the 64 squares of the chessboard. (See Problem 15 for a description of an admissible knight move.) Write a program to simulate 1,000 such trips for a knight to determine counts of how many times each square was reached at the end of a trip. These counts should be presented as an 8-by-8 table displaying the counts for the 64 squares. A value for N is to be input. (Use an 8-by-8 array to record the number of times each square was reached at the end of a trip.)

17. Let a function $y = f(x)$ have positive values for all x between A and B, as in the following diagram:

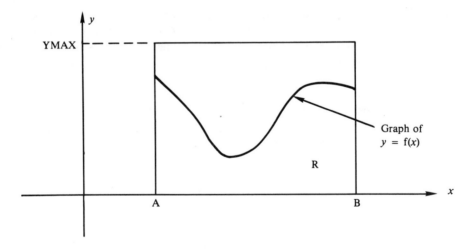

A point (x, y) with $A < x < B$ will lie in the region R if $0 < y < f(x)$. If YMAX is a number such that $f(x) \leq$ YMAX for all such x, the area of the rectangle of height YMAX shown in the diagram is YMAX*(B − A). Use the method of Section 13.6 (Monte Carlo) to approximate the area R. Try your program for the following cases:

  a. $y = 1 - x^3$, $A = 0$, $B = 1$.
  b. $y = \sin(x)$, $A = 0$, $B = \pi/2$.
  c. $y = \sin(x)/x$, $A = 0$, $B = 1$.

13.9 Review True-or-False Quiz

1. If 100 numbers are generated by the statement R = RANF(0), then approximately one-half of these numbers will be less than 50. T F
2. If 100 integers are generated by the statement I = IFIX(2.*RANF(0)), then approximately one-half will be 0 and one-half will be 1. T F
3. If 100 integers are generated by the statement

   I = IFIX(2.*RANF(0)) + IFIX(2.*RANF(0))

   then each of the values 0, 1, and 2 will be generated approximately 33 times. T F
4. RANF(0)/RANF(0) = 1. T F
5. RANF(0) − RANF(0) is not necessarily zero. T F
6. A certain experiment has two possible outcomes, Outcome 1 and Outcome 2. To simulate this experiment on the computer, we can generate a number R = RANF(0) and specify that Outcome 1 occurs if R is less than .5 and Outcome 2 occurs otherwise. T F
7. Let LIST be an array of 100 different integers. If we wish to select exactly 20 of these integers randomly, we can generate 100 random numbers between 0 and 1 and select the Ith integer in LIST if the Ith number generated is less than 0.2. T F
8. The value of the expression IFIX(17.*RANF(0)) + 1 is an integer between 1 and 17, inclusive. T F
9. The value of the expression IFIX(5.*RANF(0)) + 5 is an integer between 5 and 10, inclusive. T F
10. If a FORTRAN system does not have a RANF function, it is a simple matter to include in any program a function subprogram that performs its role. T F

14
Data
Files

In all applications considered to this point, we have assumed that input data have been presented to the computer on data cards (batch systems) or typed at the terminal (conversational systems). Both of these methods, though adequate for many applications, have their disadvantages and limitations—typing large quantities of data is tedious and handling large decks of cards is cumbersome. It may also happen that the output values of one program are required as the input values of another program, or even of several other programs. For these reasons, FORTRAN systems allow I/O operations that utilize high-speed external storage devices such as magnetic tape and disk units. In this chapter we describe how the WRITE statement can be used to direct output to a tape or disk, and how the READ statement can be used to read information previously recorded on a tape or disk.

14.1 Sequential Data Files

We have used the term "record" to denote a single line of input (input record) or a single line of output (output record).

A **sequential data file** is a *sequence* of related records that can be referenced by a program.

Thus, a collection of data cards is an instance of a sequential file. In this chapter we restrict our attention to sequential files that are stored on magnetic tapes or disks and will refer to them simply as files.

Associated with each file you use in a program is a **unit number** (positive integer) that is used to reference the file. To write the value of the variable VAR1 on the file with unit number K, you can use the WRITE statement

WRITE(K,10)VAR1

To read a value for VAR1, you can use

```
          READ(K,10)VAR1
```

In each case, 10 is the statement number of a FORMAT statement. (Files with unformatted data are discussed in Section 14.3.)

EXAMPLE 1. Here is a program segment to write two records on the file with unit number 3:

```
       M=77
       N=41
       K=M+N
       WRITE(3,10)M,N
       WRITE(3,11)K
   10 FORMAT(I6,I4)
   11 FORMAT(I8)
```

The first WRITE statement writes the integers 77 and 41 as a single record using the format specification (I6,I4). The second WRITE statement uses the specification (I8) to write a second record containing the value 118.

Remark: Note that neither output format specification begins with the descriptor 1X. Carriage control characters are not used when writing on files.

The program segment shown in Example 1 causes no output that we can "see." The output was directed to a tape or disk unit, and not to a printer. The program segment shown in the next example can be used to examine this output file.

EXAMPLE 2. Here is a program segment to read and print the contents of the file created in Example 1:

```
       READ(3,20)NUM1,NUM2
       READ(3,21)NUM3
       WRITE(6,22)NUM1,NUM2,NUM3
   20 FORMAT(I6,I4)
   21 FORMAT(I8)
   22 FORMAT(1X,3I6)
```

The first READ statement reads values for NUM1 and NUM2. The unit designator 3 says to read these input data from the file with unit number 3. Note that the format specification used to read the file is the same as that used to write it. Thus, NUM1 = 77 and NUM2 = 41. The second READ statement reads the next record from the file according to the I8 descriptor and assigns the value 118 to NUM3. Once read, the three values can, of course, be printed with any suitable format specification—we used (1X,3I6).

Remark: Although we can't "see" the numbers written on the file in Example 1, the file can be visualized as follows:

```
          1         2
12345678901234567890
   77  41
    118
```

These two records can be read by using any format specification. Thus, if we used (2I5) for the first and I6 for the second, the assignment would be NUM1 = 7, NUM2 = 70041, and NUM3 = 1, hardly what was desired. If you want to retrieve data from a file it is important to match up the format specifications used to write and read it.

At this point certain questions may come to mind. How do we know there is a file to be written on? Is the file available when we want to read it? Must we use the same number to read a file as was used to write it? The answers to these questions depend on the system being used.

On some systems, each unit number refers to a specific I/O device such as a card reader, a data terminal keyboard, a printer, a card punch, or a tape drive. If you designate the unit number 3 in a WRITE statement, the output is directed to the specific device specified as unit number 3. For this reason, a file with unit number K is often referred to as the *file connected to unit* K. On other systems, unit numbers do not necessarily correspond to specific I/O devices and your program must contain an opening statement designating a name and a unit number for each file to be referenced. Two commonly used opening statements are the OPEN statement and the PROGRAM statement. If your system requires the OPEN statement, you can write

    OPEN 3 FILE = DATA1

to specify a file with name DATA1 and unit number 3. We say that DATA1 is the file connected to unit 3. If there is no file named DATA1 at this time, the OPEN statement creates an empty file with that name and allows your program to write on it. If DATA1 is a previously created file, the OPEN statement makes it available for your program to read. The user's manual for your system will give you the necessary details for creating and saving files for later use. (The form of the PROGRAM statement differs from system to system and will not be considered in this text.)

14.2 File Control Statements

In this section, we illustrate FORTRAN statements designed to carry out certain necessary file manipulation chores.

EXAMPLE 3. Illustration of the ENDFILE statement. (This program assumes that the file DATA is connected to unit 8.)

```
C THIS PROGRAM CREATES A FILE CONTAINING ALL
C INPUT VALUES. 9999 IS AN EOD-TAG.
    1 READ(6,10)N
         IF(N.EQ.9999) GO TO 2
         WRITE(8,10)N
      GO TO 1
    2 ENDFILE 8
   10 FORMAT(I5)
      STOP
      END
```

Input Data:

```
         1         2
123456789012345678 90
   27
  243
    6
 9999
```

The READ statement reads an input value, and, if it is not the EOD-tag 9999, the WRITE statement writes it on the file DATA.

When the EOD-tag is read, control transfers to the statement ENDFILE 8. This statement writes a special character, called an **end-of-file mark,** following the last record that was written on the file. This end-of-file mark serves two purposes.

1. During any subsequent reading of the file, the end-of-file mark will be sensed by the computer. Any attempt to read information from the file after the end-of-file mark has been reached will result in an error diagnostic and program execution will terminate.

2. As shown in the next example, an END= specifier can be included in a READ statement to transfer control to any executable statement when the end-of-file mark is sensed.

EXAMPLE 4. Here is a program to read the file created in Example 3. This program illustrates the END= specifier. (The file DATA is assumed to be connected to unit 4.)

```
 1 READ(4,10,END=2)K
      WRITE(6,11)K
   GO TO 1
 2 STOP
10 FORMAT(I5)
11 FORMAT(1X,I4)
   END
```

Output:

```
 27
243
  6
```

The END=2 specifier in the READ statement causes the computer to check for the end-of-file mark just *before* the READ statement is executed. When it is detected, control passes to the STOP statement labeled 2.

Remark: Note that the file DATA read by this program does not contain an EOD-tag as its last entry. When reading from a file you can always use an END= specifier to ensure that no attempt will be made to read more information than was written on the file.

The files considered in this chapter are called *sequential files* because they contain a *sequence* of records—that is, a first record, a second record, and so on. To read a particular record from a sequential file, you must first read all records preceding it. If the file is positioned at the fifth record, a READ statement, that reads a single record, will read this fifth record and cause the file to be positioned at the sixth record.*

FORTRAN contains two statements to control the positioning of files. The statement

REWIND K

positions the file connected to unit number K at the beginning of its first record. The REWIND statement is used for the following three purposes.

1. REWIND statements are often placed at the beginning of a program to ensure that all files are positioned at their first record. (This operation is automatic on some, but not all, FORTRAN systems. The safest policy is to rewind all files as described.)
2. REWIND statements are also used to rewind all files just before program execution terminates. If you do not use REWIND statements in this manner, you may have trouble reading your files at a later time. (Again, the safest policy is to rewind all files before a STOP statement is encountered.)
3. Placing a REWIND statement at any point in a program will position the file at its first record so that the data can be read again or so that an updated version of the file can be created. (This latter application is illustrated in Section 14.4.)

The BACKSPACE statement allows the file to be positioned before the previous record. Thus, the statement

*To say that a file is positioned at its fifth record makes sense if the file is stored on a magnetic tape—it simply means that the tape reel has been wound so that the beginning of its fifth record is positioned at the read/write head. Although this terminology is not accurate for files stored on rotating disks, it is still used. Indeed, most of the current terminology concerning sequential files is a carry-over from earlier days of computing when tapes were used almost exclusively for storing files.

BACKSPACE 8

"backspaces" the file connected to unit number 8 one record, and

```
    DO 1 I=1,4
       BACKSPACE 8
  1 CONTINUE
```

"backspaces" the same file four records.

By way of summary, we present the general forms of the three file control statements introduced in this section:

REWIND *u*
ENDFILE *u*
BACKSPACE *u*

In each case, *u* denotes an integer constant or integer variable whose value is the unit number of the file.

14.3 Unformatted Files

A file created with formatted WRITE statements must be read with formatted READ statements. Moreover, to ensure that the "correct" values are read, the input format specifications must match the format specifications used to write the file. This requirement can lead to obvious difficulties if you are not sure just how a file was created. These difficulties can be avoided by using unformatted WRITE statements to create files and unformatted READ statements to read them.

The statement

WRITE(3)A,N

will write the values of A and N on the file connected to unit 3 in a form that corresponds *exactly* to the binary representations of these two values in the computer's memory unit. This means that the sequences of 0's and 1's representing A and N are copied directly onto the file without being reformatted to fit a format specification. If, later, these two values are read with the unformatted READ statement

READ(3)B,M

these sequences of 0's and 1's are copied directly into the memory locations reserved for the variables B and M. Thus, we have avoided any potential problems related to incorrect format specifications; not only that, but the computer does not have to reformat the data being transferred between main memory and tape or disk units. For this reason, the unformatted transfer of data to and from a tape or disk unit is faster than the formatted transfer of data. In addition, it takes less space on a tape or disk to record unformatted data than formatted data. Hence, unformatted WRITE statements are more efficient in terms of space as well as time.

Caution: Formatted and unformatted input/output should not be used on the same file.

In Example 5 we use an unformatted WRITE statement to create a file, and in Example 6 we show a program that uses this unformatted file as an input file. Using the output file of one program as an input file for another program is a common use of files.

EXAMPLE 5. Here is a program to create an unformatted file named MONTH containing the monthly incomes from the previous 12 months for the O'Halloran Shoe Company. (This program assumes that the file MONTH is connected to unit 9.)

```
C PROGRAM TO CREATE A FILE CONTAINING
C TWELVE MONTHLY INCOME AMOUNTS
        REAL INCOME
        REWIND 9
        DO 1 MONTH=1,12
          READ(5,10)INCOME
          WRITE(9)INCOME
      1 CONTINUE
        ENDFILE 9
        REWIND 9
        STOP
     10 FORMAT(F10.2)
        END
```

Input Data:

```
         1         2
12345678901234567890
   13200.57
   11402.48
    9248.23
    9200.94
   11825.50
   12158.07
   11028.40
   22804.22
   18009.40
   12607.25
   19423.36
   24922.50
```

When this program is executed, nothing will be printed, but the 12 income figures will be written on the file connected to unit number 9—that is, on the file named MONTH. To test such a program, you would insert program statements to cause some or all of the output to be printed. Once you are convinced that the program is correct, delete these lines.

Remark 1: The file was written with an unformatted WRITE statement and each record contains one real number. Hence, it should be read with an unformatted READ statement that reads a single real number from each record.

Remark 2: The statement REWIND 9 appearing at the outset ensures that the output file MONTH is positioned at its beginning. This means that any information previously written on the file MONTH will be written over and, hence, lost. Thus, if you must run this program more than once to debug it, you can be sure that each time, you will create an entirely new file. What would happen if no REWIND statements were used is system dependent and, hence, unpredictable.

EXAMPLE 6. Here is a program to determine the average monthly income and the number of months in which the income exceeds the average. (The file MONTH is assumed to be connected to unit 7.)

```
C PROGRAM TO FIND AVERAGE MONTHLY INCOME AND
C NUMBER OF MONTHS IN WHICH INCOME EXCEEDS THE AVERAGE

C   INCOME = MONTHLY INCOME
C   SUM    = SUM OF MONTHLY INCOMES
C   AVE    = AVERAGE MONTHLY INCOME
C   NUM    = NUMBER OF MONTHS IN WHICH AVERAGE IS EXCEEDED
C
      REAL INCOME,SUM,AVE
      INTEGER NUM
C READ FILE AND FIND AVERAGE
      REWIND 7
      SUM=0.
      DO 1 MONTH=1,12
         READ(7,END=3)INCOME
         SUM=SUM+INCOME
    1 CONTINUE
      AVE=SUM/12.
C READ FILE AGAIN TO FIND NUMBER OF
C MONTHS AVERAGE IS EXCEEDED
      REWIND 7
      NUM=0
      DO 2 MONTH=1,12
         READ(7)INCOME
         IF(INCOME.GT.AVE) NUM=NUM+1
    2 CONTINUE
C PRINT RESULTS
      WRITE(6,10)AVE
      WRITE(6,11)NUM
   10 FORMAT(1X,'AVERAGE MONTHLY INCOME',F10.2)
   11 FORMAT(1X,'NUMBER OF MONTHS INCOME EXCEEDS AVERAGE',I3)
    3 REWIND 7
      STOP
      END
```

Input: (From file MONTH created in Example 5.)

Output:

```
AVERAGE MONTHLY INCOME  14652.53
NUMBER OF MONTHS INCOME EXCEEDS AVERAGE  4
```

Remark 1: Note that having the values written on the file provided an easy access to these same values when needed a second time.

Remark 2: The first time the input file is read, the END = 3 specifier terminates the program run with no output if 12 income amounts are not included in the file. The second time the input file is read, there is no need for this END = specifier, since the second READ statement is not reached if the 12 amounts are not included in the file. (Of course, in this case, the input file is correct; it was created by using the program shown in Example 5.)

14.4 Problems

1. Below are two programs and accompanying input that create files FILE1 and FILE2. Assuming that FILE1 and FILE2 are connected to units 8 and 3, respectively, what will be printed when each program in parts (a) through (d) is run?

Program to create file FILE1:

```
      REWIND 8
    1 READ(5,10)NUM1,NUM2
        IF(NUM.EQ.9999) GO TO 2
        WRITE(8,11)NUM1,NUM2
      GO TO 1
    2 ENDFILE 8
      REWIND 8
      STOP
   10 FORMAT(2I5)
   11 FORMAT(2I6)
      END
```

Input Data:

```
          1         2
12345678901234567890
    35    4
   121    8
    63   31
   200    2
    16    6
  9999    4
```

Program to create file FILE2:

```
      REWIND 3
    1 READ(5,20)I,J,K
        IF(I.EQ.0) GO TO 2
        WRITE(3)I,J,K
      GO TO 1
    2 ENDFILE 3
      REWIND 3
      STOP
   20 FORMAT(3I4)
      END
```

Input Data:

```
          1         2
12345678901234567890
    6    5    9
    3    1    3
    4    2    1
    8    3    7
    1    6    2
    0    4    4
```

a.
```
      REWIND 8
    1 READ(8,30,END=2)INT,KOUNT
        WRITE(6,31)INT,KOUNT
      GO TO 1
    2 REWIND 8
      STOP
   30 FORMAT(I6,I6)
   31 FORMAT(1X,I4,I3)
      END
```

b.
```
      INTEGER SUM
      REWIND 3
    1 READ(3,END=2)M,N,J
        SUM=M+N+J
        WRITE(6,40)SUM
      GO TO 1
    2 REWIND 3
      STOP
   40 FORMAT(1X,I5)
      END
```

c.
```
      REWIND 8
      REWIND 3
      DO 1 I=1,5000
        IF(I.EQ.3)BACKSPACE 3
        READ(8,50,END=2)II,JJ
        READ(3,END=2)NUM1,NUM2,NUM3
        WRITE(6,60)II,JJ,NUM1,NUM2,NUM3
    1 CONTINUE
      WRITE(6,70)
    2 REWIND 8
      REWIND 3
      STOP
   50 FORMAT(2I6)
   60 FORMAT(1X,5I5)
   70 FORMAT(1X,'END OF FILE NOT REACHED')
      END
```

d.
```
      REWIND 3
      REWIND 8
      DO 1 I=1,5
        READ(3)J,K,L
        READ(8,10)M,N
        WRITE(6,11)L,N
        IF(L.EQ.N) GO TO 2
    1 CONTINUE
      WRITE(6,12)
    2 REWIND 3
      REWIND 8
      STOP
   10 FORMAT(2I6)
   11 FORMAT(1X,2I5)
   12 FORMAT(1X,'BAD DATA')
      END
```

2. Write a program to create a file named INFO containing the following information about employees of the Libel Insurance Company. The file INFO is to be used as an input file in Problems 3–7, so you should "save" it. (1 and 2 denote male and female, respectively.)

ID	Sex	Age	Years of service	Annual salary
2735	1	47	13	20,200.00
2980	2	33	6	14,300.00
3865	2	41	15	23,900.00
4222	1	22	2	11,400.00
4740	1	59	7	19,200.00
5200	2	25	3	13,000.00
5803	1	33	13	21,500.00
7242	2	28	4	13,400.00
7341	1	68	30	25,500.00
8004	1	35	6	14,300.00
9327	2	21	3	9,200.00

Problems 3–7 refer to the file INFO *created in Problem 2.*

3. Print a five-column report with a title and appropriate column headings displaying the employee information contained in the file INFO. (The sex column is to contain MALE or FEMALE, and not 1 or 2.)

4. Print two reports showing the employee information contained in INFO by sex. Each report is to be titled and is to have four appropriately labeled columns.

5. Print a two-column report showing ID numbers and annual salaries of all employees whose annual salary exceeds $15,000.00. In addition to printing column headings, be sure the report has an appropriate title.

6. Print a two-column report as described in Problem 5 for all employees whose annual salaries exceed the average annual salary of all Libel employees. Following the report, display the total annual salary earned by these employees. The title of the report should include the average salary of all Libel employees.

7. Print a report showing the ID numbers, years of service, and salaries of all employees who have been with the firm for more than five years.

14.5 File Maintenance

Maintaining and updating existing data files are common programming applications. In this section, we give an example illustrating this practice. The example involves updating a short, simplified inventory file. However, it should be remarked that, in practice, data files usually are not short and require rather complicated programs to maintain them. Our objective is simply to show that file maintenance is possible. A complete discussion of the many techniques used in file-maintenance programs is beyond the scope of an introductory text such as this one.

EXAMPLE 7. A file named INVTRY contains the following data:

```
            1         2
 12345678901234567890
 A100  2000
 A101  4450
 C229  1060
 D402  2300
 X992   500
 X993   650
 Y880  1050
 Y881   400
```

The first entry in each record represents an item code and the second entry gives the quantity (number of units) on hand. Our task is to write a program to update INVTRY to reflect all transactions since the last update.

Problem Analysis:

The input data for the program to be written will be the file INVTRY and a list of input records containing, for each item to be changed, the item code, the number of units shipped since the last update of INVTRY, and the number of units received since the last update. Let's agree to present these changes to the computer in the following form:

```
            1         2         3
123456789012345678901234567890
A100    1200    1000
A101    1000     550
D402    1800    2000
Y880     300       0
XXXX       0       0
```

The three entries in each of these records show the item code, the number of units shipped, and the number of units received. The last record will be used as an EOD-tag. These input records may be punched on cards (batch systems) or typed at a terminal keyboard (conversational systems).

A person carrying out this task by hand might proceed as follows:

a. Read the code number of an item to be changed.
b. Search the file INVTRY for this code and change the units-on-hand figure as required.
c. If more changes are to be made, go to step (a).
d. Have the updated copy of INVTRY typed.

Step (b) poses a problem. FORTRAN does not allow you to write over a single number that is recorded on a sequential file. When a file must be changed, a common practice is to read all information from the file into one or more arrays, make any necessary changes in these arrays, and then make a completely new copy of the file from the data stored in these arrays. Before rewriting this procedure in a form suitable for a FORTRAN program, let's choose variable names.

ICODE = the list of item codes from file INVTRY.
QTY   = the corresponding list of quantities from INVTRY.
NREC = the number of records in the file INVTRY.
CODE = an item code to be input.
SHIP   = the quantity shipped.
RCVD = the quantity received.

The Algorithm:

a. Input arrays ICODE and QTY from the file INVTRY.
b. Read an item code CODE and the corresponding values SHIP and RCVD.
c. If CODE is the EOD-tag XXXX, create an updated version of INVTRY and stop.
d. Find I such that ICODE(I)=CODE. If CODE is not in the array ICODE, print an appropriate message and go to step (b).
e. Add RCVD-SHIP to QTY(I) and go to step (b).

The flowchart shown in Figure 14.1 was drawn to display the steps in this algorithm in greater detail. By using the flowchart as a guide, a program is easily written. The program is shown in Figure 14.2.

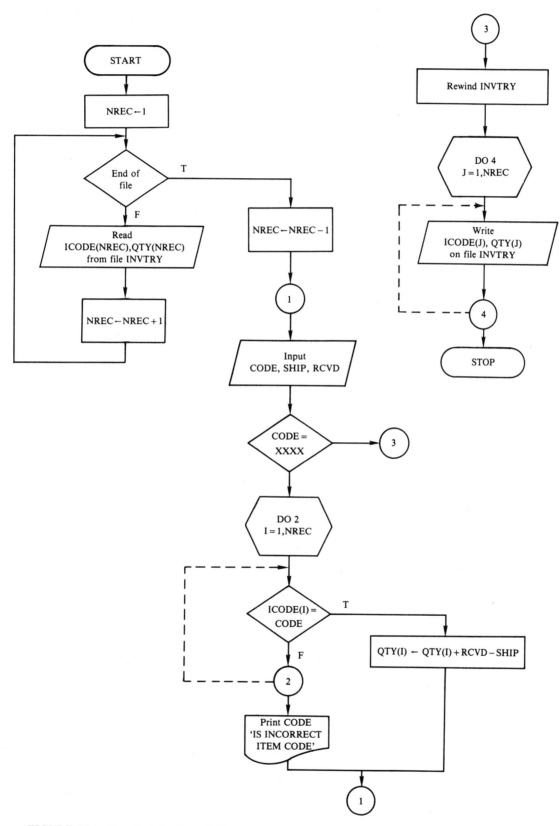

FIGURE 14.1. Flowchart for Example 7.

```
C *************** INVENTORY UPDATE PROGRAM ***************
C         ICODE = LIST OF ITEM CODES FROM FILE INVTRY
C         QTY   = LIST OF QUANTITIES FROM FILE INVTRY
C         NREC  = NUMBER OF RECORDS IN FILE INVTRY
C         CODE  = ITEM CODE TO BE INPUT
C         SHIP  = QUANTITY SHIPPED (OF ITEM CODE)
C         RCVD  = QUANTITY RECEIVED (OF ITEM CODE).
      INTEGER ICODE(100),QTY(100),NREC,CODE,SHIP,RCVD
      DATA LAST/'XXXX'/
      REWIND 8
C READ ARRAYS ICODE AND QTY FROM FILE INVTRY
      DO 1 NREC=1,100
         READ(8,20,END=2)ICODE(NREC),QTY(NREC)
    1 CONTINUE
      WRITE(6,21)
      STOP
    2 NREC=NREC-1
C READ CODE,SHIP,AND RCVD TO UPDATE ARRAY QTY
    3 READ(5,22)CODE,SHIP,RCVD
         IF(CODE.EQ.LAST) GO TO 6
C         SEARCH ARRAY ICODE FOR CODE
         DO 4 I=1,NREC
            IF(ICODE(I).EQ.CODE) GO TO 5
    4    CONTINUE
C         CODE IS NOT IN FILE INVTRY
         WRITE(6,23)
         GO TO 3
    5    QTY(I)=QTY(I)+RCVD-SHIP
      GO TO 3
    6 WRITE(6,24)
C CREATE AN UPDATED FILE INVTRY CONTAINING THE INFORMATION
C CONTAINED IN THE ARRAYS ICODE AND QTY.
      REWIND 8
      DO 7 J=1,NREC
         WRITE(8,20)ICODE(J),QTY(J)
    7 CONTINUE
      ENDFILE 8
      REWIND 8
      STOP
   20 FORMAT(A4,1X,I5)
   21 FORMAT(1X,'INADEQUATE ARRAY DIMENSIONS')
   22 FORMAT(A4,2X,I5,2X,I5)
   23 FORMAT(1X,I5,' IS NOT A CORRECT ITEM CODE.')
   24 FORMAT(1X,'INVENTORY IS UPDATED')
      END
```

FIGURE 14.2. Program for the algorithm displayed in Figure 14.1.

Although this program creates an updated file INVTRY, we cannot "see" it. The only printed output is the message INVENTORY IS UPDATED. To get a printed copy of the contents of INVTRY, we can include the following program segment just before the STOP statement:

```
      WRITE(6,25)
      DO 8 I=1,NREC
         WRITE(6,26)CODE(I),QTY(I)
    8 CONTINUE
   25 FORMAT(/1X,'ITEM CODE      UNITS ON HAND')
   26 FORMAT(1X,3X,A4,10X,I5)
```

Suppose we had done this by using the input data:

Input Data:

From card reader or
terminal keyboard

	1	2	3
1234567890	1234567890	1234567890	
A100	1200	1000	
A101	1000	550	
D402	1800	2000	
Y880	300	0	
XXXX	0	0	

From file INVTRY
(connected to unit 8)

	1	2	3
1234567890	1234567890	1234567890	
A100	2000		
A101	4450		
C229	1060		
D402	2300		
X992	500		
X993	650		
Y880	1050		
Y881	400		

Then the output would be as follows:

Output:

```
INVENTORY IS UPDATED

ITEM CODE      UNITS ON HAND
   A100             1800
   A101             4000
   C229             1060
   D402             2500
   X992              500
   X993              650
   Y880              750
   Y881              400
```

Remark: Note that the flowchart symbol used to denote output to a file is not the one used to denote output to a printer. The standard practice is to use the same symbol for all I/O operations that transfer data to and from files.

File-maintenance programs are most often used to modify large existing files that serve as input files for other programs. Printed copies of what is contained in these files are usually not needed; hence, including WRITE statements to print their contents serves only to tie up a printer needlessly. Should a copy of a file be needed, another program can be used to read and print its contents. Thus, although we showed how the program to update the file INVTRY could be modified to print the contents of the updated file, you should not do this without good reason.

14.6 Problems

1. Below are two programs and accompanying input that create files DATA1 and DATA2. If DATA1 and DATA2 are connected to units 2 and 3 respectively, what will be printed when each program in parts (a) through (e) is run? You are to assume that each variable containing character data each can store at least four characters.

Program to create file DATA1:

```
    REWIND 2
    DO 1 I=1,5
       READ(5,10)J,N,K
       WRITE(2,10)J,N,K
  1 CONTINUE
    ENDFILE 2
    REWIND 2
    STOP
 10 FORMAT(I4,2X,A4,2X,I4)
    END
```

Input Data:

```
          1         2         3
12345678901234567890123456789 0
   10   JOAN   78
   20   SAM    75
   30   GREG   86
   40   MARY   81
   50   MARK   93
```

Program to create file DATA2:

```
    REWIND 3
    DO 1 I=1,5
       READ(5,20)JJ,KK
       WRITE(3)JJ,KK
  1 CONTINUE
    ENDFILE 3
    REWIND 3
    STOP
 20 FORMAT(A4,1X,I4)
    END
```

Input Data:

```
          1         2
12345678901234567890
SAL    64
JILL   72
JACK   88
JANE   95
PETE   79
```

a.
```
    REWIND 2
    READ(2,30,END=2)NAM,NUM
    WRITE(6,31)NUM,NAM
  2 REWIND 2
    STOP
 30 FORMAT(6X,A4,I6)
 31 FORMAT(1X,I2,1X,A4)
    END
```

b.
```
    REWIND 3
    READ(3) I,J,K,L
    WRITE(6,20)I,J,K,L
    REWIND 3
    STOP
 20 FORMAT(1X,A4,2X,I3)
    END
```

c.
```
    REWIND 2
    READ(2,10)K,M,N
    DO 1 J=1,4
       READ(2,10)KK,MM,NN
       IF(NN.GT.N) WRITE(6,11)MM,NN
  1 CONTINUE
    REWIND 2
    STOP
 10 FORMAT(I6,A4,3X,I3)
 11 FORMAT(1X,A4,I6)
    END
```

d.
```
    DIMENSION N(10),M(10)
    REWIND 2
    REWIND 3
    DO 1 I=1,9,2
       READ(3)N(I),M(I)
       READ(2,11)N(I+1),M(I+1)
  1 CONTINUE
    DO 2 I=1,10
       WRITE(6,12)N(I),M(I)
  2 CONTINUE
    REWIND 2
    REWIND 3
    STOP
 11 FORMAT(6X,A4,I6)
 12 FORMAT(1X,A4,I4)
    END
```

Problems 2–4 refer to the following product survey.

A manufacturing company sends a package consisting of eight new products to each of ten families and asks each family to rate each product on the following scale:

        0 = poor;   1 = fair;   2 = good;   3 = very good;   4 = excellent.

Here are the results in tabular form:

Family number

		1	2	3	4	5	6	7	8	9	10
	1	0	1	1	2	1	2	2	1	0	1
	2	2	3	3	0	3	2	2	3	4	1
	3	1	3	4	4	4	1	4	2	3	2
	4	3	4	2	4	3	1	3	4	2	4
Product number	5	0	1	3	2	2	2	1	3	0	1
	6	4	4	4	3	2	1	4	4	1	1
	7	1	3	1	3	2	4	1	4	3	4
	8	2	2	3	4	2	2	3	4	2	3

2. Write a program to create a file RATE containing the information in this table. Then use this file to print a two-column report showing the product numbers and the average rating for each product.

3. Use the file RATE to print a report as in Problem 2. However, the average ratings are to appear from smallest to largest.

4. Use the file RATE to print a two-column report as follows. The first column is to give the product numbers receiving at least six ratings of 3 or better. The second column is to give the number of these ratings obtained.

5. Write a program to create a file named SST containing the following information about employees of the Sevard Company. The file SST is to be used in Problems 6–8, so you should "save" it.

Employee ID	Year-to-date income	Hourly rate
24168	12,442.40	7.35
13725	17,250.13	11.41
34104	10,425.00	6.50
28636	11,474.25	6.75
35777	15,450.35	10.45
15742	14,452.00	10.05

Problems 6–8 refer to the file SST created in Problem 5.

6. A Social Security tax deduction of 6.65% is taken on the first \$29,700 earned by an employee. Once this amount is reached, no further deduction is made. Each of the following six input records gives an employee ID number and the number of hours worked this week:

```
          1          2
1234567890123456789O
24168     40
13725     36
34104     32
28636     40
35777     40
15742     30
```

Use these input data and the file SST to print a report giving the ID number, the current week's gross pay, and this week's Social Security deduction for each employee.

7. Write a program that uses the input data given in Problem 6 to update the year-to-date income figures in the file SST.

8. Using the file SST and the input data given in Problem 6, print a list of all employees who have satisfied the Social Security tax requirement for the current year. With each ID number printed, give the year-to-date income figure.

9. Write a program to create a file GRADE containing the following information. After the file has been written, its contents should be read and printed. It should then be saved.

```
2
Edwards           75   93
Lebak             91   65
Myers             41   83
Nolan             89   51
Post              78   63
Sovenson          56   87
Block             82   82
```

10. The two numbers following each name in the file GRADE created for Problem 9 represent grades; the first value in the file, the number 2, tells how many grades have previously been recorded on the file for each student. Write a program that will allow an additional grade to be input for each student. Your program should update the file GRADE, and print a listing of student names and averages.

14.7 Review True-or-False Quiz

1. Files created with formatted WRITE statements should be read with formatted READ statements.   T   F

2. The END= specifier obviates the need to use an EOD-tag as the last record in a data file.   T   F

3. A program can use no more than one file for input and one for output.   T   F

4. A programmer must make a choice as to whether input should be made in the usual way (from the card reader or terminal keyboard) or whether it should be from a file, since both methods cannot be used in the same program.   T   F

5. If a file is created with a formatted WRITE statement, it must be read by using the same format specification.   T   F

6. Any edit descriptor can be used with formatted input/output files.   T   F

7. The statement BACKSPACE 5 informs the computer to "backspace" 5 records.   T   F

15
Sorting and Searching

Many computer applications require sorting data according to some specified order. The most obvious of these concern programming tasks to produce printed reports with columns of figures appearing in ascending or descending order, or columns of names appearing in alphabetical order. Less obvious, but equally important, applications of sorting concern programming tasks that require searching given collections of data for specified values. In this text, we have considered several examples that involved searching lists of numbers or lists of strings, and, in each case, a sequential search was performed; that is, the value being sought was compared with the successive list entries, starting with the first, until a match was found. If nothing is known about how the list entries are ordered, then this method is as good as any. However, lists whose entries are sorted according to some specified order can be searched much more efficiently.

For the reasons cited, much attention has been given to the problem of sorting and many different sorting algorithms have been developed. The *bubble sort* algorithm described in Section 9.6 is but one of these. Although this algorithm can be used for many of the applications encountered by beginning programmers, it is very inefficient and not suitable for a great many programming tasks. In this chapter, we will describe some of the techniques used in sorting.

In addition, we will present a very efficient search algorithm. Although only numerical lists will be considered, the techniques presented are also applicable to problems involving nonnumerical data such as lists of names. (A comprehensive treatment of all topics covered in this chapter, and many more, can be found in the text *Sorting and Searching,* by Donald Knuth.*)

The Art of Computer Programming, Vol. 3: Sorting and Searching, by Donald E. Knuth, Addison-Wesley, Reading, Mass., 1973.

15.1 Insertion Sort

The sorting algorithm described in this section is called an *insertion sort* and is somewhat more efficient than the bubble sort (about twice as fast). Although it is not one of the most efficient sorting algorithms, it is easy to understand and will help us describe an algorithm that is very efficient.

Suppose the list A(1), A(2), . . . , A(N) is to be sorted in ascending order. We start with a list containing only the one entry A(1). Then we compare the next term A(2) with A(1) and these are swapped if necessary to give a list with the two entries

A(1),A(2)

in the proper order. Next A(3) is compared with A(2) and, if necessary, with A(1) to determine where it should be inserted. We illustrate with the following list:

3 2 5 4 1

Start with a single entry list:	3
Insert the 2 before the 3:	2, 3
Place 5 after the 3:	2, 3, 5
Insert 4 between 3 and 5:	2, 3, 4, 5
Insert 1 before the 2:	1, 2, 3, 4, 5

Let us examine this process of insertion more carefully. Suppose the items

A(1), A(2), A(3), . . . , A(I)

are in order and A(I + 1) is to be inserted in its proper place. Temporarily assigning the value of A(I + 1) to the variable T, we proceed as follows.

If $T \geqslant A(I)$	no swap is necessary and no further comparisons are required.
If $T < A(I)$	let A(I + 1) = A(I). (This moves A(I) one position to the right.) Note that T "remembers" the original value of A(I + 1).
If $T \geqslant A(I-1)$	let A(I) = T and the insertion is complete.
If $T < A(I-1)$	let A(I) = A(I − 1). (This moves A(I − 1) one position to the right.) T still remembers the original value of A(I + 1).

         •   •
         •   •
         •   •

(Continue this process until T, the original value of A(I + 1), has been inserted in its proper place.)

The following algorithm describes this process:

    a. Let J = I and T = A(I + 1) (to compare A(J) with T).
    b. If $T \geqslant A(J)$, let A(J + 1) = T and stop.
    c. Let A(J + 1) = A(J) (moves A(J) one position to the right).
    d. Let J = J − 1.
    e. If $J \geqslant 1$, go to step (b). Otherwise, let A(J + 1) = T and stop.

To sort a list A(1), A(2), . . . , A(N), this procedure must be repeated for each value of I from 1 to N − 1. This is accomplished as shown in the flowchart of Figure 15.1 on page 320. The following subroutine INSORT is based on this flowchart. It can be used in any program to sort, into ascending order, any one-dimensional array A of size N. (If the array A contains names, they will be alphabetized.)

```
C ************** SUBROUTINE INSORT ***************
C SUBROUTINE TO SORT THE ENTRIES OF ARRAY A
C INTO ASCENDING ORDER USING THE INSERTION METHOD
      SUBROUTINE INSORT(A,N)
      DIMENSION A(N)
      NM1=N-1
      DO 3 I=1,NM1
        J=I
        T=A(I+1)
 1      IF(T.GE.A(J)) GO TO 2
          A(J+1)=A(J)
          J=J-1
        IF(J.GE.1) GO TO 1
 2        A(J+1)=T
 3 CONTINUE
      RETURN
      END
```

15.2 Shell's Method (Shell-Sort)

A principal reason for the inefficiency of the bubble sort is that it moves list entries at most one position at a time. (Recall that in the bubble sort all comparisons involve adjacent array entries A(I) and A(I + 1), which are swapped if they are out of order.) The insertion sort improves slightly on this technique, but not much. For example, consider the following list:

4 2 3 1 7 8 9

Either of the two methods will make numerous comparisons and swaps to sort this list, even though only one swap is actually needed. Certainly, no sorting algorithm should be expected to recognize this one swap. However, the example does suggest that we might do better than the two methods presented. The key is to allow comparisons and swaps between array entries that are not next to each other. The method we now describe is called Shell's method.*

The idea behind Shell's method is to precede the insertion algorithm by a process that moves the "smallest" values to the left and "largest" values to the right more quickly. To illustrate the method, we'll sort the following list:

7 1 6 3 4 2

First imagine the list divided into two parts, and make the comparisons indicated:

7 1 6 3 4 2

Thus, 7 and 3 will be swapped, 1 and 4 will not be, and 6 and 2 will be. This gives us a new list:

3 1 2 7 4 6

Note that these three comparisons resulted in moving the "small" values 2 and 3 to the left and the "large" values 6 and 7 to the right, each by more than one position.

*"A High-Speed Sorting Procedure," by Donald L. Shell, *Comm. of the ACM*, Vol. 2, July 1959 (30–32).

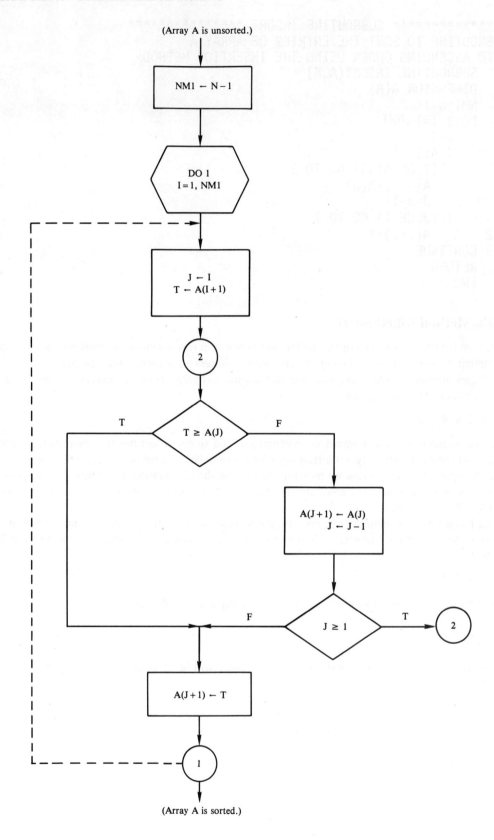

FIGURE 15.1. Flowchart to sort an array by the insertion method.

Dividing the original list of six entries into two parts led us to compare entries three positions apart. Similarly, we can compare entries that are two positions apart and make the following comparisons:

3 1 2 7 4 6

Note that 2 is compared with 3 and swapped. Then 4 is compared with 3, which was moved to the third position. But this is just an application of the insertion method applied to the list

3 2 4

Similarly, comparing 7 with 1 and 6 with 7 is the same as using the insertion method for the list

1 7 6

These comparisons leave us with

2 1 3 6 4 7

The final step is to compare entries one position apart. But this is the insertion method applied to the list of all six terms, so we know the list will be sorted.

Let's summarize the process just used to sort a list of length 6:

A(1), A(2), A(3), A(4), A(5), A(6)

First, the list was rearranged so that entries three positions apart were in order—that is, each of the following two-element lists was sorted:

A(1),A(4)
A(2),A(5)
A(3),A(6)

Next, the list obtained was rearranged so that entries two positions apart were in order—that is, each of the following three-element lists was sorted:

A(1),A(3),A(5)
A(2),A(4),A(6)

Finally, the list was rearranged so that entries one position apart were in order, which resulted in a completely sorted list. The important thing to note is that each of these partial sorts used the insertion method.

We now describe Shell's method for sorting a one-dimensional array A of size N.

a. Select an integer M from 1 to N/2.
b. Sort the list so that entries M positions apart are in order.
c. If M = 1, stop. The list is sorted.
d. Pick a new and smaller M (M $\geq$ 1), and go to Step (b).

For the list with six entries, the values M = 3, M = 2, and M = 1 were chosen. Of course, the successive values M = 3, 2, 1 are not always to be used. The sequence of M values that yields the fastest sort is not known. The most common practice is to use the sequence of values obtained by successively dividing N, the array size, by 2. Thus, the starting value of M (Step (a)) is M = N/2 (integer arithmetic), and the "next" M value (Step (d)) is obtained by replacing M with M/2 (integer arithmetic).

The only difficult part of Shell's algorithm is Step (b). To accomplish this, each of the following M lists must be sorted:

A(1), A(1+M), A(1+2M), A(1+3M), . . .
A(2), A(2+M), A(2+2M), A(2+3M) . . .
.
.
.
A(M), A(M+M), A(M+2M), A(M+3M) . . .

As indicated in the worked-out example, a modification of the insertion algorithm is used. The flowchart in Figure 15.2 which sorts the list

$$A(K), A(K+M), A(K+2M), \ldots$$

is identical to the insertion-algorithm flowchart (Figure 15.1) except that it uses increments of M rather than increments of 1. The following subroutine SHELL uses this flowchart for each K from 1 to M. This subroutine can be used in any program to sort, into ascending order, any one-dimensional array A of size N. It is very fast.

```
C ************* SUBROUTINE SHELL *************
C SUBROUTINE TO SORT THE ENTRIES OF ARRAY A
C INTO ASCENDING ORDER USING SHELL'S METHOD
      SUBROUTINE SHELL(A,N)
      DIMENSION A(N)
      M=N
    1 M=M/2
      IF(M.LT.1) RETURN
C        SORT ARRAY A SO THAT ENTRIES M
C        POSITIONS APART ARE IN ORDER.
      DO 5 K=1,M
        NMM=N-M
        DO 4 I=K,NMM,M
          J=I
          T=A(I+M)
    2     IF(T.GE.A(J)) GO TO 3
            A(J+M)=A(J)
            J=J-M
          IF(J.GE.1) GO TO 2
    3       A(J+M)=T
    4   CONTINUE
    5 CONTINUE
      GO TO 1
      END
```

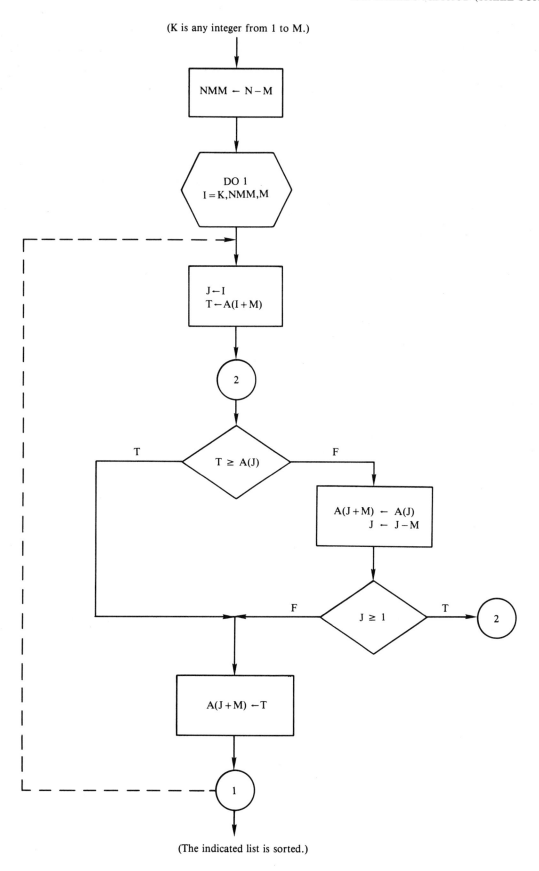

(K is any integer from 1 to M.)

(The indicated list is sorted.)

FIGURE 15.2. Flowchart to sort the list A(K), A(K + M), A(K + 2M), ...

15.3 Binary Search

Suppose a one-dimensional array A of length N has been sorted in ascending order. The first step in a "binary" search for a specified value VAL is to compare VAL with the "middle" term A(MID). When this is done one of three things will happen:

VAL = A(MID)   in which case VAL is found.
VAL < A(MID)   in which case VAL is in the left half of the list, if at all.
VAL > A(MID)   in which case VAL is in the right half of the list, if at all.

Thus, if VAL is not found by these three comparisons, the search may be confined to a list half the length of the original list. The next step would be to compare VAL with the "middle" term of this smaller list. If this "middle" term is VAL, the search is complete. If not, the number of terms to be considered is again halved. Continuing in this manner, we can search the entire list very quickly. We illustrate by searching the following list of 13 numbers for the value VAL = 67:

28   31   39   43   48   52   60   62   67   73   77   86   89

VAL = 67 is compared with the middle term, 60. Since it is larger, only the last six terms need be considered:

62   67   73   77   86   89

This shorter list has two "middle" terms. When this happens, let's agree to use the leftmost of these. Thus, VAL = 67 is compared with 73. Since it is smaller, the search is confined to the two values

62   67

These final two values are both "middle" terms, so 62 is used. VAL = 67 is larger than 62, which leaves only the term 67. This final comparison results in a match, and VAL = 67 is found.

Note that VAL was compared with just four "middle" terms. In the same manner, a search of this list for any value VAL can be completed by comparing VAL with at most four such "middle" terms. If none of these four values is VAL, it must be concluded that VAL is not in the list. Using this method on a list with as many as 2^N terms, we will either find VAL by comparing it with at most N "middle" terms or be sure that VAL is not in the list. Thus, a list with $2^{10} = 1,024$ terms requires ten or fewer steps to find VAL or to conclude that it is not present. (A sequential search of a list with 1,024 terms will take 512 steps, on the average, to do the same thing.)

As simple as a binary search may appear, care must be taken to state the algorithm precisely so that it can be programmed (coded) without bugs. Perhaps the safest way to do this is to use two variables, say LEFT and RIGHT, to store the leftmost and rightmost positions yet to be searched. Thus, at the outset LEFT = 1, RIGHT = N, and the position of the middle term is MID = (LEFT + RIGHT)/2 (integer arithmetic). If VAL < A(MID), only the terms in positions LEFT through MID − 1 need be considered, so RIGHT will be set equal to MID − 1. Similarly, if VAL > A(MID), LEFT will be set equal to MID + 1. As long as LEFT ≤ RIGHT, VAL must be compared with A(MID). However, if LEFT > RIGHT, no more comparisons are required and we must conclude that VAL is not in the list.

Binary-search algorithm (to search an array A of size N for the value VAL):

a. Initialize LEFT = 1 and RIGHT = N.
b. Let MID = (LEFT + RIGHT)/2 (integer arithmetic).
c. If VAL = A(MID), stop; the search is complete.
d. If VAL < A(MID), let RIGHT = MID − 1. Otherwise let LEFT = MID + 1.
e. If LEFT ≤ RIGHT, go to Step (b). Otherwise, stop; VAL is not in the list.

The flowchart shown in Figure 15.3 describes a subroutine to perform this binary search. The value MID = 0 is returned to the calling program to indicate that VAL was not found. Otherwise, the value of MID indicates the position of VAL in the list. The following subroutine SEARCH is based on this flowchart. It is very fast.

```
C ********** SUBROUTINE SEARCH **********
C SUBROUTINE TO CARRY OUT A BINARY SEARCH
C OF THE ARRAY A FOR THE VALUE VAL.
C MID=0 IS RETURNED IF VAL IS NOT IN ARRAY A.
C OTHERWISE,MID IS SUCH THAT A(MID)=VAL.
      SUBROUTINE SEARCH(A,N,VAL,MID)
      INTEGER LEFT,RIGHT
      LEFT=1
      RIGHT=N
    1 MID=(LEFT+RIGHT)/2
      IF(VAL.EQ.A(MID)) RETURN
      IF(VAL.LT.A(MID)) THEN
         RIGHT=MID-1
      ELSE
         LEFT=MID+1
      END IF
      IF(LEFT.LE.RIGHT) GO TO 1
      MID=0
      RETURN
      END
```

15.4 Merge Sorting

The bubble sort, insertion sort, and Shell-sort algorithms are instances of **internal-sorting algorithms.** This term is used to indicate that all of the data being sorted are stored in the computer's main memory at the same time. If the data to be sorted do not fit into memory, the usual practice is to sort them in parts, store these parts as files by using one or more secondary storage devices (tape units or disk units), and then merge these files into a single sorted file. This process is called **external sorting**—the data to be sorted are stored on external storage devices, and are never stored in their entirety in the computer's main memory.

(Array A of size N is in ascending order and V is given.)

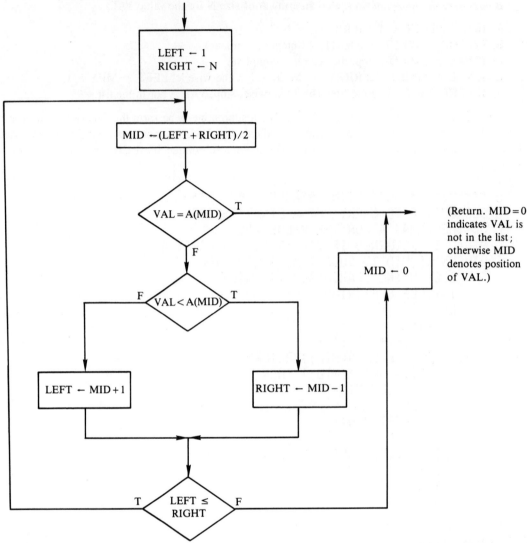

FIGURE 15.3. Flowchart: binary-search subroutine.

In this section we describe one of the many methods used to merge sorted files into a single sorted file. We illustrate the method by showing how two lists of numbers

$$A_1 \leq A_2 \leq A_3 \leq \cdots \leq A_m$$

and

$$B_1 \leq B_2 \leq B_3 \leq \cdots \leq B_n$$

can be merged into a single list

$$C_1 \leq C_2 \leq C_3 \leq \cdots \leq C_{m+n}$$

First, we compare A_1 with B_1 and store the smaller as C_1. Suppose B_1 is smaller. Then $C_1 = B_1$ and we compare A_1 with B_2. If this time A_1 is smaller, then $C_2 = A_1$ and we compare A_2 with B_2. (If it happens that two values being compared are equal, we will assign the A entry to list C.) We continue in this manner until all terms in one of the two lists have been stored as C entries. The remaining terms in the other list are then placed in the C list as they appear. This process is called a *merge-sort* process since two sorted lists are *merged* into a single *sorted* list.

Applying this merge-sort method to the lists

$$A = 3\ 4\ 6\ 8\ 9\ 10\ 13$$
$$B = 5\ 8\ 8$$

we obtain

$C_1 = 3$ since $3 \leq 5$
$C_2 = 4$ since $4 \leq 5$
$C_3 = 5$ since $6 > 5$
$C_4 = 6$ since $6 \leq 8$
$C_5 = 8$ since $8 \leq 8$
$C_6 = 8$ since $9 > 8$
$C_7 = 8$ since $9 > 8$
$C_8 = 9$
$C_9 = 10$ } since all of list B has been stored in C.
$C_{10} = 13$

If two lists, stored as File 1 and File 2, are to be merged into File 3, the same method can be used. The flowchart in Figure 15.4 shows one way to do this. In the flowchart, A and B denote single values read from File 1 and File 2, respectively. Note that each flowchart symbol to read a value from a file is preceded by an end-of-file test. You will recall that such a test can be coded in FORTRAN by using an END= specifier in a READ statement. For example, the flowchart segment

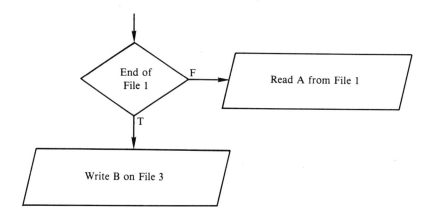

can be coded as

    READ(1,END=5)A

where 5 is the statement number of a statement that writes B on File 3.

The merge-sort program shown in Figure 15.5 is based directly on the merge-sort flowchart in Figure 15.4. As written, it will merge files containing unformatted real data. To merge integer files, simply include the type statement

    INTEGER A,B

It is also easily modified to merge files with formatted data.

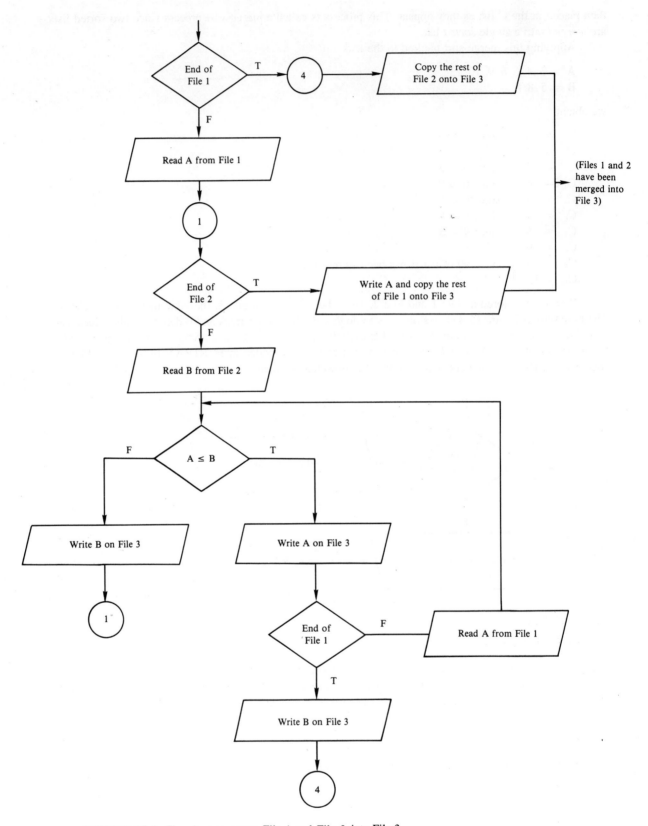

FIGURE 15.4. Flowchart to merge File 1 and File 2 into File 3.

```
C PROGRAM TO MERGE FILES 1 AND 2 INTO FILE 3.
C FILE 3 WILL BE IN ASCENDING ORDER IF FILES 1 and 2 ARE.
C ALL FILES CONTAIN UNFORMATTED REAL DATA.
C TO MERGE INTEGER FILES,DECLARE A AND B AS INTEGERS.
C
C A DENOTES A VALUE READ FROM FILE 1.
C B DENOTES A VALUE READ FROM FILE 2.
C
      REWIND 1
      REWIND 2
      REWIND 3
      READ(1,END=4)A
    1 READ(2,END=6)B
C WRITE THE SMALLER OF A AND B ON FILE 3.
    2 IF(A.LE.B) GO TO 3
          WRITE(3)B
      GO TO 1
    3     WRITE(3)A
          READ(1,END=5)A
      GO TO 2
C COPY THE REST OF FILE 2 ONTO FILE 3.
    4     READ(2,END=7)B
    5     WRITE(3)B
      GO TO 4
C COPY THE REST OF FILE 1 ONTO FILE 3.
    6     WRITE(3)A
          READ(1,END=7)A
      GO TO 6
C MERGE IS COMPLETE.
    7 REWIND 1
      REWIND 2
      REWIND 3
      STOP
      END
```

FIGURE 15.5. Program for the algorithm displayed in Figure 15.4.

The method described for merging two files into a single file can be generalized to allow more than two files to be merged. The subroutine MERGE shown in Figure 15.6 can be used to merge files numbered 1 through K into a single file numbered L. The subroutine is based on the following algorithm.

Merge Algorithm: to merge K files, numbered 1 through K, into a single file, numbered L. One or more of the K files to be merged may be empty files. If the entries in each of files 1 through K are in ascending order, the entries in file L will be in ascending order.

a. Read the first entries of files 1 through K into $A(1), A(2), \ldots, A(K)$. If file number I is empty, assign the "large" number 1E30 to $A(I)$.
b. Find J such that $A(J)$ is the smallest of $A(1), A(2), \ldots, A(K)$.
c. If $A(J) = 1E30$, stop; the merge is complete.
d. Write $A(J)$ onto file L and read another value for $A(J)$ from file J. But if the end of file J is encountered, assign 1E30 to $A(J)$.
e. Go to Step (b).

```
C ******************* SUBROUTINE MERGE *******************
C SUBROUTINE TO MERGE INPUT FILES 1 THROUGH K INTO FILE L.
C K MUST NOT EXCEED 6 AND L MUST BE GREATER THAN K.
C IF THE INPUT FILES ARE SORTED IN ASCENDING ORDER,
C FILE L WILL ALSO BE SORTED IN ASCENDING ORDER.
C ALL FILES CONTAIN UNFORMATTED REAL DATA.
C
C A(I) DENOTES A VALUE READ FROM INPUT FILE I.
C
      SUBROUTINE MERGE(K,L)
      DIMENSION A(6)
C REWIND ALL FILES
      REWIND L
      DO 1 I=1,K
        REWIND I
    1 CONTINUE
C READ FIRST ENTRIES OF INPUT FILES INTO ARRAY A.
C SET A(I)=1E30 IF FILE I IS EMPTY.
      DO 3 I=1,K
        READ(I,END=2)A(I)
        GO TO 3
    2   A(I)=1E30
    3 CONTINUE
C FIND J SUCH THAT A(J) IS LEAST.
    4 J=1
      DO 5 I=2,K
        IF(A(I).LT.A(J)) J=I
    5 CONTINUE
C TEST FOR MERGE COMPLETION
      IF(A(J).EQ.1E30) GO TO 7
C WRITE A(J) ON FILE L AND READ ANOTHER VALUE FROM FILE J.
      WRITE(L)A(J)
      READ(J,END=6)A(J)
      GO TO 4
    6 A(J)=1E30
      GO TO 4
C MERGE IS COMPLETE-REWIND FILES
    7 REWIND L
      DO 8 I=1,K
        REWIND I
    8 CONTINUE
      RETURN
      END
```

FIGURE 15.6. Subroutine to merge up to six files.

15.5 Problems

Write a program to perform each task specified in Problems 1–10. The subroutines presented in this chapter may be used where appropriate. Be sure to use the top-down approach.

1. Read a list of positive integers into arrays L1 and L2 with all integers from 1 to 69 being assigned to L1 and the others to L2. Sort L1 and L2 into ascending order and print them as adjacent columns with the headings LIST1 and LIST2. Use input format specifications that allow you to use the following input data as a test set:

```
        1         2
12345678901234567890
 95 90 87 63 68 71
 84 60 55 70 45 53
 65 78 79 79 84 86
 99 80 60 43 68 75
 82 65 93
```

2. Read a list of positive integers into an array L and then create arrays L1 and L2 with L1 containing those values that exceed the average of all input values and with L2 containing the others. Sort L1 and L2 into descending order and print them as adjacent columns with the headings LIST1 and LIST2. Use input format specifications as stated in Problem 1.

3. Read a list of positive integers into an array L and then create arrays L1 and L2 as follows. L1 is to contain those integers that exceed the *median* of the input list and L2 is to contain the others. L1 and L2 are to be printed as adjacent columns and each column is to appear in ascending order. (The median of a list of numbers $a_1 \le a_2 \le a_3 \cdots \le a_n$ is the middle term if n is odd and the average of the two "middle" terms if n is even.) Use input format specifications as stated in Problem 1. (*Remark:* Only the list L needs to be sorted.)

4. Two input lists of positive integers, each appearing in ascending order, are to be read into arrays L1 and L2. The two arrays are then to be merged into a single array L whose entries are also in ascending order. L is to be printed, five numbers to the line. Use input format specifications that allow you to use the following input data as test data. (-1 is used as an EOD-tag for each input list.)

```
        1         2
12345678901234567890
 10 14 18 27 36 45
 59 73 79 85 87 88
 92 95 -1
 11 13 15 24 39 44
 45 62 68 79 86 88
 89 95 98 99 -1
```

5. Two input lists of positive integers, each appearing in ascending order, are to be read into arrays L1 and L2. The contents of these two arrays are then to be printed as a single column, from smallest to largest. The arrays L1 and L2 are not to be merged into a single array. Use input format specifications as stated in Problem 4.

6. Create an array A containing 5,000 numbers. Print every 100th entry of A, sort A into ascending order by using a bubble sort or insertion sort subroutine, and then print every 100th entry of the sorted array A. Next, replace the sorting subroutine used by the Shell-sort subroutine and run the program again. (Any numbers will do for the array A. For instance, you can use the function RANF, described in Chapter 13, to generate 5,000 "random" numbers, all lying between 0 and 1.)

7. Create an array LIST of 1,000 integers with

LIST(I) = $I^2 - I + 1$

Search this array for each of the following ten numbers. (They are to be input.)

205663   676507   3131   225   62751   810901   202951   164212   678153   723351

As each number is read, it is to be printed along with the I value indicating its position in the list. If it is not in the list, an appropriate message should be printed. Use a binary search. (You do not have to sort LIST. It is in ascending order.)

8. Let LIST be as described in Problem 7. For each integer J from 1 to 1,000, search LIST for the value

VAL = MOD(J**4 − J**2 + 1,1000000)

(VAL is the remainder when $J^4 - J^2 + 1$ is divided by 1,000,000, hence it will be an integer from 0 to 999,999. You may check that all entries in LIST are also in this range.) For each VAL found in LIST, print VAL, the J that gave it, and the subscript M indicating the position of VAL in the array LIST. (Use a binary search. A sequential search will take too long. Try it and see.)

9. Write a short program to create a file with 1,000 real numbers. (Any numbers will do. See the suggestion in Problem 6.) Create a new file containing these 1,000 numbers in ascending order and then print a two-column table with the first column showing every 50th entry in the unsorted file and the second showing every 50th entry in the sorted file. Use an array A of size 1,000 to carry out an internal sort.

10. Carry out the task specified in Problem 9 under the restriction that you can use at most one array in your program, and can store at most 400 real values in the array.

In Problems 11 and 12, describe an algorithm for the given task, prepare a flowchart from this algorithm, and write a corresponding subroutine. In each case write a short program to test the subroutine.

11. If we are given an array A, we can create a file containing the entries of A in ascending order by the following method. Find the smallest value in A and write it on the output file. If A(K) is this smallest value, replace it with a very large number. Next, select the smallest value in the modified array A and write it on the file. Again, if A(K) is this smallest value, replace it with the same large number. Repeat this process until all entries of A have been written on the output file. (This is an example of a selection sort. The smallest value is selected first, then the next smallest, and so on.)

12. Problem 11 describes a selection sort that can be used to copy the entries of an array onto a file in ascending order. A selection sort to rearrange the terms of an array A so that they are in ascending order can be described as follows. The first term A(1) of a list of length N is successively compared with A(2), A(3), . . . , A(N). Whenever A(1) is larger than a term A(K), A(1) and A(K) are swapped. These N − 1 comparisons will leave the smallest value in A(1). Next, A(2) is compared with A(3), A(4), . . . , A(N), swapping A(2) with A(K) whenever A(2) is larger than a term A(K). This process leaves the next smallest value in A(2). Repeating this process for A(3), then for A(4), and so on, will arrange the entire list in ascending order. (This algorithm is reasonably easy to remember and code, but it is only about as fast as the bubble sort algorithm.)

15.6 Review True-or-False Quiz

1. A list must be sorted in ascending order before a sequential search may be made.   T F

2. It is desirable to use sorting algorithms that compare and swap only adjacent entries, for such algorithms will not only be easier to understand but will generally be very efficient.   T F

3. The idea behind the insertion sort is to build a list by starting with one value and then placing each successive value in its proper position relative to all values included to that point.   T F

4. The idea of the Shell-sort is to use the insertion method on shorter and shorter lists.   T F

5. One reason the Shell-sort is efficient is that "small" values are moved to the left by more than one position at a time.   T F

6. A binary search can be made only on lists that are sorted.   T F

7. Each step in a binary search for a value VAL involves comparing VAL with a list entry A(MID) to determine if VAL = A(MID), VAL < A(MID), or VAL > A(MID). Fewer than 15 such steps are required to determine if a value VAL is included in a list of length 2,000.   T F

8. Algorithms used to sort data that are stored in a computer's main memory are called *internal-sorting algorithms*.   T F

9. The expressions *external-sorting* and *merging* are synonymous.   T F

10. External-sorting algorithms can be used to sort data that will not fit in the computer's main memory.   T F

11. External-sorting procedures often utilize internal-sorting algorithms.   T F

16
Specification Statements

Specification statements give the compiler certain information necessary to compile a program. They cause no action to take place during program execution; hence, they are nonexecutable. The DIMENSION, EXTERNAL, and type statements described previously are specification statements. The DIMENSION statement is used to specify array names and dimensions, and EXTERNAL statements are used to specify that certain symbolic names are names of subprograms. We have also used type statements throughout the text to specify that certain symbolic names are names of real, integer, or character entities.

In this chapter we describe three kinds of specification statements. In Sections 16.1 and 16.2 we consider type statements that allow you to process data types other than real data, integer data, and character data. In Section 16.4 we describe the EQUIVALENCE statement that is used to identify two or more variable names as being equivalent—that is, as sharing the same memory storage unit. In Sections 16.5 and 16.6 we describe the COMMON and labeled COMMON statements. These are used to set up one or more blocks of memory that can be referenced in any program unit. Doing so provides a means of communication between program units other than the communication through the correspondence set up between actual and dummy arguments.

All specification statements are placed near the beginning of a program unit before the first executable statement. The order of statements in any program unit is given in Appendix A.

In addition to the specification statements, we describe, in Section 16.7, the BLOCKDATA subprograms. These are nonexecutable subprograms (they contain only nonexecutable statements) that use DATA statements to initialize variables during program compilation.

16.1 Type Statements

FORTRAN allows several data types in addition to the types integer, real, and character. These include double precision, complex, and logical data.

Double Precision Data

Every computer has a limitation on the number of significant digits that it can store in a single storage unit. A common maximum number is seven. However, on some occasions, greater accuracy than this is needed. FORTRAN allows this greater accuracy through *double precision* arithmetic. Each double precision value uses two storage units, thereby approximately doubling the number of significant digits stored.

Double precision constants are written as ordinary numbers with a decimal point, or in the exponential form

nDm

where n denotes an integer or a decimal and m denotes an integer. This form is analogous to the nEm form of real constants and the interpretation of D is exactly that of E. Thus,

$$464.378614D2 = 464.378614 \times 10^2 = 46437.8614$$

Double precision variables must be declared explicitly in a type statement. For instance, the statements

```
DOUBLE PRECISION A,B
A = 464.378614D2
B = 1.234567890123
```

declare A and B as double precision variables and assign the values 46437.8614 and 1.234567890123 to A and B, respectively. As we have stated, the number of digits that will be retained is system dependent, but it will be approximately twice the number retained for reals.

To read and print double precision values, the F and D edit descriptors are used. The descriptor $Fw.d$ edits input and output data just as it does for real variables and $Dw.d$ has the same meaning as $Ew.d$. The only difference is that more significant digits can be stored or printed when double precision variables are used.

Mixed-mode expressions involving real and double precision data are allowed by most FORTRAN compilers. Your FORTRAN manual will explain how such expressions are treated—the usual situation is that double precision arithmetic is used.

Complex Data

FORTRAN allows the processing of *complex* data by including the standard operations for *complex numbers* as part of the language. Recall that a complex number is an ordered pair of real numbers. Two standard forms for writing complex numbers are (a, b) and $a + bi$ where a and b are real numbers and $i = \sqrt{-1}$; a is called the real part and b the imaginary part of $a + bi$. FORTRAN uses the form (a, b).

Complex variables must be declared as such in COMPLEX type statements. The statements

```
COMPLEX Z1,Z2,W1,W2
Z1 = (5.3, -2.5)
Z2 = (7.12E1, 3.0E-1)
```

assign the values $(5.3, -2.5)$ and $(7.12E1, 3.0E-1)$ (equivalently, $5.3 - 2.5i$ and $71.2 + 0.3i$) to Z1 and Z2, respectively. When storing a value of a complex number, FORTRAN uses two storage units, one for the real part and the second for the imaginary part; however, the number is referenced by a single variable name. Thus, the statements

```
W1 = Z1 + Z2
W2 = Z1*Z2
```

evaluate the sum† $Z1 + Z2 = (76.5, -2.2)$ and the product† $Z1*Z2 = (378.11, -176.41)$ and assign these values to W1 and W2, respectively.

No special edit descriptor is necessary for reading or printing complex values. Since the real and imaginary parts of the number are real, a *pair* of E or F descriptors can be used.

---

†$(a,b) + (c,d) = (a+c, b+d)$ and $(a,b)*(c,d) = (ac-bd, ad+bc)$.

EXAMPLE 1.

```
      COMPLEX Z1,Z2,W
      READ(5,10)Z1,Z2
   10 FORMAT(4F4.0)
      W=Z1*Z2
      WRITE(6,11)W
   11 FORMAT(1X,F4.1,'+',F4.1,"I")
      STOP
      END
```

Input Data:

```
          1         2         3
123456789012345678901234567890
   3.0 2.0 5.0 6.0
```

Output:

```
   3.0+28.0I
```

Mixed-mode expressions involving real and complex data are allowed by most FORTRAN compilers. If W is a complex variable, the assignment statement

```
W=2.5+(3.0,4.0)
```

will treat 2.5 as the real part of a complex number to obtain the value

```
W=(5.5,4.0)
```

Your FORTRAN manual will explain how such mixed-mode expressions are treated.

Logical Data

Logical expressions are expressions that have one of the two values *true* and *false*—in FORTRAN these are written .TRUE. and .FALSE.. The expression (A.LT.B) appearing as the condition in a logical IF statement is a logical expression; its value is .TRUE. if A is less than B, and otherwise is .FALSE.. FORTRAN allows you to use the assignment statement to assign the value (.TRUE. or .FALSE.) of any logical expression to any variable that has been declared in a LOGICAL type statement. For example, the statements

```
LOGICAL LOGVAL
READ(5,10)A,B
LOGVAL=(A.GT.B)
```

declare LOGVAL as a *logical* variable, read input values for the *real* variables A and B, and assign .TRUE. to LOGVAL if A is greater than B and .FALSE. if A is not greater than B.

The general form of the assignment statement as it applies to logical variables is

a = e

where **a** denotes any logical variable and **e** denotes any logical expression. The following are admissible assignment statements. The variables L1, L2, M1, M2, and M3 are logical variables, and A and B are real variables.

```
M1=.TRUE.
M2=(A.LT.B).OR..FALSE.
M3=.NOT.(L1.AND.L2)
```

The first assigns the value .TRUE. to M1, the second assigns .TRUE. to M2 if A is less than B, and the third assigns .TRUE. to M3 if L1 and L2 are not both .TRUE..

EXAMPLE 2. Here is a program to determine if three input values are ordered—that is, if they appear either from smallest to largest or largest to smallest.

```
      INTEGER N1,N2,N3
      LOGICAL J,K
      READ(5,10)N1,N2,N3
      J=(N1.LE.N2).AND.(N2.LE.N3)
      K=(N1.GE.N2).AND.(N2.GE.N3)
      IF(J.OR.K) THEN
          WRITE(6,11)
      ELSE
          WRITE(6,12)
      END IF
      STOP
   10 FORMAT(3I5)
   11 FORMAT(1X,'VALUES ARE ORDERED')
   12 FORMAT(1X,'VALUES ARE NOT ORDERED')
      END
```

The L edit descriptor is used to read and print logical data. Its form is Lw, where w denotes the width of the input or output field. On input, the value .TRUE. or .FALSE. is assigned to the variable depending on whether the first nonblank character in the input field is T or F. (What happens if T or F is not included in the input field is system dependent.) On output, the Lw descriptor will cause a T or an F to be printed right-justified in the output field—that is, in the last position of the field.

EXAMPLE 3.

```
      LOGICAL M(9)
      READ(5,10)M
   10 FORMAT(3L6)
      WRITE(6,11)M
   11 FORMAT(3L2)
      STOP
      END
```

Input Data:

```
        1         2         3
12345678901234567890123456789 0
 TRUE FALSE TRUE
F    T    T
    F    T    F
```

Output:

```
 T F T
 F T T
 F T F
```

The logical statement specifies M as a one-dimensional logical array of size 9. The READ statement reads nine logical values (.TRUE. or .FALSE.) for the array M. The 3 in the input specification (3L6) says to read three values from each input record; the 6 says that each input value appears in a field of width 6; and the letter L says to assign the value .TRUE. or .FALSE. depending on whether the first nonblank character is a T or an F. (Characters in an input field following the letter T or F are ignored.)

The WRITE statement prints the contents of the array M by using the output format specification (3L2). Thus, each output record (line) contains three logical values (the letters T and F) printed right-justified in an output field of width 2.

The general form of the type statement is

type a, b, c, . . .

where **type** denotes one of INTEGER, REAL, DOUBLE PRECISION, COMPLEX, or LOGICAL, and **a, b, c, . . .** denote names of variables, arrays, array declarators, or functions. (The form of the type statement CHARACTER differs from this, as shown in Chapter 12.)

16.2 The IMPLICIT Statement

The IMPLICIT statement allows you to "type" variables in any program unit by the first letter of their names. For instance, the statement

IMPLICIT INTEGER(A,W-Z), COMPLEX(M-P)

tells the compiler to regard all variable names beginning with A, W, X, Y, or Z as integer variable names and all those beginning with M, N, O, or P as complex. Variable names beginning with any letter not appearing in the IMPLICIT statement are covered by the usual I through N convention. Thus, in this example, names beginning with I, J, K, and L will be integer names and all others not listed will be real.

An explicit type statement will override the effect of an IMPLICIT statement. For instance, the statements

IMPLICIT INTEGER(A-K),COMPLEX(M-W)
REAL BAL
INTEGER NUM

declare BAL a real variable even though the IMPLICIT statement "types" variables beginning with B as integer variables. Similarly, NUM is an integer variable. The form of the implicit statement is

IMPLICIT **type**$_1$ (a$_1$,a$_2$, . . .), **type**$_2$ (b$_1$,b$_2$, . . .), . . .

where **type**$_i$ denotes one of INTEGER, REAL, DOUBLE PRECISION, COMPLEX, or LOGICAL, and each **a**$_i$ and **b**$_i$ denotes either a single letter or two letters separated by a dash. If the second form of **a**$_i$ or **b**$_i$ is used, the two letters must be in alphabetical order.

16.3 Problems

1. Find and correct all errors.

a.
```
C PRINT ALL INTEGERS
C FROM FIRST TO LAST.
      INTEGER FIRST,LAST
      READ(5,10)FIRST,LAST
      IF (FIRST.GT.LAST) STOP
      DO 1 I=FIRST,LAST
         WRITE(6,11)I
    1 CONTINUE
      STOP
   10 FORMAT(F5.0,I5)
   11 FORMAT(1X,I5)
      END
```

b.
```
C READ TWO REAL VALUES AND PRINT
C THE INTEGER PART OF THEIR SUM
      READ(5,10)A,B
      SUM=A+B
      INTEGER SUM
      WRITE(6,11)SUM
      STOP
   10 FORMAT(2F7.2)
   11 FORMAT(1X,I7)
      END
```

c.
```
C READ 10 VALUES INTO A REAL
C ARRAY LIST AND PRINT THEM
C IN REVERSE ORDER
      IMPLICIT REAL(A-L)
      DIMENSION LIST(10)
      DO 1 N=1,10
        READ(5,10)LIST(N)
    1 CONTINUE
      DO 2 I=1,10
        J=11-I
        WRITE(6,11)LIST(J)
    2 CONTINUE
      STOP
   10 FORMAT(F7.2)
   11 FORMAT(1X,F7.2)
      END
```

d.
```
C READ A DOUBLE PRECISION VALUE AND
C PRINT THE WORD TRUE IF IT IS
C NEGATIVE; OTHERWISE PRINT FALSE.
      DOUBLE PRECISION A
      LOGICAL L
      READ(5,10)A
      IF (A.LT.0.) L=.TRUE.
      IF (A.GE.0.) L=.FALSE.
      WRITE(6,11)L
      STOP
   10 FORMAT(F12.4)
   11 FORMAT(1X,L5)
      END
```

2. Assuming that the following four type statements appear in a program unit, give the type of each variable name shown in parts (a)–(l):

```
IMPLICIT INTEGER(A-D),COMPLEX(G-K),LOGICAL(R-T)
DOUBLE PRECISION BETA,SUM
REAL COST,INT
INTEGER YRS
```

a.	ALPHA	**b.**	ISUM	**c.**	NAME	**d.**	SUM
e.	TRUE	**f.**	FALSE	**g.**	JYEARS	**h.**	YRS
i.	COST	**j.**	COMM	**k.**	ZZZ	**l.**	BETA

3. What will be printed when each program is run?

a.
```
      IMPLICIT COMPLEX(A-K)
      READ(5,10)A,B,C
      D=A-B*C
      WRITE(6,11)D
   10 FORMAT(2F5.0)
   11 FORMAT(1X,2F7.2)
      STOP
      END
```

Input Data:

```
         1         2
12345678901234567890
 1.0  5.0
-3.0  2.0
 4.0 -6.0
```

b.
```
      COMPLEX J,K
      J=(4.0,-3.0)
      K=(-8.0,5.0)
      J=J/K*K
      WRITE(6,10)J
   10 FORMAT(1X,F6.2,3X,F6.2)
      STOP
      END
```

c.
```
      IMPLICIT LOGICAL(A-D),INTEGER(E-N)
      E=5
      F=2
      A=E.LE.F
      B=.TRUE.
      C=(A.OR.B).AND.(F**2.GT.E)
      WRITE(6,10)C,B,A
   10 FORMAT(1X,3L3)
      STOP
      END
```

d.
```
      LOGICAL M,N,O,R,S,T
      WRITE(6,10)
   10 FORMAT(1X,'P',3X,'Q',3X,'P.AND.Q',
     +3X,'P.OR.Q',3X,'P IMPLIES Q'/)
      DO 1 I=1,4
         READ(5,11)M,N
         S=M.AND.N
         T=M.OR.N
         R=.NOT.M.OR.N
         WRITE(6,12)M,N,S,T,R
    1 CONTINUE
   11 FORMAT(2L4)
   12 FORMAT(1X,2(L1,3X),L4,L9,L12)
      STOP
      END
```

Input Data:

```
              1         2
    12345678901234567890
       T    T
       T    F
       F    T
       F    F
```

4. Each of the first 30 positions of an input record contains one of the letters T and F. Use a one-dimensional logical array of size 30 to read this input record, print counts of how many of each letter are included, and print all of the T's and F's, six to a line.

5. Each of six different bacterial cultures is examined at five incubation times (1, 2, 3, 4, and 5 hours) to determine the presence or absence of a certain attribute. Write a program to input a string of five T's and F's for each culture—T denotes the presence, and F the absence, of the attribute. A report is to be printed showing, for each culture, the incubation times at which the attribute was present.

6. Write a program to print a table of values for the complex function
$$w = 1 + z + z^2 \quad \text{for} \quad z = 0, 1+i, 2+2i, 3+3i, \ldots, 10+10i.$$

7. For any angle A (radian measure), let $w = \cos A + i \sin A$. Write a program to print a three-column table as follows. The first column is to show the values of A from 0 to 2π in increments of 0.2; the second column is to show the corresponding value of w; and the third column is to show the absolute value of w. (One way to determine w is to use the statement W = COS(A)+(0.,1.)*SIN(A).)

16.4 The EQUIVALENCE Statement

The EQUIVALENCE statement allows you to have more than one variable name share the same storage unit in the computer's memory. In a program unit containing the statement

    EQUIVALENCE (A,ALPHA,FIRST)

the variables A, ALPHA, and FIRST share the same storage unit and, hence, have the same value. Changing the value of any one of these variables changes the value of all three. A, ALPHA, and FIRST must be of the same type.

Similarly, the statement

EQUIVALENCE (N,NUM), (NPAY,NETPAY,NET), (X,XX,Y)

specifies that only three storage units are to be allotted for the eight variables, one for N and NUM, a second for NPAY, NETPAY, and NET, and a third for X, XX, and Y. Again, only variables in the program unit containing the EQUIVALENCE statement are affected.

The EQUIVALENCE statement serves two purposes. First, suppose that after writing a long program, you discover that different names (or different spellings of the same name) are used to denote the same quantity. Should this happen you need not rewrite the program. Instead, you can insert an EQUIVALENCE statement that will associate all of these names with the same storage unit. This means that the variables will be *equivalent;* that is, their values will always be identical.

The second use of the EQUIVALENCE statement is to minimize the amount of memory space needed to execute a program. This applies especially to the multiple use of storage units reserved for arrays. Suppose the beginning of a program requires a two-dimensional array TABLE and later in the program, after all references to TABLE are concluded, a one-dimensional array LIST is needed. You can save a significant number of memory locations by using the same storage units for both of these arrays. For example, if TABLE must be a 100-by-25 array and LIST a one-dimensional array of size 1000, you can write

REAL TABLE(100,25), LIST(1000)
EQUIVALENCE (TABLE(1,1), LIST(1))

The EQUIVALENCE statement says only that the *first* entry of the array TABLE and the *first* entry of the array LIST share the same storage unit. However, the effect will be to reserve 2,500 storage units, as needed for the array TABLE, and use the first 1,000 of these for the array LIST. Schematically, the correspondence between the entries in the two arrays is as follows. In this instance, the number of storage units needed is reduced by one thousand.

EQUIVALENCE statements can be used to associate any entries (not just the first entries) in two arrays with the same storage unit. For example, the statements

DIMENSION A(20),B(5),C(5),D(10)
EQUIVALENCE (A(1),B(1)), (A(6),C (1)), (A(11),D(1))

will reserve only twenty storage units as follows:

```
A(1)   ┌──────┐   B(1)
  ⋮    │  ⋮   │    ⋮
A(5)   ├──────┤   B(5)
A(6)   ├──────┤   C(1)
  ⋮    │  ⋮   │    ⋮
A(10)  ├──────┤   C(5)
A(11)  ├──────┤   D(1)
  ⋮    │  ⋮   │    ⋮
A(20)  └──────┘   D(10)
```

When the name of the *first* entry in an array is to be used in an EQUIVALENCE statement, it is permitted to use the array name in its place. Thus, the preceding EQUIVALENCE statement can be written as

EQUIVALENCE (A,B) (A(6),C), (A(11),D)

The general form of the EQUIVALENCE statement is

EQUIVALENCE (**list$_1$**), (**list$_2$**), . . . ,

where **list$_i$** denotes a list of variable names, array names, or names of array entries. Each **list$_i$** must contain at least two such names.

16.5 The COMMON Statement

We emphasized in Chapter 11 that variable names are local to the program unit in which they appear and that communication between program units is accomplished through the correspondence set up between dummy and actual arguments. FORTRAN allows for additional communication between program units by the use of the COMMON statement. Its purpose is to set up a **common storage area** (called a **common block**) that can be used by any program unit, thus allowing variables from different program units to share the same memory locations.

EXAMPLE 4.

Main Program:

```
DIMENSION A(3),B(2,2)
COMMON A,C,I,B
         .
         .
         .

CALL DMN(X)
         .
         .
         .


END
```

Subprogram:

```
SUBROUTINE DMN(X)
DIMENSION A(3),B(2,2)
COMMON A,C,I,B
         .
         .
         .

RETURN
END
```

The COMMON statement in the main program sets up the following common block:

A(1)
A(2)
A(3)
C
I
B(1,1)
B(2,1)
B(1,2)
B(2,2)

The COMMON statement in the subprogram instructs the compiler (COMMON statements are nonexecutable) to use this block of storage units for the subprogram variables and arrays A, C, I, and B. Thus, the values stored in any one of these locations can be changed by either program unit.

Following are three rules governing the use of COMMON statements.

1. Arrays can be dimensioned in a COMMON statement, rather than in a separate DIMENSION or type statement. The single statement

   COMMON A(3),C,I,B(2,2)

   is equivalent to the two statements

   DIMENSION A(3),B(2,2)
   COMMON A,C,I,B

   An array must not be declared in both a COMMON statement and a DIMENSION or type statement.

2. Several COMMON statements can appear in one program unit, but only one common block is set up. The pair of statements

   COMMON M,N,A
   COMMON L(100),TERM(100)

   is equivalent to the single statement

   COMMON M,N,A,L(100),TERM(100)

3. The storage units in the common block can be associated with different variable names in different program units. For example, placing the statement

   COMMON A(5),M,N

   in a main program sets up the common block

A(1)
A(2)
A(3)
A(4)
A(5)
M
N

If a subprogram contains the statement

COMMON B(5),NUM,M

the following correspondence is set up:

```
A(1)  ┌──────────┐  B(1)
A(2)  │          │  B(2)
A(3)  │          │  B(3)
A(4)  │          │  B(4)
A(5)  │          │  B(5)
M     │          │  NUM
N     └──────────┘  M
```

Note that the storage units reserved for M and N in the main program are used by NUM and M, respectively, in the subprogram. Thus, changing M in the subprogram changes the value of the main program variable N (and not M). Of course, variables referring to the same common storage unit must be of the same type. If another subprogram contains the statement

COMMON X,Y,Z

the variables X, Y, Z are associated with the first three storage units in the common block. Changing the value of Y in this subprogram has the effect of changing A(2) in the main program, and B(2) in the first subprogram.

16.6 Labeled COMMON Blocks

As shown in Section 16.5, COMMON statements appearing in a main program set up a single common block. To provide more than one common block, the labeled COMMON statement is used. It allows different common blocks to be referred to by different names.

EXAMPLE 5.

Main Program:

```
COMMON/STOR1/A(5),B(3)/STOR2/I,J(5)
CALL SUBA(X)
   .
   .
   .
CALL SUBB(X)
   .
   .
   .
END
```

Subroutines:

```
SUBROUTINE SUBA(Y)
COMMON/STOR1/D(8)
   .
   .
   .
RETURN
END
SUBROUTINE SUBB(Z)
COMMON/STOR2/K(4),M,N
   .
   .
   .
RETURN
END
```

The main program sets up two common storage areas called **labeled common blocks.** The first is labeled STOR1 and is used by both the main program and the subroutine SUBA. The other, labeled STOR2, is used by the main program and the subroutine SUBB. The association of variables with the storage units in these labeled common blocks is as follows:

STOR1   STOR2

A(1) ☐ D(1)   I   ☐ K(1)
A(2) ☐ D(2)   J(1) ☐ K(2)
A(3) ☐ D(3)   J(2) ☐ K(3)
A(4) ☐ D(4)   J(3) ☐ K(4)
A(5) ☐ D(5)   J(4) ☐ M
B(1) ☐ D(6)   J(5) ☐ N
B(2) ☐ D(7)
B(3) ☐ D(8)

The COMMON statements

COMMON X(5),A(7)/MEM/I(50))

and

COMMON//X(5),A(7)/MEM/I(50)

are equivalent. Both set up two common blocks, but only the second is a labeled common block. The double slash (//) appearing after COMMON denotes the absence of a label for the first common block. Common blocks that are not labeled are called **blank common blocks.** As shown, FORTRAN permits both blank and labeled common blocks to be defined in the same COMMON statement.

Some rules governing the use of labeled COMMON statements:

1. The names of the common blocks must appear between slashes.
2. The name of any labeled common block shared by two program units must appear in a COMMON statement in both.
3. Although the names of the variables referencing the storage units in a labeled common block may differ in different program units, the number of such variables must be the same.

The general form of the COMMON statement is

COMMON /block$_1$/list$_1$/block$_2$/list$_2$ . . .

where **block$_i$** denotes the name of a common block and **list$_i$** denotes a list of variable names, array names, and array declarators. The labels **block$_i$** can be omitted, but if they appear they must be enclosed in slashes.

16.7 BLOCKDATA Subprograms

You have seen how the nonexecutable DATA statement can be used to initialize program variables and arrays. DATA statements alone are not adequate for initializing variables and arrays associated with *labeled* common blocks. To initialize such variables and arrays during program compilation you must use a BLOCKDATA subprogram as illustrated in the next example.

EXAMPLE 6. If a main program contains the statement

```
COMMON/BLOC3/ALPHA(5)/BLOC4/P,Q,K(4)
```

the following subprogram will initialize the arrays ALPHA and K as indicated:

```
BLOCKDATA VALUES
COMMON/BLOC3/ALPHA(5)/BLOC4/P,Q,K(4)
DATA ALPHA/5*0/,K/5,3,6,8/
END
```

BLOC3

ALPHA(1)	0
ALPHA(2)	0
ALPHA(3)	0
ALPHA(4)	0
ALPHA(5)	0

BLOC4

P	
Q	
K(1)	5
K(2)	3
K(3)	6
K(4)	8

The BLOCKDATA statement specifies the name VALUES for the subprogram (names are optional). The COMMON statement associates the array ALPHA with the five storage units in the block labeled BLOC3, and P, Q, and the array K with the storage units in the block labeled BLOC4. The DATA statement initializes ALPHA and K as shown.

Remark: Although we used the same variable names in the BLOCKDATA subprogram as in the main program, it is not necessary to do this. However, it is important that the number and types of the variables associated with a block correspond exactly to the number and types of the storage units in the block. For instance, the COMMON statement in the subprogram associates P, Q, and the array K with the block BLOC4 even though P and Q are not to be initialized.

BLOCKDATA subprograms are used only to initialize variables during program compilation. For this reason they must contain only nonexecutable statements. In particular, a BLOCKDATA subprogram must begin with a BLOCKDATA statement, and can include only DIMENSION, COMMON, EQUIVALENCE, DATA, and type statements. It must conclude with an END statement.

16.8 Problems

What will be printed when each program is run?

1.
```
      EQUIVALENCE(A,B,C),(I,J)
      A=7
      J=12
      B=A+C
      I=J+6
      C=A+B
      J=I-2
      WRITE(6,10)B,I
   10 FORMAT(1X,F7.2,I5)
      STOP
      END
```

2.
```
      DIMENSION J(8),K(5)
      EQUIVALENCE(M,J(1)),(K(1),J(2))
      DO 1 I=1,8
         J(I)=I**2
    1 CONTINUE
      DO 2 L=1,5
         K(L)=K(L)+2
    2 CONTINUE
      M=8
      WRITE(6,10)(J(I),I=2,8,2)
   10 FORMAT(1X,8I6)
      STOP
      END
```

```
3.    INTEGER A,B,C
      DIMENSION A(7),B(2,3)
      EQUIVALENCE(A(2),B(1,1))
      READ(5,10)A
      DO 1 I=1,2
         C=B(I,3)
         B(I,3)=B(I,2)
         B(I,2)=C
   1  CONTINUE
      WRITE(6,11)(A(I),I=1,7)
  10  FORMAT(7I3)
  11  FORMAT(1X,7I3)
      STOP
      END
```

Input Data:

```
              1         2         3
    123456789012345678901234567890
       6   4   8   2   9   6   5
```

```
5.    COMMON M,K,NUM(3,3)
      M=9
      K=9
      DO 1 I=1,3
         DO 2 J=1,3
            NUM(I,J)=I+J
   2     CONTINUE
   1  CONTINUE
      CALL B1Z(K)
      WRITE(6,10)M,K
      WRITE(6,10)((NUM(I,J),J=1,3)I=1,3)
  10  FORMAT(1X,3I4)
      STOP
      END

      SUBROUTINE B1Z(N)
      COMMON I,J,LIST(9)
      DO 1 L=1,N
         LIST(L)=LIST(L)+L
   1  CONTINUE
      RETURN
      END
```

```
4.    COMMON IX(4),J,M
      M=4
      J=M-4
      DO 1 K=1,M
         IX(K)=J+K
   1  CONTINUE
      CALL SUB3(M)
      WRITE(6,10)(IX(K),K=1,M)
  10  FORMAT(1X,4I6)
      STOP
      END

      SUBROUTINE SUB3(N)
      COMMON JOHN(4)
      DO 1 M=1,N
         JOHN(M)=JOHN(M)+M
   1  CONTINUE
      RETURN
      END
```

```
6.    COMMON /A/I,J,K,L/B/M,N
      I=5
      J=4
      K=I+J
      L=I*J
      CALL ALPHA(X)
      WRITE(6,10)I,J,K,L,M,N
  10  FORMAT(1X,6I4)
      STOP
      END

      SUBROUTINE ALPHA(X)
      COMMON /A/N1,N2,N3,N4/B/I,J
      I=N1+N2
      J=10+N4
      RETURN
      END
```

```
7.    DIMENSION N(5),M(5)
      COMMON /B1/N/B2/M
      CALL SUB1(X)
      CALL SUB2(Y)
      WRITE(6,10)(N(I),M(I),I=1,5)
   10 FORMAT(1X,2I4)
      STOP
      END

      SUBROUTINE SUB1(X)
      COMMON /B1/LIST(5)
      DO 1 I=1,5
         LIST(I)=I
    1 CONTINUE
      RETURN
      END

      SUBROUTINE SUB2(X)
      COMMON /B2/LIST(5)
      DO 1 I=1,5
         LIST(I)=I**2
    1 CONTINUE
      RETURN
      END
```

```
8.    COMMON /BLOK1/M,N,I,J/BLOK2/MN,NQ,K
      CALL SUB1(X)
      CALL SUB2(Y)
      STOP
      END

      SUBROUTINE SUB1(Q)
      COMMON /BLOK1/J,I,K,NUM
      WRITE(6,10)K,NUM
   10 FORMAT(1X,2I5)
      RETURN
      END

      SUBROUTINE SUB2(A)
      COMMON /BLOK2/N(3)
      WRITE(6,10)N
   10 FORMAT(1X,3I3)
      RETURN
      END

      BLOCKDATA
      COMMON /BLOK1/L(4)/BLOK2/I(3)
      DATA L/4*3/,I/2,3,4/
      END
```

16.9 Review True-or-False Quiz

1. Specification statements are instructions to a compiler.   T F
2. The variable name CNTRL cannot be used as the control variable in a DO-loop.   T F
3. There is nothing wrong with the statement REAL A,B,M(3,4),N.   T F
4. The only way to declare FIRST as the name of an integer variable is to include it in an INTEGER statement.   T F
5. A DIMENSION statement and a LOGICAL statement are needed to declare LGCL as a logical array.   T F
6. If a computer can store only eight significant digits for each real value, all significant digits in the number 123400000.0 will be retained if it is assigned to a double precision variable but not if it is assigned to a real variable.   T F
7. Whereas 1.0E1 represents the real number 10.0, 1.0D1 represents the double precision number 100.0.   T F
8. The logical expression (TRUE.EQ.FALSE) can never be true in FORTRAN.   T F
9. If a program unit contains the statement IMPLICIT LOGICAL(A-Z), it is not necessarily true that every variable in the program unit will be a logical variable.   T F
10. The statement EQUIVALENCE(A,B) is perfectly acceptable even if A denotes a real array and B denotes a real variable.   T F
11. Variable names associated with the storage units in a common block must all be of the same type.   T F
12. The expressions *common block* and *common storage area* are used synonymously.   T F
13. The expression *blank common block* refers to a common storage area containing no data or else blank data.   T F
14. COMMON statements provide a means of communication between program units other than the communication allowed by the correspondence set up between dummy and actual arguments.   T F
15. BLOCKDATA subprograms serve only one purpose—when executed, they assign values to variables.   T F

The Order of Appearance of FORTRAN Statements in Any Program Unit

The statements in any program unit must conform to the order given by the eight categories in the following outline. The statements in any numbered category must appear before the statements in a higher numbered category. However,

Comment statements can appear anywhere in a program unit before the END statement.

FORMAT statements can appear anywhere in a program unit after the PROGRAM, FUNCTION, SUBROUTINE, or BLOCKDATA statement and before the END statement.

1. a. Main Program. PROGRAM statement (if required by system).
   b. Subprogram. FUNCTION, SUBROUTINE, or BLOCKDATA statement.
2. IMPLICIT statement.
3. Type statements:

   INTEGER
   REAL
   COMPLEX
   DOUBLE PRECISION
   LOGICAL
   CHARACTER

4. Other specification statements:

   DIMENSION
   EQUIVALENCE
   COMMON
   EXTERNAL

5. DATA statement.
6. Statement Function Statement.
7. Executable statements:

    Arithmetic IF
    Assignment statement
    BACKSPACE
    Block IF
    CALL
    CONTINUE
    DO
    ELSE
    ELSE IF
    END IF
    ENDFILE
    GO TO
    IF–THEN
    IF–THEN–ELSE
    Logical IF
    OPEN
    PRINT
    READ
    RETURN
    REWIND
    STOP
    WRITE

8. END statement.

B
FORTRAN
Intrinsic Functions

In this appendix the following abbreviations apply:

I	=	Integer
R	=	Real
D	=	Double precision
C	=	Complex
Ch	=	Character
L	=	Logical

B.1 Numeric functions

Function name	Number of arguments	Type of arguments	Type of function	Purpose
INT	1	R	I	Converts argument to an integer value.
IFIX	1	R	I	
IDINT	1	D	I	
FLOAT	1	I	R	Converts argument to a real value.
REAL	1	I	R	
SNGL	1	D	R	
DBLE	1	I	D	Converts argument to a double precision
DBLE	1	R	D	value.
CMPLX	1 or 2	I	C	Converts argument(s) to a complex
CMPLX	1 or 2	R	C	value. (If one argument, imaginary
CMPLX	1 or 2	D	C	part is zero.)

B.1 *(continued)*

Function name	Number of arguments	Type of arguments	Type of function	Purpose
AINT	1	R	R	Drops the fractional part of argument.
DINT	1	D	D	
ABS	1	R	R	Gives the absolute value of the argument.
IABS	1	I	I	
DABS	1	D	D	
CABS	1	C	R	If $z = a + bi$, $CABS(z) = \sqrt{a^2 + b^2}$.
NINT	1	R	I	Rounds argument to the nearest integer.
IDNINT	1	D	I	
ANINT	1	R	R	
DNINT	1	D	D	
MOD	2	I	I	Gives the remainder when the first argument is divided by the second.
AMOD	2	R	R	
DMOD	2	D	D	
MAX0	2 or more	I	I	Gives the largest of all the arguments.
AMAX0	2 or more	I	R	
AMAX1	2 or more	R	R	
MAX1	2 or more	R	I	
DMAX1	2 or more	D	D	
MIN0	2 or more	I	I	Gives the smallest of all the arguments.
AMIN0	2 or more	I	R	
AMIN1	2 or more	R	R	
MIN1	2 or more	R	I	
DMIN1	2 or more	D	D	
SQRT	1	R	R	Gives the square root of the argument.
DSQRT	1	D	D	
CSQRT	1	C	C	
REAL	1	C	R	Gives real part of complex argument.
AIMAG	1	C	R	Gives the imaginary part of complex argument.
CONJG	1	C	C	Gives complex conjugate of argument.
SIN	1	R	R	Calculates the sine of the argument. (Argument in radian measure.)
DSIN	1	D	D	
CSIN	1	C	C	
COS	1	R	R	Calculates the cosine of the argument. (Argument in radian measure.)
DCOS	1	D	D	
CCOS	1	C	C	
TAN	1	R	R	Calculates the tangent of the argument. (Argument in radian measure.)
DTAN	1	D	D	
ASIN	1	R	R	Calculates the arcsine of argument a. $\|a\| \leq 1$ and $-\pi/2 \leq (D)ASIN(a) \leq \pi/2$.
DASIN	1	D	D	
ACOS	1	R	R	Calculates the arccosine of argument a. $\|a\| \leq 1$ and $0 \leq (D)ACOS(a) \leq \pi$
DACOS	1	D	D	

B.1 *(continued)*

Function name	Number of arguments	Type of arguments	Type of function	Purpose
ATAN	1	R	R	Calculates the arctangent of argument a.
DATAN	1	D	D	$-\pi/2 < \text{(D)ATAN}(a) < \pi/2$.
EXP	1	R	R	Calculates the exponential e^a of the ar-
DEXP	1	D	D	gument a, where $e = 2.71828\ldots$
CEXP	1	C	C	is the base of the natural logarithms.
ALOG	1	R	R	Calculates the natural logarithm $\ln(a)$ of
DLOG	1	D	D	the argument a.
CLOG	1	C	C	
ALOG10	1	R	R	Calculates the common logarithm $\log_{10}(a)$
DLOG10	1	D	D	of the argument a.

B.2 Character functions

Function name	Number of arguments	Type of arguments	Type of function	Purpose
ICHAR	1	Ch	I	ICHAR(c) is the numeric code (see Figure 12.1) of the character c.
CHAR	1	I	Ch	CHAR(i) is the character that corresponds to the numeric code i (see Figure 12.1).
LGE	2	Ch	L	Gives a value true if the first argument does not precede the second in alphabetical order; otherwise false.
LGT	2	Ch	L	Gives a value true if the first argument follows the second in alphabetical order; otherwise false.
LLE	2	Ch	L	Gives a value true if the first argument does not follow the second in alphabetical order; otherwise false.
LLT	2	Ch	L	Gives a value true if the first argument precedes the second in alphabetical order; otherwise false.

C

Answers to Selected Problems

SECTION 1.3

1. T   **2.** F   **3.** F   **4.** F   **5.** F   **6.** T   **7.** T   **8.** F   **9.** F
10. T   **11.** F   **12.** F

SECTION 2.3

1. 5% discount   **2.** Decide whether the discount is applicable.   **3.** 693.50   **4.** 250.00
5. 80.00 and 0, 128.00 and 0, 176.00 and 48.00, 206.00 and 78.00
6. X is pay for hours over 32. G is gross pay.   **7.** 4 dollars.   **8.** 6 dollars per hour.   **9.** 21

10. 1   1
    2   2
    3   6
    4   24
    5   120
    6   720

11. 55   **12.** 2,4,7,8,14,28,64

13. Variable names:
    NAME   = name of an item.
    COST   = fixed cost for the item NAME.
    PRICE   = sale price for the item NAME.
    QTY   = number of units of NAME sold.
    GROSS   = gross sales for the item NAME.
    INCOME = income from the item NAME.

Algorithm:

a. Print column headings as specified.
b. Read NAME and values for COST, PRICE, and QTY, for one item.
c. Assign the value of the product QTY × PRICE to GROSS.
d. Multiply QTY times (PRICE − COST) to obtain a value for INCOME.
e. Enter NAME and the values GROSS and INCOME under the appropriate column headings.
f. Return to step (b) until the report is complete.

15. Variables:

CORP   = corporation name.
SHARES = number of shares.
PRICE   = current price for one share.
EARN   = earnings for one share.
EQTY   = equity represented by all shares of corporation CORP.
PE   = price/earnings ratio for one share.

Algorithm:

a. Print column headings as specified.
b. Read CORP and values for SHARES, PRICE, and EARN.
c. Assign the value of the product SHARES × PRICE to EQTY.
d. Divide PRICE by EARN to obtain a value for PE.
e. Enter CORP and the values SHARE, EARN, EQTY, and PE under the appropriate column headings.
f. Return to step (b) until the report is complete.

17. a. Start with SUM = 0 and COUNT = 0.
b. Add the number on the top card to SUM and add 1 to COUNT.
c. Remove the top card and return to step (b) until all cards have been processed.
d. Divide SUM by COUNT to obtain the average AV and proceed to step (e) with the original stack of cards in hand.
e. If the number on the top card exceeds AV, write the letter G on the card; otherwise write the letter L.
f. Remove the top card and return to step (e) until all cards have been examined.

SECTION 2.4

1. F   **2.** T   **3.** T   **4.** F   **5.** F   **6.** F   **7.** T

SECTION 3.2

1. a. 275   **b.** −124   **c.** 620   **d.** 95   **e.** 13500   **f.** 21743   **g.** 200   **h.** 910

2. a. 2346. and 2.346E + 03   **b.** 26500. and 265E + 02   **c.** 14.6 and 1.46E + 01
d. 12. and 1.2E + 01   **e.** 0.000123 and 1.23E − 04   **f.** 123500 and 1.235E + 06
g. 5.6 and 5.6E + 00   **h.** 100000. and 1E5

3. a. 29,340   **b.** 12.3   **c.** 0.0101   **d.** 1   **e.** 100,002   **f.** .0000000000001

4. a. Inadmissible. Comma.   **b.** Inadmissible. It is a sum.
e. Inadmissible. Only integer can follow E.   All others are admissible.

5. a. Admissible. Real.   **b.** Admissible. Integer.   **c.** Inadmissible. − not allowed.
d. Inadmissible. Period not allowed.   **e.** Admissible. Integer.
f. Inadmissible. First character not a letter.   **g.** Admissible. Integer.
h. Inadmissible. − not allowed.   **i.** Inadmissible. Too many characters.
j. Admissible. Integer.   **k.** Admissible. Real.   **l.** Inadmissible. # not allowed.

SECTION 3.5

1. a. 4.   **b.** 4   **c.** −2   **d.** −6   **e.** −2   **f.** −2   **g.** .25   **h.** 0
i. 0   **j.** 1   **k.** 8   **l.** 8.   **m.** −9   **n.** 0   **o.** 4.

2. a. 3.333 . . .   **b.** 36.   **c.** 27.   **d.** 84.   **e.** 0.   **f.** 25   **g.** 25.
h. 81.   **i.** 243.   **j.** 4   **k.** 0   **l.** 1

3. a. Inadmissible. * is missing.   **c.** Inadmissible. Mixed mode.   **d.** Inadmissible. Mixed mode.
e. Inadmissible. 2X is not a variable name.   **h.** Inadmissible. Adjacent operation symbols.
i. Inadmissible. Adjacent operation symbols.   **j.** Inadmissible. 2B is not a variable name.
k. Inadmissible. 2N is not a variable name.   All others are admissible.

4. a. $(-3+(-7))*2$; -20 **b.** Admissible; 4   **c.** Admissible; -12 **d.** $(7+2)/(-4)$; -2
e. Admissible; 9   **f.** Admissible; -9 **g.** $2.*(3.1+2.2)$; 10.6   **h.** Admissible; -5
i. Admissible; .0084   **j.** $7.*1.2E-03$; .0084   **k.** Admissible; 8400.   **l.** Admissible; 4
m. $9.**(1./2.)$; 3.   **n.** Admissible; 4.5   **o.** $(2.+7.+6.)/FLOAT(3)$; 5.

5. a. $5.*X+2.*Y$ **b.** $1./(A*B)$ **c.** $(A+B)/(C+D)$ **d.** $2.*X**2-9$.
e. $FLOAT(M+N)/2$.   **f.** $(X**2+Y**2)**(1./2.)$

SECTION 3.7

1. a. Incorrect. * missing.   **c.** Incorrect. 2FJ is not a variable name.
e. Incorrect. VALUE135 is not a variable name and $41+4*Y$ is mixed mode.
f. Incorrect. $I+J$ cannot appear to the left of = sign.   **h.** Incorrect. 0.5 cannot follow E.

2. a. $M=7$ **b.** $X=S+X$ **c.** $N=N+7$ **d.** $S=S+7$.   **e.** $A=(1.0+R)**10$
f. $H=2.*H$ **g.** $X=X-2.*Y$ **h.** $Y=Y+FLOAT(M)$

3. a. $A=5.5$ **b.** $Z=4$.   **c.** $K=1$ **d.** $A=1.2$ **e.** $T=2$.   **f.** $N=2$
g. $S=3.333\ldots$ **h.** $S=2.666\ldots$ **i.** $P=8$.   **j.** $M=27$

4. a.

I	J	K
1	–	–
1	2	–
1	2	1
1	2	3
4	2	3
4	5	3
4	5	2
4	20	2
5	20	2

c.

X	Y	I
1.5	–	–
1.5	0.6	–
−1.5	0.6	–
−1.5	−3.	–
−1.5	−3.	−4
−1.5	−3.	4
−1.5	−3.	16

SECTION 3.10

1. a. Incorrect. Comma missing between 6 and 10.   **b.** Incorrect. Unit number and statement label missing.
c. Incorrect. 'SUM IS' cannot appear in WRITE statement.
d. Incorrect. Commas missing between edit descriptors.   **e.** Incorrect. DEPT IS must be in quotes.
f. Correct.

2.
```
                  1         2
         12345678901234567890
    a.        12    36
    b.     12    36    12
    c.        LARGEST 36
    d.        FIRST  12
         SUM=   48.000
    e.   ANSWER        0.686
    f.       RESULT    0.00
    g.   TWO NUMBERS
              12    36
    h.     1239.00  1239
```

3.
```
                  1         2
         123456789012345678901 2345
    a.        70    48
    b.     138.83 48
    c.   NUMBERS 70 48
         SUM 118.00
    d.   QUOTIENT        0.686
    e.   QUOTIENT 1.00
    f.   TWO NUMBERS
              70   139.
```

4. a. QUOTIENT has too many characters; I4 is incorrect.   **b.** Change 'SUM',SUM to 'SUM',F6.2.
c. Prints TEAFORTWO   **d.** Words will not line up properly.

5. a. PRINT 10,Q   **b.** PRINT 11,SUM   **c.** PRINT 13
d. PRINT 14 and PRINT 15   (Errors are as described for Problem 4.)

6. a.

X	Y	S	Output
12.69	–	–	
12.69	–	–	X = ΔΔΔ13.
12.69	5.	–	
12.69	5.	17.69	
12.69	5.	17.69	ΔΔ5.00
12.69	5.	17.69	SUM ISΔΔΔ17.7

b.

X	Y	P	Output
14.915	–	–	
14.915	–	–	ΔΔΔ15.
14.915	20.918	–	
14.915	20.918	–	Y = ΔΔΔ20.92
14.915	20.918	209.18	
14.915	20.918	209.18	ΔΔΔΔΔ209.2

SECTION 3.11

1. F   **2.** T   **3.** F   **4.** T   **5.** F   **6.** F   **7.** F   **8.** F   **9.** T
10. T   **11.** F   **12.** T   **13.** F   **14.** T   **15.** F

SECTION 4.2

1. List:

```
10 M=24
20 N=M-5
30 WRITE(6,20)N
40 20 FORMAT(1X,'DIFF',I4)
50 STOP
60 END
```

Output: 19

4. List:

```
10 X=5.
20 Y=X/4.+X**2
30+  +3.*X+20.
50 WRITE(6,10)Y,X
60 10 FORMAT(1X,F10.4,3X,F10.4)
65 STOP
70 END
```

Output:

```
61.2500        5.0000
```

5. Syntax:

```
30 D=23000
```

Programming:

```
50 A=(R/100.)*D
```

6. Programming:

```
15 REAL MEAN
40 MEAN=FLOAT(NUM1+NUM2)/2.
```

7. Syntax and Programming:

```
60 X=-B/A
```

8. Syntax:

```
10C ASSIGN VALUES
40C INTERCHANGE M AND N
80 10 FORMAT(1X,I5,2X,I5)
```

Programming:

```
50 K=M
55 M=N
60 N=K
```

SECTION 4.7

1. F **2.** T **3.** T **4.** F **5.** F **6.** T **7.** F **8.** F
9. F **10.** T **11.** F **12.** T **13.** F **14.** F **15.** F **16.** F
17. F **18.** T **19.** F **20.** F

SECTION 5.2

1. a. 653 **b.** 500 **c.** −4300 **d.** 743006 **e.** 805043 **f.** −430 **g.** 0

2. a. 53.76 **b.** 8408.05 **c.** 83400.04 **d.** 54103.7 **e.** 4.43 **f.** −3510.53
g. 4.693 **h.** −1.864

3. N1 = 64 **5.** ID = 8715 **7.** COUNT = 3.55
N2 = 31 RATE = 10.85 NAME = 4420
N3 = 85162 HOURS = 44.5 VALUE = 278.625
SALE = 2.45
NEXT = 356

9.
```
READ(5,80)C,D,M,BETA,NUM

          1         2
123456789012345678901245
 42.3       84  68.35 7
```

11.
```
        READ(5,20)X,N1
        READ(5,21)Y,MEM7
     20 FORMAT(F7.2,I8)
     21 FORMAT(F7.2,I6)
```

SECTION 5.8

```
1.      READ(5,10)X                    3.      READ(5,10)X
   10 FORMAT(F10.2)                       10 FORMAT(F7.2)
        A=X/52.                                A=X+.045*X
        WRITE(6,11)A                           WRITE(6,11)A
   11 FORMAT(1X,'WEEKLY SALARY:',F8.2)    11 FORMAT(1X,'TOTAL COST:',F8.2)


5.      READ(5,10)X
   10 FORMAT(F5.1)
        A=X/19.2
        WRITE(6,11)X
   11 FORMAT(1X,'FUEL COST PER MILE(CENTS):',F5.1)


13.     READ(5,10)X
   10 FORMAT(F5.0)
        A=((4000.*5280.+X)**2-(4000.*5280.)**2)**.5/5280.
        WRITE(6,11)X
   11 FORMAT(1X,'DISTANCE IN MILES TO HORIZON:',F5.0)
```

SECTION 5.10

1. a. C needed in line 2

```
1 READ(5.10)A,B
  IF(A.EQ.99.) GO TO 2
     DIFF=A-B
     WRITE(6,11)DIFF
  GO TO 1
```

b. Insert N = N + 1 after the WRITE statement.
Replace (N.EQ.10) by (N.GT.10).
c. Initialize SUM = 0.
Replace SUM = X by SUM = SUM + X.
Replace (N.LT.25) by (N.LE.25).
d. Replace lines 8, 9, and 10 by IF(N.LT.77) GO TO 1
                                    IF(N.GT.145) GO TO 1

SECTION 5.11

1. T   **2.** F   **3.** T   **4.** F   **5.** T   **6.** F   **7.** T   **8.** F   **9.** T   **10.** T

SECTION 6.3

1. a. T   **b.** T   **c.** F   **d.** T   **e.** F   **f.** T   **g.** T   **h.** F

2. a. Syntax. $(X - Y)*(X + Y)$ is not a logical expression.
b. Syntax. There should not be a comma.
c. Syntax. M>N is not a logical expression.
d. Programming. If I<J, infinite loop.
e. Syntax. Right parenthesis missing.
f. Syntax. Need parentheses around SUM.EQ.TOTAL.
g. Syntax. NOT.(I/3) is not a logical expression.
h. Syntax. (A.LT.B.LT.C) is not allowed.

3. a. The WRITE statement should be labeled 1 instead of the statement N = 1. Incorrect edit descriptor.

b. The statement WRITE(6,30) should appear before the loop is entered.

c. Change R = N**1/2 to 2 R = FLOAT(N)**.5 and delete the 2 in the WRITE statement.

d. Remove the first STOP statement.

4. a.

K	M	Output	
1	–		
1	1		
1	1		
1	1	1	1
2	1		
2	2		
2	2	2	2
3	2		
3	6		
3	6	3	6
4	6		
4	24		
4	24	4	24
5	24		

c.

I	J	K	Output
1	–	–	
1	–	–	1
1	1	–	
1	1	–	1
1	1	2	
1	1	2	2
1	1	2	
1	2	2	
1	2	3	
1	2	3	3
2	2	3	
2	3	3	
2	3	5	
2	3	5	5

d.

I	J	K	Output
0	–	–	
0	0	–	
0	0	11	
2	0	11	
2	1	11	
2	1	10	
5	1	10	
5	2	10	
5	2	9	
9	2	9	
9	3	9	
9	3	8	
9	3	8	3

SECTION 6.8

1. a. 1806   **c.** 90.00   99.00
                        120.00   144.00
                        200.00   240.00

2. a.
```
VAL=0.
IF(SUM.LT.100.) THEN
  VAL=.10*SUM
  N=N+1
END IF
WRITE(6,10)N,VAL
```

c.
```
IF(X*Y.GT.0.) THEN
  IF(X.LT.0) THEN
    WRITE(6,10)
  ELSE
    WRITE(6,11)
  END IF
END IF
WRITE(6,12)X,Y
```

SECTION 6.11

1. F   **2.** T   **3.** T   **4.** F   **5.** F   **6.** T   **7.** T   **8.** T   **9.** F
10. T   **11.** F   **12.** F   **13.** F   **14.** T   **15.** F   **16.** F   **17.** F

SECTION 7.3

1. a. 2 4   **b.** 9   **c.** 1   **d.** 0.9167
　　　　　　　　　　　　　3
　　　　　　　　　　　　　5
　　　　　　　　　　　　　7
　　　　　　　　　　　　　9

2. a. Compile time: There is no statement labeled 2.
Replace GO TO 1 with 2 CONTINUE.

　b. Programming: Replace FLOAT(1/K) by 1./FLOAT(K)

　c. Run time: Division by zero.

　d. Compile time: FORMAT statements are not executable and cannot be the terminal statement of a DO-loop.

　e. Compile time: The statement labeled 6 is not allowed as the terminal statement of a DO-loop.

　f. Syntax and programming in the assignment statement.

SECTION 7.5

1. a. 1 2 3   **c.** 3   **e.** 1! =   1
　　　　1 3 4　　　　　3　　　　2! =   2
　　　　2 2 4　　　　　3　　　　3! =   6
　　　　2 3 5　　　　　5　　　　4! =   24
　　　　3 2 5　　　　　5　　　　5! =   120
　　　　3 3 6　　　　　5　　　　6! =   720

2. a. Compilation: Improper nesting of loops.

　b. Compilation: Improper terminal statement for a DO-loop.

　c. Programming: Replace the first two lines by
```
DO 1 I=1,3
K=I+1
DO 1 J=K,4
```

　d. Programming: Change IF-END IF segment to
```
  IF(I.EQ.2) THEN
    DO 2 J=1,3
      WRITE(6,11)
2   CONTINUE
  ELSE
    WRITE(6,10)
  END IF
```

SECTION 7.6

1. F   **2.** T   **3.** T   **4.** F   **5.** F   **6.** F   **7.** T   **8.** T
9. F   **10.** T   **11.** T   **12.** T

SECTION 8.5·

1.
```
              1         2
12345678901234567890012345
```
a.   24 43
     -35
b.   203.65
          24
     -13.41
          43
     12.34
          -35
c.   COUNT   VALUE

     24   203.7
     43   -13.4
d.   204.

         -13.

         12.
e.   24

     43

     -35
f.   X= 203.650
     Y= -13.410

2. a. N1 = 12345
           N2 = 23456
           N3 = 34567

b. JOB = 1
        MIN = 567
        LARGE = 2
        NUM = 678

c. A = 12.34
        B = 12.34
        C = 2.345
        D = 34.56
        E = 234.56

d. M = 890
        N = 12

e. A = 12.34
        B = 567.89
        C = 34.56
        D = 789.01

f. N1 = 90
        N2 = 90
        N3 = 12
        N4 = 12

g. N1 = 901
        N2 = 12
        N3 = 345
        N4 = 456

h. I = 1234
        J = 4567
        K = 7890

3. a.
```
      X          X**2
     -----       ----
      1           1
      2           4
      3           9
      4          16
      5          25
```

b.
```
PROBABILITY     COUNT
   0.35          20
   0.65          10

EXPECTED VALUE IS  13.50
```

c.
```
(1.5,2.5)
(3.5,4.5)
---------
(5.0,7.0)
```

d. TOTAL EMPLOYEES 104

e. ITEM1924   INVENTORY 1480
        ITEM4326   INVENTORY 1000

f. TOTAL SALES=$120314.11

4. a.
```
     WRITE(6,10)
 10 FORMAT(1X,'LINE1'/1X,1X,'LINE2'/1X,2X,'LINE3')
```

b.
```
     WRITE(6,11)
 11 FORMAT(1X,8X,'ONE'/1X,5X,'TWO',3X,'TWO'/1X,'THREE ,9X,'THREE')
```

SECTION 8.8

1.
```
         1         2
12345678901234567890123456
```
a.   27   123.46
    216   -45.27

b. 123.457 -45.273

```
        27    2.6
```
c. -----INTEGERS-----
        27   216

d.   XXXXX
      XXXX
      XXX

e. FIRST VALUE 27 SECOND VALUE 123.46

    FIRST VALUE 216 SECOND VALUE -45.27

f. *
    XX
    XXX

2. **a.** $A = 1.234E + 3 = 1234.$
   $B = 1.234E004 = 12340.$

   b. $A = 12.34E + 3 = 12340.$
   $B = 56.78E - 3 = .05678$
   $C = 1.234E004 = 12340.$

   c. $A = 123.4E + 3 = 123400.$
   $B = 567.8E - 03 = .5678$
   $C = .234E004 = 2340.$

   d. $A = 12.34$
   $B = .5678E - 30$
   $C = 1.234$

3. **a.** TIME NO. 1*****   1
   TIME NO. 2*****   12
   TIME NO. 3***** 123
   TIME NO. 4***** 1234
   TIME NO. 5*****12345

   b.
   ```
   H     H
   H     H
   H     H
   HHHHHHH
   H     H
   H     H
   H     H
   ```

SECTION 8.9

1. T **2.** F **3.** T **4.** T **5.** F **6.** T **7.** F **8.** T
9. F **10.** T **11.** T **12.** F **13.** F

SECTION 9.3

1. **a.** 5 **b.** 3
      4   1
             5

2. **a.** DIMENSION statement must appear before the first executable statement.
   b. Replace the type statement by INTEGER LIST(100),SUM and place it first.
   c. When the J in the J loop becomes 6 the subscript 2*J is out of range.
   d. Entries L(6),L(7), . . . , L(10) are lost.

SECTION 9.5

1.

```
                1           2           3           4
      12345678901234567890123456789012345678901234567890
a.    100   101   102   103   104
b.          135.0
            140.3
            150.5
            160.8
c.    100   100
       18    18
      101   101
d.     18   275  3500   104
e.    0 0 0 0 3 0 0 0 0 1 3 5
      0 0 0 0 1 0 0
f.   12345
     1234
     123
     12
     1
g.     1   1
       1   2
       1   3
       1   4
       1   5
h.   1
     1 1
     1 1 1
     1 1 1 1
     1 1 1 1 1
     1 1 1 1 1 1
```

SECTION 9.9

1.

```
                    1           2           3
          12345678901234567890123456789012345678901234567890
   a.     1   4   9  16
   b.     1 1 1 1
          0 1 1 1
          0 0 1 1
          0 0 0 1
   c.     1.0 3.0 5.0 2.0 4.0 6.0
   d.     1.0 2.0 3.0
          4.0 5.0 6.0
   e.     10 30
          20 40
   f.     4 5 6
```

2. a. The statement S = 0 must be moved between the two DO statements.
   b. Change DO 1 J = 1,5 to DO 1 J = I,5. Declare N to be real.
   c. Replace the J loop by WRITE(6,11)(A(I,J),J = 1,5)
   d. In WRITE statement replace A(I,5) by A(5,I). Replace DATA statement by

```
DO 1 I=1,5
  DO 1 J=1,5
    A(I,J)=0.
1 CONTINUE
```

SECTION 9.10

1. F   **2.** T   **3.** F   **4.** F   **5.** F   **6.** F   **7.** F   **8.** T
9. F   **10.** F   **11.** T   **12.** F

SECTION 10.2

1. a. 6.   **b.** 6.   **c.** 1   **d.** 2   **e.** 2   **f.** 3   **g.** 3.   **h.** 42.4   **i.** 3.565
j. 0.9   **k.** 5   **l.** 3   **m.** 3   **n.** −1   **o.** 10

2. a. 2.   **b.** 2.   **c.** 1   **d.** 1   **e.** 2   **f.** 3   **g.** 3   **h.** 6   **i.** 22
j. −4.   **k.** −4.3   **l.** 5.9

3. a.

		b.		**c.**	**d.**	
1	8	1	30	14.0000	4	
2	6	2	15	13.9000	7	
3	2	3	10	13.9300	2	
4	4	5	6	13.9270	5	
				13.9274		

4. a. Y = ANINT(10.*X)/10.
   b. Y = ANINT(100.*X)/100.
   c. Y = ANINT(1000.*X)/1000.
   d. Y = ANINT(.01*X)/.01
   e. Y = ANINT(.001*X)/.001

SECTION 10.4

1. a.

a.	**b.**		**c.**		**d.**	
1	1	4	2	10.00	1	45.0
2	2	5	3	15.00	2	29.0
3	3	6	4	20.00	3	53.0
0			5	25.00	4	117.0
1						
1						

2. a. Change F(V) = .06*U to F(U) = .06*U
      Change V = F(U) to V = F(Y).
   b. Change SQ(I) = N**2 to SQ(I) = I**2.
   c. Change the function statement to RECIP(I) = FLOAT(N)/FLOAT(I).
   d. FN1 is a function of 2 variables, so FN1(R) is not admissible.
      FN2 is a function of 1 variable, so FN2(FN1(R),R) is not admissible.

3. a. TENTH(X) = ANINT(10.*X)/10.
   c. SPRICE(X,Y) = X − X*Y/100.
   e. DMILES(F) = F/5280.
   g. F(C) = 9./5.*C + 32.
   i. DKIL(X) = 1.6093*X
   k. HYPOT(A,B) = SQRT(A**2 + B**2)
   m. RADIUS(A) = SQRT(A/3.14159)
   o. DEGTAN(A) = TAN(3.14159/180.*A)

SECTION 10.5

1. F   **2.** F   **3.** T   **4.** T   **5.** F   **6.** F   **7.** T   **8.** F
9. T   **10.** F   **11.** T

SECTION 11.3

1. a. 1   **b.** 0   **c.** −1   **d.** −1   **e.** 1   **f.** 1

2. a. The expression X + Y cannot be a dummy argument.
  b. Is allowed.
  c. There is no function name.
  d. The expressions (A + B)/2. and (A − B)/2. cannot be dummy arguments. AVERAGES is too long.

3. a. The function name EVAL is not assigned a value in the subprogram.
  b. The array LIST is not dimensioned in the subprogram.
  c. The variable SUM is not initialized to zero in the subprogram.

SECTION 11.8

1. a. I = 5   **b.** N1 = 3   **c.** I = 1   **d.** K = 5
  J = 3   N2 = 6   J = 2   L = 5
  K = 7   N3 = 4   K = 3   M = 5
  N1 = 5   M = 6   N1 = 2   N = 0
  N2 = 3   N = 4   N2 = 2

2. a. K = 2   **b.** N = 5
  AV = 4.5   ANS = 25.

3. a. Is correct.
  b. The expression X + 1 cannot be a dummy argument.
  c. Subroutine has no name.
  d. The expressions (I + J)/2 and (I*J)/2 cannot be dummy arguments.

4. a. A value cannot be assigned to a subroutine name.
  b. The dummy array A is not dimensioned in the subroutine.
  c. SUM is not initialized to zero before summing.

SECTION 11.9

1. F   **2.** T   **3.** T   **4.** F   **5.** F   **6.** T   **7.** F   **8.** T
9. F   **10.** T   **11.** T   **12.** F   **13.** T

SECTION 12.4

1. **a.** I=ABCD   **b.** I=ABCD△△△△△△
             J=EF△△   J=EFGHIJKL△△
             K=IJKL   K=MN△△△△△△△△

             Output: ABCDEF△△IJKL   Output: ABCD△△EFGHIJMN△△

       c. I=A   **d.** I=ABCD
             J=1   J=1234
             K=A   K=A1B2

             Output: A   Output: △△△△ABCD
                      1   △△△△1234
                      A   △△△△A1B2

e. I=ABCDΔΔ
    J=12ΔΔΔΔ
    K=A1B2C3

    Output: ABCD
              12ΔΔ
              A1B2

f. I=ABCDEΔΔΔΔΔ
    J=6789012345
    K=A1B2C3D4E5

    Output: ABCDEΔΔΔΔΔ
              6789012345
              A1B2C3D4E5

2. a. RIVERBOAT
         BOATSWAIN

b. *
       **
       ***

SECTION 12.7

1.a. N(1)=AΔΔΔ
          N(2)=KΔΔΔ
          N(3)=1ΔΔΔ
          N(4)=1ΔΔΔ
          N(5)=AΔΔΔ
          N(6)=FΔΔΔ

          Output: A   K   1   1
                   A   F

b. N(1)=ABCD
        N(2)=EFGH
        N(3)=IJKL
        N(4)=MNOP

        Output: ABCD
                  EFGH
                  IJKL
                  MNOP

c. N(1)=KLΔΔ
        N(2)=MNΔΔ
        N(3)=OPΔΔ
        N(4)=F6ΔΔ
        N(5)=G6ΔΔ

        Output: KL
                  MN
                  OP
                  F6
                  G7

d. N(1)=A
        N(2)=B
        N(3)=C
        N(4)=D
        N(5)=E
        N(6)=F
        N(7)=G
        N(8)=H
        N(9)=I
        N(10)=J
        N(11)=K
        N(12)=L

        Output: A B C D E F G H I J K L

2. a. SEN
          DBE
          NDL

b. SEN
       DBE
       NDL

c. *****
       ****
       ***
       **
       *

d. ABCD
       BCD
       CD
       D

SECTION 12.8

1. F   **2.** F   **3.** T   **4.** T   **5.** T   **6.** F   **7.** F   **8.** F

SECTION 13.8

1. a. $X = 4.*RANF(0)$ **b.** $Y = 6.*RANF(0) + 5.$
c. $Z = 8.*RANF(0) - 5.$ **d.** $I = IFIX(7.*RANF(0)) + 6$
e. $J = (IFIX(5.*RANF(0)))*2$ **f.** $K = (IFIX(5.*RANF(0)))*2 + 1$

2. a. T or F **b.** F **c.** T **d.** T **e.** T or F **f.** T **g.** T **h.** T or F

3. a. 1, 2 equally likely. **b.** 0
c. $-2, -1, 0, 1, 2$ equally likely. **d.** 2, 3, 4 not equally likely.
e. 2, 3, 4, . . . , 12 not equally likely. **f.** 1, 2, 3, 4, 6, 9 not equally likely.

SECTION 13.9

1. F **2.** T **3.** F **4.** F **5.** T **6.** F **7.** F **8.** T **9.** F **10.** T

SECTION 14.4

1. a. 35 4 **b.** 20
121 8 7
63 31 7
200 2 18
16 6 9
8

SECTION 14.6

1. a. 78 JOAN **b.** SAL 64
JILL 72

SECTION 14.7

1. T **2.** T **3.** F **4.** F **5.** F **6.** T **7.** F

SECTION 15.6

1. F **2.** F **3.** T **4.** F **5.** T **6.** T **7.** T **8.** T
9. F **10.** T **11.** T

SECTION 16.3

1. a. Change 10 FORMAT(F5.0,I5) to 10 FORMAT(I5,I5).
b. The statement INTEGER SUM must appear before the first executable statement.
c. Since I and J are covered by the IMPLICIT REAL(A-L) statement, the statement INTEGER I,J should be inserted before the first DO-loop.
d. The program will print T or F, not TRUE or FALSE.

2. a. Integer. **b.** Complex. **c.** Integer. **d.** Double precision. **e.** Logical. **f.** Real.
g. Complex. **h.** Integer. **i.** Real. **j.** Integer. **k.** Real. **l.** Double precision.

3. a. $1.00 - 21.00$ **b.** $4.00 \quad -3.00$
c. F T F **d.**

P	Q	P.AND.Q	P.OR.Q	P IMPLIES Q
T	T	T	T	T
T	F	F	T	F
F	T	F	T	T
F	F	F	F	T

SECTION 16.8

```
                    1                   2                   3
          1234567890123456789012345678 90
1.        28.00      16
2.             6      18        38          64
3.        6  4   8   6   5   2   9
4.           2        4        6          8
5.           9    9
             3    7   11
             5    9   13
             7   11   15
6.           5    4    9   20    9   30
7.           1    1
             2    4
             3    9
             4   16
             5   25
8.              3        3
          2   3    4
```

SECTION 16.9

1. T   **2.** F   **3.** T   **4.** F   **5.** F   **6.** F   **7.** F   **8.** F
9. T   **10.** T   **11.** F   **12.** T   **13.** F   **14.** T   **15.** F

Index